D1564793

Critical Essays on
D. H. Lawrence

Critical Essays on
D. H. Lawrence

Dennis Jackson and
Fleda Brown Jackson

G. K. Hall & Co. • Boston, Massachusetts

Critical essays on D. H. Lawrence / [edited by] Dennis Jackson and
    Fleda Brown Jackson.
        p. cm. — (Critical essays on British literature)
    Includes index.
    ISBN 0-8161-8765-7 (alk. paper)
    1. Lawrence, D. H. (David Herbert), 1885–1930 — Criticism and
interpretation. I. Jackson, Dennis, 1945–   . II. Jackson, Fleda
Brown, 1944–   . III. Series.
PR6023.A93Z62325 1988
823'.912 — dc19   87-33111
                                                                    CIP

This publication is printed on permanent/durable acid-free paper
MANUFACTURED IN THE UNITED STATES OF AMERICA

CRITICAL ESSAYS ON BRITISH LITERATURE

The Critical Essays on British Literature series attempts to provide a variety of approaches to both the classical writers of Britain and Ireland, and the best contemporary authors. The formats of the volumes in the series vary with the thematic designs of individual editors, and with the number and nature of existing reviews, criticism, and scholarship. In general, the series seeks to represent the best in published criticism, augmented, where appropriate, with original essays by recognized authorities. It is hoped that each volume will be unique in developing a new overall perspective on its particular author.

In their long introductory essay, the Jacksons summarize and assess the history of major Lawrence criticism. Previous summaries have dealt with the critical approaches through 1960, but none has produced so precise an analysis of the available criticism of Lawrence as the present volume. Most of their analysis deals with the last thirty years, the bulk being the prolific period from 1970–85. The essays selected cover a range of Lawrence's work including the best-known novels, short stories, poetry, plays, and even letters. The two concluding essays deal with the entire Lawrentian canon.

ZACK BOWEN, GENERAL EDITOR

University of Miami

116826

CONTENTS

INTRODUCTION

D. H. Lawrence's Critical Reception:
An Overview

Though during his lifetime Lawrence was never a big success in the marketplace and his books were often misjudged or misrepresented by reviewers, he was certainly never neglected by the literary community: from the time *Sons and Lovers* was published in 1913, his books were regularly reviewed in the most influential British and American literary organs of his day, he was profiled in a number of literary histories, and his works were discussed — often sympathetically — in books by Conrad Aiken, Douglas Goldring, Harold Monro, Henry Seidel Canby, Paul Rosenfeld, Stuart Sherman, Bonamy Dobrée, and other of his contemporaries. Moreover, several entire books — Herbert Seligmann's *D. H. Lawrence: An American Interpretation* (1924), Edward McDonald's useful *A Bibliography of the Writings of D. H. Lawrence* (1925), and Richard Aldington's warmly appreciative *D. H. Lawrence: An Indiscretion* (1927) — were devoted to him.

Still, Lawrence biographers have been correct in stating that he was often severely undervalued as an artist during his lifetime. The reception given his works before his death in 1930 can be well illustrated by reference to the various reviews and essays by Edward Shanks, for a time the assistant editor of the *London Mercury*.[1] He regularly reviewed Lawrence's major works as they were published. Recognizing that Lawrence, whom he called "a fine novelist and poet, a man of great intellectual and spiritual energy and originality," had something vital to offer, Shanks clearly *wanted* to like and to understand Lawrence's books. So long as the artist expressed "what he had to say in terms of ordinary life realistically described," so long as his narratives fit the Victorian paradigm of the novel of "personal" character and situation, Shanks was an admirer. But he was too much a prisoner of the prepotent literary conventions to accept the break that Lawrence made from traditionally disciplined narrative procedures in the novels that followed *Sons and Lovers*, and he voiced the often-made complaint that those later novels were "shapeless." Like many other reviewers, Shanks was baffled by Lawrence's innovative use in *The Rainbow* and later novels of dynamic symbols to convey inward states. Moreover, the novelist's rebellious social theory and "peculiar dark philoso-

1

phy" seemed to him "simply incomprehensible." By the time *The Plumed Serpent* was published in 1926, Shanks was thoroughly confused by what Lawrence was trying to express. Reluctantly he came to hold the view that Lawrence had betrayed the promise of *Sons and Lovers*, that he had let his talent disintegrate, that he had "allowed the thinker to swamp the artist" in his later writings. Shanks complained, too, that after *Sons and Lovers* Lawrence had lost touch with "normality" and had begun excessively to glorify the salvific possibilities of sexual love. In all of these attitudes, Shanks typified the responses that Lawrence's writings elicited from a good portion of the literary journalists of his day.

The sexual explicitness in Lawrence's writings increasingly drew the ire of reviewers, and from the time *The Rainbow* was successfully prosecuted for obscenity and ordered to be destroyed in 1915, his public image was increasingly one of notoriety. Some of his works of the late 1920s — *Lady Chatterley's Lover*, *Pansies*, and paintings he exhibited at the Warren Gallery in London — encountered further troubles with censoring authorities, and when he died, newspapers the world over bore the inevitable headlines announcing the death of this "Much Censored Celebrity," this "Stormy Petrel of Literature" who had been an "Outspoken Writer on Sex Problems."

The 1930s

But it was simply not true, what Mark Schorer asserted in a March 1974 *Atlantic Monthly* article, that the "tattered state" of Lawrence's reputation at the time of his death "was dramatized by his obituary press, which was almost universally scurrilous."[2] A survey of over two hundred English-language newspapers and journals from 1930 shows that the news of Lawrence's death generated an impressive outpouring of print, and that overall this obituary press gave him considerably more praise and sympathy than condemnation.[3] With Lawrence's death, journalists and critics the world over felt a sudden challenge to discuss the "shape" of his career and to try to predict how he would fare in future literary discussions. This effort inevitably yielded a bumper crop of nonsense, but in those months following Lawrence's death there were also some surprisingly accurate assessments, particularly those by E. M. Forster, Arnold Bennett, Desmond MacCarthy, Paul Rosenfeld, and Lionel Trilling, and one can perceive in some of the obituaries and articles of 1930 the first faint outlines of the sort of balanced, intelligently sympathetic criticism that a quarter of a century hence would spark a revival of popularity for Lawrence's works.

There was lively contention among the obituarists over what, exactly, Lawrence had accomplished. Joseph Wood Krutch expressed in the *Nation*

(3/19/30) his doubts that Lawrence would emerge as a novelist of the first importance.[4] George Currie in the *Brooklyn Daily Eagle* (3/5/30) assessed him as a "one-book man" who would be remembered by 1980 only for *Sons and Lovers* — the other books Currie dismissed as "gestures of revolt."[5] *Sons and Lovers* was indeed generally regarded in 1930 as Lawrence's masterpiece, and, interestingly, the other novel extensively admired by the obituarists as one of his "best" two books was *The Lost Girl*. *The Rainbow* and *Women in Love*, today considered his preeminent artistic accomplishments, rarely received high praise in the death notices, especially in England (*The Rainbow* was largely ignored), and *Lady Chatterley* was likewise little appreciated. The other novels only rarely drew individual comment. A few in the obituary press thought Lawrence's most enduring art was his poetry, while his talents as a dramatist and essayist went virtually unrecognized.

Of all who wrote about Lawrence in 1930, it was his fellow authors Forster and Bennett who gave the most daring and accurate predictions of how future generations would respond to his work.[6] Forster declared in the *Listener* (4/30/30) that the day was "not far off" when Lawrence would "become famous" with readers, and Bennett stated in the London *Evening Standard* (4/10/30): "I would say that no finer work has yet been done in our time than Lawrence's finest. He is not yet understood, even by the majority of his admirers, but he will be, and meanwhile his work must accept injustice."

The most immediate injustice came in the form of ten book-length memoirs by Lawrence's friends and relatives in the decade following his death. These memoirists — Jessie Chambers, Ada Lawrence, John Middleton Murry (who wrote two books on Lawrence during the 1930s), Catherine Carswell, Mabel Dodge Luhan, Dorothy Brett, Knud Merrild, Earl and Achsah Brewster, and Frieda Lawrence — presented information invaluable to later scholars, but each individual was deeply involved in Lawrence's life, and, therefore, could hardly be expected to view him dispassionately. Several memoirists portrayed him as a savior of the modern age, while others pictured him as a petulant, bizarre genius. A few attempted to dissect the neuroses, fixations, and complexes they perceived in the autobiographical stratum of his work. Murry, for instance, argued in his influential *Son of Woman* (1931) that the weaknesses in Lawrence's art and personality derived from his crippling relationship with his mother. The neurotic "sex-crucified" failure portrayed in *Son of Woman* was counterbalanced impressively by the portrait that Aldous Huxley offered in his splendid introduction to *The Letters of D. H. Lawrence* (1932), of Lawrence as a sensitive and intelligent artist whose loyalty to his extraordinary "gift — the immediate perception and artistic rendering of divine otherness" accounted "for all that the world found strange in his beliefs and his behaviour." The memoirs by Murry and the others clouded the issue of Lawrence's artistry and served to keep the public focused, instead, on his personality.

For at least the first half dozen years after his death, there was some stir of interest in Lawrence. Eleven of his books were reissued in a small "uniform" edition by Albert and Charles Boni, and his posthumously published works, including *Apocalypse* (1931), *The Letters of D. H. Lawrence, Etruscan Places, Last Poems* (all 1932), and the *Phoenix* essays (1936), were widely and often more sympathetically reviewed than those published during his lifetime.

Lawrence's value as an "artist first of all" (to use Huxley's phrase) was noted also by F. R. Leavis and Horace Gregory, who in the early 1930s each wrote outstanding studies of Lawrence. Leavis in his pamphlet *D. H. Lawrence* (1930) argued for his subject's recognition as an original and important writer, anticipating the even stronger case that he was to make on the artist's behalf two decades hence, when he would spearhead the Lawrence "revival." Like Stephen Potter's less illuminating *D. H. Lawrence: A First Study* (1930), Gregory's *Pilgrim of the Apocalypse* (1933) was one of the earliest attempts to place all of Lawrence's writings in critical perspective, and his tracing of Lawrence's themes and his argument that Lawrence was essentially a romantic poet-prophet in the tradition of Shelley and Whitman constituted some of the most perceptive commentary on Lawrence during the two decades following his death.

During the 1930s over 40 books were written about Lawrence (roughly one-third of them in languages other than English), and most of the ones not devoted to dissecting his personality concentrated on the task of sorting out—usually for the purpose of defending or attacking—the various aspects of his "metaphysic," in particular his intense rejection of the Christian-democratic ethos. The publication of such late works as *The Man Who Died* and *Apocalypse* elicited further condemnation of what some writers perceived to be his destructive "neo-paganism" and "heresy," but other writers took issue with that position and with T. S. Eliot's charge in *After Strange Gods* (1934) that Lawrence's vision had been "spiritually sick," that he had been an "instrument" for "daemonic forces" in modern times.[7] Lawrence's "cosmic mysticism" drew extensive commentary from Frederick Carter in *D. H. Lawrence and the Body Mystical* (1932) and Helen Corke in *Lawrence and Apocalypse* (1933), and Saul Colin, Anaïs Nin, and several others who wrote books on Lawrence during the period made enthusiastic defenses of Lawrence as a deeply religious modern mystic. His mysticism fared not so well, however, in the pages of William York Tindall's provocative *D. H. Lawrence and Susan His Cow* (1939). Attempting to place Lawrence historically within the intellectual, social, and literary context of the early twentieth century, Tindall's book treated him as a romantic irrationalist intent on founding a "private religion" which, Tindall argued, Lawrence had been unable to keep separate from his art.[8] Tindall's summations of Lawrence's theories were uniformly reductive and ironic, but he was one of the first scholars to research Lawrence's interest in animism, theosophy, and yoga, and to explore the anthropological sources for *The Plumed Serpent*.

While Tindall dismissed Lawrence's social, political, and economic theories as inconsistent and impractical, others during the thirties took his ideas more seriously, as the worldwide Depression and the upsurge of communism and fascism were casting a perilous shadow over Europe. Lawrence's indictment of democracy made him attractive to writers of both the Left and the Right as the political tug-of-war raged during the decade. His own working-class origins and his antagonism toward capitalistic industrial society drew the attention of such Socialist critics as John Strachey and Christopher Caudwell, though each ultimately condemned Lawrence as an ineffectual "bourgeois artist" whose revolutionary solution was Fascist rather than Communist. A considerable number of writers in the thirties proposed that Lawrence's hatred of reason, his advocacy of vitalistic "blood-consciousness" and primitive "dark" gods, his call (in *The Plumed Serpent* and elsewhere) for an elite class of charismatic dictatorial "leaders," and his own messianic impulse made him a "proto-Fascist." French critic Ernest Seillière in *David Herbert Lawrence et les récentes idéologies allemandes* in 1936 argued — on slim evidence — that Lawrence had been influenced by certain German pre-Hitlerite writers. Tindall in his chapter "Lawrence among the Fascists" mounted a lukewarm defense, noting that Lawrence's "stubborn individualism" would have prevented his ever deferring to any authoritarian leader, and contending that he was more a "theocratic Fascist" bent on using politics to advance his religion, rather than the other way round.[9] Others, like Danish critic Elias Bredsdorff, waged stronger defenses against the charge of Lawrence's "Nazi tendencies," but this issue was to continue to draw critics into combat for many years beyond World War II.

As the thirties progressed and readers became more and more preoccupied with the deepening economic and political troubles afflicting nations in Europe and elsewhere, Lawrence's own writings began to seem to them outmoded. As Horace Gregory had remarked prophetically in a December 1932 issue of the *New Republic*, "The world is moving away from Lawrence's need for personal salvation, his 'dark religion' is not a substitute for economic planning."[10] Readers turned to new literature pervaded by a new social and political consciousness, and Lawrence's reputation took a severe downward swing. By 1937 Leavis was complaining in *Scrutiny* that Lawrence had become "distinctly passé" among "ruling literary intellectuals," and that while he was "generally accepted" as a "genius," it was as a "muddle-headed" one no longer to be taken seriously as an intellectual and spiritual force (if ever he had been so taken).[11] On the tenth anniversary of Lawrence's death, Harry T. Moore lamented in the *Saturday Review of Literature* that the British author had become "The Great Unread."[12]

The 1940s

For a time it appeared that Frank Swinnerton's prophecy in *The Georgian Scene* (1934), that Lawrence's reputation was destined to decline, might prove accurate. Dial Press issued *The First Lady Chatterley* in 1944, causing a mild flurry of interest when an effort was made in New York to suppress its publication, but Lawrence's works otherwise received little public attention in the forties. Between 1943 and 1948, only three of his novels, *Sons and Lovers, Women in Love,* and *The Plumed Serpent,* were published (by Heinemann), and except for small editions of a few minor collections of stories and poems, the rest of his works were by mid-decade generally unobtainable. His reputation reached its nadir in about 1942: in that year, fewer than a dozen items were published about him (as opposed to almost a hundred in 1932). At least 45 books and pamphlets were written about Lawrence in the 1930s, but only four were published in the 1940s, three of those in Italy.

By the late 1940s there were some signs of a quickening interest in Lawrence's works, after the lull. Viking published *The Portable D. H. Lawrence* (1947), an anthology of works in various genres, and other presses published *D. H. Lawrence: Selected Poems* (1947) and *D. H. Lawrence's Letters to Bertrand Russell* (ed. Harry Moore, 1948). Though some reviewers complained that Diana Trilling had selected the wrong works for inclusion in *The Portable D. H. Lawrence* and that her introduction was too apologetic, that collection marked a turning point in the reception of Lawrence's literature, and both it and the *Selected Poems* with Kenneth Rexroth's introduction have since remained in print. More significantly, Heinemann published "uniform" editions of *Aaron's Rod* and *Women in Love* in 1949, and within two years added seven more novels and a number of other works, and these and especially the "Phoenix" editions of Lawrence's works which Heinemann also published in the 1950s played a major part in the renascence of interest in him during that decade.

While acknowledging that Lawrence was seldom being read in the 1940s, novelist Elizabeth Bowen contended that he had become part "of the English bloodstream" and that his "trail" could be picked up "across the work of most English novelists making their mark now."[13] "This is his day," she declared. "He has outlived his denouncers." Lawrence's prophecies had been substantiated by the passage of time, she argued, especially the way he had foreseen how the prevalent attitudes in modern civilization would lead to the cataclysm of a second world war. Other writers agreed. As he had in *D. H. Lawrence and Susan His Cow,* Tindall in *Forces in Modern British Literature, 1885–1946* (1947) still argued that most of Lawrence's novels were "not first rate," "their beauties [being] lost among the sermons," but from his post-Hiroshima perspective Tindall found new relevance in Lawrence's dire warnings against modern man's overreliance on scientific, technical rationalism.[14] Lawrence's "crusade against science," Tindall wrote, "seems less absurd today than it used to seem."

Mark Schorer's important article "Technique as Discovery," in the *Hudson Review* in spring 1948, used *Sons and Lovers* as a negative illustration for his thesis that form in the novel determines content or function (a view essentially the opposite of Lawrence's own aesthetic ideas).[15] Tracing the "confusions between intention and performance" in *Sons and Lovers*, Schorer echoed the many complaints by earlier critics about Lawrence's seeming "formlessness." That same year, E. W. Tedlock, Jr., edited *The Frieda Lawrence Collection of D. H. Lawrence Manuscripts: A Descriptive Bibliography*, which valuably displayed the writer's working methods and helped, as Schorer's keenly analytical essay did also, to focus further attention on Lawrence's literary techniques.

The 1950s

Several things help to explain why the climate of opinion regarding Lawrence's status changed so markedly during the 1950s. Enough time had passed to allow the battle smoke to clear from most of the violent controversies that his life and art had sparked decades earlier. Moreover, as Tindall had observed, Lawrence's ideas seemed more serious and acceptable to readers at mid-century. Also, western society by that time had developed more permissive standards regarding sexual behavior, so Lawrence's writings about sex no longer seemed as shockingly "licentious" as they had to earlier readers. Thus the way was cleared for readers to make a more discerning estimate of his life and work, and by mid-century a critical and biographical "revival" of his reputation was under way. Concurrent with and more important than all the writings being published about Lawrence then was the large-scale reprinting of his own works in England and America. During the decade Heinemann published in its hardbound "Phoenix" series ten of his novels and a good deal of the rest of his canon, and Penguin Books issued many of his works in cheap paperback editions, thus making his literature available to a much wider audience.

Perhaps more so than is true of any other author, a reader gains understanding of Lawrence's literature through familiarity with his personal history. The most significant of the biographical studies so far produced about him were published during the 1950s. The earliest in English had been Hugh Kingsmill's occasionally disparaging *The Life of D. H. Lawrence* in 1938, largely an unadmirable cut-and-paste compilation from published memoirs and letters. The first of the biographies in the 1950s, Richard Aldington's *D. H. Lawrence: Portrait of a Genius, But . . .* (1950), more an appreciative "portrait" than a detailed biography, introduced little new information, as was the case also with Eliot Fay's *Lorenzo in Search of the Sun* (1953).

By far the most original, informative, and ultimately influential of the biographical works thus far published on Lawrence have been books produced during the 1950s by two American academics, Harry T. Moore and Edward Nehls. Of all who have written on Lawrence, the most assiduous researcher into his personal history has been Harry T. Moore. He wrote or edited six books on Lawrence during the fifties, and it was his biographical and critical labors and F. R. Leavis's provocative critical commentary that contributed the most to the effort to elevate Lawrence's literary status. Moore's *The Life and Works of D. H. Lawrence* (1951), *The Intelligent Heart* (1954), and *Poste Restante: A Lawrence Travel Calendar* (1956) were all sound scholarly examinations of Lawrence's material and creative existence. In *The Life and Works*, Moore gave perspective to Lawrence's career by dividing it into four "phases" — the first (1900–12) characterized by Lawrence's treatments of his youth, through his completion of *Sons and Lovers*; the second (1913–19) by his treatment of modern love and his "important psychological explorations into the emotional consciousness," especially in *The Rainbow* and *Women in Love*; the third (1920–25), his "wander years," by his treatment of mystical and political themes in works such as *The Plumed Serpent*; and the last (1926–30), by his treatment of sexual and religious themes in works such as *Lady Chatterley* and *Apocalypse*.[16] Scholars the world over have since made frequent use of Moore's shaping of Lawrence's literary development. *The Intelligent Heart* and *Poste Restante* each included fresh biographical information culled in part from the impressive cache of unpublished letters Moore had tracked down. For the next two decades he continued his effort to reconstruct the details of Lawrence's life and career, first revising and amplifying *The Life and Works* and *The Intelligent Heart* in the early 1960s and later revising the latter book again, publishing it in 1974 as *The Priest of Love*. In that version, still recognized as the standard Lawrence biography, he attempted to incorporate details from the many new Lawrence letters recovered and published since the fifties and to accommodate the new critical assessments of Lawrence offered during that interval.

Nehls's *D. H. Lawrence: A Composite Biography* (1957–59) was an extraordinary, original work of literary scholarship. In this three-volume biography of almost two thousand pages, Nehls compiled a montage of extracts from published memoirs, newly solicited reminiscences, fictional portraits, diary entries, letters, official documents, newspaper articles, radio interviews, essays by various contemporaries of Lawrence, snippets from his own imaginative writings, and many other such clippings, and arranged them chronologically according to their content, so that the events of Lawrence's life and career were seen from numerous shifting points of view. Lawrence's own comments on people and situations in his life were juxtaposed to opinions expressed by his contemporaries, and from this montage emerged a more objective portrait of him than had ever been recorded.

The rounded and ultimately sympathetic accounts of Lawrence's life by Moore and Nehls offered a meaningful corrective to the distorted image — of Lawrence as a diabolic, erratic, and often neurotic genius — created by some of the earlier critics and memoirists, and the research performed by these two biographers implemented and complemented the fresh critical reception which Lawrence's art had begun receiving at mid-century.

Many of the earlier commentaries on Lawrence's writings had been impassioned observations on "the meaning of Lawrence," but such impressionistic essays gave way after mid-century to more deeply analytic studies of his ideas as they were expressed in the separate novels and tales. As F. R. Leavis's title suggested, it was *D. H. Lawrence: Novelist* (1955) that predominantly drew critics' interest in the fifties. Huxley, in his introduction to the 1932 *Letters*, had acknowledged that his friend's efforts to show the "carbon" of human character, to express "psychological reality," had made his novels "so curiously difficult to get through," and for several decades after Huxley had noted this "strangeness" in Lawrence's fiction, readers had continued frequently to express puzzlement over the meaning and value of the novels that had followed *Sons and Lovers*. But in the fifties critics began to "get through" the novels in a fresh, illuminating way, and, particularly because of the compelling arguments of Leavis, *The Rainbow* and *Women in Love* were by the end of the decade generally decreed to stand above all Lawrence's other fiction. *Sons and Lovers*, still admired, slipped to third in this new hierarchical view of the novels, and though *Lady Chatterley* was still drawing fire for what Anglican priest William Tiverton called its "solemn pornographics" — its four-letter words — and its explicit treatment of sexuality, that novel, too, was finding a few more defenders.

Even in the most valuable of the 1950s critical books there remained a slightly too-insistent tone, as the various authors defended Lawrence against the long-standing charges that he had lacked cultural roots; that he had been a proto-Fascist, a pornographer, or a philosopher of demonism; that despite his intuitive genius he had lacked artistic discretion and the ability to structure his works and to create characters who were not projections of himself; that he had allowed the "medicine man" to overwhelm the artist in his later writings. No critic was more a polemicist on Lawrence's behalf than Leavis, the distinguished British critic, who responded to these and other charges in *D. H. Lawrence: Novelist*, to this day the most influential book on Lawrence. In Leavis's eyes, Lawrence was "the great creative genius" of "our phase of civilization," a "master" novelist, "surely the supreme master of short fiction," "a great social historian" — and these are but a sampling of the encomia heaped on the artist by Leavis. Today, readers might be puzzled over what seems an inordinately combative tone throughout *D. H. Lawrence: Novelist*, but at mid-century Leavis felt — and with some justification — that he was taking on the entire British literary establishment that had refused to give Lawrence his "due" recognition as a great artist.

Leavis insisted that criticism of Lawrence's doctrine could not be separated from judgments concerning his art, and one of the main values of *D. H. Lawrence: Novelist* was the way it demonstrated Lawrence's achievement specifically as an *artist*.[17] Using New Critical tactics, Leavis showed that Lawrence's more successful long fictions, in particular *The Rainbow* and *Women in Love*, could be viewed as admirably constructed "dramatic poems"—that is, as complex and subtle organisms of meaning wherein every scene, action, character, or image has been carefully deployed by the artist to forward the organized development of his themes.

Leavis vigorously and systematically rebutted the pronouncements Eliot had made in *After Strange Gods* (1934) and elsewhere against Lawrence's snobbishness and class-consciousness, his lack of a sense of humor, his sexual morbidity, his "lack of intellectual and social training," his "incapacity for what is ordinarily called thinking," his inability to make a finished work of art, and his religious "ignorance." Most significantly, against Eliot's orthodoxy and his labeling of Lawrence as heretical, Leavis insisted on Lawrence's having been a "moral" and "affirmative" writer the greatness of whose art had lain in its "normative" bearings. Lawrence had possessed an "almost infallible sense for health and sanity," Leavis argued, and he placed him with Austen, George Eliot, James, and Conrad in what he called "the great tradition" of the English novel, a line of writers whose works showed "a vital capacity for experience, a kind of reverent openness before life, and a marked moral intensity."[18] He further asserted that Lawrence's insistence on individual regeneration and "full spontaneous being," his focus on the organic "oneness" of human life, and his advocacy of one's reestablishing a "responsive relation with the cosmos" were all fundamentally "religious" concerns, vital in an uprooted age.

A good number of other books during the fifties similarly emphasized the "religious" dimension of Lawrence's writings. Father William Tiverton surveyed the prose works aesthetically and ideologically in *D. H. Lawrence and Human Existence* in 1951 and concluded that Lawrence's pantheism and notions on the importance and potentially sacramental nature of human sexuality had been not at all inimical to Christian thought. The same year, Sinhalese novelist Martin Wickramasinghe noted in *The Mysticism of D. H. Lawrence* the affinity of his occultism and his attitudes toward sex to the old Indian mystic philosophy known as Tantricism. Lawrence's mysticism was likewise the focus of *Brave Men: D. H. Lawrence and Simone Weil* (1958), wherein Richard Rees praised the efforts Lawrence and the French mystic had each made to counteract the loss of the religious sense in the modern world by emphasizing a vitalistic religion of love. Mark Spilka's impressive commentary on *The Love Ethic of D. H. Lawrence* (1955) built on Tiverton and Leavis, further exploring the ways Lawrence's work had been "governed by religious ends." Works such as *Lady Chatterley* and *The Man Who Died*, Spilka declared, "give us . . . a fund of rejuvenated ideals, a creative pattern for the future."[19]

Two other writers in the fifties made noteworthy comprehensive efforts to analyze Lawrence's leading ideas. Neither Mary Freeman in *D. H. Lawrence: A Basic Study of His Ideas* (1955) nor Graham Hough in *The Dark Sun* (1956) were especially original, but each usefully summarized the previous commentaries on Lawrence, and contributed to his critical rehabilitation. Perhaps more successfully than most writers of the fifties, Hough illustrated the fusion of the aesthetic and prophetic halves of Lawrence's work, as he explained how the artist, with his "disrupting and fertilising" vitalism, had been "near the centre" of "a great revolution of sensibility" earlier in the century. Freeman's often tendentious book focused more exclusively on Lawrence as prophet, concentrating on his "social ethics" and the development of his ideas (for example, his flirtation with and ultimate rejections of futurism, fascism, and socialism) as he had moved from novel to novel. Like most major Lawrence critics during the fifties, Freeman concluded that he had been an affirmative prophet whose literature held normative value for readers.

The title of a Harry T. Moore article in the 12 March 1955 *Saturday Review* proclaimed "The Return of D. H. Lawrence," and by the end of the decade the artist had indeed emerged from the shadows and had begun to take his place alongside Joyce, Faulkner, Mann, Proust, and other "classic" modern novelists.

The 1960s

As the 1950s ended, editions of his various works were proliferating. Sales of *Sons and Lovers* were stimulated in 1960 by a popular Twentieth-Century Fox film version, and after heavily publicized censorship trials in America in 1959 and England in 1960, *Lady Chatterley's Lover* was published in those countries for the first time in its unexpurgated form and immediately rose near the top of best-seller lists. Penguin Books published the novel in fall 1960, and between 10 November of that year and June 1961, sold well over three million copies in England alone. According to Gerald J. Pollinger, literary executor of the Lawrence estate, sales figures for *Lady Chatterley* during the 1960s and 1970s exceeded 4,500,000 copies.[20] *Sons and Lovers*, *Women in Love*, and *The Rainbow*, in that order, have been Lawrence's next three best-selling books, but sales figures for none of them have approached those of *Lady Chatterley*. The biggest-ever sales period for his books occurred during 1960–69, when worldwide sales totalled roughly ten million copies. The extensive press coverage given the *Lady Chatterley* trials had brought Lawrence's other books to the attention of a new reading public on a scale that would have seemed unimaginable during the years in which his reputation had been in eclipse.

Except for *Movements in European History* and a few of the lesser-known novels, travel books, and translations, all of Lawrence's books were in print during the sixties, and some of his previously unpublished or long-out-of-print writings were newly published. His *Phoenix* collection, long out of print, was reprinted in England in 1961, inspiring Leavis to declare it "the finest body of criticism in existence,"[21] and it was reissued in America by Viking in 1968 as a companion to another such Lawrence miscellany that editors Warren Roberts and Harry Moore called *Phoenix II*. Many of the sixty-one essays, stories, and sundry short pieces in *Phoenix II* had previously been uncollected or generally unavailable, and a few items had never been published. Interest in Lawrence's expository writings was stimulated also by the publication of *The Symbolic Meaning* (ed. Armin Arnold, 1962), a collection of the early versions of his essays on American literature. *The Collected Letters of D. H. Lawrence* (ed. Harry Moore, 1962) and other new collections of his correspondence introduced hundreds of important letters during the 1960s, helping readers further flesh out that "biography of an emotional and inner life" that Lawrence had spoken of in the preface to his collected poems. And further indices of the burgeoning interest in his art during the decade were the assembling of large collections of *The Paintings of D. H. Lawrence* (ed. Mervyn Levy, 1964); *The Complete Plays of D. H. Lawrence* (1966); and *The Complete Poems of D. H. Lawrence* (ed. Vivian de Sola Pinto and F. Warren Roberts, 1964).

Critical books and journal articles about Lawrence were on the increase (especially in America) during the 1960s, furthering his transformation from an idiosyncratic figure into a major writer in the history of the English novel. By the end of the decade *The D. H. Lawrence Review* was established by editor James C. Cowan as a forum for criticism and scholarship (and that journal has continued to thrive). Many of the outstanding critical books of the sixties—those by George Ford, Julian Moynahan, and H. M. Daleski come most quickly to mind—have become "standards" that Lawrence scholars ever since have felt it their duty to assimilate. Feeling less need to defend Lawrence's place in the literary pantheon, critics were generally able to forgo polemics in favor of New Critical analyses of his novels. Also, several studies perceptively examined his essays as keys to the novels. The most notable of such efforts, Daleski's *The Forked Flame* (1965), used "Study of Thomas Hardy" as the basis for a thorough exploration of Lawrence's concepts about "dualism" as they are reflected in his novels. His creative work, Daleski proposed, was a lifelong effort to reconcile the opposed male and female principles within himself, but because he was more strongly feminine than masculine, he was unable ever to effect such a reconciliation. This theory of Lawrence's dualism became a means of Daleski's gauging the value of the novels: the finest (in particular *The Rainbow*) are those wherein the author attempts a polarity between the two principles; the poorest (*Aaron's Rod, Kangaroo, The Plumed Serpent*), those in which, against his own nature, he insists on masculine domination.

Lawrence's poems, plays, essays, travel books, and letters received some critical attention during the sixties, but usually only insofar as they were useful in illuminating his fiction. The novels—especially *Sons and Lovers, The Rainbow*, and *Women in Love*—remained the prime interest for most scholars. Leavis had passed over *Sons and Lovers* lightly, but Daniel Weiss and other critics in the sixties examined that novel closely, focusing especially on its oedipal theme, its structure, and Lawrence's problematic handling of point-of-view. As the decade progressed, a radical shift occurred in the way *Women in Love* was being interpreted. One catalyst of this shift was the appearance, in the *Texas Quarterly* in 1963 and later in *Phoenix II*, of the controversial "Prologue to *Women in Love*." This cancelled first chapter of the novel, which extensively explores Birkin's attraction to men, figured centrally in the fresh interpretations Colin Clarke, David Cavitch, and others in the late 1960s were to make of the ethical and aesthetic values of the most complex of Lawrence's fictions.

The Plumed Serpent and *Lady Chatterley* also received fairly intensive treatment from critics during the sixties, though most commentators agreed with Eliseo Vivas's estimation (in *D. H. Lawrence: The Failure and the Triumph of Art*, 1960) that both novels were aesthetic "failures." Since Tindall's high valuation of *The Plumed Serpent* in the 1930s, it had seldom found defenders, and frequent objections had been voiced about its "formlessness" and about its ideology—its advocacy of "Fascistic" leadership, "mindless" paganism, and male-dominated sexual politics. But L. D. Clark in *Dark Night of the Body* (1964)—to this day the best study of *The Plumed Serpent*—defended its "peculiar brilliance," claiming that, despite its excesses of language and prophecy, the book is saved from its author and his polemic intentions by two things: his "profound sympathy with the land he was writing about, and his uncanny skill at synthesizing form and setting and symbol."[22] *Lady Chatterley* similarly found defenders in Moynahan and Daleski, whose respective treatments of its symbolism and themes formed the most sensitive critical assessments that book received prior to the 1970s. Most who commented on *Lady Chatterley* during the sixties, however, repeated the familiar complaints, that the "message" overwhelms the art (Vivas); that its symbols and realistic dimensions fail to cohere (Ian Gregor); that it falsifies sexual experience (David Holbrook); that its solutions for modern social problems are "oversimple" (Colin Clarke). Much of the commentary about *Lady Chatterley* during the decade dealt less with aesthetic matters than with censorship, the book's sexual ideology, or other controversial issues raised by the recent trials involving the novel.

A substantial portion of the books on Lawrence during the 1960s were primarily concerned either with endorsing or challenging Leavis's pronouncements. That critic's version of Lawrence as a "normative" artist and as a "life"-affirming moralist was confirmed and elaborated, for instance, in insightful studies by George Panichas (*Adventure in Consciousness: The Meaning of D. H. Lawrence's Religious Quest*, 1964), Laurence Lerner (*The Truthtellers*, 1967), Keith Sagar, and Julian Moynahan. But whereas Leavis had cast Lawrence as the inheritor of the "great tradition of the English novel," Sagar concentrated *The Art of D. H. Lawrence* (1966) "more on Lawrence's reaction *against* the English realist tradition" and on placing him alongside Sophocles, Shakespeare, Tolstoy, and Hardy in a larger, older (and less parochial) tradition of writers who "[set] behind the small action of [their] protagonists the terrific action of unfathomed nature."[23] Moynahan likewise found the "moral tradition of the English novel" too constricting a designation for Lawrence's fictions, but he nonetheless ended *The Deed of Life* (1963) with a Leavisian acclamation of Lawrence as a Moses-like prophet leading modern men out of a material and spiritual industrial wasteland toward a vitalistic transformation of being and "a human community that is suffused with reverence for life."[24]

Throughout the 1960s, however, numerous other commentators were reacting against what Eugene Goodheart called the "sterile classicizing"[25] of Lawrence by Leavis and his followers. Arguing that these scholars had gone too far in "normalizing" Lawrence, the anti-Leavisites themselves focused anew on what they considered the more problematic—and, to them, more interesting—aspects of Lawrence's life and writings, for example, on: (1) his use of art as "therapy" for his own neuroses and repressions; (2) the "perverse" elements of his "love ethic" (for instance, the anal preoccupations, homoeroticism, and misogyny exhibited by some of his protagonists in love); (3) his moral nihilism and "Dionysiac" enthusiasms; (4) his social rage and reactionary political views; (5) the paradoxic and often self-contradictory nature of his ideas; and (6) his failure to achieve psychic "integration" in any of his protagonists. As Mark Spilka and others subsequently observed, the diabolic, Fascistic, rebellious, perverse, and maladjusted writer portrayed by anti-Leavisite critics in the 1960s and 1970s often seemed strangely like the scandalous Lawrence of old, that "stormy petrel of literature" who had previously drawn such rabid disapprobation from so many critics, clerics, and censors. But there was nonetheless a substantial difference between the way Lawrence was treated in most of the books of the sixties and the way the earlier negative commentators had appraised his work. With few exceptions (notably, John Stoll and John Harrison, who seemed wholly unsympathetic to Lawrence), the anti-Leavisites of the sixties and later were not reluctant to grant Lawrence a lofty place in literary history; they simply preferred to revere his books less for their being high-moral visions than for their being brilliantly equivocal, revolutionary, and apocalyptic. In short, they often valued his art most for its idiosyncratic depictions of the extremities of human experience, for its precisely *not* having that "normative" value Leavis and his followers assigned to it.

The first challenge to Leavis's "abandoned panegyrics" on Lawrence was that thrown up by the American aesthetician Eliseo Vivas in *D. H. Lawrence: The Failure and the Triumph of Art*. The "triumphs," Vivas proclaimed, were *Sons and Lovers*, *The Rainbow*, and *Women in Love*, where the novelist successfully creates a fictional world through dramatic interactions of his characters, without the intercession of the "pamphleteer" who spoils all the other novels. Vivas countered Leavis's claims for Lawrence's prophetic art by asserting that the writer's moral, social, and political philosophy had been warped by his own emotional disorders and consequently "is a mixture of sense and nonsense . . . wisdom and corruption."[26] In particular Vivas condemned Lawrence's "love ethic," arguing that his "radical alienation" and incapacity to love led him to reject "agape" and serve only "eros," to advocate cruel and corrosive passion while overlooking tenderness. Also, though the questions of Lawrence's "Fascist" tendencies had been resolved to the satisfaction of most readers by Mary Freeman in the fifties, Vivas raised it again, and the issue surfaced as well in other books of the sixties, in those by David Cavitch and Stoll and especially in Harrison's *The Reactionaries* (1966), where Lawrence is lumped with Yeats, Pound, Eliot, and Wyndham Lewis — the "anti-democratic intelligentsia" of their day — and scolded for his "viciousness of temperament" and advocacy of brutal authoritarian societies.

The focus of both Kingsley Widmer in *The Art of Perversity* (1962) and E. W. Tedlock, Jr., in *D. H. Lawrence Artist and Rebel* (1963) was the "rebellious," "nihilistic," and "vitalistic" dimensions of Lawrence's fiction, but whereas Tedlock asserted that the artist's "militant vitalism" predominates over his nihilism, Widmer audaciously asserted the counterview, that Lawrence's vitalism is an aspect of his nihilistic embracing of "the reality of nothingness." According to Widmer, the short fiction often evidences a fascination with "strange and annihilating extremes" of feeling and conduct which, Lawrence believed, could lead an individual toward regeneration into vital "fulness" of being. "Such perversity," Widmer concluded, "is true art."[27] Contrary to Raymond Williams's assertion in *Culture and Society* (1958) that Lawrence's gesture toward community is more essential than the fact of his alienation, Widmer, Tedlock, and Eugene Goodheart portrayed him as a modern romantic "rebel" necessarily operating *outside* of civilization in order to effect changes in human consciousness. Goodheart concluded *The Utopian Vision of D. H. Lawrence* (1963) declaring that Lawrence simply cannot properly be made "to serve the gods of a humanistic civilization" unless his words are severely misunderstood.[28] Given Lawrence's "power-urge," his hostility to Christianity, his dynamic egoism, and his dangerous and provocative prophetic

vision, Goodheart propounded, he fits better into the tradition of vision-
ary "tablet-breakers" with writers like Blake, Dostoyevski, Nietzsche, and
Rilke than into the confining English ethical and artistic traditions where
Leavis had embedded him.

Leavis also had found no basic contradictions in Lawrence's art and
psyche, but Goodheart, Widmer, George Ford, Colin Clarke, and others
writing in the sixties emphasized and often praised the self-contradictions
and unresolved oppositions that they believed give Lawrence's best works
some of their special dramatic force. Ford's *Double Measure* (1965)
brilliantly explored the conflicting "rhythm of creating and destroying,"
the "double measure" between "life and death forces," and the drives
"toward isolation" and "toward union" that inform *Women in Love* and
Lawrence's other major works.[29] Contravening the views of the Leavisites,
Ford asserted that Lawrence's aim is never to resolve such paradoxes and
thereby to supply absolutes or paradigms for human behavior, but rather
to show, through the juxtapositions of "compelling opposites," the human
situation as it *is*.

The moral ambiguities of Lawrence's fictions were even more intensively investigated by Colin Clarke in *River of Dissolution: D. H. Lawrence and English Romanticism* (1969). Clarke's provocative thesis was
that a reader errs in assuming "that, quite simply, Lawrence spoke for life
and growth against mechanism and the flux of corruption."[30] According to
Clarke, Lawrence inherited from the English Romantic poets a tradition
of concepts and images which expresses a deeply ambiguous, paradoxic
attitude toward corruption, reduction, and disintegration, and this is
evidenced particularly in *Women in Love* where the author often seems
darkly equivocal toward the processes of decay and at times even
sanctions the forces of "perversity" that he elsewhere in the novel attacks.
With his homoerotic attraction to Gerald and his practice of anal sex with
Ursula, Birkin embraces the same "corruption" embodied in Crich,
Gudrun, and Loerke, observed Clarke, but Lawrence's hero is finally able
to pass beyond this paradoxically life-giving dissolution to a new germina-
tion and relative wholeness of being.

Clarke's insistence on the centrality of anal-eroticism in Lawrence's
art renewed contention among critics. Earlier in the sixties, G. Wilson
Knight, William Empson, John Sparrow and others had waged a lively
skirmish in the pages of *Essays in Criticism* and *Encounter* over whether
or not Lawrence celebrates anal penetration in *Lady Chatterley* and, if so,
how that should affect the reader's understanding of the novel. With
variations, this debate was renewed, for several years, following the
publication of *River of Dissolution*. Some commentators, such as R. E.
Pritchard in *D. H. Lawrence: Body of Darkness* (1971), extended Clarke's
arguments. Others hotly challenged Clarke and those who concurred with
his view that Lawrence assigns strong value to the modes of "disintegra-

tion" in his fiction. For example, Spilka in a review essay, "Lawrence Up-Tight, or the Anal Phase Once Over,"[31] reasserted the moralistic reading of *Women in Love* and *Lady Chatterley*, arguing that anal sex in those novels is a mere "final therapeutic purging" that occurs *after* the lovers have undergone their basic sexual regeneration.

Though *River of Dissolution* was widely condemned, Clarke's study did contribute to the important reassessment being made of Leavis's view of *Women in Love*. David Cavitch's *D. H. Lawrence and the New World* (1969) similarly proposed a radical new perspective on that novel. Drawing heavily on the "Prologue to *Women in Love*," Cavitch claimed that much of Lawrence's fictional art is motivated by suppressed homoeroticism. In *Women in Love*, he proposed, Lawrence transfers to Gudrun all the sexual fears and fantasies "that would have been Birkin's if his homosexuality had become explicitly the central issue in the fiction," and her "distorted" sexual feelings have their psychological genesis in Lawrence himself.[32] Likewise, Cavitch suggested, the heroines in the fictions of Lawrence's American period who submit to brutal male force, are each Lawrence's own persona. But sometime during the author's "new world" experience, Cavitch argued, he realized the psychic conflict underlying his art, realized that even in America he could not freely be his androgynous self, and thus thereafter wrote only escapist idylls filled with fear of male sexuality.

A growing number of critics in the sixties were similarly taking a psychoanalytic approach to Lawrence. As Cavitch acknowledged, his study was indebted to another Freudian reading of Lawrence done earlier in the decade by Daniel Weiss. Weiss, refuting the view expressed by Tiverton and others that Lawrence had successfully shed his Oedipus complex in writing *Sons and Lovers*, contended instead in *Oedipus in Nottingham* (1962) that Lawrence's unresolved feelings for his mother and father informed the structure of works throughout his career, up through *Lady Chatterley*, where we finally see "the perfection of his reactive anti-Oedipal vision of life," as, for the first time, he fully identifies "with the once-despised father" in his delineation of the gamekeeper.[33] Weiss thus perceived the full movement of Lawrence's writings as a victorious emergence from the oedipal drama. John Stoll disagreed, in his own "modified Freudian" study, *D. H. Lawrence's "Sons and Lovers": Self-Encounter and the Unknown Self* (1968), contending that Lawrence, because of his "abnormal" sexual and psychological views and his overvaluing of "blood-consciousness," never achieved any sort of resolution or harmony within his psyche.[34] Whatever their conclusion about Lawrence's triumphs and failures, these psychoanalytic critics of the sixties, using his works as documents to analyze his subconscious drives and neuroses, certainly arrived at a version of Lawrence substantively different from that perceived by Leavis and his followers.

1970–1985

Lawrence studies in the seventies and eighties were especially energized by three important events: (1) the launching of the Cambridge University Press (CUP) scholarly editions of his *Letters* and *Works*; (2) the fiftieth anniversary of his death, marked in 1980 by festivals at Eastwood, at Taos, and at other sites around the world; and (3) the 1985 centenary anniversary of his birth, celebrated by conferences and festivals in England, America, France, and India and commemorated by the unveiling of a memorial stone to Lawrence in Poets' Corner of Westminster Abbey and by many special publications.

Books about Lawrence — more than 200 in all — continued to cascade from the world's academic and commercial presses between 1970 and 1985. Certain trends were evident: (1) much new energy was being devoted to textual and bibliographical matters, making available to scholars a full range of reliable materials; (2) perceptions of Lawrence's creative processes, of his methods of revising, were changing radically; (3) Lawrence's works in genres other than the novel were receiving far more intense critical attention than before (there were even books devoted to his work as a translator and as a painter); (4) increased and subtler attention was likewise being paid to the literature of his "leadership" period of the early 1920s, and to such late works as *Lady Chatterley* and *Apocalypse*; (5) scholars were taking more eclectic critical-interpretive approaches to his literature and life (there were, for example, numerous biographical, feminist, psychological, mythological, genetic, stylistic, historical or sociological, and influence and comparative studies); and (6) critics were focusing more closely on his technique and appraising his art much more objectively than had most of the earlier commentators.

Publication of Lawrence's Works.   By the 1970s, literally all of his previously published writings were in print, most of them available in paperback, and sales of his books continued to flourish not only in England and America, but also in Germany, France, and Italy, and — during recent years especially — in Japan, Spain, and South Korea. Probably the most remarkable aspect of the developing history of Lawrence's reputation has been the continuing introduction — in literally every decade since his death — of his own works, important materials published either for the first time or in forms radically different from previous publications. The publishing events of most import to Lawrence scholars in the 1970s and 1980s were: (1) the initial appearance in English of version two of *Lady Chatterley*, given the title *John Thomas and Lady Jane* (1972); (2) the publication of *Sons and Lovers: A Facsimile of the Manuscript* (1977); and (3) the momentous inauguration of the CUP editions of *The Letters of D. H. Lawrence* (1979–   ) and *The Works of D. H. Lawrence* (1980–   ), which should prove invaluable to biographers, literary critics, cultural historians, and future generations of readers.

Slowly over the years since his death, Lawrence's letters have been making their way into print, in a bewildering assortment of books and periodicals, but with the publication of the CUP *Letters* we have the promise of seeing all of his known surviving correspondence gathered in one standard edition. With an international team of respected scholars serving as editors, the eight CUP volumes (the last will be a grand index) will contain fifty-five hundred letters, including over two thousand published for the first time. The three huge, copiously annotated volumes of these *Letters* published through the mid-1980s were widely hailed for the proficient job done by General Editor James Boulton of the University of Nottingham and his coeditors. The CUP *Letters* will undoubtedly serve further to enhance Lawrence's reputation as being, with Byron and Keats, among the greatest letter-writers in English literature. Charged with the same creative energy as his imaginative writings, his letters are characteristically absorbing and lively, full of his own intensely interesting, mercurial personality and his often percipient observations on his life and times, and when the CUP *Letters* are completed, we should have, as Eugene Goodheart ventured in a review, "one of the great autobiographies of world literature."[35]

The projected thirty volumes of the CUP *Works of D. H. Lawrence* will comprise the first full-scale scholarly edition of the canon of a modern author. Each work is being critically edited by a knowledgeable Lawrence scholar and prepared after careful collation of the printed texts, extant manuscripts and typescripts, and other evidence. General Editors for the *Works* are James Boulton and Warren Roberts. Through the mid-1980s, eight CUP editions had appeared—*The Trespasser, The White Peacock, The Lost Girl, Mr Noon*, two collections of short fiction, and two volumes of expository writing—and they were welcomed by scholars who had long decried the unreliable, misprint-riddled texts of most earlier editions of Lawrence's works. As Michael Black and several other essayists pointed out in the critical anthology *D. H. Lawrence: The Man Who Lived* (ed. Robert Partlow and Harry Moore, 1980), Lawrence's texts have suffered myriad vicissitudes: they were tailored to placate timorous publishers and to appease censors and to avoid libel suits; they were sometimes cut radically by editors seeking to impose "form" on his fiction; they were tightened to answer space restrictions in periodicals; they were also often marred by Lawrence himself, as he inadvertently created errors during revision or proofreading. But now, assiduous efforts are being made to rectify these mistakes, and authoritative texts are being produced that are, the CUP editors say, as near as can be determined to what Lawrence himself would have wished to see printed. The debut volume, *"Apocalypse" and Other Writings on Revelation* (1980), sensitively and intelligently edited by Mara Kalnins, typified the rich offerings of all the subsequent CUP editions. In addition to the text of *Apocalypse* (based on the typescript version) and two short related pieces previously printed, the CUP edition included over 50 pages of previously unpublished deleted fragments of *Apocalypse*, extensive annotations, full textual apparatus, and a substantive introduction treating the genesis of the work and its critical reception.

Of the CUP *Works* published through the mid-1980s, the one that generated the most interest among readers was *Mr Noon* (1984), a novel only recently reconstructed from a manuscript lost for fifty years. As edited by Lindeth Vasey, it became the thirteenth published novel in the Lawrence canon (and the seventh in order of composition). Part 1 of *Mr Noon* had been previously published as a self-contained short story in *A Modern Lover* (1934), but part 2 (almost two hundred pages as published) had never appeared in print. The more substantial and engaging part 2 is a thinly disguised recountal of Lawrence's first few months with Frieda, when the two had eloped to the Continent in 1912. The novel ends in mid-sentence, and apparently Lawrence never reworked the story or pursued its publication. As reconstituted in the CUP edition, *Mr Noon* is certainly no major work in Lawrence's canon, but it is significant because it includes some of his most directly autobiographical writing and because it sheds light on his other novels of the early 1920s and on the general course of his artistic development. The appearance of *Mr Noon* evoked a rapid cross-fire of opinions from reviewers. One declared in the *Spectator*,[36] "It is bad, giving little evidence of the imagination at work." Others found fault with the book's capricious narrator, with his incessant invocations to the "Dear Reader" and his distracting disquisitions on sundry topics, and several reviewers echoed Raymond Williams's complaint in the 13 September 1984 *Guardian* that the two sections of the novel do not cohere (a charge convincingly countered by Blanchard's essay in this volume). But *Mr Noon* did find reviewers willing to praise at least some of its features, for instance its frequently sharp comedy or its fine travel and nature writing. David Lodge's opinion of the book paralleled that expressed by a good portion of the reviewers: while conceding that *Mr Noon* is a "flawed and broken-backed" novel, he asserted, "[B]ut it crackles with energy. It is a reckless, risky book that makes much of our own contemporary fiction seem over-anxious to please and impress. Its belated appearance is cause for . . . celebration."[37]

Bibliographies.   Since 1970 scholars have made meaningful contributions to the continuing effort to trace the development of Lawrence's publishing career and the history of his critical reputation. The most valuable bibliographic work on Lawrence, Warren Robert's *A Bibliography of D. H. Lawrence*, first published in 1963, was issued in a newly expanded and revised second edition in 1982. Because at various times

Lawrence switched publishers, printed books at private presses, revised or expurgated works to meet difficulties regarding censorship, and, to complicate things further, had his works stolen by publishing pirates, extraordinary bibliographical problems have faced scholars attempting to document his publishing career, but for over three decades Roberts made a commendable effort to compile an accurate and comprehensive primary bibliography.

In 1970 R. P. Draper collected in *D. H. Lawrence: The Critical Heritage* nearly 100 reviews (dating through 1933) which, taken together, presented a useful history of the reception given Lawrence's works by his contemporaries. The history of his reputation can be traced even more thoroughly in the two-volume *D. H. Lawrence: An Annotated Bibliography of Writings about Him* (1982, 1985), edited by James Cowan. These authoritative volumes, covering the years 1910–75, abstracted over forty-six hundred books and articles, and more recent bibliographies in *The D. H. Lawrence Review* and other periodicals listed well over fifteen hundred more works on Lawrence written since 1975. Another annotated bibliography, Thomas Jackson Rice's *D. H. Lawrence: A Guide to Research* (1983) was less comprehensive than Cowan's, but the information was accurate and accessible. By contrast, John Stoll's *D. H. Lawrence: A Bibliography 1911–1975* (1977) was unhelpfully formatted and shamefully riddled with mistakes.

Studies of the Novels. Of all the genres in which he worked, Lawrence's novels continued during the 1970s and 1980s to elicit the most critical attention. Much closer scrutiny was made of their verbal and aesthetic densities, of their literary structures and inner dynamics. Furthermore, increasing use was made of Lawrence's expository prose to illuminate the novels: for instance, both Baruch Hochman in *Another Ego: The Changing View of Self and Society in the Work of D. H. Lawrence* (1970) and Stephen Miko in *Toward "Women in Love": The Emergence of a Lawrentian Aesthetic* (1971) examined the fiction through the lens of some of Lawrence's more difficult and sometimes contradictory essays, such as "Study of Thomas Hardy" and "The Crown." Miko related Lawrence's "developing mind" to his "developing art" in his first five novels, and Gavriel Ben-Ephraim in *The Moon's Dominion: Narrative Dichotomy and Female Dominance in Lawrence's Early Novels* (1981) similarly concentrated on only those five works as he elaborated on the dichotomy between "tale" and teller" in each novel through *Women in Love*. A handful of other critics, such as John Stoll in *The Novels of D. H. Lawrence: A Search for Integration* (1971), Alastair Niven in *D. H. Lawrence: The Novels* (1978), and John Worthen in *D. H. Lawrence and the Idea of the Novel* (1979), attempted wider ranging surveys of all or most of the novels. Of these studies, Worthen's was by far the most incisive. Whereas Stoll merely elaborated an argument he had presented in an earlier book on Lawrence, and Niven managed only to re-argue the Leavisian notion of "Lawrence's greatness" as an artist and social diagnostician, Worthen—one of the editors of the CUP editions—drew extensively on unpublished materials and newly discovered textual history of each of ten novels to establish insightful critical readings. Worthen traced precisely the novelist's "changing relationship with his audience" as he moved toward a stronger sense of his artistic mission.

In the fifties and sixties, Leavis and others had convincingly established *Women in Love* and *The Rainbow* as Lawrence's masterworks, with *Sons and Lovers* falling a bit behind, and later criticism has not altered that view. After 1970, scholars continued taking basically formalistic approaches to *The Rainbow* and *Women in Love*. They continued to investigate Lawrence's theory of allotropic characterization, his experimentation with a new mode of expressing feeling, and his original style in the novels (see, for example, Jack Stewart's 1980 essay in this volume). And they continued to focus on problematic features of the novels, for example, on whether the ending of *The Rainbow* is supported by the story's preceding events; on the meaning there of Ursula's encounter with the horses and of the rainbow symbol; on Lawrence's ambivalent treatment of "corruption" in *Women in Love*; and, predictably, on both novels' sexual politics (Kate Millett and many others were fascinated with Ursula as heroine). Some critics, most notably Scott Sanders in *D. H. Lawrence: The World of the Major Novels* (1973), attempted to assess the value of the two books as diagnoses of cultural ills. Perhaps the most important work on *The Rainbow* and *Women in Love* during the 1970s and 1980s was the meticulous tracing by scholars, especially Mark Kinkead-Weekes, Pierre Vitoux, and Charles Ross, of the genesis and evolution of "The Sisters" manuscript. In *The Composition of "The Rainbow" and "Women in Love"* (1979), Ross built on Kinkead-Weekes's earlier analysis of the evolution of *The Rainbow* manuscripts and then reconstructed the history of *Women in Love* from available manuscripts, demonstrating from the copious interlinear alterations in the holographs and typescripts that Lawrence was much more a self-conscious artist than had been generally acknowledged.

Sons and Lovers seemed to engage critics less intensely in the seventies and eighties than in the two previous decades. Still, it remained among the most admired of Lawrence's works, and a few critics, such as Peter Scheckner and Graham Holderness, continued in the 1980s to champion it over all of Lawrence's other novels for its social realism. Some fresh critical interest in the novel was stirred in 1977 by the publication in *Sons and Lovers: A Facsimile of the Manuscript* of a full-size replica of the complete final holograph. It showed Lawrence's very legible final alterations along with the excisions (totalling roughly one-tenth of the manuscript) made by the publisher's reader, Edward Garnett, and thus the *Facsimile* made it possible for scholars easily to assess the effect of Garnett's pruning. In his interesting introduction to the *Facsimile*, editor Mark Schorer called Garnett a "brilliant editor" whose cuts made the novel "tighter and more smoothly paced." But it remains to be seen whether Carl Baron, who is editing the novel for the CUP editions, will agree, or whether he will restore some or all of Garnett's cuts to the body of the text.

Probably the most noticeable difference between the way Lawrence's novels were treated in the seventies and eighties and the way they had been considered earlier was that a great deal more serious exegetical attention was being paid to *Lady Chatterley* and to his other lesser-known novels, with these individual works sometimes being explicated in entire books. No longer considered just a tract for Lawrence's sexual politics and social vision, *Lady Chatterley* began to be examined carefully for its literary artistry — for the effectiveness of its structure, characterization, imagery, allusions, and other technical matters. In fact, many critics ignored the novel's treatment of sex altogether, for instance preferring instead to discuss the book as a version of the utopian, as pastoral, or as a retelling of myth or medieval romance. Particular interest in the novel was generated in 1972 by the initial publication in English of *John Thomas and Lady Jane*, Lawrence's second version of the story, by Heinemann and Viking presses, which simultaneously reissued *The First Lady Chatterley*. Some reviewers expressed preference for *John Thomas and Lady Jane*, which had previously been published only in a 1954 Italian translation. Harry T. Moore, for instance, argued that it "presents the story more intensely" and includes characters "more believable and more vital" than those in the third version.[38] But most critics now hold that Lawrence well knew what he was doing in revising, that the third and final version more powerfully expresses the "phallic reality" in which he saw possibilities of regeneration for modern people. The publication of the Chatterley saga in such multiple forms provided a new sort of laboratory for studying the gestation of a novel, and a number of critics subsequently traced the story's evolution from the realistic-naturalistic narrative of *The First Lady Chatterley* into the far-ranging symbolist romance it became under Lawrence's revising hand. Michael Squires, the editor of the forthcoming CUP *Lady Chatterley*, did the most and the most valuable work on the novel's progressive mutations. In *The Creation of "Lady Chatterley's Lover"* (1983), Squires scrupulously recounted the novel's genesis and development, and concluded that as Lawrence rewrote, he radically improved the "aesthetic shape of his work." Also, with Dennis Jackson, Squires coedited *D. H. Lawrence's "Lady": A New Look at "Lady Chatterley's Lover"* (1985), a collection of twelve original essays that examined the novel from a variety of perspectives and helped to support the editors' contention that, while not being Lawrence's masterpiece, *Lady Chatterley* is "a work of major social, intellectual, and literary importance — a work that has centrally shaped our culture."[39] Of course, the novel continued to draw fire from feminists and from Marxist critics (who considered it "escapist" literature), and from certain other commentators such as John Worthen, who claimed in *The Idea of the Novel* that, by 1928, Lawrence had become so "isolated," he could no longer speak to or of the "community" of England.

His other novels likewise received more intense analyses and often more appreciation in the 1970s and 1980s. For example, *Aaron's Rod* became the focus of two books, Henry Miller's *Notes on "Aaron's Rod"* (1980), interesting more for Miller's own passionate engagement with Lawrence's text than for any critical insights, and Paul Baker's *A Reassessment of D. H. Lawrence's "Aaron's Rod"* (1983), which more usefully traced the novel's evolution and analyzed its themes and characterization. Baker made strong—but not ultimately convincing—claims for this "boldly experimental" novel's "considerable artistic merit" and its pivotal importance in Lawrence's development as a novelist. The later "leadership" novels, *Kangaroo* and *The Plumed Serpent*, also elicited substantial commentary during this period. For instance, Robert Darroch's *D. H. Lawrence in Australia* (1981) extensively examined Lawrence's sources for *Kangaroo*, to show that his depiction of Australia's political situation was—despite assertions to the contrary by many Australian commentators—grounded in fact. Among other recent critics, John Worthen and Alastair Niven made good cases for a reappraisal of the novel, and Anthony Burgess in *Flame Into Being* (1985) called *Kangaroo* "the strangest but in some ways the most satisfying novel of [Lawrence's] entire career."[40] The long-standing problem of how to evaluate *The Plumed Serpent* was not resolved, but especially illuminating work on the novel was done by James Cowan in *D. H. Lawrence's American Journey* (1970) and by Ross Parmenter, who devoted a long chapter of *Lawrence in Oaxaca* (1984) to assessing the revisions Lawrence made on the *Plumed Serpent* manuscript during his winter 1924–25 stay in Mexico. Even Lawrence's first two novels, *The White Peacock* and *The Trespasser*, which had so often received low marks from critics, were frequently discussed extensively by prominent critics during the 1970s and 1980s. For instance, Miko's *Toward "Women in Love"* gave—in separate chapters—much fuller treatment to *The White Peacock* and *The Trespasser* than had been usual in books of previous decades, as he thoughtfully explored problems implicit in each novel's characterization and structuring. And Burgess in *Flame Into Being* also devoted impressive space to *The White Peacock*, which he surprisingly declared an "important novel."

Studies of the Short Fiction.   Lawrence and Joyce are now frequently proclaimed the premier tellers of tales from the British Isles. Joseph Flora's Introduction to *The English Short Story, 1880–1945* (1985), for example, described Lawrence's place in the history of the modern British short story as "multidimensional and major." But even though his short story volumes had drawn more complimentary reviews during his lifetime than had the novels, his more than sixty tales elicited little distinctive criticism prior to the 1960s, when Widmer, Tedlock, Moynahan, Weiss, Ford, and several others wrote books that meaningfully examined them. In *The Art of Perversity* (1962), the first comprehensive analysis of the short fiction, Widmer went so far as to argue that the tales were Lawrence's "central writings."

In the decades following Widmer's study, Lawrence's stories were the focus of a plethora of journal articles characteristically concerned with *explication de texte*. Lawrence himself never made a public statement about the aesthetic of the short story, as he did about the novel, and no doubt partially for that reason, some critics have suggested that he did not really care about the short story form, that he wrote stories just to earn — as he himself put it in a 1912 letter to Edward Garnett — "running money." But his numerous alterations suggest otherwise: even after his stories had been published, he usually revised again before they were collected into volumes. These revisions have recently been inspected intensively by critics seeking to draw some conclusions about the development of his technique. For example, Keith Cushman in *D. H. Lawrence at Work: The Emergence of the "Prussian Officer" Stories* (1978) percipiently traced the development of the early tales through successive revisions in their manuscript, magazine, and collected book versions, showing how Lawrence discovered his distinctive literary voice and vision during the time (around 1914) when he was writing *The Rainbow* and recasting his earlier short stories. Janice Harris's *The Short Fiction of D. H. Lawrence* (1984) similarly demonstrated how he improved his stories while revising. Only the second full-length study of all the tales, Harris's book traced Lawrence's development from his early "realistic" stories through his "visionary" short fiction (after 1912) to "fabulation" and satire (in stories after the mid-1920s), while offering useful observations on the dialectic, or conversation, of themes and imagery among various Lawrence stories.

Studies of the Poetry.   Though from the beginning Lawrence's poetry had often been hailed for its passion and spirit, it was only during the 1970s and 1980s that critics began examining and appreciating the poems as conscious art. The chief barrier to that approach had been, of course, Lawrence's predominantly free verse form. Early reviewers such as Edward Garnett tended to assign him to the category of "demonic" poet and "natural genius," thus excusing him his "hasty" technique.[41] But when the question of Lawrence's metrics arose, his contemporaries found little positive to say beyond a comparison of his free rhythm with the sort popularized by translations from the Chinese. Lawrence himself, in his preface to the American edition of *New Poems* in 1920, denied that breaking "the lovely forms of metrical verse" and dishing up the fragments as *vers libre* was any way to compose free verse. His point was that free verse had its own nature and its own law, which "must come new each time from within." His organic format, a part of the general tendency of English and American prosody in the first quarter of the twentieth century, shaped itself into a biography of the spirit, especially as he chronologically arranged the poems in *Look! We Have Come Through!* Naturally, this organization contributed to the later focus on the poems as autobiographical adjuncts to the novels, and as studies in the poet's psychic development.

R. P. Blackmur's 1935 essay "D. H. Lawrence and Expressive Form" held sway over critical evaluation of Lawrence's eleven books of poetry for several generations. Blackmur's principal accusation was that Lawrence committed "the fallacy of expressive form," that is, the poetry "fails to its own disadvantage to employ the formal devices of the art in which . . . [the insight of the poem] is couched."[42] It was not until the 1950s that critics such as Graham Hough (in *The Dark Sun*) felt compelled to answer Blackmur by agreeing to abandon a purely formal standard to evaluate Lawrence's poetic form. But while Hough expressed admiration for much of the poetry, he valued it chiefly as commentary on the artist's fiction, and his general lack of concern with Lawrence's poetic technique was typical of the studies of that decade. So was Dallas Kenmare's effusive *Fire-bird* (1952), which concerned itself largely with Lawrence's "message" — especially his condemnation of war.

In 1960 in *Start With the Sun*, James Miller, Karl Shapiro, and Bernice Slote placed Lawrence's technique in "the Whitman tradition," but few other studies of the decade focused meaningfully on the style of the poems. *The Complete Poems of D. H. Lawrence* (1964), edited by Vivian de Sola Pinto and Warren Roberts, was a valuable first attempt at a complete edition of the poetry and included a good number of previously uncollected poems from both printed and manuscript sources, as well as numerous variants and early drafts of published poems, scholarly notes, and a substantial introduction by Pinto. This collection prompted the strongest praise for Lawrence's poetry since his death. Kenneth Rexroth's review in the *Nation*, for instance, called Lawrence "one of the major poets of the Twentieth Century," a leader in the "rejection of rhetoric and Symbolism and the return of poetry to colloquial honesty and presentational immediacy."[43] But it is fair to say that before the 1970s most of those concerned with Lawrence's work agreed with Moynahan's view, in *Deed of Life*, that while there was excellence in much of Lawrence's poetry and non-fiction prose, he was "a novelist and writer of tales first and last."[44]

The early 1970s represented a watershed in the recognition of Lawrence's poetry. Although Tom Marshall's *The Psychic Mariner* in 1970 found almost half of Lawrence's poetry a formal failure, that book's biographical and critical data provided a milieu in which to read the poems: it was the first significant comprehensive study of the poetry. The same year, T. A. Smailes's less ambitious volume, *Some Comments on the Verse of D. H. Lawrence*, evaluated the growth stages of the poetry through close reading of several poems, and Reloy Garcia and James Karabatsos's *Concordance to the Poetry of D. H. Lawrence* marked the first, albeit awkward, computer application to Lawrence scholarship. Sandra Gilbert's *Acts of Attention* (1972) was clearly the most competent critical examination of the poetry during the decade. In the process of establishing Lawrence as a fully conscious major poet of the century, she discussed his poetry as an artistic achievement within the tradition of not only Wordsworth and Whitman, but also of Swift, Yeats, Herbert, and others.

More recently, Ross Murfin's *The Poetry of D. H. Lawrence* (1983) explored the crosscurrents of what Murfin called "interfluence" through the poet's three major "lustres" or phases, showing that Lawrence's poetic language, although it seems liberated from all recognizable form, is actually an amalgam of Lawrence's models (Milton, Whitman, various romantic and Victorian poets), reshaped. And another recent major study, Gail Porter Mandell's *The Phoenix Paradox: A Study of Renewal through Change in the "Collected Poems" and "Last Poems" of D. H. Lawrence* (1984), examined for the first time his revisions and the way he rearranged *Collected Poems* into a narrative order that embodies "implicit" myths in the early poems. Both Murfin's and Mandell's intense engagement with the text evidenced a growing perception of Lawrence the poet as deliberate craftsman.

Studies of the Drama.   Recognition of Lawrence as a skilled playwright was an even slower process. Sean O'Casey lamented in 1934 (in a review reprinted in this volume) that "a little more experience, a little more encouragement, and, in Lawrence, England might have had a great dramatist." But because Lawrence's naturalistic plays of working-class life lay outside the conventions of the theater of his day, only two of his eight plays were produced in his lifetime. All were more or less forgotten until 1965, when, for the first time, they were gathered into one volume, *The Complete Plays of D. H. Lawrence.* Because this collection of his eight dramas (and two fragments) included no editorial commentary or annotation of any sort, it seemed a curiously unambitious project, but along with the successful staging of three of his plays at London's Royal Court Theatre three years later, *The Complete Plays* stirred new interest in Lawrence as a playwright. Prior to that flush of activity in the late 1960s, most critics had concurred with Arthur Waterman's assessment (in a 1960 *Modern Drama* essay) that Lawrence had not taken his dramatic work very seriously, that the plays are not good drama, and that they contain "nothing new in dramatic technique."

In theory, Lawrence reacted against the new Royal Court Theatre tradition, against what he called, in a February 1913 letter, the "bony, bloodless drama" of Shaw, Galsworthy, Ibsen, Strindberg — all his immediate predecessors.[45] Reviewers of the early productions sometimes faulted the stark naturalism of Lawrence's setting and movement on stage, sometimes the heavy-handed theorizing by his characters. But, too, they sometimes faulted the audience's ability to understand what they saw.

As Lawrence said in that 1913 letter, he himself believed that "an audience might be found in England for some of my stuff, if there were a man to whip 'em in,"[46] but it was not until 1968 that producer Peter Gill's sensitive productions of *A Collier's Friday Night*, *The Daughter-in-Law*, and *The Widowing of Mrs Holroyd* at the Royal Court Theatre in London finally established Lawrence as a successful dramatist. Gill's extensive research of all the plays, the criticism, and many of the novels enabled him to achieve in his production of the three plays an admirable faithfulness to Lawrence and to his environment. A reviewer in the *New Yorker* declared the plays "the real stuff of life, strong and nourishing";[47] the *London Sunday Times* reported that the productions "revealed a dramatist of outstanding talent who, though famous in other connections, has been unaccountably neglected on stage";[48] and others praised the plays for their open-ended, exploratory nature, their intelligent attempt to work through the problems of human relationship. Since 1968, Lawrence's dramas have continued to be staged occasionally in provincial playhouses, usually to critical acclaim.

The first and still the only significant book-length study of the drama was Sylvia Sklar's *The Plays of D. H. Lawrence* (1975). A staunch defender of Lawrence as a playwright, Sklar examined the plays both in themselves and as expressions of the author's recurring themes, making an interesting analysis of the way his "unspoken dialogue" modifies the "preaching" in his drama. To date there have been only two other short books on Lawrence's plays, both considerably less insightful than Sklar's, and fewer than a dozen substantial essays on the topic.

Studies of the Criticism.   Lawrence as a critic has certainly never achieved the status of, say, a Henry James or a T. S. Eliot. From Lawrence's death until the 1960s, most commentators would have endorsed his own statement in an August 1912 letter that he was "no critic at all." Until the reprinting of many of his essays in the fifties and sixties, much of his criticism stayed buried in little periodicals and in unpublished letters, and partly for that reason, up to and during those two decades any history of modern literary criticism would have included only scant — if any — mention of Lawrence's critical ideas.

David Gordon's *D. H. Lawrence as Literary Critic* (1966) was the first book-length study on that topic, and remains the best. Noting that the prime concern of Lawrence's literary criticism is always "art in relation to morality," Gordon called him "the last Romantic, the last of those radical individuals who set themselves against an entire culture and still stood for something meaningful."[49] Adopting a medial position between Leavis's acclaim of Lawrence as "an incomparable literary critic" and Eliot's disdain for Lawrence's instinctual responses to what he read, Gordon convincingly argued that the literary criticism "must rank as a major area of Lawrence's achievement." After Gordon's study, books by Indian scholars Ileana Cura-Sazdanic, Aruna Sitesh, K. K. Sharma, and Tajindar Singh similarly focused on Lawrence's critical ideas, but often reached derivative or unenlightening conclusions. The best among these was Singh's *The Literary Criticism of D. H. Lawrence* (1984), which argued that, despite their unacademic peculiarities and stylistic excesses, the "Study of Thomas Hardy" and *Studies in Classic American Literature* contain high-quality commentary that adheres to "fairly coherent critical principles."

Lawrence's criticism has been most profoundly influential in the way it has affected American literary criticism. When *Studies in Classic American Literature* was published in 1923, the essays — with their strident, cocky, often staccato outpourings of the critic's feelings about America, its writers, and the motivating impulses in their art — frequently were disparaged by reviewers for their "murky mysticism" and Lawrence's "tiresome," "spoofing style," but his views nonetheless had far-reaching effects on the way America's literature was perceived and read in subsequent decades. Richard Chase, Leslie Fiedler, and other eminent American critics have often acknowledged their debt to Lawrence's readings of nineteenth-century American novels, particularly to his persuasive emphasis on the way that fiction so often portrays the solitary individual in unavoidable conflict with his society. Richard Poirier in *A World Elsewhere: The Place of Style in American Literature* (1966) proclaimed Lawrence's *Studies* "probably the crucial study of American literature," and later, in a 1975 *American Quarterly* review of books on American literature, Michael Colacurcio noted that Lawrence's "passionate impressionism" is "now part of the received critical wisdom."

Studies of the Travel Writings.   Before the 1980s, *Twilight in Italy, Sea and Sardinia, Mornings in Mexico*, and *Etruscan Places* were considered chiefly as appendages to and sourcebooks for Lawrence's novels. Though Harry T. Moore's *Poste Restante: A Lawrence Travel Calendar* (1956) had carefully traced the artist's peregrinations through England, Germany, Italy, Australia, and the American Southwest, very few sustained attempts had been made to assess Lawrence's writings about those travels. But in the early eighties, four books — L. D. Clark's *The Minoan Distance: The Symbolism of Travel in D. H. Lawrence* (1980), Del Ivan Janik's *The Curve of Return: D. H. Lawrence's Travel Books* (1981), Billy Tracy's *D. H. Lawrence and the Literature of Travel* (1983), and Maya Hostettler's less useful *D. H. Lawrence: Travel Books and Fiction* (1985) — focused on the travel books, on Lawrence's place in the tradition of English travel literature, and on the distinctive way he inhaled the "vital effluence, different vibration, different chemical exhalation" of each land he visited (the words are his own, from his essay "The Spirit of Place"). The best of those new studies (and one of the most knowledgeable of all recent works on Lawrence), Clark's book examined how place became symbol in Lawrence's poetry and fiction, how his psychology directed and shaped the varied places he visited, turning them into art.

Several studies in the 1970s and 1980s focused specifically on Lawrence's relationship to a particular country or landscape. Leo Hamalian's *D. H. Lawrence and Italy* (1982) and Jeffrey Meyers's *D. H. Lawrence and the Experience of Italy* (1982) each demonstrated that country's power to shape Lawrence's mind and art, and Robert Darroch's useful journalistic account, *D. H. Lawrence in Australia* (1981), similarly showed how the writer's experiences in that country were fed into *Kangaroo*. Growing numbers of critics in recent decades have likewise examined the literary aspects of Lawrence's encounter with the North American continent. The first such major study, Armin Arnold's *D. H. Lawrence and America* (1958), was superseded by more specialized studies. Cavitch's *D. H. Lawrence and the New World* (1969) related the artist's escape to that world to his effort to liberate himself psychically and sensually. Cowan's *D. H. Lawrence's American Journey* (1970) also considered America as the arena in which Lawrence hoped to heal his psychic ambivalences. But while Cavitch argued that Lawrence's New World experiences were ultimately not curative, Cowan claimed Lawrence experienced in the Southwest a personal and artistic regeneration. Three other recent studies treated Lawrence's reaction to Mexico. Douglas Veitch's *Lawrence, Greene and Lowry: The Fictional Landscape of Mexico* (1978) and Ronald Walker's *Infernal Paradise: Mexico and the Modern English Novel* (1978) demonstrated a relationship between the authors' experiences (Walker also adds Huxley) of the Mexican landscape and their feelings of personal alienation and apocalypse. The third book, Ross Parmenter's loosely organized and charmingly anecdotal *Lawrence in Oaxaca: A Quest for the Novelist in Mexico* (1984), more thoroughly treated the writer's aesthetic and personal experiences there and in the whole American Southwest.

Biographical Studies.   No writer has ever infused his own experiences into his art more profoundly than Lawrence, and his colorful, intense life has continued to intrigue writers. Rather remarkably—since most of Lawrence's contemporaries have died—memoirs by his friends have continued to the present day to be newly published. Those introduced in recent decades have been of mixed value: Joseph Foster's gushing tribute *D. H. Lawrence in Taos* (1972) merely reheated passages from earlier books by and about Lawrence, while G. H. Neville's *A Memoir of D. H. Lawrence (The Betrayal)* (ed. Carl Baron, 1982) was a worthwhile account of Lawrence's early life, the period fictionalized in *The White Peacock* and *Sons and Lovers*, by a man who was his closest male friend through adolescence.

Of the dozen or so biographical studies since 1970, the most compelling and valuable were those by Harry T. Moore, Emile Delavenay, Paul Delany, and Keith Sagar. Whereas Moore's *The Priest of Love* (1974) championed Lawrence as a life-affirmative moralist, a very different Lawrence emerged from Delavenay's controversial *D. H. Lawrence: The Man and His Work: The Formative Years: 1885–1919* (in English, 1972). Delavenay's Lawrence was a tormented, self-centered, asocial personality who betrayed friends, who exhibited homosexual impulses and was a precursor of fascism, and who wrote novels that were flawed because he had not achieved the needed artistic detachment. Critics subsequently faulted this perception of Lawrence, but Delavenay's 590-page study did make two useful contributions: it presented fresh facts about Lawrence's early life that the biographer had obtained in the 1930s through letters and interviews with some of Lawrence's family and friends (Jessie Chambers, for instance); it also made a game effort to discover the "psychological origins and the creative sources" of Lawrence's art, for instance, arguing provocatively—but not always convincingly—that Edward Carpenter (the Yorkshire socialist and sexologist), Houston Stewart Chamberlain (the proto-Nazi ideologist), Mme H. P. Blavatsky, Havelock Ellis, Otto Weininger, and other such figures helped shape Lawrence in his "formative years."[50] Paul Delany took fewer risks in *D. H. Lawrence's Nightmare: The Writer and His Circle in the Years of the Great War* (1978), but his biography was no less engaging, especially in its description of how profoundly the war intensified Lawrence's apocalyptic vision and consequently affected the creation of *Women in Love*. Keith Sagar's *D. H. Lawrence: A Calendar of His Works* (1979) presented the most thorough and reliable listing yet compiled of *when* Lawrence was writing or revising each of his individual works. Issued almost simultaneously was Sagar's *The Life of D. H. Lawrence: An Illustrated Biography* (1980), and though that volume introduced only bits of new information, it did provide, for general readers, the most readable short biography on Lawrence. Sagar also compiled useful information in editing *A D. H. Lawrence Handbook* (1982), which collected various biographical, historical, geographical, bibliographical, and linguistic ancillaries to the study of Lawrence's life and literature.

In 1962, in reviewing Moore's edition of Lawrence's *Letters*, Frank Kermode declared: "They are squaring and hewing the material. After Nehls's work the biography could be regarded as virtually complete."[51] That remark has, of course, proven to be highly inaccurate, for one thing because such significant new knowledge about Lawrence's life, publishing career, and writing methods is being generated by the work on the CUP *Works* and *Letters*, and now Cambridge has announced plans to publish, between 1989 and 1991, a new three-volume biography tentatively titled *D. H. Lawrence: A Life*, separate volumes to be written by John Worthen, Mark Kinkead-Weekes, and David Ellis. In combination with the other biographies mentioned here, this CUP *Life* shows promise of being, at last, that "virtually complete" biography of which Kermode spoke prematurely a quarter of a century ago.

Feminist Studies.   As the international debate over sexual roles and sexual relationships intensified during recent decades, it was inevitable that the self-proclaimed Priest of Love's relationships with and attitudes toward women would come under increased scrutiny. Lawrence's life was, as Emily Hahn noted in her gossipy *D. H. Lawrence and the Women Who Loved Him* (1975), "dominated by women," and interest has remained high over the years regarding the women who in one way or another inspired his art. Several of the women portrayed in Hahn's book have recently had their own books published or have had biographies written about them. For instance, the colorful American *saloniste* (and writer of modest talents) Mabel Dodge Luhan, who figured importantly in Lawrence's life and art during the twenties, was the subject of books by Emily Hahn (1977), Lois Palken Rudnick (1984), and Winifred L. Frazer (1984). But of most import to Lawrence studies, among the various books by or about women linked to Lawrence, were the recent volumes about his strong-willed, amoral, disorderly, but vital and intelligent mate, Frieda, who was, as Huxley noted (in his introduction to the *Letters*), "Lawrence's only deep and abiding human relationship." In the 1970s, Frieda was the subject of two ample biographies, Robert Lucas's entertaining but largely derivative *Frieda Lawrence* (1973) and Martin Green's *The von Richthofen Sisters: The Triumphant and the Tragic Modes of Love* (1974), and more recently Harry T. Moore and Dale Montague edited *Frieda Lawrence and Her Circle: Letters from, to, and about Frieda Lawrence* (1981), which added little to what we had learned about the Lawrences in her earlier memoirs *Not I, But the Wind . . .* (1934) and *Frieda Lawrence: The Memoirs and Correspondence* (1961). Of the three recent books on Frieda, Green's speculative consideration of her role as the "muse" of Lawrence's "erotic imagination" was by far the most rewarding. Green convincingly argued that Lawrence's writings after 1912 were informed meaningfully by ideas on instinct and eroticism that Frieda had brought to their marriage from her experiences with Otto Gross and the German intellectuals she had known among the "Cosmic Circle" in Schwabing-Munich. None of the books on Frieda or on Lawrence's other female acquaintances were examples of feminist scholarship, but probably all had implications for contemporary feminism.

Lawrence's most vocal antagonists from 1970 to 1985 were the feminist literary critics, many of whom decried him as the epitome of male chauvinism. There was irony in this. As Kate Millett noted in *Sexual Politics* (1970), the "sexual revolution" of the 1960s "had done a great deal to free female sexuality," and through that decade Lawrence had been hailed as a prophet of that liberated sexuality. But Millett argued that

Lawrence was really "the evangelist of quite another cause—'phallic consciousness,' " and was to be condemned for his "doctrinaire male-supremacist ethic."[52] She was not the first to assert this. Early reviewers had occasionally faulted his sexual politics, and other writers such as Simone de Beauvoir (in *The Second Sex*, 1953) had further developed the case against him. Millett was simply playing variations on de Beauvoir's basic theme concerning Lawrence's "Phallic Pride." But it was Millett's book that focused and catalyzed the feminist attack waged on Lawrence after 1970. Calling him the "most talented" of "sexual politicians," she disparaged his creation of what she perceived as passive, nonintellectual heroines who must each relinquish self and individuality to be "awakened" by domineering Lawrentian males. Her own critics (among the many, Norman Mailer, Carol Dix, and Janice Harris) have charged Millett with using questionable critical methods to reach distorted readings of Lawrence's works, but the questions she raised about his art and metaphysic have continued to reverberate in Lawrence criticism.

As editor Anne Smith noted in her opening essay in *D. H. Lawrence and Women* (a collection of nine lively essays on the topic, by diverse hands, 1978), several of Lawrence's friends during his early manhood supported the suffragette movement. His changing attitudes toward that movement were precisely traced in Hilary Simpson's *D. H. Lawrence and Feminism* (1982), one of the best studies of Lawrence by a feminist scholar. For a brief time before and during the Great War, Simpson maintained, Lawrence "espoused feminism," but near the war's end, his attitude toward women underwent a "volte-face": perceiving the public changes in women's status and behavior during the war, he decided uneasily that women had become the dominant sex, and thus developed his notions of the need for a "masculine revolution" that would restore harmony in sexual relations.[53] An earlier study, R. P. Draper's 1966 essay reprinted in this volume, had ably demonstrated how Lawrence's "anti-feminist" attitudes profoundly affected some of his postwar fiction, and no one has ever successfully defended him against the charge of male chauvinism in *Aaron's Rod*, *The Plumed Serpent*, "The Woman Who Rode Away," and other works from the middle years of his career.

Though Sheila Macleod claimed in *Lawrence's Men and Women* (1985) to "have scarcely been able to find a woman in the 1980s who has a good word to say for him," a substantial number of writers—female and male—during the seventies and eighties expressed admiration for his sensitive insight into the nature and temperament of the heroines in his major works. In *Men and Feminism in Modern Literature* (1985) Declan Kiberd asserted (as had Anaïs Nin, decades earlier) that Lawrence is not a male propagandist, but rather an androgynous artist attuned to the lives of both sexes. Lawrence himself remarked, in an April 1914 letter, that his aim in *The Rainbow* was to show "woman becoming individual, self-responsible, taking her own initiative,"[54] and Carol Dix (in her spirited defense of him in *D. H. Lawrence and Women*, 1980), Lydia Blanchard, Janice Harris, and others writing in the seventies and eighties affirmed that he did indeed realize that goal in the characters of Ursula Brangwen and other heroines. Lawrence's defenders also noted that his male protagonists are crushed by female dominance as often as his women characters are damaged by domineering men, and, further, that the most autobiographical of his figures typically seek relationships in which they can, with their mate, maintain separate integrities balanced in polarity.

Other critics, including Mark Schorer and John Humma, also stressed that Lawrence never lets his dogmatic male chauvinist heroes go unchallenged in their views, that his fictive females usually provide a counterpoint, corrective view, and thus that Lawrence's own sexual metaphysic within a given story is customarily criticized within that work through the presentation of multiple points of view. Lawrence's defenders further protested that many feminist critics were treating him as if he had remained monolithic in his views toward women throughout his career, and were reading his novels as tracts rather than as a series of imaginative trials and explorations regarding ideas of male-female relationships. Mark Spilka and Norman Mailer stoutly argued that Lawrence's male-supremacist ideas in the middle years of his career were (to quote Mailer's *The Prisoner of Sex*, 1971) "only a way station on the line of Lawrence's ideas." In his 1967 article reprinted in this collection, and in several other essays, Spilka asserted that toward the end of his career (notably in *Lady Chatterley*), Lawrence purged himself of his hostility to willful and egoistic women and turned toward a new sexual ethic characterized by reciprocity and "tenderness" between men and women.

Psychological Studies.   Like many of the earlier psychoanalytic approaches, R. E. Pritchard's *D. H. Lawrence: Body of Darkness* in 1971 was a reductive psychobiographical study with a Freudian bias. But the nature of psychoanalytic criticism of Lawrence's life and literature changed in the years following Pritchard's study. For example, Judith Ruderman and Daniel Dervin applied post-Freudian psychoanalytic theory, producing a more complex and less reductive criticism that concentrated more rigorously on intrinsic literary concerns. Ruderman's *D. H. Lawrence and the Devouring Mother* (1984) and Dervin's *A "Strange Sapience": The Creative Imagination of D. H. Lawrence* (1984) each focused not so much on the classic father-son conflict emphasized in such earlier works as Weiss's *Oedipus in Nottingham*, but rather on the preoedipal period of individuation, the tug-of-war between regression and selfhood. Ruderman identified in writings from Lawrence's "leadership" period "a pattern of preoedipal concerns and conflicts" that depicts the assertion of male supremacy and godhead as Lawrence's struggle against the nurturing/smothering female. Unlike Ruderman, Dervin concluded that Lawrence eventually overcame his view of woman as a "devouring mother," and Dervin in his psychoanalytic study of the creative process in Lawrence identified the source of the artist's creativity as his need to reinvent imaginatively his inadequate parents, pointing toward *Lady Chatterley* and *The Man Who Died* as the triumphant culmination of that attempt.

Lawrence's own psychological theories received increasing attention in the seventies and eighties. Daniel Schneider, building on work by Philip Rieff and others, constructed in *D. H. Lawrence: The Artist as Psychologist* (1984) the most comprehensive analysis yet made of the ideas in *Psychoanalysis and the Unconscious* and *Fantasia of the Unconscious*. Like Baruch Hochman in *Another Ego: The Changing View of Self and Society in D. H. Lawrence* (1970), Schneider found in Lawrence's psychological vision a strong theoretical base. Schneider's conclusion that Lawrence's theories form "a coherent psychology with well-defined assumptions and a logical development of the implications of those assumptions"[55] also paralleled arguments in Leavis's final book, *Thought, Words, and Creativity: Art and Thought in Lawrence* (1976). But while Leavis, in his attempt to show how the thinker is originally related to the novelist in *The Plumed Serpent*, *Women in Love*, *The Captain's Doll*, and *The Rainbow*, contented himself chiefly with assertions and generalizations and offered little new evidence, Schneider much more convincingly demonstrated Lawrence's success in integrating his psychology into his novels.

As Marguerite Beede Howe in *The Art of the Self in D. H. Lawrence* and Robert Langbaum in *The Mysteries of Identity: A Theme in Modern Literature* each noted in 1977, theirs was an "egocentric age" in which *self* and *identity* had become the subject of much intense scrutiny. Lawrence's own conceptions of "selfhood" received substantial attention in a dozen or so books published during the 1970s and 1980s. Writers frequently noted how his career-long insistence on modern man's need to regain "wholeness of being" — to integrate unconscious, intuitive awareness and rationality into a meaningful self — anticipated much of what was being written in their own time by ego psychologists, by proponents of the "consciousness revolution," and by other academic and popular writers. But while the "vitalist" critics of the 1950s and 1960s had believed that Lawrence in his major works successfully reconciles the demands of the individual's conscious and unconscious selves and integrates the social self and vital self, the more recent critics frequently challenged that view.

Contending that identity and "the fragmented self" are Lawrence's main concern, Howe traced the shifts in his ego psychology as they are registered through his novels, showing how his notions of personality serve to organize his art. Elizabeth Brody Tenenbaum in *The Problematic Self: Approaches to Identity in Stendhal, D. H. Lawrence, and Malraux* (1977) strove to show how Lawrence's characters reflect the Rousseauistic idea of the intrinsic self, and how, for the British author, being what one truly *is* leads not to a consistent self but to "spontaneous mutability" in response to the impulse of man's "natural" self, which is continually evolving (and which one can either actualize or repress). Lawrence's sense of this "evolving" nature of the self, Roger Ebbatson proposed in *The Evolutionary Self: Hardy, Forster, Lawrence* (1983), was directly influenced by Darwin's theory of evolution, "with its emphasis on change and process." But Howe, John Stoll, and others reached the (arguable) conclusion that, despite Lawrence's insistence on the importance of the individual's evolution into conscious being, the novelist was ultimately unable to achieve unity of "self" in any of his various protagonists.

Arguing that Lawrence never really *wanted* true psychic integration, but rather the total victory of the vital, dark self over "mental or social consciousness," Stoll in *The Novels of D. H. Lawrence: A Search for Integration* (1971) further contended that Lawrence failed also in his other professed goal of harmonizing self and society. In *Another Ego*, Baruch Hochman proposed that Lawrence moved from a "radical individualism" in his early works (through *Women in Love*) to a "radical communalism." Thus, said that critic, the goal of the Lawrentian hero became not only the realization (usually through erotic experience) of the vital blood-conscious "natural self," but also the creation of a "communal consciousness," the realization of what Aidan Burns in *Nature and Culture in D. H. Lawrence* (1981) called the "social infrastructure of the self." Like Hochman, Stoll, Calvin Bedient (in *Architects of the Self: George Eliot, D. H. Lawrence, and E. M. Forster*, 1972), and many others who addressed this subject, Burns concluded that Lawrence was never able in his novels to construct a "living, believing community" in which "the true freedom of the self can be realized." And yet, all these and most other recent commentators agreed that Lawrence, despite his failure to create fully integrated individual characters or to resolve the conflict between personal and social modes of feeling, made one of the most admirable contributions to what Bedient called "the post-Christian disputes over the best blueprint of human character."

Mythological Studies. Our growing awareness of the powerful mythic and archetypal dimensions of Lawrence's art was enhanced significantly in recent decades, notably by James Cowan and John Vickery. Cowan's *D. H. Lawrence's American Journey: A Study in Literature and Myth* (1970) identified that journey as "essentially a quest for the symbols and myths whereby what he regarded as the waste land of modern western civilization might be revived."[56] Lawrence's own quest—his separation from stagnant and dying Europe, his reestablishment of his relationship with the cosmos in America, and his return—paralleled "the pattern of the quest of the hero of romance," a paradigm which, Cowan believed, became "the dominant structural and thematic image" in various fictions of Lawrence's American period. Vickery, in several essays reprinted in his books, *The Literary Impact of "The Golden Bough"* (1973) and *Myths and*

Texts: Strategies of Incorporation and Displacement (1983), demonstrated further how mythic patterns are woven into sundry Lawrence works. Of special value was Vickery's tracing of the influence that Cambridge anthropologist Sir James George Frazer's writings about Ancient Near East vegetative myths had on Lawrence's artistic imagination, particularly in the short fiction and *The Plumed Serpent*. Dennis Jackson's essay in this volume extends Vickery's findings, to show how Lawrence uses ancient myth and ritual elements to reinforce themes and motifs in *Lady Chatterley's Lover* and to help give that novel its form.

Genetic and Stylistic Studies.   Aldous Huxley noted in 1937 that Lawrence's surviving manuscripts could "furnish material for a most interesting study in the psychology of composition,"[57] but for decades after, scholars made no such effort. They continued to accept the myth— originated by Huxley—that Lawrence was a careless romantic artist who scorned the Flaubertian habit of revising locally or reworking parts in favor of starting fresh and dashing off the whole work again, in order that his "indwelling daemon" could generate the proper creative flow. But beginning in the late 1970s, a chain of books examining how Lawrence's achieved works of art emerged in drafts and revisions demolished the misconception that he could not correct or patch his writings. To the contrary, he was perceived in the new studies as a daring, resourceful, often painstaking craftsman who was usually very wise in making artistic choices during revision. The most illuminating of the genetic approaches were Keith Cushman's *D. H. Lawrence at Work: The Emergence of the "Prussian Officer" Stories* (1978), Charles Ross's *The Composition of "The Rainbow" and "Women in Love"* (1979), and Michael Squires's *The Creation of "Lady Chatterley's Lover"* (1983), each of which focused intently on the artist's imaginative processes. Increasingly through the 1980s, other critics drew on the textual history of Lawrence's individual works to help establish their critical readings (see, for example, Mandell's book on the poetry and Worthen's on the novels).

Prior to 1970, sustained critical attention was seldom paid to what Northrop Frye would call the *lexis* or verbal texture of Lawrence's writing. but commentators thereafter often showed keener interest in his language and idiosyncratic style. Squires, for example, elaborated on the anaphoric "loop method" of composition and other techniques in *Lady Chatterley*, and concluded, as Avrom Fleishman similarly did in his 1985 essay on "Lawrence's Later Style,"[58] that Lawrence still had firm command of his "artful style" (Fleishman's phrase) in the 1920s, a view that ran counter to the belief expressed by many other critics, that Lawrence suffered an artistic "decline" in his later years. Fleishman proposed that in *St. Mawr*, Lawrence shows himself "a grand master of the oral, dialectical, parodic, and polyglot manner" that Mikhail Bakhtin has established for Dostoyevski. Among other works appraising Lawrence's stylistic achievement, two of the best were Garrett Stewart's 1976 essay, "Lawrence, 'Being,' and the Allotropic Style"[59] and Michael Ragussis's *The Subterfuge of Art: Language and the Romantic Tradition* (1978). Stewart closely analyzed Lawrence's diction, grammar, and rhetoric, and remarked on how his "revolutionary emphasis on allotropes of the self in fictional narrative" mandated "a change in the very nature of novelistic prose." Ragussis based his book's title on Lawrence's idea that the writer is "a damned liar," his art "a sort of subterfuge," and perceptively explored the impact that view had on the functioning of language in *Women in Love*. Authors of other books in the seventies and eighties investigated various particular features of Lawrence's style: Keith Alldritt and Marianna Torgovnick, for instance, described the "visual" or "pictorial" quality of the prose, and Kenneth Inniss traced the uses Lawrence makes of animal imagery and symbols to express his metaphysic. Thus far, Lawrence's writings seem largely to have been ignored by linguistic and stylistic / statistical critics, though a small number of essayists, such as John Russell in *Style in Modern British Fiction* (1978), have taken that approach to his fiction.

Sociological/Historical Studies. Lawrence's disillusionment with liberalism and democracy and his prophetic warnings about the effects of capitalism and industrialism were examined intensively through the 1970s and 1980s, as the long-waged debate over the value of his socio-political ideas continued. Terry Eagleton asserted in *Exiles and Émigrés* (1970) that, "if few twentieth-century writers have paralleled Lawrence in his uncompromisingly total and revolutionary critique of English society, few also have achieved his inward understanding of its character,"[60] but many critics, such as Emile Delavenay, have continued to characterize his social criticism as irrational, impractical, and puerile.

Several writers insisted that, in order to be properly understood, Lawrence's prophetic stance must first be considered carefully within its social/historical/political context. Thus, three noteworthy recent studies, Scott Sanders's *D. H. Lawrence: The World of the Major Novels* (1973), Graham Holderness's *D. H. Lawrence: History, Ideology, and Fiction* (1982), and Peter Scheckner's *Class, Politics, and the Individual: A Study of the Major Works of D. H. Lawrence* (1985), all of them influenced by the Marxist cultural criticism of Raymond Williams and Georg Lukacs, anchored their argument in Lawrence's own historical circumstances. Sanders's calmly persuasive and sometimes penetrating book reduced the five major novels to varying projections of Lawrence's sense of the ongoing conflict between "nature" and "society" (which on one level corresponds to the division of labor between workers and managers). Both Sanders and Holderness found Lawrence still struggling, still admirably yearning for community (or, as Holderness called it, "realism") in his final novel, *Lady Chatterley*, but each critic discounted as a necessarily damaged product of an oppressive industrial society the Lawrence who returns to a personal, "natural" metaphysic, who can find no solution to that oppression except aestheticism or personal evasion. Holderness demonstrated the progression of that conflict in the three versions of *Lady Chatterley's Lover*, expressing preference for the "realistic" *First Lady Chatterley* over the romantic and mythic later versions. Scheckner, too, in his less reductive study, preferred the first version for its realism in class issues and further insisted that the final version "fogs" any effort to assess Lawrence's political commitments. Arguing from the realistic social context of Lawrence's work, and using a wider range of Lawrence's writings than did Sanders or Holderness, Scheckner made a strong case for class consciousness as Lawrence's core issue, and demonstrated how the radical yet ambivalent author responded in his work to immediate social events.

Influence and Comparative Studies.   Before the 1970s a few critics had pointed out Lawrence's affinities to certain other writers, for example, to Whitman, Tolstoy, Dostoyevski, and various Victorians, but not until that decade did the long-needed project of tracing the literary influences on Lawrence get substantially under way. Concomitant with that was a beginning effort to trace his own literary and cultural endowment on later writers.

The task of mapping and assessing other authors' influence on Lawrence's writings has been made especially difficult by the diversity of his reading. In recounting her friend's "Literary Formation," in *D. H. Lawrence: A Personal Record*, Jessie Chambers recalled that he "seemed to read everything," and Rose Marie Burwell's useful "Checklist of Lawrence's Reading" (in Sagar's *A D. H. Lawrence Handbook*) evidenced that Lawrence did indeed read an extraordinary number of books — literature in several languages, psychology, anthropology, philosophy, history, science — throughout his lifetime. He himself seemed to encourage his own anxiety of influence: about his efforts to write plays, he wrote to Edward Garnett in February 1913 that "we have to hate our immediate predecessors, to get free from their authority."[61] John Burt Foster, Jr., in *Heirs to Dionysus* (1981) noted that "Lawrence puts the entire emphasis on discovering rivals rather than acknowledging models: he overlooks the persistent action on him of writers who had helped to mold his imagination."[62]

Foster's erudite treatment of Nietzsche's impact on Lawrence and on Gide, Mann, and Malraux was one among a handful of worthwhile books in the seventies and eighties that considered the imprint of Lawrence's predecessors on his work. Another was Green's *The von Richthofen Sisters* (1974), which speculated that German intellectuals among the Munich Cosmic Circle may have influenced Lawrence. George Zytaruk's *D. H. Lawrence's Response to Russian Literature* (1971) perceptively traced the influence of V. V. Rozanov's "phallic vision" on *The Man Who Died* and

Lady Chatterley. Richard Swigg's broader study, *Lawrence, Hardy, and American Literature* (1972), claimed that the "expressions of tragic dilemma" in Hardy, Poe, Hawthorne, Melville, and Cooper helped Lawrence (especially in *The Rainbow* and *Women in Love*) to crystallize his understanding of the way (to quote Lawrence's preface to *Touch and Go*) "tragedy is the working out of some passional problem within the soul of man." And a recent collection of essays, *D. H. Lawrence and Tradition* (ed. Jeffrey Meyers, 1985), attempted to sharpen the definition of "influence" to mean something like "tradition," but the essays, only a few of which were outstanding, had little to do with what might truly be considered "tradition."

Emile Delavenay and Ross Murfin each produced two books about Lawrence that extensively explored the impact various other writers had on his art and ideas. Delavenay's *D. H. Lawrence: The Man and His Work* (1972) discussed the influence of Schopenhauer, Nietzsche, Whitman, Bergson, Blake, and others on Lawrence (many of Delavenay's leads were further pursued in Daniel Schneider's two 1980s books on Lawrence). In *D. H. Lawrence and Edward Carpenter* (1971), Delavenay was unable to prove that Lawrence had ever met or read the Yorkshire socialist, sexologist, and mystic, but he presented strong internal evidence that Lawrence's debt to that writer was considerable, particularly in the system of ideas present in *The Rainbow* and *Women in Love*. In *Swinburne, Hardy, Lawrence and the Burden of Belief* (1978), Murfin similarly strove to demonstrate how Hardy influenced Lawrence's aesthetic and philosophy, and how "each of the three writers, independently, reacted against and revised an inherited set of metaphysical and aesthetic laws."[63] Murfin's *The Poetry of D. H. Lawrence* (1983) again considered Lawrence's "anxiety of influence" in relation to several traditions: the subjectivity of Shelley; the objectivity of Milton, Wordsworth, Coleridge, and Keats; and the liberating influence of Blake and Whitman.

A few scattered critical essays recently began the imposing task of tracing Lawrence's own cultural and literary influence, on such authors of the past half-century as Stephen Spender, W. H. Auden, Ted Hughes, Doris Lessing, Bernard Malamud, John Fowles, Norman Mailer, Lawrence Durrell, Seamus Heaney, Joyce Carol Oates, Alan Sillitoe, and David Storey. Through 1985, only one critical book had been focused exclusively on Lawrence's impact on a later writer: Norman Fedder's *The Influence of D. H. Lawrence on Tennessee Williams* (1966) reached only predictable conclusions about the American playwright's debt to Lawrence.

It became particularly fashionable in the 1970s and 1980s to compare Lawrence to, and group him with, other writers, as well as to place him within wider surveys of particular traditions, themes, techniques, or genres. The yoking of Lawrence with sometimes disparate bedfellows seemed, on occasion, "a little willful," as Roger Sale observed in *Modern Heroism: Essays on D. H. Lawrence, William Empson, and J. R. R.*

Tolkien (1973). Sale himself strangely yoked those three writers as "historians of the Myth of Lost Unity," arguing that each made heroic efforts to create or achieve community. Brian John made a similar point as he more convincingly linked Lawrence to other authors in *Supreme Fictions: Studies in the Work of William Blake, Thomas Carlyle, W. B. Yeats, and D. H. Lawrence* (1974), examining the four writers in the context of the romantic vitalist tradition. Robert Kiely's distinguished and subtle *Beyond Egotism: The Fiction of James Joyce, Virginia Woolf, and D. H. Lawrence* (1980) found the three novelists likewise inspired by romantic literature, but showed how they each felt challenged to subdue that inspiration. Kiely focused on the similarities in basic human and aesthetic relationships among the major novels of the three authors.

A number of helpful comparative studies resulted from the recent concern with "selfhood." In addition to the books by Bedient, Tenenbaum, and Ebbatson mentioned earlier, there were Daniel Albright's *Personality and Impersonality: Lawrence, Woolf, and Mann* (1978), and Margot Norris's *Beasts of Modern Imagination: Darwin, Nietzsche, Kafka, Ernst, and Lawrence* (1985). Like Ebbatson in *The Evolutionary Self*, Norris was concerned with the new conception of the self influenced by Darwinism. She explored what she called the "biocentric" tradition of modern man as a natural being, lost from his true nature, compensating for his deficiencies by creating art and thought.

The exploration of the natural self was the matrix of several studies of Lawrence's place in the tradition of the pastoral, or "naturist" fiction. The best of these, Michael Squires's *The Pastoral Novel: Studies in George Eliot, Thomas Hardy, and D. H. Lawrence* (1974), delineated with impressive subtlety the pastoral elements in *The White Peacock* and *Lady Chatterley's Lover*, though in arguing that "the pastoral pattern of retreat-reorientation-return" is "beautifully embodied" in the later novel, Squires failed to indicate that Connie and Mellors make no real "return" from the green world (rather, they seem, at story's end, set to make yet another "retreat" from society). Related but less useful studies were John Alcorn's somewhat sketchy treatment of *The Nature Novel from Hardy to Lawrence* (1977) and Roger Ebbatson's occasionally reductive commentary on *Lawrence and the Nature Tradition: A Theme in English Fiction, 1859–1914* (1980).

Several studies provided a broader perspective as they placed Lawrence with other authors in a specific literary or cultural tradition. Kim Herzinger's *D. H. Lawrence in His Time: 1908–1915* (1982) emphasized his relationship with Georgianism, but also showed how he worked within and often against the milieu of the Imagists, Vorticists, and the Bloomsbury Group. More inclusive were George Levine's *The Realistic Imagination: English Fiction from "Frankenstein" to "Lady Chatterly"* (1981), Ragussis's *The Subterfuge of Art: Language and the Romantic Tradition* (1978), and Gregory Lucente's *The Narrative of Realism and Myth: Verga,*

Lawrence, Faulkner, Pavese (1981). The most enlightened of these was Levine's study, which claimed that Lawrence reverses the trend of realism by embracing the impersonal, organic life that previously had been depicted as "monstrous": Conrad's "horror" becomes for Lawrence a vibrant and awesome psychological realism.

Centenary Publications.   The 1985 Centenary of Lawrence's birth yielded a predictable bonanza for publishers and scholars. At least half a dozen academic journals around the world published commemorative collections of essays on Lawrence, and at least eighteen books about him were issued in that year. Two of those books were impressive anthologies, *D. H. Lawrence: Centenary Essays* (ed. Mara Kalnins, 1985), which gathered commentaries by British Commonwealth scholars, and *D. H. Lawrence: A Centenary Consideration* (ed. Peter Balbert and Phillip Marcus, 1985), which collected essays by North American critics.

Three of the most interesting books marking the Centenary were Anthony Burgess's *Flame Into Being: The Life and Work of D. H. Lawrence* (1985), Keith Sagar's *D. H. Lawrence: Life into Art* (1985), and Daniel Schneider's *The Consciousness of D. H. Lawrence: An Intellectual Biography* (January 1986), all directly concerned with the intimate links between Lawrence's life and his literature, with how one informs and interprets the other. Burgess's anecdotal book paralleled Lawrence's career with his own, to reinforce the portrait of an artist whose life becomes his art. Among the fascinating aspects of the introductory study were Burgess's iconoclastic valuations of Lawrence's major works and his repeated expressions of admiration for Lawrence as a truth-telling "subversive." Sagar's book was more critically substantial. Drawing on his thirty years of dedicated work as a Lawrence critic and biographer, he produced a comprehensive (though not particularly ground-breaking) examination of "the genesis of the art in the life," the best such study — with the exception of Clark's *The Minoan Distance* — yet done. Perhaps the finest of all the critical books marking the Centenary, Schneider's *The Consciousness of D. H. Lawrence* concentrated on the development of the author's religious consciousness. This erudite and original "inner biography" stressed influences on and emphases in Lawrence's thought that had necessarily received less attention in the broader biographies of Moore, Delavenay, and others.

The Future of Lawrence Studies

Since the late 1950s, reviewers have frequently growled about the flourishing "Lawrence industry" of critical studies and about what they viewed as the regrettable "academization" or "literary institutionalization" of the artist. Although it seems particularly romantic and Lawrentian to complain that Lawrence's power to disturb is suffering entombment in repetitious, stock, and static exegeses, it is obvious that any writer who can elicit over six thousand books and articles about his work has hardly lost any of his power to inspire and provoke. Moreover, much remains to be done on Lawrence, for example, on his relationship to other major Modernists (the further removed we are from Lawrence's day, the more he appears — in spite of his idiosyncracies — highly representative of his time), on his influence on later writers both within and outside the English-language tradition, and on his work as an essayist and as a letter writer, to name but a few of the topics that seem likely to engage more scholars in coming years. Although most commentaries on Lawrence to date have been by traditional humanistic scholars more interested in the controlling ideas in his work than in his language, he is slowly beginning to attract poststructural critical theorists, and it seems inevitable that in the next decade his work will increasingly become a subject of their scrutiny.

Scholars have struggled for years to assemble Lawrence's canon, so that all his various works could be seen as a whole and the multiple sides of his genius could be properly appraised, but this endeavor has been slowed by Lawrence's own astonishing creative diversity — his forty or so books include work in seven genres — and by the ongoing publication over the past six decades of his previously unpublished works. But now, with the CUP publications of his *Works* and *Letters*, scholars are being given the opportunity to form a fuller, much more coherent image of the creative artist. Lying ahead is a period of consolidation, during which readers will almost certainly have to again readjust their estimate of Lawrence's intentions and achievements.

And he will undoubtedly continue to lure new readers and commentators, for, as Cambridge scholar Carl Baron once noted, Lawrence stands at the confluence of so many vital human interests: "One of the great fascinations of D. H. Lawrence is that there is *so* much on record by and about him that his life and work is one of the places where the minds of many people can meet to contemplate human nature."[64]

The essays and reviews in this collection were selected, first of all, for their intrinsic quality. Most of our choices were from journals (rather than from other books on Lawrence). Three of the essays, those by Clark, Jackson, and Cowan, were extensively revised for this collection, and the essays by Blanchard, Mace, and Laird were written specifically for this book. We tried to include essays and reviews that would meet the needs of both Lawrence specialists and students. Keeping that in mind, we sought essays that focused on Lawrence's major works or on other of his writings most frequently taught, and at the same time we tried to select essays typifying some of the major interests and critical approaches of Lawrence scholars during the past quarter-century. In other words, this collection is intended to be as eclectic as possible within the constraints of quality and concern with Lawrence's major texts.

DENNIS JACKSON and FLEDA BROWN JACKSON

University of Delaware

Notes

1. For a sampling of his commentaries on Lawrence, see Shanks's reviews/essays in the *London Mercury* issues for December 1920, August 1921, October 1922, May 1923, October 1924, March 1926, August 1928, and December 1933, and his articles in the London *Evening Standard* for 3 March 1930 and *John O'London's Weekly* for 22 March 1930.

2. Mark Schorer, "D. H. Lawrence: Then, During, Now," *Atlantic Monthly*, March 1974, p. 84.

3. See Dennis Jackson, " 'The Stormy Petrel of Literature is Dead': The World Press Reports D. H. Lawrence's Death," *D. H. Lawrence Review* 14 (Spring 1981): 33–72.

4. Joseph Wood Krutch, "D. H. Lawrence," *Nation*, 19 March 1950, p. 320.

5. George Currie, "Passed in Review," *Brooklyn Daily Eagle*, 15 March 1930, p. 23.

6. E. M. Forster, "D. H. Lawrence," *Listener*, 30 April 1930, pp. 343–47; and Arnold Bennett, "D. H. Lawrence's Delusion," London *Evening Standard*, 10 April 1930, p. 9.

7. T. S. Eliot, *After Strange Gods: A Primer of Modern Heresy* (New York: Harcourt, Brace & Co., 1934), pp. 38–43, 62–67.

8. William York Tindall, *D. H. Lawrence and Susan His Cow* (New York: Columbia University Press, 1939), p. 207.

9. Ibid., pp. 177, 179.

10. Horace Gregory, "D. H. Lawrence: The Phoenix and the Grave," *New Republic*, December 1932, pp. 131–33.

11. F. R. Leavis, "The Wild, Untutored Phoenix," *Scrutiny*, December 1937, pp. 352–58.

12. Harry T. Moore, "The Great Unread," *Saturday Review of Literature*, 2 March 1940, pp. 8.

13. Elizabeth Bowen, "D. H. Lawrence: Reappraising His Literary Influence," *New York Times Book Review*, 9 February 1947, Sect. 7, p. 4.

14. William York Tindall, *Forces in Modern British Literature, 1885–1946* (New York: Knopf, 1947); revised and reprinted as *Forces in Modern British Literature, 1885–1956* (New York: Vintage Books, 1956), pp. 172, 222–26.

15. Mark Schorer, "Technique as Discovery," *Hudson Review*, Spring 1946, pp. 67–87,

16. Harry T. Moore, *The Life and Works of D. H. Lawrence* (London: Allen & Unwin, 1951).

17. F. R. Leavis, *D. H. Lawrence: Novelist* (London: Chatto and Windus, 1955).

18. This quotation is from Leavis's *The Great Tradition: George Eliot, Henry James, Joseph Conrad* (London: Chatto and Windus, 1948), p. 17. All other observations are from *D. H. Lawrence: Novelist*.

19. Mark Spilka, *The Love Ethic of D. H. Lawrence* (Bloomington: Indiana University Press, 1955), p. 231.

20. The data on sales from Lawrence's books are from personal correspondence with Pollinger (letter of 23 February 1984). See also Gerald J. Pollinger, "*Lady Chatterley's Lover*: A View from Lawrence's Literary Executor," in *D. H. Lawrence's "Lady": A New Look at*

"Lady Chatterley's Lover," ed. Michael Squires and Dennis Jackson (Athens: University of Georgia Press, 1985), p. 238.

21. F. R. Leavis, "Genius as Critic," *Spectator*, 24 March 1961, pp. 412, 414.

22. L. D. Clark, *Dark Night of the Body* (Austin: University of Texas Press, 1964), p. 13.

23. Keith Sagar, *The Art of D. H. Lawrence* (Cambridge: Cambridge University Press, 1966), p. 5.

24. Julian Moynahan, *The Deed of Life: The Novels and Tales of D. H. Lawrence* (Princeton, N.J.: Princeton University Press, 1963), p. 226.

25. Eugene Goodheart, "Lawrence and the Critics," *Chicago Review* 16, no. 3 (1963): 128.

26. Eliseo Vivas, *D. H. Lawrence: The Failure and the Triumph of Art* (Evanston, Ill.: Northwestern University Press, 1960), p. ix.

27. Kingsley Widmer, *The Art of Perversity: D. H. Lawrence's Shorter Fictions* (Seattle: University of Washington Press, 1962), p. 220.

28. Eugene Goodheart, *The Utopian Vision of D. H. Lawrence* (Chicago: The University of Chicago Press, 1963), p. 173.

29. George Ford, *Double Measure* (New York: Holt, Rinehart and Winston, 1965).

30. Colin Clarke, *River of Dissolution: D. H. Lawrence and English Romanticism* (London: Routledge and Kegan Paul; New York: Barnes and Noble, 1969), p. 20.

31. Mark Spilka, "Lawrence Up-Tight, or the Anal Phase Once Over," *Novel* 4 (1971): 257–67.

32. David Cavitch, *D. H. Lawrence and the New World* (London: Oxford University Press, 1969), p. 67.

33. Daniel A. Weiss, *Oedipus in Nottingham: D. H. Lawrence* (Seattle: University of Washington Press, 1962), p. 109.

34. John Stoll, *D. H. Lawrence's "Sons and Lovers": Self-Encounter and the Unknown Self* (Muncie, Ind.: Ball State University, 1968).

35. Eugene Goodheart, "Letters from a Son and Lover," *Books and Arts*, 9 November 1979, p. 6.

36. Christopher Hawtree, "The Crawling Snail," *Spectator*, 15 September 1984, p. 30.

37. David Lodge, "Comedy of Eros," *New Republic*, 10 December 1984, p. 100.

38. Harry T. Moore, *"John Thomas and Lady Jane," New York Times Book Review*, 7 August 1972, p. 7.

39. Squires and Jackson, Introduction to *D. H. Lawrence's "Lady": A New Look at "Lady Chatterley's Lover,"* p. xi.

40. Anthony Burgess, *Flame Into Being* (New York: Arbor House, 1985), p. 176.

41. Edward Garnett, "Art and the Moralists: Mr. D. H. Lawrence's Work," *Dial*, 16 November 1916, pp. 379–81.

42. R. P. Blackmur, "D. H. Lawrence and Expressive Form," in *Language as Gesture* (New York: Arrow Editions, 1935), pp. 103–20.

43. Kenneth Rexroth, "Poet in a Fugitive Cause," *Nation*, 23 November 1964, pp. 382–83.

44. Moynahan, *Deed of Life*, p. xiv.

45. Letter from Lawrence to Edward Garnett, 1 February 1913, in *The Letters of D. H. Lawrence, Volume I: 1901–1913*, ed. James T. Boulton (Cambridge: Cambridge University Press, 1979), p. 509.

46. Ibid.

47. Mollie Panter-Downes, "Letter from London," *New Yorker*, 11 May 1968, pp. 101–2.

48. Harold Hobson, "Oratoria on the Terraces," London *Sunday Times*, 17 March 1968, p. 490.

49. David Gordon, *D. H. Lawrence as Literary Critic* (New Haven and London: Yale University Press [Yale Studies in English vol. 161], 1966), pp. 40, 151.

50. Emile Delavenay, *D. H. Lawrence: The Man and His Work: The Formative Years: 1885–1919*, trans. Katharine M. Delavenay (London: William Heinemann; Carbondale: Southern Illinois University Press, 1972).

51. Frank Kermode, "Lawrence in His Letters," *New Statesman*, 23 March 1962, pp. 422.

52. Kate Millett, *Sexual Politics* (Garden City, N.Y.: Doubleday, 1970), p. 257.

53. Hilary Simpson, *D. H. Lawrence and Feminism* (DeKalb, Ill.: Northern Illinois University Press, 1982), p. 17.

54. Letter from Lawrence to Edward Garnett, 22 April 1914, in *The Letters of D. H. Lawrence, Volume II: 1913–1916*, ed. George J. Zytaruk and James T. Boulton (Cambridge: Cambridge University Press, 1981), p. 165.

55. Daniel J. Schneider, *D. H. Lawrence: The Artist as Psychologist* (Lawrence: University Press of Kansas, 1984), p. 73.

56. James C. Cowan, *D. H. Lawrence's American Journey: A Study in Literature and Myth* (Cleveland and London: The Press of Case Western Reserve University, 1970), p. 1.

57. See Huxley's Foreword to *The Manuscripts of D. H. Lawrence: A Descriptive Catalogue*, by Lawrence Clark Powell (Los Angeles: Public Library, 1937), pp. ix–xi. Huxley also commented on Lawrence's writing habits in his introduction to *The Letters of D. H. Lawrence* (London: Heinemann, 1932).

58. "He Do the Polis in Different Voices: Lawrence's Later Style," in *D. H. Lawrence: A Centenary Consideration*, ed. Peter Balbert and Phillip Marcus (Ithaca, N.Y.: Cornell University Press, 1985), pp. 162–79.

59. Garrett Stewart, "Lawrence, 'Being,' and the Allotropic Style," *Novel* 9 (Spring 1976): 217–42.

60. Terry Eagleton, *Exiles and Émigrés* (New York: Schocken Books, 1970), p. 218.

61. Letter from Lawrence to Edward Garnett, 1 February 1913, in *The Letters of D. H. Lawrence, Volume 1*, p. 509.

62. John Burt Foster, Jr., *Heirs to Dionysus: A Nietzschean Current in Literary Modernism* (Princeton, N.J.: Princeton University Press, 1981), p. 180.

63. Ross Murfin, *Swinburne, Hardy, Lawrence, and the Burden of Belief* (Chicago: University of Chicago Press, 1978), p. ix.

64. "The Nottingham Festival D. H. Lawrence Exhibition, 1972," *D. H. Lawrence Review* 7 (Spring 1974): 19.

On the Novels

Portrait of Miriam: A Study in the Design of *Sons and Lovers*

Louis L. Martz*

[i]

The girl was romantic in her soul.

And she was cut off from ordinary life by her religious intensity which made the world for her either a nunnery garden or a paradise, where sin and knowledge were not, or else an ugly, cruel thing.

And in sacrifice she was proud, in renunciation she was strong, for she did not trust herself to support everyday life.

"You don't want to love—your eternal and abnormal craving is to be loved. You aren't positive, you're negative. You absorb, absorb, as if you must fill yourself up with love, because you've got a shortage somewhere."[1]

With very few exceptions, the commentators on Lawrence's *Sons and Lovers* have tended to accept the view of Miriam's character as thus described by the narrator and by Paul Morel. Mark Spilka, for example, in his stimulating book, bases his interpretation of the novel on the assumption that Miriam has "an unhealthy spirituality," is truly "negative," that she really "wheedles the soul out of things," as Paul Morel says, and that "because of the stifling nature of Miriam's love, Paul refuses to marry her"—justifiably, since "Miriam's frigidity is rooted in her own nature."[2] But I believe that the portrait of Miriam is far more complex than either Paul or the narrator will allow, and that a study of her part in the book will cast some light upon the puzzling and peculiar technique of narration that Lawrence adopts when he comes to the central section of his novel, the five tormented chapters (7–11) running from "Lad-and-Girl Love" through "The Test on Miriam."

As everyone has noticed, Part I of the novel (the first third of the

*Reprinted from *Imagined Worlds: Essays on Some English Novels and Novelists in Honour of John Butt*, ed. Maynard Mack and Ian Gregor (London: Methuen & Co., 1968), 343–69, by permission of Methuen & Co. and the author.

book, concluding with the death of William) is written in the manner of
Victorian realism: the omniscient narrator, working with firm control, sets
forth the facts objectively. The countryside, the mining village, the family
conflicts, the daily life of the household—all is given in clear, precise,
convincing detail. The use of local dialect, the echoes of biblical style, the
short, concise sentences combine to create in us a confidence in the
narrator's command of his materials. His fairness to everyone is evident. If
the father is predominantly shown as brutal and drunken, in those savage
quarrels with the mother, he is also shown in his younger glory as a man
who might have flourished with a different wife: "Gertrude Coppard
watched the young miner as he danced, a certain subtle exultation like
glamour in his movement, and his face the flower of his body, ruddy, with
tumbled black hair, and laughing alike whatever partner he bowed above"
(pp. 9–10). Even when the wife has turned away from him she can enjoy
his music:

> Quite early, before six o'clock, she heard him whistling away to himself
> downstairs. He had a pleasant way of whistling, lively and musical. He
> nearly always whistled hymns. He had been a choir-boy with a beautiful
> voice, and had taken solos in Southwell cathedral. His morning whis-
> tling alone betrayed it.
> His wife lay listening to him tinkering away in the garden, his
> whistling ringing out as he sawed and hammered away. It always gave
> her a sense of warmth and peace to hear him thus as she lay in bed, the
> children not yet awake, in the bright early morning, happy in his man's
> fashion.
>
> (p. 18)

We watch Morel's relish in getting his breakfast and his joy in walking
across the fields to his work in the early morning; we learn of those happy
times when Morel is cobbling the family's boots, or mending kettles, or
making fuses; we recognize his faithful labour at his gruelling job; and
particularly we notice the love for him felt by the youngest child Arthur:
"Mrs. Morel was glad this child loved the father" (p. 47). All these things
give a sense of balance and proportion to Part I, making it clear that Paul's
view is partial, unfair to the father, ignoring his basic humanity.

Paul's blindness towards his father's very existence as a human being is
cruelly shown in the scene where Morel emerges from the pit to hear of
William's death:

> "And William is dead, and my mother's in London, and what will
> she be doing?" the boy asked himself, as if it were a conundrum.
> He watched chair after chair come up, and still no father. At last,
> standing beside a waggon, a man's form! The chair sank on its rests,
> Morel stepped off. He was slightly lame from an accident.
> "Is it thee, Paul? Is 'e worse?"
> "You've got to go to London."
> The two walked off the pit-bank, where men were watching

curiously. As they came out and went along the railway, with the sunny autumn field on one side and a wall of trucks on the other, Morel said in a frightened voice:

"" 'E's niver gone, child?""

"Yes."

"When wor't?"

The miner's voice was terrified.[3]

"Last night. We had a telegram from my mother."

Morel walked on a few strides, then leaned up against a truck side, his hand over his eyes. He was not crying. Paul stood looking round, waiting. On the weighing-machine a truck trundled slowly. Paul saw everything, except his father leaning against the truck as if he were tired.

(p. 137)

"Paul saw everything, except his father." Only the omniscient narrator reveals the man Morel, battered from his work, frightened for his son's life, sunk in dumb agony at the news, while his intimate dialect plays off pitifully against the formal language of Paul, to stress the total division between the two.

Part I, then, is a triumph of narration in the old Victorian style. It is a long prologue, in which the issues are clearly defined, and in which, above all, the mother's overpowering influence is shown in the death of one son, while she turns toward Paul as her only remaining hope: "" 'I should have watched the living, not the dead,' she told herself" (p. 140).

Meanwhile, as William is engaged in his fatal courtship, the figure of Miriam has been quietly introduced, in the natural, harmonious setting of the farm: "Mother and son went into the small railed garden, where was a scent of red gillivers. By the open door were some floury loaves, put out to cool. A hen was just coming to peck them. Then, in the doorway suddenly appeared a girl in a dirty apron. She was about fourteen years old, had a rosy dark face, a bunch of short black curls, very fine and free, and dark eyes; shy, questioning, a little resentful of the strangers, she disappeared" (pp. 124-5). Shortly after this follows the vivid incident in which the brothers jeer at Miriam for being afraid to let the hen peck the corn out of her hand:

"Now, Miriam," said Maurice, "you come an' 'ave a go."

"No," she cried, shrinking back.

"Ha! baby. The mardy-kid!" said her brothers.

"It doesn't hurt a bit," said Paul. "It only just nips rather nicely."

"No," she still cried, shaking her black curls and shrinking.

"She dursn't," said Geoffrey. "She niver durst do anything except recite poitry."

"Dursn't jump off a gate, dursn't tweedle, dursn't go on a slide, dursn't stop a girl hittin' her. She can do nowt but go about thinkin' herself somebody. 'The Lady of the Lake.' Yah!" cried Maurice.

(p. 126)

We are bound to align this with the later incident of the swing, both of which might be taken "as revelations of Miriam's diminished vitality, her tendency to shrink back from life, whether she is making love, feeding chickens, trying to cope with Mrs. Morel's dislike of her, or merely looking at flowers."[4] But we should note that immediately after the passage just quoted Paul witnesses another aspect of Miriam:

> As he went round the back, he saw Miriam kneeling in front of the hen-coop, some maize in her hand, biting her lip, and crouching in an intense attitude. The hen was eyeing her wickedly. Very gingerly she put forward her hand. The hen bobbed for her. She drew back quickly with a cry, half of fear, half of chagrin.
>
> "It won't hurt you," said Paul.
>
> She flushed crimson and started up.
>
> "I only wanted to try," she said in a low voice.
>
> "See, it doesn't hurt," he said, and, putting only two corns in his palm, he let the hen peck, peck, peck at his bare hand. "It only makes you laugh," he said.
>
> She put her hand forward, and dragged it away, tried again, and started back with a cry. He frowned.
>
> "Why, I'd let her take corn from my face," said Paul, "only she bumps a bit. She's ever so neat. If she wasn't, look how much ground she'd peck up every day."
>
> He waited grimly, and watched. At last Miriam let the bird peck from her hand. She gave a little cry — fear, and pain because of fear — rather pathetic. But she had done it, and she did it again.
>
> "There, you see," said the boy. "It doesn't hurt, does it?"
>
> She looked at him with dilated dark eyes.
>
> "No," she laughed, trembling.
>
> (p. 127–8)

The scene shows more than timidity; it shows, also, her extreme sensitivity, along with her shy desire for new experience: she wants to try, she wants to learn; if rightly encouraged she will and can learn, and then she can respond with laughter and trembling excitement. This first view of Miriam, seen through the eyes of the objective narrator, is astir with life: for all her shyness and shrinking she is nevertheless capable of a strong response. The whole initial sketch is suffused with her "beautiful warm colouring" and accompanied by her "musical, quiet voice." She is a girl of rich potential.

[ii]

As Part II opens we become at once aware of a drastic shift in method. The first two pages are given over to an elaborate interpretation of Miriam's character before she again appears, "nearly sixteen, very beautiful, with her warm colouring, her gravity, her eyes dilating suddenly like an ecstasy" (p. 144). No such extended analysis of anyone has appeared in Part I; there the characters have been allowed to act out their parts before us, with only brief guiding touches by the objective narrator. But here we sense a peculiar intensity in the analysis: the narrator seems to be preparing the way for some new and difficult problem, and in so doing he seems to be dropping his manner of impartiality. He is determined to set our minds in a certain direction, and this aim is reflected in the drifting length and involution of the sentences. The style of writing here seems designed to reflect the "mistiness" of the character he is describing, her remoteness from life:

> Her great companion was her mother. They were both brown-eyed, and inclined to be mystical, such women as treasure religion inside them, breathe it in their nostrils, and see the whole of life in a mist thereof. So to Miriam, Christ and God made one great figure, which she loved tremblingly and passionately when a tremendous sunset burned out the western sky, and Ediths, and Lucys, and Rowenas, Brian de Bois Guilberts, Rob Roys, and Guy Mannerings, rustled the sunny leaves in the morning, or sat in her bedroom aloft, alone, when it snowed. That was life to her. For the rest, she drudged in the house, which work she would not have minded had not her clean red floor been mucked up immediately by the trampling farm-boots of her brothers. She madly wanted her little brother of four to let her swathe him and stifle him in her love; she went to church reverently, with bowed head, and quivered in anguish from the vulgarity of the other choir-girls and from the common-sounding voice of the curate; she fought with her brothers, whom she considered brutal louts; and she held not her father in too high esteem because he did not carry any mystical ideals cherished in his heart, but only wanted to have as easy a time as he could, and his meals when he was ready for them.
>
> (pp. 142–3)

She is also a girl who is "mad to have learning whereon to pride herself"; and for all these causes she neglects and ignores her physical being: "Her beauty — that of a shy, wild, quiveringly sensitive thing — seemed nothing to her. Even her soul, so strong for rhapsody, was not enough. She must have something to reinforce her pride, because she felt different from other people." At the same time, her misty emotions lead her towards a desire to dominate Paul: "Then he was so ill, and she felt he would be weak. Then she would be stronger than he. Then she could love him. If she could be mistress of him in his weakness, take care of him, if he could depend on her, if she could, as it were, have him in her arms, how she would love him!" (p. 143).

In all this the narrator is anticipating the views of Miriam frequently expressed by Paul himself: that she is too spiritual, too abstract, that she shrinks away from physical reality, and that she has a stifling desire to absorb and possess his soul. The incident of the swing that follows shortly after (pp. 149–51) would seem to bear out some of this: she is afraid to let

Paul swing her high, and Lawrence phrases her fear in language that has unmistakable sexual overtones: "She felt the accuracy with which he caught her, exactly at the right moment, and the exactly proportionate strength of his thrust, and she was afraid. Down to her bowels went the hot wave of fear. She was in his hands. Again, firm and inevitable came the thrust at the right moment. She gripped the rope, almost swooning" (p. 151). Yet she has led Paul to the swing, and she is fascinated by his free swinging: "It roused a warmth in her. It were almost as if he were a flame that had lit a warmth in her whilst he swung in the middle air." Who can say that Miriam is unable to learn this too, as she has learned with the hen, and as she is later shown to overcome her fear of crossing fences?

> Occasionally she ran with Paul down the fields. Then her eyes blazed naked in a kind of ecstasy that frightened him. But she was physically afraid. If she were getting over a stile, she gripped his hands in a little hard anguish, and began to lose her presence of mind. And he could not persuade her to jump from even a small height. Her eyes dilated, became exposed and palpitating.
> "No!" she cried, half laughing in terror — "no!"
> "You shall!" he cried once, and, jerking her forward, he brought her falling from the fence. But her wild "Ah!" of pain, as if she were losing consciousness, cut him. She landed on her feet safely, and afterwards had courage in this respect.
>
> (p. 154)

Certainly she wants to learn; only a few lines after the swing episode we find this all-important passage:

> But the girl gradually sought him out. If he brought up his sketch-book, it was she who pondered longest over the last picture. Then she would look up at him. Suddenly, her dark eyes alight like water that shakes with a stream of gold in the dark, she would ask:
> "Why do I like this so?"
> Always something in his breast shrank from these close, intimate, dazzled looks of hers.
> "Why *do* you?" he asked.
> "I don't know. It seems so true."
> "It's because — it's because there is scarcely any shadow in it; it's more shimmery, as if I'd painted the shimmering protoplasm in the leaves and everywhere, and not the stiffness of the shape. That seems dead to me. Only this shimmeriness is the real living. The shape is a dead crust. The shimmer is inside really."
> And she, with her little finger in her mouth, would ponder these sayings. They gave her a feeling of life again, and vivified things which had meant nothing to her. She managed to find some meaning in his struggling, abstract speeches. And they were the medium through which she came distinctly at her beloved objects.
>
> (p. 152)

It seems as though she is learning to reach out towards the "shimmeriness" that is the "real living"; with his help she is coming out of her "mist" towards a distinct sight of "her beloved objects." *She* is learning, while *he* shrinks away from her intimate, shimmering eyes ("like water that shakes with a stream of gold in the dark"). She senses the meaning of his "abstract speeches," she gets "so near him," she creates in him "a strange, roused sensation" (p. 153) — and as a result she enrages him for reasons that he cannot grasp. Is it because he is refusing to face the shimmer that is really inside Miriam?

So, when he sees her embracing her youngest brother "almost as if she were in a trance, and swaying also as if she were swooned in an ecstasy of love," he bursts out with his irritation:

> "What do you make such a *fuss* for?" cried Paul, all in suffering because of her extreme emotion. "Why can't you be ordinary with him?"
>
> She let the child go, and rose, and said nothing. Her intensity which would leave no emotion on a normal plane, irritated the youth into a frenzy. And this fearful, naked contact of her on small occasions shocked him. He was used to his mother's reserve. And on such occasions he was thankful in his heart and soul that he had his mother, so sane and wholesome.
>
> (p. 153)

One senses, as Miriam does at a later point, an alien influence here, twisting the mind of Paul and the narrator away from Miriam. Two pages later we see a dramatic juxtaposition of two warring actualities:

> He used to tell his mother all these things.
>
> "I'm going to teach Miriam algebra," he said.
>
> "Well," replied Mrs. Morel, "I hope she'll get fat on it."
>
> When he went up to the farm on the Monday evening, it was drawing twilight. Miriam was just sweeping up the kitchen, and was kneeling at the hearth when he entered. Everyone was out but her. She looked round at him, flushed, her dark eyes shining, her fine hair falling about her face.
>
> "Hello!" she said, soft and musical. "I knew it was you."
>
> "How?"
>
> "I knew your step. Nobody treads so quick and firm."
>
> He sat down, sighing.
>
> "Ready to do some algebra?" he asked, drawing a little book from his pocket.
>
> (p. 155)

Who is sane and wholesome, we may well ask? And whose thoughts are abstracted from life? We are beginning to learn that we cannot wholly trust the narrator's remarks in this central portion of the book, for his commentary represents mainly an extension of Paul's consciousness; everywhere, in this portion of the book, the voice of the narrator tends to echo and magnify the confusions that are arising within Paul himself. These are the contradictions in which some readers have seen a failure or a faltering in the novel, because "the point of view is never adequately objectified and sustained to tell us which is true."[5] But I feel rather that Lawrence has invented a successful technique by which he can manage the deep autobiographical problems that underlie the book. We are watching the strong graft of a stream of consciousness growing out of the live trunk of that Victorian prologue, and intertwining with the objectively presented action. The point of view adopted is that of Paul; but since confusion, self-deception, and desperate self-justification are essential to that point of view, we can never tell, from that stream of consciousness alone, where the real truth lies. But we can tell it from the action; we can tell it by seeking out the portrait of Miriam that lies beneath the overpainted commentary of the Paul-narrator. This technique of painting and overpainting produces a strange and unique tension in this part of the novel. The image of Miriam appears and then is clouded over; it is as though we were looking at her through a clouded window that is constantly being cleared, and fogged, and cleared again. It is an unprecedented and inimitable technique, discovered for this one necessary occasion. But it works.

How it works, we may see by looking once again at the frequently quoted passage where Miriam leads Paul, despite his reluctance ("They grumble so if I'm late") into the woods at dusk to find the "wild-rose bush she had discovered."

> The tree was tall and straggling. It had thrown its briers over a hawthorn-bush, and its long streamers trailed thick, right down to the grass, splashing the darkness everywhere with great split stars, pure white. In bosses of ivory and in large splashed stars the roses gleamed on the darkness of foliage and stems and grass. Paul and Miriam stood close together, silent, and watched. Point after point the steady roses shone out to them, seeming to kindle something in their souls. The dusk came like smoke around, and still did not put out the roses.
>
> Paul looked into Miriam's eyes. She was pale and expectant with wonder, her lips were parted, and her dark eyes lay open to him. His look seemed to travel down into her. Her soul quivered. It was the communion she wanted. He turned aside, as if pained. He turned to the bush.
>
> "They seem as if they walk like butterflies, and shake themselves," he said.
>
> She looked at her roses. They were white, some incurved and holy, others expanded in an ecstasy. The tree was dark as a shadow. She lifted her hand impulsively to the flowers; she went forward and touched them in worship.
>
> "Let us go," he said.
>
> There was a cool scent of ivory roses—a white, virgin scent. Something made him feel anxious and imprisoned. The two walked in silence.
>
> (pp. 159–60)

What is this "something" that makes him "feel anxious and imprisoned"? Is he like the hawthorn-bush, caught in the trailing streamers of the rose-bush? Is it because she has insisted on a moment of soul-communion which represents her tendency towards "a blasphemous possessorship"?[6] The narrator seems to be urging us in this direction. Yet in itself the scene may be taken to represent, amid this wild profusion of natural growth, a moment of natural communion in the human relationship, a potential marriage of senses and the soul. This is, for Miriam, an "ecstasy" in which nature is not abstracted, but realized in all its wild perfection. Paul breaks the mood and runs away towards home. And when he reaches home we may grasp the true manner of his imprisonment:

> Always when he went with Miriam, and it grew rather late, he knew his mother was fretting and getting angry about him — why, he could not understand. As he went into the house, flinging down his cap, his mother looked up at the clock. She had been sitting thinking, because a chill to her eyes prevented her reading. She could feel Paul being drawn away by this girl. And she did not care for Miriam. "She is one of those who will want to suck a man's soul out till he has none of his own left," she said to herself; "and he is just such a gaby as to let himself be absorbed. She will never let him become a man; she never will." So, while he was away with Miriam, Mrs. Morel grew more and more worked up.
> She glanced at the clock and said, coldly and rather tired:
> "You have been far enough to-night."
> His soul, warm and exposed from contact with the girl, shrank.
>   (pp. 160–1)

Miriam offers him the freedom of natural growth within a mature relation, though Paul soon adopts the mother's view of Miriam's "posses-sive" nature. He cannot help himself, but there is no reason why readers of the book should accept the mother's view of Miriam, which is everywhere shown to be motivated by the mother's own possessiveness. The mother has described only herself in the above quotation; she has not described Miriam, who is quite a different being and has quite a different effect on Paul. The fact is that Paul needs both his mother and Miriam for his true development, as he seems to realize quite early in the conflict: "A sketch finished, he always wanted to take it to Miriam. Then he was stimulated into knowledge of the work he had produced unconsciously. In contact with Miriam he gained insight; his vision went deeper. From his mother he drew the life-warmth, the strength to produce; Miriam urged this warmth into intensity like a white light" (p. 158). Or earlier we hear that Miriam's family "kindled him and made him glow to his work, whereas his mother's influence was to make him quietly determined, patient, dogged, unwear-ied" (p. 149).

But the mother cannot bear to release him. Miriam must be met by her with cold, unfriendly curtness, while the married woman, Clara, may receive a friendly welcome from the mother. Clara offers no threat: "Mrs. Morel measured herself against the younger woman, and found herself easily stronger" (p. 321). "Yes, I liked her," she says in answer to Paul's inquiry. "But you'll tire of her, my son; you know you will" (p. 329). And so she encourages the affair with Clara: the adulterous relation will serve the son's physical needs, while the mother can retain the son's deeper love and loyalty. Mrs. Morel senses what she is doing, but evades the facts: "Mrs. Morel considered. She would have been glad now for her son to fall in love with some woman who would—she did not know what. But he fretted so, got so furious suddenly, and again was melancholic. She wished he knew some nice woman—She did not know what she wished, but left it vague. At any rate she was not hostile to the idea of Clara" (pp. 242–3). The mother's devices are pitiful, and at the same time contemptible, as we have already seen from the painful episode in which she overwhelms her son with raw and naked emotion:

> He had taken off his collar and tie, and rose, bare-throated, to go to bed. As he stooped to kiss his mother, she threw her arms round his neck, hid her face on his shoulder, and cried, in a whimpering voice, so unlike her own that he writhed in agony:
> "I can't bear it. I could let another woman—but not her. She'd leave me no room, not a bit of room—"
> And immediately he hated Miriam bitterly.
> "And I've never—you know Paul—I've never had a husband—not really—"
> He stroked his mother's hair, and his mouth was on her throat.
> "And she exults so in taking you from me—she's not like ordinary girls."
> "Well, I don't love her, mother," he murmured, bowing his head and hiding his eyes on her shoulder in misery. His mother kissed him a long, fervent kiss.
> "My boy!" she said, in a voice trembling with passionate love.
> (p. 213)

"At your mischief again?" says the father, "venomously," as he interrupts this scene of illicitly possessive passion. Mischief it is, corrosive and destructive to the marriage that Paul needs, the full relationship that Miriam offers, with her intimate love for nature.

It will be evident that I do not agree with the view that Spilka and others have taken of that flower-picking episode with Miriam and Clara, the view that takes the scene as a revelation of a basic flaw in Miriam: "she kills life and has no right to it."[7]

> "Ah!" cried Miriam, and she looked at Paul, her dark eyes dilating. He smiled. Together they enjoyed the field of flowers. Clara, a little way off, was looking at the cowslips disconsolately. Paul and Miriam stayed close together, talking in subdued tones. He kneeled on one knee, quickly gathering the best blossoms, moving from tuft to tuft restlessly,

talking softly all the time. Miriam plucked the flowers lovingly, lingering over them. He always seemed to her too quick and almost scientific.
Yet his bunches had a natural beauty more than hers. He loved them,
but as if they were his and he had a right to them. She had more
reverence for them: they held something she had not.

(p. 237)

The last clause has a wonderful ambiguity. If we take Paul's point of view,
we will say that she is "negative," that she lacks true life. If we ponder the
whole action of the book, we will say that what she lacks is the full organic
life of the flower, sexually complete within itself. She cannot grow into her
full life without the principle that Paul, with his masculine creativity, here
displays. The passage shows a man and a woman who are true counterparts, in mind and body. When, a little later, Paul sprinkles the flowers
over Clara, he is performing an exclusively sensuous ritual that threatens
more than a pagan love-death:

> Her breasts swung slightly in her blouse. The arching curve of her back
> was beautiful and strong; she wore no stays. Suddenly, without know-
> ing, he was scattering a handful of cowslips over her hair and neck,
> saying:
>
> > "Ashes to ashes, and dust to dust,
> > If the Lord won't have you the devil must."
>
> The chill flowers fell on her neck. She looked up at him, with
> almost pitiful, scared grey eyes, wondering what he was doing. Flowers
> fell on her face, and she shut her eyes.
> Suddenly, standing there above her, he felt awkward.
> "I thought you wanted a funeral," he said, ill at ease.

(pp. 238–9)

It is Paul, under his mother's domination, who kills life, by refusing
to move in organic relation with Miriam:

> He would not have it that they were lovers. The intimacy between
> them had been kept so abstract, such a matter of the soul, all thought
> and weary struggle into consciousness, that he saw it only as a platonic
> friendship. He stoutly denied there was anything else between them.
> Miriam was silent, or else she very quietly agreed. He was a fool who
> did not know what was happening to himself. By tacit agreement they
> ignored the remarks and insinuations of their acquaintances.
> "We aren't lovers, we are friends," he said to her. "*We* know it. Let
> them talk. What does it matter what they say."
> Sometimes, as they were walking together, she slipped her arm
> timidly into his. But he always resented it, and she knew it. It caused a
> violent conflict in him. With Miriam he was always on the high plane of
> abstraction, when his natural fire of love was transmitted into the fine
> steam[8] of thought. She would have it so.

(pp. 172–3)

The last sentence is a fine example of the way in which the commentary of the Paul-narrator can contradict the tenor of the action: "she slipped her arm timidly into his." Clara knows better and tells Paul the truth in that revealing conversation just before "the test on Miriam." Paul has been describing how Miriam "wants the soul out of my body": "I know she wants a sort of soul union."

> "But how do you know what she wants?"
> "I've been with her for seven years."
> "And you haven't found out the very first thing about her."
> "What's that?"
> "That she doesn't want any of your soul communion. That's your own imagination. She wants you."
> He pondered over this. Perhaps he was wrong.
> "But she seems—" he began.
> "You've never tried," she answered.
>
> (pp. 277–8)

This is not to deny that Miriam is shy, intense, spiritual, and, as a result of her upbringing, fearful and evasive of sexual facts. All these qualities belong to her character, for she is young, sensitive, and modest. My point is that her portrait does not consist simply of a static presentation of these aspects: her portrait is being enriched dynamically and progressively before our eyes, over a long period of years, from her early adolescence, through an awakening and potential fulfillment, to the utter extinction of her inner life and hope.

The truth of Clara's view has been borne out long before, as far back as that scene where Paul accuses Miriam of never laughing real laughter:

> "But"—and she looked up at him with eyes frightened and struggling—"I do laugh at you—I *do*."
> "Never! There's always a kind of intensity. When you laugh I could always cry; it seems as if it shows up your suffering. Oh, you make me knit the brows of my very soul and cogitate."
> Slowly she shook her head despairingly.
> "I'm sure I don't want to," she said.
> "I'm so damned spiritual with *you* always!" he cried.
> She remained silent, thinking, "Then why don't you be otherwise." But he saw her crouching, brooding figure, and it seemed to tear him in two.
>
> (p. 188)

And then, on the next page, as Paul repairs the bicycle tyre, we have an unmistakable glimpse of the vital image of Miriam, her strong physical feeling for him, and her true laughter:

> "Fetch me a drop of water in a bowl," he said to her. "I shall be late, and then I s'll catch it."
> He lighted the hurricane lamp, took off his coat, turned up the

bicycle, and set speedily to work. Miriam came with the bowl of water
and stood close to him, watching. She loved to see his hands doing
things. He was slim and vigorous, with a kind of easiness even in his
most hasty movements. And busy at his work, he seemed to forget her.
She loved him absorbedly. She wanted to run her hands down his sides.
She always wanted to embrace him, so long as he did not want her.

"There!" he said, rising suddenly. "Now, could you have done it
quicker?"

"No!" she laughed.

He straightened himself. His back was towards her. She put her
two hands on his sides, and ran them quickly down.

"You are so *fine!*" she said.

He laughed, hating her voice, but his blood roused to a wave of
flame by her hands. She did not seem to realise *him* in all this. He might
have been an object. She never realised the male he was.

(p. 189)

Those last three sentences, the outgrowth of his torment, and the earlier
remark, "so long as he did not want her," provide clear examples of the
way in which the overpainted commentary tends to obscure the basic
portrait of Miriam. It is the same in the episode at Nethermere: "He could
not bear to look at Miriam. She seemed to want him, and he resisted. He
resisted all the time. He wanted now to give her passion and tenderness,
and he could not. He felt that she wanted the soul out of his body, and not
him."

He went on, in his dead fashion:

"If only you could want *me*, and not want what I can reel off for
you!"

"I!" she cried bitterly—"I! Why, when would you let me take
you?"

(p. 194)

His bursts of anger and "hate," his feeling that Miriam is pulling the soul
out of his body, are only his own tormented reactions to the agony he feels
in being pulled so strongly away from his mother, as Daniel Weiss has said:
"It is that for the first time in his life he is facing a mature relationship
between himself and another woman, *not* his mother, and that a different
mode of love is being demanded from him. It is Miriam's refusal to allow
him to regress to the Nirvana, the paradisal state of the infant, her
insistence that he recognize her, that fills him with anguish."[9]

As though to warn us against accepting Paul's responses and interpretations, Lawrence inserts in the middle of the crucial chapter, "Strife in
Love," a long, vigorous, attractive, and surprising scene where the father is
shown totally in command of the household, on a Friday evening, when
the miners make their reckoning in Morel's house. Complaining with
warm, vigorous dialect about the cold room, as he emerges from his bath,
Morel draws even his wife into laughter and reminiscent admiration:

Morel looked down ruefully at his sides.

"Me!" he exclaimed. "I'm nowt b'r a skinned rabbit. My bones fair juts out on me."

"I should like to know where," retorted his wife.

"Iv'ry-wheer! I'm nobbut a sack o' faggots."

Mrs. Morel laughed. He had still a wonderfully young body, muscular, without any fat. His skin was smooth and clear. It might have been the body of a man of twenty-eight, except that there were, perhaps, too many blue scars, like tattoo-marks, where the coal-dust remained under the skin, and that his chest was too hairy. But he put his hand on his side ruefully. It was his fixed belief that, because he did not get fat, he was as thin as a starved rat.

Paul looked at his father's thick, brownish hands all scarred, with broken nails, rubbing the fine smoothness of his sides, and the incongruity struck him. It seemed strange they were the same flesh.

"I suppose," he said to his father, "you had a good figure once."

"Eh!" exclaimed the miner, glancing round, startled and timid, like a child.

"He had," exclaimed Mrs. Morel, "if he didn't hurtle himself up as if he was trying to get in the smallest space he could."

"Me!" exclaimed Morel — "me a good figure! I wor niver much more n'r a skeleton."

"Man!" cried his wife, "don't be such a pulamiter!"

" 'Strewth!" he said. "Tha's niver knowed me but what I looked as if I wor goin' off in a rapid decline."

She sat and laughed.

"You've had a constitution like iron," she said; "and never a man had a better start, if it was body that counted. You should have seen him as a young man," she cried suddenly to Paul, drawing herself up to imitate her husband's once handsome bearing.

Morel watched her shyly. He saw again the passion she had had for him. It blazed upon her for a moment. He was shy, rather scared, and humble. Yet again he felt his old glow. And then immediately he felt the ruin he had made during these years. He wanted to bustle about, to run away from it.

(p. 197)

Paul is the "outsider" here, the one who does not enter into the family warmth, as we have seen a few lines earlier from his cold comment on his father's vigorous exclamations ("Why is a door-knob deader than anything else?"), and as we see a little later from the way in which he turns "impatiently" from his books and pencil, after his father has asked him "humbly" to count up the money. And at the close of the episode he dismisses his father viciously: "It won't be long," he says to his mother. "You can have my money. Let him go to hell" (p. 201). Morel does not deserve this, we feel, after all the warmth and vigour of his action here. Paul is cruel to anyone who threatens his mother's dominion, however briefly.

This Miriam feels instinctively, a few minutes later, when she looks at the stencilled design that Paul has made for his mother:

> "Ah, how beautiful!" she cried.
>
> The spread cloth, with its wonderful reddish roses and dark green stems, all so simple, and somehow so wicked-looking, lay at her feet. She went on her knees before it, her dark curls dropping. He saw her crouched voluptuously before his work, and his heart beat quickly. Suddenly she looked up at him.
>
> "Why does it seem cruel?" she asked.
>
> "What?"
>
> "There seems a feeling of cruelty about it," she said.
>
> "It's jolly good, whether or not," he replied, folding up his work with a lover's hands.
>
> (p. 201–2)

He has also made a "smaller piece" for Miriam; but when he sees her fingering the work "with trembling hands" he can only turn with embarrassment to tend the bread in the oven, and when she looks up at him "with her dark eyes one flame of love" he can only laugh "uncomfortably" and begin to talk "about the design." "All his passion, all his wild blood, went into this intercourse with her, when he talked and conceived his work. She brought forth to him his imaginations. She did not understand, any more than a woman understands when she conceives a child in her womb. But this was life for her and for him" (p. 202). But, as the imagery of conception ironically implies, such talk is not all of life for either of them.

Immediately after this, the physical scuffle and flirtation with Beatrice shows another need, which Miriam recognizes and would like to satisfy: "His thick hair was tumbled over his forehead. Why might she not push it back for him, and remove the marks of Beatrice's comb? Why might she not press his body with her two hands? It looked so firm, and every whit living. And he would let other girls, why not her?" (p. 207). A moment later, as usual, Paul tries to "abstract" their relationship into a French lesson, only to find that her French diary is "mostly a love-letter" to him:

> "Look," he said quietly, "the past participle conjugated with *avoir* agrees with the direct object when it precedes."
>
> She bent forward, trying to see and to understand. Her free, fine curls tickled his face. He started as if they had been red hot, shuddering. He saw her peering forward at the page, her red lips parted piteously, the black hair springing in fine strands across her tawny, ruddy cheek. She was coloured like a pomegranate for richness. His breath came short as he watched her. Suddenly she looked up at him. Her dark eyes were naked with their love, afraid, and yearning. His eyes, too, were dark, and they hurt her. They seemed to master her. She lost all her self-control, was exposed in fear. And he knew, before he could kiss her, he

must drive something out of himself. And a touch of hate for her crept back again into his heart. He returned to her exercise.

(p. 208)

Miriam does not bear the slightest blame for the failure of this relationship: she is "like a pomegranate for richness," like the bride in the Song of Solomon; she combines a pure beauty of sensuous appeal with all the soul that Paul the artist needs for his further development. And like that bride she is not passive, she tries to draw Paul out of his imprisonment, tries to draw his attention towards the wild beauty of "the yellow, bursten flowers." His response is to level at her the most cruel of all his desperate charges:

> "Aren't they magnificent?" she murmured.
> "Magnificent! it's a bit thick—they're pretty!"
> She bowed again to her flowers at his censure of her praise. He watched her crouching, sipping the flowers with fervid kisses.
> "Why must you always be fondling things!" he said irritably.
> "But I love to touch them," she replied, hurt.
> "Can you never like things without clutching them as if you wanted to pull the heart out of them? Why don't you have a bit more restraint, or reserve, or something?"
> She looked up at him full of pain, then continued slowly to stroke her lips against a ruffled flower. Their scent, as she smelled it, was so much kinder than he; it almost made her cry.
> "You wheedle the soul out of things," he said. "I would never wheedle—at any rate, I'd go straight."
> He scarcely knew what he was saying. These things came from him mechanically. She looked at him. His body seemed one weapon, firm and hard against her.
> "You're always begging things to love you," he said, "as if you were a beggar for love. Even the flowers, you have to fawn on them—"
> Rhythmically, Miriam was swaying and stroking the flower with her mouth, inhaling the scent which ever after made her shudder as it came to her nostrils.
> "You don't want to love—your eternal and abnormal craving is to be loved. You aren't positive, you're negative. You absorb, absorb, as if you must fill yourself up with love, because you've got a shortage somewhere."
> She was stunned by his cruelty, and did not hear. He had not the faintest notion of what he was saying. It was as if his fretted, tortured soul, run hot by thwarted passion, jetted off these sayings like sparks from electricity.

(p. 218)

The shortage is in Paul; and she fondles the flowers so warmly because they offer solace from his ruthless rejection of her natural being. Her closeness to flowers throughout the book shows her as an innocent Persephone who needs only to be carried away by the power that Paul might possess if he were a whole man. But he is not. He is a child, with a child's limited outlook. His mother's influence has reduced all other human beings to unreality. This the narrator makes plain in one of his rare moments of illumination:

> He had come back to his mother. Hers was the strongest tie in his life. When he thought round, Miriam shrank away. There was a vague, unreal feel about her. And nobody else mattered. There was one place in the world that stood solid and did not melt into unreality: the place where his mother was. Everybody else could grow shadowy, almost non-existent to him, but she could not. It was as if the pivot and pole of his life, from which he could not escape, was his mother.
>
> (p. 222)

So then for Paul the warm reality of Miriam must fade away into spirituality and soulfulness, and she must suffer the cruel accusation summed up in the falsely composed letter that he writes at the end of the chapter, "Defeat of Miriam" — a letter of stilted, inflated rhetoric, false in every way:

> "May I speak of our old, worn love, this last time. It, too, is changing, is it not? Say, has not the body of that love died, and left you its invulnerable soul? You see, I can give you a spirit love, I have given it you this long, long time; but not embodied passion. See, you are a nun. I have given you what I would give a holy nun — as a mystic monk to a mystic nun. Surely you esteem it best. Yet you regret — no, have regretted — the other. In all our relations no body enters. I do not talk to you through the senses — rather through the spirit. That is why we cannot love in the common sense. Ours is not an everyday affection. As yet we are mortal, and to live side by side with one another would be dreadful, for somehow with you I cannot long be trivial, and, you know, to be always beyond this mortal state would be to lose it. If people marry, they must live together as affectionate humans, who may be common-place with each other without feeling awkward — not as two souls. So I feel it."
>
> (p. 251)

So she feels it too, and the hopeless rejection of her true character gives a death-blow to her inner vitality. " 'You are a nun — you are a nun.' The words went into her heart again and again. Nothing he ever had said had gone into her so deeply, fixedly, like a mortal wound" (p. 252).

After such a wound, his later effort to carry on sexual relations with her is bound to be a failure. She tries, as she always has tried, but her inner life is ebbing. This is not the marriage that she yearns for, not the union that he needs. Paul hardly knows that she is there, as a person; indeed he does not want to know her as a human being. "He had always, almost wilfully, to put her out of count, and act from the brute strength of his own feelings" (p. 290). The title of the chapter, "The Test on Miriam," is bitterly ironic, for what the chapter presents is the test on Paul's ability to free himself from the imprisonment which he feels, but does not understand. This is clear from Paul's stream of consciousness at the very outset of the chapter: "There was some obstacle; and what was the obstacle? It lay in the physical bondage. He shrank from the physical contact. But why? With her he felt bound up inside himself. He could not go out to her" (p. 278). His only refuge is to turn towards a sort of mindless evasion of his torments, a rejection of his own humanity:

> He courted her now like a lover. Often, when he grew hot, she put his face from her, held it between her hands, and looked in his eyes. He could not meet her gaze. Her dark eyes, full of love, earnest and searching, made him turn away. Not for an instant would she let him forget. Back again he had to torture himself into a sense of his responsibility and hers. Never any relaxing, never any leaving himself to the great hunger and impersonality of passion; he must be brought back to a deliberate, reflective creature. As if from a swoon of passion she called him back to the littleness, the personal relationship.
>
> (p. 284)

So Paul, near the end of this chapter, is reduced to pitiful, even contemptible, littleness. Miriam, in her violent despair, at last cries out the essential truth: "It has been one long battle between us — you fighting away from me" (p. 298). His response is shock and utter amazement: in his self-absorption he has never even begun to see it from her point of view. And he turns at once towards a painful series of self-justifications, throwing the blame on her: "He was full of a feeling that she had deceived him. She had despised him when he thought she worshipped him. She had let him say wrong things, and had not contradicted him. She had let him fight alone . . . She had not played fair" (p. 298). Yet at the very end of the chapter, the bitter truth of what he has done to her emerges poignantly out of his self-deception:

> "She never thought she'd have me, mother, not from the first, and so she's not disappointed."
> "I'm afraid," said his mother, "she doesn't give up hopes of you yet."
> "No," he said, "perhaps not."
> "You'll find it's better to have done," she said.
> "*I* don't know," he said desperately.
> "Well, leave her alone," replied his mother.
> So he left her, and she was alone. Very few people cared for her, and she for very few people. She remained alone with herself, waiting.
>
> (p. 300)

[iii]

Now all the tension of that doomed affair is over, and for the last four chapters of the book the method of the objective narrator may be resumed.

With the opening of chapter XII everything comes back into clarity and firmness. Paul is making progress with his designs, he believes in his work, and the clear tone of this conclusion is struck at once as we read: "He was twenty-four when he said his first confident thing to his mother" about his art. Had Lawrence been a more conventional craftsman, he might have put the heading "Part III" at the top of this chapter, so that we could see clearly the essential structure of the book, that of a triptych, with the major scene of suffering in the centre, and two smaller scenes on either side, focusing our eyes towards the centre of the drama.

The portrait of Clara Dawes is not in any way designed to rival that of Miriam. Clara is second-best, and second-hand, for all her beauty. "Some part, big and vital in him, she had no hold over; nor did she ever try to get it, or even to realize what it was. And he knew in some way that she held herself still as Mrs. Dawes" (pp. 360–1). Their physical passion is significant, not for itself, but for the clarifying, purgatorial effect upon both of them, leading them to find a truth that lies beyond those times when they "included in their meeting the thrust of the manifold grass-stems, the cry of the peewit, the wheel of the stars" (p. 353). This sort of immersion in mindlessness plays an essential part in Lawrence's later philosophy of love; but it is only a part, and it is here shown to be utterly insufficient. For Paul, the immediate result of the affair is the feeling that Clara is "not much more than a big white pebble on the beach." "What does she mean to me, after all?" he asks. "She represents something, like a bubble of foam represents the sea. But what is *she*? It's not her I care for" (pp. 357–8).

It has been, from the beginning, a flawed relationship, with unpleasant overtones of the mother-substitute.[10] During that trip to Lincoln with his mother, we recall, Paul had complained bitterly of his mother's aging: "Why can't a man have a *young* mother?" he cries (p. 242). So now he has her, in Clara, only six or seven years older than he, a woman married, like his mother, to a rough workman who has, she says, treated her badly. There is a striking resemblance between Baxter Dawes and Paul's father— their use of dialect, their roughness, and their collapse into drunkenness and apathy, with outbursts of violence. Clara is "reserved" and "superior," like his mother; and she has the mother's deep discontent, her independent spirit, her sharp tongue, her bitterness against life and against men. This is an affair which, as the ominous flower ritual has prophesied, carries in itself the sources of its own death; and the affair dies as the mother is dying: "She [Clara] was afraid of the man who was not there with her, whom she could feel behind this make-believe lover: somebody sinister, that filled her with horror. She began to have a kind of horror of him. It was almost as if he were a criminal. He wanted her—he had her—and it made her feel as if death itself had her in its grip" (p. 387). For Paul, at its best, the affair has been a blind rushing, an escape from thought, like being swept away in the torrent of the Trent: "Gradually, the little criticisms, the little sensations, were lost, thought also went, everything borne along in one flood. He became, not a man with a mind, but a great instinct" (p. 363).

Yet the result of this immersion is a new clarity of vision in Paul and a consequent clarity and precision in the remarks of the narrator. The whole effect is summed up in the remarkable self-understanding that Paul displays in chapter XIII, in the luminous conversation with his mother about his feeling for Clara: "You know, mother, I think there must be something the matter with me, that I *can't* love . . . I feel sometimes as if I wronged my women, mother."

> "How wronged them, my son?"
> "I don't know."
> He went on painting rather despairingly; he had touched the quick of the trouble.
> "And as for wanting to marry," said his mother, "there's plenty of time yet."
> "But no, mother. I even love Clara, and I did Miriam; but to *give* myself to them in marriage I couldn't. I couldn't belong to them. They seem to want *me*, and I can't ever give it them."
> "You haven't met the right woman."
> "And I never shall meet the right woman while you live," he said.
> She was very quiet. Now she began to feel again tired, as if she were done.
>
> (p. 350–51)

His growth in understanding, his realization of the importance, the bigness of the human relationship, is shown in his sympathy for Dawes, in his deepened understanding of the basic relationship between his mother and father (p. 317), and in his final reconciliation of Clara and her husband. In this way, perhaps, he can make amends to his father, by reconciling the surrogates of father and mother. And finally, the superb clarity of the whole objective vision now is shown in the long passage of the mother's dying, where she becomes in death a youthful bride in Paul's eyes, and Paul says his long farewell to his only love.

But for Miriam, nothing can be done, as we see in that last sad interview, after the mother's death: "Still, the curls were fine and free, but her face was much older, the brown throat much thinner. She seemed old to him, older than Clara. Her bloom of youth had quickly gone. A sort of stiffness, almost of woodenness, had come upon her" (p. 416). She is the walking ghost of her former self. He knows what he has done to her, but he cannot help her, for she no longer attracts him. The mother's influence has stifled the vitality in Miriam that once drew them together. Inevitably, he rejects her pathetic proposal with the mother's reasoning: "But — you love me so much, you want to put me in your pocket. And I should die there smothered" (p. 417).

" 'Mother!' he whimpered — 'mother!' " we read on the book's last page. It is the clearest judgement of the book. For *whimpered* is precisely the right word[11] to describe the bondage that has held him from Miriam. Yet there remains in him his mother's tough, unyielding will; maimed and damaged as he is, "he would not give in." The phrase has been three times applied to the mother in her fatal illness, and the words are perfectly in line with the whole tragic story. Whatever happens to others, he will survive: his mother's will drives him on into a pilgrimage of pain. But there is no reason to feel that his pilgrimage, however painful to him, will always be only destructive to others. His growth in self-knowledge offers a better hope. Paul has within himself a vital, creative spark; when that energy is frustrated, the results are bitterly destructive; but when, however briefly, that energy can be released, the results may be beneficent and beautiful. He has still, potentially, an artist's vision that can bring all things into harmony:

> "What a pity there is a coal-pit here where it is so pretty!" said Clara.
> "Do you think so?" he answered. "You see, I am so used to it I should miss it. No; and I like the pits here and there. I like the rows of trucks, and the headstocks, and the steam in the daytime, and the lights at night. When I was a boy, I always thought a pillar of cloud by day and a pillar of fire by night was a pit, with its steam, and its lights, and the burning bank, — and I thought the Lord was always at the pit-top."
>
> (p. 320)

Notes

1. Quotations are taken from the first English edition of *Sons and Lovers* (London, (1913), but page references are made to the currently available editions in the Modern Library and Compass Books (Viking Press), where the texts are numbered 1–420 (older editions in these two series have different pagination, along with a somewhat more reliable text). The above quotations come from pages 142, 148, 215–16, 218.

2. Mark Spilka, *The Love Ethic of D. H. Lawrence* (Bloomington, 1955), pp. 45, 51, 56, 66. A notable exception to this view is presented by Graham Hough, *The Dark Sun: A Study of D. H. Lawrence* (New York, 1956), pp. 39–47, where Hough sees "the co-presence in the Paul and Miriam parts of *Sons and Lovers* of two different kinds of experience — more or less simple recollection, checked and assisted by Jessie Chambers; and a later interpretation of the whole sequence of events." The very early Freudian interpretation by Alfred Booth Kuttner also shows clearly the way in which Paul is being unfair to the character of Miriam: see the reprint of this essay of 1916 in the valuable collection edited by E. W. Tedlock, Jr., *D. H. Lawrence and "Sons and Lovers": Sources and Criticism* (New York, 1965); see especially pp. 81–6. For the later Freudian study by Daniel Weiss, see note 9 below.

3. This important line is omitted in the current texts of the Modern Library and Compass Books.

4. Julian Moynahan, *The Deed of Life: The Novels and Tales of D. H. Lawrence* (Princeton, 1963), p. 17.

5. Mark Schorer, "Technique as Discovery," in *The Modern Critical Spectrum*, ed. Gerald and Nancy Goldberg (Engelwood Cliffs, 1962), pp. 76–7; the essay originally

appeared in *The Hudson Review* (1948). See also the interesting essay by Seymour Betsky in *The Achievement of D. H. Lawrence*, ed. Frederick J. Hoffman and Harry T. Moore (Norman, 1953), esp. pp. 138–40.

6. The phrase is applied to Miriam by Dorothy Van Ghent on the later occasion when Miriam is caressing the daffodils and draws down Paul's harshest charges: see *The English Novel: Form and Function* (New York, 1953), p. 256.

7. Spilka, pp. 51–3.

8. Many later editions read "stream."

9. Daniel A. Weiss, *Oedipus in Nottingham: D. H. Lawrence* (Seattle, 1962), p. 53. Though Weiss sees Miriam primarily as "a static figure . . . the Ophelia, the virginal side of the maternal image" (p. 82), his book is excellent for the light it throws on the causes of Paul's misunderstanding.

10. Weiss's book is excellent on this point too, particularly in its treatment of the significance of the similarity between Clara's husband and Paul's father. See especially pp. 26–37.

11. The current Modern Library, Compass, and Penguin texts all erroneously read "whispered": see the comment on this textual crux by Harry T. Moore in Tedlock's collection, p. 63. (The older printings in the Modern Library and in Compass Books, however, retain the plates that read "whimpered.")

The Fictions of Autobiographical Fiction [*Sons and Lovers*]   Avrom Fleishman*

D. H. Lawrence's *Sons and Lovers* is so much an autobiographical novel that our knowledge of its roots in the author's life threatens to overwhelm our critical appreciation of the book. So powerful are these links between life and art that its composition was influenced by Lawrence's (and others') concern for its autobiographical accuracy, so that, e.g., the girl who provided the model for Miriam in the novel could read an early draft and suggest changes in characterization (including her own) to make it more true-to-life — a rare instance of an esthetic object debating about itself with its creator.[1] There has been a commendable effort in recent criticism to get away from assessing the novel on the grounds of its psychological revelations alone, and to evaluate its embodiment of love and growth in symbolic forms.

Sons and Lovers has been seen as structured by a symbolic pattern that runs throughout Lawrence's work: the simultaneous attraction and repulsion between a fair, sexually repressed girl and a dark, sexually virile man — often recalling the seduction and (partial) conquest of Persephone by Pluto in the classical myth. Lawrence is by now recognized not only as a student of mythologies from a wide variety of cultures but also as a

*Reprinted from "The Fictions of Autobiographical Fiction" in *Genre* 9 (Spring 1976):73–86, by permission of the author and the journal. This excerpt is from pages 82–86 in that issue of *Genre*.

myth-maker in his own right, and it is no longer surprising that he portrayed the members of his own family and the ordinary folk of modern England in the trappings of eternal personality types or archetypes.

It is also widely acknowledged that Lawrence was a student of the Bible and owes a greater debt to Scriptural style and imagery than any major artist in England since Blake. This dominance of patriarchal and prophetic elements from the Bible is less obvious but no less prominent in *Sons and Lovers* than in *The Rainbow* or *The Man Who Died*. There is no self-contradiction in the idea that a highly personal novel may have such an elaborate religious background, for Lawrence's preoccupation with the cycle of the generations, sibling rivalries, and parental preferences for younger and older sons finds an echo in the stories with which Genesis, especially, is filled. The groundwork for Scriptural references is well prepared by the fact that the characters — particularly the hero's mother, Mrs. Morel — are themselves imbued with the Bible-centered, "low-church" Protestant tradition in which Lawrence grew up. This community of culture allows Lawrence to find images of his own early years in the well-known patterns of the Bible, and to place these analogies not only in the situations of the story but in the speech of the characters who enact them.

From birth, Paul Morel, Lawrence's surrogate in the novel, is conceived as a Biblical hero of continuing fascination: Joseph. Mrs. Morel establishes the younger son as her favorite in the struggle against her husband, and we are invited to see the family struggle as a modern instance of the succession of younger sons, like Jacob and Isaac, who are preferred to the elder. Mrs. Morel herself is conscious of the tradition, as she walks in the fields with the newly-born Paul: "A few shocks of corn in a corner of the fallow stood up as if alive; she imagined them bowing; perhaps her son would be a Joseph" (II, 36). The preference for the younger in the novel takes the form not of conflict between the brothers but rather of an alliance of the mother and the favorite son: "She felt as if the navel string that had connected its frail little body with hers had not been broken. . . . She thrust the infant forward to the crimson, throbbing sun, almost with relief. She saw him lift his little fist. Then she put him to her bosom again, ashamed almost of her impulse to give him back again whence he came" (II, 37). The child is established as a specially-favored, if not a divinely endowed one, and in his gesture of raising his fist one can sense that he is born for struggle if not for conquest — as Freud noted about such intensely mother-loved sons.

The mythic dimensions of Lawrence's image of himself are enhanced by his relationship with the next of his lovers, his childhood sweetheart Miriam.[2] She is presented mainly in terms of virginal heroines: St. Catherine, the Virgin Mary at the annunciation, and cloistered nuns in general. But in contact with Paul she plays a role in an Old Testament scene, leading him to a "revelation" of the virile force in nature as focussed in a wild-rose bush: "In bosses of ivory and in large splashed stars the roses gleamed on the darkness of foliage and stems and grass. Paul and Miriam stood close together, silent, and watched. Point after point the steady roses shone out to them, seeming to kindle something in their souls. The dusk came like smoke around and still did not put out the roses" (VII, 160). Their responses to the burning bush are indicative of their spiritual energies: Miriam wants "communion" with Paul in a shared emotional relationship, while Paul is absorbed less by tender emotions and more by the manifestation of power: "It was the communion she wanted. He turned aside, as if pained. He turned to the bush" (VII, 160). Although the Moses-figure does not achieve as much prominence in *Sons and Lovers* as it does later in *Aaron's Rod*, there is enough mythic heightening in the scene at the bush to give the hero the stature of an isolated but enlightened prophet in touch with the mysteries of the universe.

"But there was a serpent in her Eden" (VII, 171). This is Miriam's response to Paul's refusal to accept her spiritualized sexuality as the dominant bond of their love. She imagines a love imbued with secularized Christianity: "she fell into that rapture of self-sacrifice, identifying herself with a God who was sacrificed, which gives to so many human souls their deepest bliss" (VII, 172). But Paul affirms a religion not of spirituality but of power: "I don't believe God knows such a lot about Himself. . . . God doesn't *know* things. He *is* things. And I'm sure He's not soulful" (IX, 251). The serpent in Miriam's Eden is, of course, sex, but the mythos developed in *Sons and Lovers* transvaluates Biblical values and sees her aversion to sexuality as original sin.

In place of her fastidiousness, Clara Dawes provides the full response of mature womanhood: "And after such an evening they both were very still, having known the immensity of passion. They felt small, half-afraid, childish and wondering, like Adam and Eve when they lost their innocence and realised the magnificence of the power which drove them out of Paradise and across the great night and the great day of humanity. It was for each of them an initiation and a satisfaction" (XIII, 353–54). So the original loss of innocence is depicted in Lawrencian mythology as the dawn of full humanity; the unblushing sexuality of Clara-Eve makes a fulfilled Adam of Paul. Although the later Lawrence was to see himself magnified in the figure of Christ—misunderstood by men, and striving to trade his spirituality for a healthy human body—in *Sons and Lovers* Lawrence could see himself as having reached a height of human maturity in sexual love—becoming the essential Adam of all men. For Clara, let there be no mistake, is modelled after Frieda, the woman Lawrence had eloped with just before writing the final draft of the novel.

Having progressed through a range of Biblical heroes—from the Joseph-figure caught up in the rivalries and passions of the family, to the Moses-figure coming into contact with the naked power of the universe, to the Adam-figure realizing his humanity in guiltless repetition of the primal act of sex — Lawrence brings his hero to a consummate stage of existence in the final pages of the novel. His mother having died, his other lovers having been cast off, his own urge to death dominant in him, Paul walks out into the night:

> In the country all was dead still. Little stars shone high up; little stars spread far away in the flood-waters, a firmament below. Everywhere the vastness and terror of the immense night which is roused and stirred for a brief while by the day, but which returns, and will remain at last eternal, holding everything in its silence and its living gloom. There was no Time, only Space . . . Where was he? — one tiny upright speck of flesh, less than an ear of wheat lost in the field. He could not bear it. On every side the immense dark silence seemed pressing him, so tiny a spark, into extinction, and yet, almost nothing, he could not be extinct. Night, in which everything was lost, went reaching out, beyond stars and sun. Stars and sun, a few bright grains, went spinning round for terror, and holding each other in embrace, there in a darkness that outpassed them all, and left them tiny and daunted. So much, and himself, infinitesimal, at the core a nothingness, and yet not nothing.
>
> (XV, 420)

Paul's vision of the starry night is a return to the moment of creation, when the heavens and the earth, the sun and moon and the lesser lights, the day and the night, all found their respective places and time was joined to space. In this awesome context, the individual is as nothing — in the Biblical image, an "ear of wheat lost in the field." But his will to live is revived by the cosmic spectacle; life is breathed into him and he is created, too. In the course of *Sons and Lovers*, and especially in its final scene, we are shown a process of self-creation to which the individual emerges distinct from the forces that go into his making. At the close, Lawrence's hero stands as if on the day of man's first breath, prepared not so much to go out into a world already there, but to proceed to make it according to his own image.

Notes

1. Jessie Chambers, *D. H. Lawrence: A Personal Record, by "E. T."* (New York, 1965); excerpted in the Viking Critical Library edition of *Sons and Lovers*, ed. Julian Moynahan (New York, 1968), pp. 478–85. Quotations of the novel will be made from this edition, and are identified parenthetically in the text by chapter and page number.

2. The figure of Miriam in Numbers 12, who as Moses' sister is both an adjunct and a competitor to him in his prophetic role — and who is partially protected from divine displeasure by the magnanimous hero — is worth pursuing in Lawrence's conception of the novel's heroine.

Expressionism in *The Rainbow*   Jack F. Stewart*

In his essay, "Lawrence as a Painter," Herbert Read observes: "Lawrence was an expressionist," and he goes on to compare him with Nolde or Soutine.[1] Edward Lucie-Smith relates Lawrence's "advocacy of expressive form" to German expressionist poetry, and his later paintings to the work of expressionists such as Kirchner.[2] Canvases like "Red Willows" (1927) and "Dance Sketch" (1928) support this claim (although Lawrence's paintings tend to be transcriptions of "literary" ideas, lacking the subtle power of his verbal imagery). Most strikingly, Daniel Weiss illustrates the affinity between Lawrence's psychological vision in his novels and the expressionist art of Edvard Munch.[3] Such literary and painterly affinities are appropriate to the movement, for as R. S. Furness notes, "developments in literature and painting ran parallel," with some artists, such as Barlach and Kokoschka, outstanding in both media.[4] Let me therefore make clear at the outset that "expressionism" in the present study refers (directly and by analogy) to Lawrence's verbal emulation of the visual arts, rather than the distinct techniques of "literary expressionism" practised by such writers as Strindberg, Trakl, Kafka, and Joyce.[5]

According to the journal, *Der Sturm*, expressionism "is not a fashion, it is an attitude to life, an attitude moreover of the senses, not of the mind."[6] Definitions of the movement are therefore notoriously difficult. To Kristian Sotriffer, "Its underlying characteristic . . . consists of an over-intensification of experience, a rejection of the classical canon, a distortion and exaggeration bordering on the hysterical, a shattering of traditional forms and the reordering of the fragments to make vehicles for changed thinking and sensation, and a new, more critical and empathic approach to the world."[7] There is often religious impetus in the expressionist desire to create a new spiritual order. "Thus the whole of space," says Kasimir Edschmid, "becomes vision for the Expressionist artist."[8] Even such a formally oriented painter as Lyonel Feininger saw his work as a struggle to express the emotional unconscious: "From deep within rises an almost painful urge for the realization of inner experiences, an overwhelming longing, an unearthly nostalgia overcomes me at times, to bring them to light. . . ."[9] This statement bears a striking resemblance to Lawrence's "Foreword" to *Women in Love*: "Man struggles with his unborn needs and fulfilment. New unfoldings struggle up in torment in him, as buds struggle forth from the midst of a plant. . . . This struggle for verbal consciousness should not be left out in art. . . . It is the passionate struggle into conscious being."[10]

The leading painters of *Die Brücke* (1905–13) themselves rejected the "Expressionist" label. The program E. L. Kirchner engraved for them in

*Reprinted from *Novel* 13 (Spring 1980):296–315, by permission of the journal and the author.

1906 was ideological, and when he attempted a more specific Chronicle in 1913, the group split up. But expressionism, which was also the motive force behind *Die Neue Kunstlervereinigung* (1909–12) and *Der Blaue Reiter* (1911–14), had already made its impact. It would be futile to classify a genius such as Lawrence's, that can draw on sources as diverse as Renaissance art, English landscape painting, and Italian Futurism, transforming all into the stuff of his own consciousness. "Influence" is too crude a concept for Lawrence's response to the *zeitgeist*, and there is no evidence of his conscious use of expressionist techniques. Expressionist elements do abound, however, in the style of *The Rainbow*.[11] As the focus of the novel shifts from representation of "reality" to expression of the unconscious, there is a corresponding intensification, distortion, and thickening of texture. This essay is concerned with equivalences between Lawrence's language and contemporary forms of expressionism in painting. Since this radically innovative language makes a strong appeal to combined visual and visionary senses, a comparison with the visual arts may be legitimate and revealing. "If Lawrence is to remain a source of life for us," writes Martin Green, "he must be put in a new imaginative context."[12] That is what I have ventured to do in this essay, and the connections I make between *The Rainbow* and expressionist art are guided by my own sense of "imaginative relevance" (see Green, 369).

Lawrence shared the spiritual drive of expressionism towards inner being and its Source: ". . . I am a passionately religious man, and my novels must be written from the depth of my religious experience."[13] The novel, for Lawrence, is cathartic and prophetic. Using Van Gogh as a mask for his own isolation and compulsion to create, he says that art should be self-creation, and the art-work "the final expression of the created animal and man" (*L*, 233).[14] For Lawrence, "real works of art are made by the whole consciousness of man working together in unison and oneness: instinct, intuition, mind, intellect all fused into one complete consciousness, and grasping what we may call a complete truth, or a complete vision. . . ."[15] Completeness does not mean detachment. Art is to be valued not as an end in itself, but as an expression of the artist's struggle to live more abundantly. One expressionist quality of Lawrence's writing is the excitement of the act of composition it retains in its rhythms. Similarly, as Maurice Tuchman notes, "The expressionist [brushstroke] . . . implies the gesture of the artist in the painting act—a gesture of body movement. . . . Thus Van Gogh's stroke seems to burn into the canvas with savage but deliberate forcefulness."[16] If the art of Joyce and Woolf aims at a "luminous silent stasis," that of Lawrence is dynamic. He gives more of himself, does less to cover up his emotional traces, makes more insistent demands upon the reader.

In his letter of self-discovery to Garnett (*L*, 197–99), Lawrence uses the futurist manifestoes of Marinetti as an aid in defining his own visionary style.[17] It is the fermentation of futurism — its creative energy as well as its destructiveness—that attracts Lawrence. But the futurists idealized war, despised woman, and worshipped the machine, thus reflecting, for Lawrence, the disintegration of society.[18] He blames them for looking for scientific phenomena in life, instead of "the new human phenomenon." Lawrence wants to focus on *being*, rather than the easily rationalized surfaces of "character." This impulse to cut deep is akin to that of the expressionists, who revived the woodcut with its primitive discipline, polarized contrasts, and capacity to grasp "the irrational, the mystical, the transcendental."[19] "I don't so much care about what the woman *feels*," Lawrence writes. "I only care about what the woman *is*—what she is—inhumanly, physiologically, materially . . . what she *is* as a phenomenon (or as representing some greater inhuman will) . . ." (*L*, 198). The "old stable *ego* of the character" is exposed as a mere literary convention, comparable to illusionist realism in painting. "There is another *ego*," he proclaims, "according to whose action the individual is unrecognisable, and passes through . . . allotropic states . . ." (*L*, 198; italics mine). The ritual and symbolic scenes in *The Sisters* are facets—like planes in painting—of a total conception. Lawrence called his method "analytical" (*L*, 111), but Aldous Huxley points out (*L*, xxii–xxiii) that the analysis was intuitional, not scientific or intellectual—as it tended to be with the futurists.

When Lawrence called *The Rainbow* "a bit futuristic—quite unconsciously so" (*L*, 197), he was writing from Italy, where he had been reading Marinetti, Buzzi, and Soffici "on cubism and futurism" (*L*, 195). But he had also travelled through Germany (1912–13) at a time when expressionism was burgeoning, and when marriage and contact with a foreign culture were shaping his own distinctive genius. Frieda not only introduced him to Freud's ideas, she was intimate with Otto Gross, whose sexual philosophy and struggle against his father had a profound impact on literary expressionism, and with the circle of Ludwig Klages and Alfred Schuler, whose ideas on blood and sun struck a responsive chord in Lawrence (Green, 353, 355–56). "Gross's theory of the necessary opposition between the ego and the non-ego" (Green, 71) influenced expressionism, and became a keystone of Lawrence's philosophy. *The Rainbow* is dedicated to Else von Richthofen, who had a child by Gross in 1907, whose husband Edgar Jaffe owned a painting by Franz Marc, and whose struggle for intellectual emancipation is one side of Ursula's character, as Frieda's *Lebensphilosophie* is another.

The first expressionist scenes in *The Rainbow* deal with Tom Brangwen's passion for an unknown Polish lady. These scenes symbolize Tom's courtship of the unknown, and Lawrence attempts to convey the unconscious process with a shift from realism to expressionism. The turbulence of Tom's soul is projected into the violence of the elements, and the image patterns create a sense of discordance. Tom's preparations for courtship are realistically described; then the technique becomes oblique, as mood, atmosphere, and subjective feeling are expressed in a few verbal brushstrokes: "as grey twilight was falling, he went across the orchard to gather the daffodils. The wind was roaring in the apple trees, the yellow flowers swayed violently up and down, he heard even the fine whisper of their spears as he stooped to break the flattened, brittle stems . . ." (37). The reader is projected immediately into the character's world, and feels the tension that heightens his sensitivity to color, movement, sound, and touch. The rhythmic imagery is a key to Tom's agitated state, which contrasts ironically with his stiff, formal manner. The recurring image of the daffodils, combined with contrasts of darkness and light, outside and inside, has a non-logical, expressionist force that "make[s] the invisible visible."[20] The man stands outside a window in the darkness, looking in at an intimate cameo that seems to exclude him: "The mother's face was dark and still, and he saw, with a pang, that she was away back in the life that had been. The child's hair gleamed like spun glass, her face was illumi-nated till it seemed like wax lit up from the inside. The wind boomed strongly" (37). The monumental simplicity of the scene has the starkness and emotional relief of an expressionist woodcut.

Brangwen is immobilized, spellbound, listening with such acute sensitivity that he can hear "the slight crunch of the rockers" of the chair. The images that follow are discordant, abrupt, surreal, suggesting his disorientation. His gaze switches from the child's "black and dilated" eyes to "the clouds which packed in great, alarming haste across the dark sky" (38). The sense of psychological distance is suggested by images of sound, silence, and space, while the character's inner pulsation is projected on to the hurrying clouds. He stands still, yet emotionally he is rushing towards a confrontation with the unknown, and so his universe is changing around him. Strangeness, awkwardness, and compulsion characterize the scene: "She could only see the dark-clad man's figure standing there upon her, and the gripped fist of flowers. She could not see the face and the living eyes" (39). Lawrence controls the focus with a painter's eye, objectifying the emotion, which has no immediate outlet. The image of "the gripped fist of flowers" stands out with expressive force as a symbol of man and moment. "An 'Image,' " according to Ezra Pound, "is that which presents an intellectual and emotional complex in an instant of time."[21] In the novel, motifs form larger patterns, but the culminating image does allow Lawrence to pinpoint the moment against a moving background of time and change, just as Van Gogh poses his portraits against a background of space.[22] The "gripped fist" is not a characterizing image, but an expression of an emotional undersurge that leads to growth and change — and this is Lawrence's true subject.

The chapter closes with an expressionist rendering of the chaos of passion, fear, and desire in Tom's soul, as he opens himself to the unknown. Lawrence does verbally what Van Gogh does with paint in "The Starry Night": he imposes an image of man's soul upon the cosmos.[23] This is not anthropomorphism, but an act of visionary transformation:

> He went out into the wind. Big holes were blown into the sky, the moonlight blew about. Sometimes a high moon, liquid-brilliant, scudded across a hollow space and took control under electric, brown-iridescent cloud-edges. Then there was a blot of cloud, and shadow. . . . And all the sky was teeming and tearing along, a vast disorder of flying shapes and darkness and ragged fumes of light and a great brown circling halo, then the terror of a moon running liquid-brilliant into the open for a moment, hurting the eyes before she plunged under cover of cloud again.
>
> (44)

Here synaesthesia, movement, chiaroscuro create an atmosphere of turmoil projected into visual forms that have the hallucinatory strangeness of a dream. One notes the distortion and exaggeration of the objective scene, which is saturated with the character's emotion and moves to the rhythm of his being. Lawrence reaches through and beyond character to grasp the substance of emotion and project it spatially.

Phenomenological imagery pervades *The Rainbow*, giving many passages a preternatural intensity. Thus Lydia's look and Tom's response are again described with bizarre force: "Her eyes, with a blackness of memory struggling with passion, primitive and electric away at the back of them, rejected him and absorbed him at once" (43). Here Lawrence dramatizes the shock and recoil of contrary impulses. The lovers' embrace, with its promise of renewed life, also carries a threat of annihilation, recalling Edvard Munch's graphic series, "The Kiss," in which the faces of two lovers are absorbed into one blank.[24] The Lawrentian male must always struggle to preserve a core of integral being; he desires union with the unknown, yet fears absorption in woman:

> Then again, what was agony to him, with one hand lightly resting on his arm, she leaned forward a little, and with a strange, primeval suggestion of embrace, held him her mouth. It was ugly-beautiful, and he could not bear it. He put his mouth on hers, and slowly, slowly the response came, gathering force and passion, till it seemed to him she was thundering at him till he could bear no more. He drew away, white, unbreathing. Only, in his blue eyes, was something of himself concentrated. And in her eyes was a little smile upon a black void.
>
> (43)

It is the woman's prerogative to accept or reject the man who comes to her in fear and desire to seek fulfilment. Woman, in *The Rainbow*, is creator and destroyer, so that sex becomes apocalyptic. Munch seems to have shared Lawrence's ambivalence towards woman: in his "Madonna" a mythic image of woman is shown at the moment of conception.[25] Her ecstasy brings the soul of man into being, giving birth to death as well as life. Munch underlined the theme by painting a trail of sperm around the red frame and a skeletal embryo in one corner. Lawrence's Madonna has "a little smile upon a black void"; Munch's has a blood-red halo.

Unnatural intensity, chemical imagery, and incremental repetition give the kisses of Will and Anna (112, 120), and Anton and Ursula (320, 446–47, 479) an increasingly obsessional quality: "She took him in the kiss, hard her kiss seized upon him, hard and fierce and burning corrosive as the moonlight" (320). On the surface, this hardly seems like a confrontation between human beings. Lawrence's imagery of "corrosive salt" and "soft iron" keeps the focus on the allotropic interaction itself. There is a dialectical progression from the absorptive kiss of Tom and Lydia to this sadomasochistic embrace. Ursula offers herself to night and moon, identifying her being with theirs, so that her kiss burns Anton, who is alienated from these sources of natural energy. Nothing in himself, he tries to match his personal "spell" or "influence" (329) against the "magnificent godly moon" and "the blond, debonair presence of the night" (322), and his inevitable failure is a failure to *be*. In their final embrace, Ursula is metamorphosed into Woman-as-harpy-or-sphinx: "Then there in the great flare of light, she clinched hold of him, hard, as if suddenly she had the strength of destruction, she fastened her arms round him and tightened him in her grip, whilst her mouth sought his in a hard, rending, ever-increasing kiss, till his body was powerless in her grip, his heart melted in fear from the fierce, beaked, harpy's kiss" (479). The sexual anxieties expressed in this scene find graphic illustration in Munch's "Vampire" (1895) which shows a woman crouched over a man's bent neck; in "Lovers in the Waves" (1896) in which a man is entangled in a woman's hair; or in the horrendous "Harpy" (1900).[26] Certainly Lawrence's accent here is on sexual neurosis: "The fight, the struggle for consummation was terrible. It lasted till it was agony to his soul, till he succumbed, till he gave way as if dead, lay with his face buried, partly in her hair, partly in the sand, motionless . . ." (479). This is followed by a tableau vivant as stark as any graphic image by Munch:

> Her face lay like an image in the moonlight, the eyes wide open, rigid. But out of the eyes, slowly, there rolled a tear, that glittered in the moonlight as it ran down her cheek.
>
> He felt as if the knife were being pushed into his already dead body. With head strained back, he watched, drawn tense, for some minutes, watched the unaltering, rigid face like metal in the moonlight, the fixed unseeing eye, in which slowly the water gathered, shook with glittering moonlight, then surcharged, brimmed over and ran trickling, a tear with its burden of moonlight, into the darkness, to fall in the sand.
>
> (479)

The frozen concentration is so intense and dehumanizing as to approach the grotesque, although it is psychologically justified by Skrebensky's transfixed state of horror.

In the three moon scenes, with their dialectical progression from equilibrium through disequilibrium to destruction, Lawrence's visual imagery and verbal rhythms are the expressive enactment of symbolic ritual. The first scene ritualizes the courtship of Will and Anna, relating their experience to age-old rhythms of sex and fertility, until they *become* those rhythms, losing personal identity. Expressionism prefers to deal with archetypes — suffering, sickness, death, passion, puberty, jealousy, anxiety, ecstasy — rather than with individuals; for Lawrence, the hero of any great novel is "Not any of the characters, but some unnamed and nameless flame behind them all. . . . If you are *too personal, too human*, the flicker fades out. . . ."[27] Here was the problem for Munch as for Lawrence: how to develop a system of expression strong enough to penetrate the individual unconscious, and yet transcend the separate psyche.

Nature is witness to actions that incorporate human life in cycles of seedtime and harvest,[28] and the scene glows with a transcendent livingness, as does Munch's "White Night."[29] This space, with its division into moonlight and shadow, prostrate and erect, is set like a stage for the "coming and going" of the lovers — a "pulsing, frictional to-and-fro which works up to culmination" in their embrace, as it does in Lawrence's style.[30] Animism takes on sacramental overtones: "Trees stood vaguely at their distance, as if waiting like heralds, for the signal to approach. In this space of vague crystal her heart seemed like a bell ringing" (117). Anna, initiate in the symbolic action, is responding to an "inhuman will" that seeks expression through her. In offering herself to the Moon, she resembles a priestess of Diana or Astarte performing magical fertility rites. Will is a passive instrument of the life-force, who serves her "dutifully," until "a low, deep-sounding will in him" (118) — not his own — begins to "vibrate." As in primitive religious ritual, the rhythm of his being is transmuted into the impersonal rhythms of nature. He no longer draws on his own limited resources, but vibrates in unison with the source of all cosmic energy. These natural rhythms have a spellbinding effect, causing loss of self and potential liberation of being: "There was only the moving to and fro in the moonlight, engrossed, the swinging in the silence, that was marked only by the splash of sheaves, and silence, and a splash of sheaves" (119). Rhythm becomes meaning here, for the verbal rhythms are not so much the mimetic image of actions, as the direct *expression* of a fully charged state of being. The intensity and rapture of the scene — "How can you tell the dancer from the dance?" — derive not from surface impressionism, but from visionary expressionism that merges human and cosmic.

The reenactment of these rites in language recalls the rhythmic brushwork of Van Gogh's late paintings. Van Gogh "longed for the night atmosphere, the stars, and the moonlight," says A. M. Hammacher, "for in this way his links with the primeval, nocturnal life forces gained symbolic expression."[31] Paintings like "Starry Night" and "Road with Cypresses"[32] are remarkable for their lunar and spiral symbolism.[33] According to Hammacher (160), "the image of the stars at night and of the harvests . . . had gained a hold on [Van Gogh's] creativity." Similarly, Lawrence's creative impulses were galvanized almost to madness by the moon. Jessie Chambers recalls that "some dark power seemed to take possession of Lawrence, and when the final beauty of the moonrise broke upon us, something seemed to explode inside him . . . his words were wild, and he appeared to be in great distress of mind, and possibly also of body."[34] On another occasion, he "created an atmosphere not of death . . . but of an utter negation of life, as though he had become dehumanized" (128). Jessie was aware of an inner conflict in Lawrence, parallel to the split in Ursula between Dionysian being and personal self. In Lawrence, as in Van Gogh, the systole and diastole of creativity seems to have involved "a struggle against destructive forces": in Van Gogh's last paintings, "space as such gives way to an almost demonic expressiveness" (Hammacher, 122, 159).

Anna, who sees "the moonlight" flash question on [Will's] face" (118), seems to respond to the moon rather than the man, just as he embraces an essence, a potentiality, rather than a woman: "All the moonlight upon her, all the darkness within her! All the night in his arms, darkness and shine, he possessed of it all! All the night for him now, to unfold, to venture within, all the mystery to be entered, all the discovery to be made" (119). This is more than eroticism: it is what Alois Riegl calls the "profound religious excitement" of expressionism.[35] "He looked through her hair at the moon, which seemed to swim *liquid-bright*" (120; my italics). An analogy might be made here with Munch's "Man's Head in Woman's Hair,"[36] but the immediate connection is with the earlier scene, in which Tom is struck by "the terror of a moon running *liquid-brilliant* into the open for a moment . . ." (44; my italics). Exposure to moonlight—a symbol of female anima—becomes more devastating in successive phases, culminating in Anton's destruction as a sexual being. It is space, rhythm, and the unknown, rather than personal psychology, that make the dynamics of such scenes.

The second moonlight scene, between Anton and Ursula, is remarkable for its preternatural intensity, matching Van Gogh's tormented visions of nature:

> The darkness seemed to breathe like the sides of some great beast, the haystacks loomed half-revealed, a crowd of them, a dark, fecund lair just behind. Waves of delirious darkness ran through her soul. . . . She wanted to reach and be amongst the flashing stars. . . . She was mad to be gone. It was as if a hound were straining on the leash, ready to hurl itself after a nameless quarry into the dark. And she was the quarry, and she was also the hound. The darkness was passionate and breathing with

immense, unperceived heaving. It was waiting to receive her in her
flight. . . . She must leap from the known into the unknown. Her feet
and hands beat like a madness, her breast strained as if in bonds.

(315–16)

Expressionism such as this involves transformation of reality, and the
supremacy of imagination over nature — Coleridge's "esemplastic power."
Thus Franz Marc, while affirming that expressionists "wrest [their forms]
from nature," which "glows in [their] paintings," points out that "there is
something which is not quite nature but rather the mastery and interpretation of nature: art. . . . The bridge across to the realm of the spirit, the
necromancy of humanity."[37] At times the dislocation of natural perception
may resemble hallucination or madness, a "dérèglement de tous les sens."
This almost schizophrenic intensity, bordering on dreams or nightmare, is
characteristic of expressionism.

Inward and outward rhythms — Ursula's excitement, the music and
movement of the dance — merge in the image of waves, as separate
identities submerge in "the deep underwater of the dance" (316). Once
more depersonalization is the prelude to transpersonal experience, as the
lovers become "one dual movement, dancing on the slippery grass. It
would be endless, this movement. . . . It was a glaucous, intertwining,
delicious flux and contest in flux. They were both absorbed into a
profound silence, into a deep, fluid underwater energy . . ." (316). Despite
insidious hints of absorption, the transition is chiefly from consciousness
into a rapt state of being. Religious ritualists and expressionist painters
were attracted to dance for similar reasons. "What Nolde looked for in
dancing was above all a rapt, total surrender to bodily expression; in this
most primitive aspect of the dance, man himself appeared to him as a
primeval being."[38] Lawrence's supple expressionist prose conveys currents
of unconscious being, that are felt but never rationalized. This is what
Kirchner meant when he said: "religious sensuality in art is an instinct of
nature . . . [that] can never be schematized."[39] Religious sensuality (of
which Anna's naked dance before the Lord is a literal example) is a key to
allotropic expressionism in The Rainbow. In "New Mexico," Lawrence
describes his physical sense of religion in primitive dances: "For religion is
. . . an uncontrollable sensual experience, even more so than love: I use
sensual to mean an experience deep down in the senses, inexplicable and
inscrutable."[40]

Lawrence's focus frequently shifts from characters to the phenomenology in which they are immersed. Personal subjects disappear, absorbed
in a ground swell of sensation: "There was a wonderful rocking of the
darkness, slowly, a great, slow swinging of the whole night, with the music
playing lightly on the surface, making the strange, ecstatic, rippling on the
surface of the dance, but underneath only one great flood heaving slowly
backwards to the verge of oblivion, slowly forward to the other verge, the

heart sweeping along each time, and tightening with anguish as the limit was reached, and the movement, at crises, turned and swept back" (316–17). Outside of the expressionist dance of Isadora Duncan and Mary Wigman[41] (at whose studios Kirchner and Nolde made sketches), the closest analogy to such verbal rhythms would be the brushstrokes of Van Gogh, Munch, Kirchner, or Nolde. The Russian painter, K. Malewich, says of Van Gogh's kinetic form: "He saw that everything trembles as the result of a simple, universal movement. . . . [I]t was as if a current passed through every growth, and their form made contact with world-unity. . . . Van Gogh separated the textural waves from the object, the latter being for him only form, saturated with a maximum of dynamic power."[42] In expressing the rhythms of the dance as an oscillation of surface and depths, Lawrence abstracts a "universal movement" out of multiplicity. A high level of abstraction from phenomena of motion is characteristic of some forms of expressionism,[43] as it is of futurism. The main distinction is that futurism tends to focus on mechanical phenomena (such as the speed of machines), while expressionism focuses on human emotive movement and gesture. The apocalyptic image of the flood (above) is linked with a rhythmic fluctuation of consciousness and the unconscious. Thus the motor sensation of the dance — at once religious, sexual, and emotional — becomes a metaphor of being.

Out of this deep, trancelike rhythm, a new awareness develops in Ursula, which might be called "moon-consciousness." In this state of animism, she gives herself to a non-human source of energy: "She turned, and saw a great white moon looking at her over the hill. And her breast opened to it, she was cleaved like a transparent jewel to its light. She stood filled with the full moon, offering herself. Her two breasts opened to make way for it, her body opened wide like a quivering anemone, a soft, dilated invitation touched by the moon. She wanted the moon to fill in to her, she wanted more, more communion with the moon, consummation" (317). The moon is the transcendent force of Eros that transforms sexual into spiritual energy, and offers fullness of being. Skrebensky, who cannot share in this pantheistic communion, is a clog on Ursula's spirit. In her quest for "pure being," she becomes "a pillar of salt" to her lover, who cannot transcend the narrow bounds of ego. The struggle merely exacerbates the neurotic will that prevents his letting go. Lawrence here creates a visual world that is distorted — or "transfigured" — by the intensity of emotion: "They went towards the stackyard. There he saw, with something like terror, the great new stacks of corn glistening and gleaming transfigured, silvery and present under the night-blue sky, throwing dark, substantial shadows, but themselves majestic and dimly present. She, like glimmering gossamer, seemed to burn among them, as they rose like cold fires to the silvery-bluish air" (319). In this moonlit arena, Skrebensky faces the fires of transfiguration, among which Ursula is a silvery flame. The symbolic scene is a painter's composition in blue and silver, but it is no Whistler "Nocturne." It looks beyond Monet's "Haystacks"[44] to the contorted burning world of Van Gogh's "Starry Night," or the serene but eerie glow of Munch's "Starlit Night" or "White Night."[45]

There is an element of expressionist abstraction in such scenes, as man and woman merge into polarized forces of light and darkness: "She seemed a beam of gleaming power. . . . He waited there beside her like a shadow which she wanted to dissipate, destroy as the moonlight destroys a darkness . . ." (319). The tension that oversensitizes Skrebensky, so that "The stack stung him keenly with a thousand cold, sharp flames," hardens Ursula into "salt, compact brilliance" (319). The struggle that follows is expressed in a cluster of images — of salt corroding iron, dissolving, crystallizing, annihilating — that suggests the slow but violent interaction of chemical agents, one of which is bound to disintegrate the other. Here Lawrence adapts the futurist aesthetic to his own brand of spiritual expressionism — "Nature is never seen like this, but it may be experienced like this."[46] The stackyard scene is so non-natural that when Ursula comes back to "daylight consciousness" she thinks she has been "possessed."

Lawrence's expressionism takes on apocalyptic overtones in the third and final moon scene (476–80). Once more Ursula undergoes a strange allotropic state; this time she casts off Skrebensky and destroys the incubus of personal self. Lawrence's rhetoric is hypnotic, with incremental repetition of phenomenological images — "electric fire," "salt burning," "incandescent," "metallic" — while the state of being borders on Dionysian frenzy.[47] Heightened sensitivity to sight, touch, and sound matches psychological extremism, while imagery of the "non-human in humanity" recalls futurist dynamism: "the electric fire of the silk under his hands upon her limbs . . . flew over her, as he drew nearer and nearer to discovery. She vibrated like a jet of electric, firm fluid in response" (47). The language here involves abstraction from physical sensuality to a chemico-erotic essence. The phenomena of sexuality may be universal, but Lawrence's expressionist rendering of "allotropic states" brings a new note of transpersonality into the novel. Such mysticism is a recurring aspect of expressionism:[48] "Then a yearning for something unknown came over her. . . . The salt, bitter passion of the sea, its indifference to the earth, its swinging, definite motion, its strength, its attack, and its salt burning, seemed to provoke her to a pitch of madness, tantalizing her with vast suggestions of fulfilment" (477). Skrebensky is a feeble "personification" of Ursula's desires, for she is reaching for infinity.

Lawrence forces the verbal medium to convey an experience that is irrational, ecstatic, and wordless. The power of the unconscious irradiates his style,[49] and there is a primitive sense of live forces in nature challenging human lives: "Suddenly . . . Ursula lifted her head, and shrank back, momentarily frightened. There was a great whiteness confronting her, the moon was incandescent as a round furnace door, out of which came the high blast of moonlight, over the seaward half of the world, a dazzling, terrifying glare of white light. . . . [Skrebensky] felt his chest laid bare, where the secret was heavily hidden. He felt himself fusing down to nothingness, like a bead that rapidly disappears in an incandescent flame" (478). The biblical symbol of the furnace harks back to "Anna Victrix" (193), where Anna offers up the infant Ursula as a living sacrifice to the fires of regeneration. Now Ursula "seem[s] to melt into the glare, towards the moon," while Skrebensky is consumed and turned to ash.[50] There is an utter disequilibrium between her moon-conscious being and his self-conscious ego.

The spiritual intensity of moon-consciousness is balanced against the physical intensity of blood-consciousness. Anton returns from Africa inoculated with a dark sensuality. The word "darkness" (or "dark") recurs a total of sixty-four times in eight pages (445–52). The rhetorical patterns express rhythms and impulses of blood-consciousness, culminating in the couple's first sexual union. In this context, the key terms — "darkness," "vibration," "fecund," "nucleus," "potent" — pulsate with combined associations of the unconscious.

The motifs of animalization, vibration, and darkness strike an expressionist note. Franz Marc, for instance, sought to immerse himself in a religion of nature, whose medium would be the " '*Animalization*' of art." "I try to intensify my sensitivity," he wrote, "for the organic rhythm of all things; I seek pantheist empathy with the vibration and flow of the blood of nature — in the trees, in the animals, in the air."[51] Lawrence also cultivated "pantheistic sensuality"; Ursula's image of hound-and-quarry (316, quoted above) reflects the mystical sensitivity to animate nature that Lawrence explores in "Pan in America."[52] The conscious primitivism of this essay is close to Gauguin's and Van Gogh's stress "upon the deep layer of the psyche in direct communion with nature and the sources of all myth" — a line of development that led to the Fauves ("Wild Beasts"), and to expressionists like Nolde, "who was by temperament inclined to a pantheistic, mythological view of nature. . . ."[53] Like Lawrence and Marc, Nolde was a visionary pantheist: " 'I had an infinite number of visions . . . for wherever I turned my eyes nature, the sky, the clouds were alive; in each stone and in the branches of every tree, everywhere, my figures stirred and lived their still or wildly animated life . . .' " (Haftmann, 19). Nolde was, in some ways, akin to Lawrence. "In his innermost being," writes Haftmann, "there was a savage need to embrace life passionately and a fervent desire to possess reality: he was extraordinarily sensitive to the Panic element in nature." There was even in Nolde a Lawrentian duality "between the demonic and the spiritual, the chthonic and the numinous, the earthly and the supernatural . . ." (11–12) — a duality that lies behind the blood-conscious and moon-conscious scenes in *The Rainbow*.

Animalism, primitivism, and universalism are key expressionist elements in the post-African courtship:

> He burned up, he caught fire and became splendid, royal, something like a tiger. She caught his brilliant, burnished glamour. Her heart and her soul were shut away fast down below, hidden. She was free of them. She was to have her satisfaction.
>   She became proud and erect, like a flower. . . . She was no mere Ursula Brangwen. She was Woman, she was the whole of Woman in the human order. All-containing, universal, how should she be limited to individuality?
>
> (444)

This expansion from individual to archetype is a hallmark of expressionism. The "profound darkness" is a sentient substratum of being, while the river is also an archetypal symbol of the unconscious: "Dark water flowing in silence through the big, restless night made her feel wild" (445). This sensitivity to the unconscious is allied with the expressionists' empathy for the primitive.[54] Thus, in *Women in Love*, Birkin copies a drawing of geese, in order to discover "what centres [the Chinese artists] live from — what they perceive and feel — . . . the curious bitter stinging heat of a goose's blood, entering their own blood like an inoculation of corruptive fire — . . . the lotus mystery" (81–82). Lawrence sought empathy with "the blood of nature," not only "in the trees, in the animals, in the air," but in the ebb and flow of human relationships.[55]

Skrebensky, then, draws strength from an influx of blood-consciousness. To Ursula, he is no longer a man, but "a voice out of the darkness" (446), and ultimately "a dark, powerful vibration that encompassed her" (451). His capacity for regression allows him to become a mere channel of the life-force: "Gradually he transferred to her the hot, fecund darkness that possessed his own blood" (446). Again the style modulates into pure expressionism, as darkness, vibration, and fecundity become the true subject: "A turgid, teeming night, heavy with fecundity in which every molecule of matter grew big with increase, secretly urgent with fecund desire, seemed to come to pass. . . . Her limbs were rich and tense, she felt they must be vibrating with a low, profound vibration. . . . The deep vibration of the darkness could only be felt, not heard" (446). Here Lawrence's style, with its rhythmic repetitions, becomes fully expressive of the animated universe of desire and procreation. The sound and rhythm of the words, with their bewildering patterns overlapping, clustering, dissolving, ebbing and flowing, enhance the hypnotic, passional sense of touch:

> Darkness cleaving to darkness, she hung close to him, pressed herself into [the] soft flow of his kiss . . . , herself covered and enveloped in the warm, fecund flow of his kiss, that travelled over her, flowed over her, covered her, flowed over the last fibre of her, so they were one stream, one dark fecundity. . . .

So they stood in the utter, dark kiss, that triumphed over them both, subjected them, knitted them into one fecund nucleus of the fluid darkness.

(447)

Movement within a still frame is created by wavelike series of verb phrases that give a sense of inner pulsation. Volatile restlessness is typical of expressionist and futurist art. But, in the words of a Taoist text: "Only when there is stillness in movement can the spiritual rhythm appear which pervades heaven and earth."[56] Lawrence's "to-and-fro" style works towards this mystic state of equilibrium. The analogy with painting is interesting: "From a point of stability in the established picture plane, [the expressionist] creates his plastic rhythm, backward and forward, with the materials of volume, plane, color, and texture. Usually there is a dominant path of movement varied with oscillations in smaller measure. . . ."[57]

The analogies with biology and atomic physics are also interesting. Lawrence's "futuristic" emphasis on the molecular and nuclear is an adaptation of Marinetti's "intuitive physiology of matter" to human phenomena. The lovers are the sentient "nucleus" of a teeming world of matter; in a kind of reciprocal rapture, natural energy comes to consciousness in them, as they lapse out into a sea of energy. This is the sense of the term "nucleolating": the lovers become the quick of creative sexual energies that gather towards expression in them. The image of the nucleus is established a few pages earlier, as Ursula examines "some special stuff" in the laboratory. Reacting to the aptly named Dr. Frankstone's argument that life is only matter, Ursula studies the organism intently, sees "the gleam of its nucleus," and reflects on the "will" that "nodalised" its functions (441). Suddenly, she has an epiphany: ". . . the world gleamed strangely, with an intense light, like the nucleus of the creature under the microscope. . . . She could not understand what it all was. She only knew that it was not limited mechanical energy, not mere purpose of self-preservation and self-assertion. It was a consummation, a being infinite. Self was a oneness with the infinite. To be oneself was a supreme, gleaming triumph of infinity" (441). In a recent article on the "spiritual" quality of matter, Fritjof Capra describes the dance of electrons around a nucleus, and observes: "Modern physics thus pictures matter as being in a continuous dancing and vibrating motion. . . . But this is also the way in which the Eastern mystics see the material world. They all emphasize that the universe has to be grasped dynamically as it moves, vibrates, and dances; that nature is not in a static equilibrium, but that it is in a dynamic one."[58] Skrebensky cannot share this vision of unlimited being because he has accepted a finite identity. In such hollow men, we see materialization of the spirit; in Lawrence and the expressionists, "spiritualization of matter." "Is everything material—or *everything* spiritual?" asks Kandinsky.[59] Neither, Lawrence would reply, for the Rainbow symbolizes a fusion of physical and spiritual in a new form of being.

Lawrence sets off the expressionist world of darkness and desire against the "realistic" world of trains, trams, and city lights. To Ursula, who goes about in "sensual sub-consciousness," "her eyes dilated and shining like the eyes of a wild animal," being is "a dark, blind, eager wave urging blindly forward . . ." (448). Expressionism reveals undercurrents of "potential darkness" that lie behind the social façade. The intensity of Ursula's experience leads to grotesque distortions of the normal. She sees the animal behind the social mask,[60] and transforms a respectable professor into "a lurking, blood-snuffing creature with eyes peering out of the jungle darkness, sniffing for [his] desires" (448). Skrebensky, sharing this reductive vitalism, sees "the stiff goat's legs" and "puppet-action" of the citizens around him. The "animalization" of the lovers themselves runs throughout this passage. Both are compared to leopards, but Ursula's freedom is potent and positive, while Skrebensky's is irresponsible and negative. His animal identity wavers from lion to tiger to leopard, while the image of the cage suggests that his freedom is a mere interlude (he is on leave from the army) and that the patriarchal world will claim him again (as it does when he marries his colonel's daughter). Thus expressionist "animalization" need not involve a total blurring of character distinctions.[61]

The motifs of vibration and darkness culminate in an expressionistic rendering of the sex act. It is the spiritualization of the physical that marks this passage as essentially Lawrence: "She was caught up, entangled in the powerful vibration of the night. The man, what was he? — a dark, powerful vibration that encompassed her. She passed away as on a dark wind, far, far away, into the pristine darkness of paradise, into the original immortality" (451). This spiritualization puts Ursula in touch with her "permanent self," whose language is mystical-expressionist.

The invisible underworld of blood-consciousness contrasts with the visual upper world on which feelings can be directly projected. After the lovers have spent a night on the Downs, Lawrence describes dawn flooding up over the horizon:

> The rose hovered and quivered, burned, fused to flame, to a transient red, while the yellow urged out in great waves, thrown from the ever-increasing fountain, great waves of yellow flinging into the sky, scattering its spray over the darkness, which became bluer and bluer, paler, till soon it would itself be a radiance, which had been darkness.
> The sun was coming. There was a quivering, a powerful terrifying swim of molten light. Then the molten source itself surged forth, revealing itself. The sun was in the sky, too powerful to look at.
>
> (465)

This is much more than surface impressionism. It is a symbolic transformation of darkness into light, expressionistically rendered through harmonic succession of colors, clusters of verb and participial phrases, and the whole modulated movement of the long sentence, from tension to expansion to diffusion, followed by short declarative units. The sun is a living presence, just as the "living darkness" is. It is the source of all light, life, and energy, animistically perceived as by a Druid or Mithraic sun-worshipper. The religious sense of non-human energy, as opposed to mechanical human activity, is prophetically expressed: "everything was newly washed into being, in a flood of new, golden creation" (465). Ursula, moved to tears, is transfigured "in the refulgent light."

The dawn scene has its closest analogy in painting. Van Gogh wrote to his brother Theo from Arles: "Those who don't believe in this sun are real infidels."[62] His own passionate belief was expressed in "The Sower" (1888) which shows the round disc of the rising sun flooding earth and sky with energy.[63] According to Frank Elgar, Van Gogh, in Arles, "was undertaking a rite such as the ancient sun-worshippers performed in their communion with the principle of light. . . . In every source of light he saw the heavenly sphere of flame," and it became a symbol of his own "impetuous creative force."[64] Nolde, whose landscapes, flowers, waves, and clouds radiate an intense visionary quality, likewise affirmed: "I believe in the sun and the moon, for I feel their influence. I believe that there is a fire blazing in the bowels of the earth and that it influences us mortals" (in Haftmann, 12). Like Van Gogh and Nolde, Lawrence believed passionately in sun and moon as vital forces. In *Fantasia* he writes: "the sun's quick is polarized in dynamic relation with the quick of life in all living things. . . . Likewise, as the sun is the great fiery, vivifying pole of the inanimate universe, the moon is the other pole, cold and keen and vivifying . . ." (184).[65]

The novel ends with two great apocalyptic scenes: Ursula's confrontation with the horses, and her vision of the Rainbow. Lawrence draws on his own instinctive animism to project Ursula's fears, first on the forest and then on the horses. To her disordered sensibility, the trees take on a magical, phallic presence as if threatening to enclose her (486). (These living trees recall Kirchner's "inner forest" paintings, with their sweeping verticals.) A "small, living seed of fear" is in Ursula's heart, distorting the shapes around her. Unconscious claustrophobic fears rise towards crisis in her, and she must project them outward. The horses are the stimulus that draws forth the latent content of her unconscious; these menacing creatures present a fusion of psychological and natural, subjective and archetypal:

> But the horses had burst before her. In a sort of lightning of knowledge their movement travelled through her, the quiver and strain and thrust of their powerful flanks, as they burst before her and drew on, beyond.
>   . . . She was aware of their breasts gripped, clenched narrow in a hold that never relaxed, she was aware of their red nostrils flaming with long endurance, and of their haunches, so rounded, so massive, pressing, pressing, pressing to burst the grip upon their breasts, pressing for

ever till they went mad, running against the walls of time, and never bursting free. Their great haunches were smoothed and darkened with rain. But the darkness and wetness of rain could not put out the hard, urgent, massive fire that was locked within these flanks, never, never. (487)

So strong are the inner tension, fear, and passion projected on to the horses, that they seem figures of nightmare or hallucination.[66] The barrier between natural vision and unconscious imagery has broken down. Vivid images and incantatory rhythms become the medium of an intense, disordered state of being: "She was aware of the great flash of hoofs, a bluish, iridescent flash surrounding a hollow of darkness" (487). This irrational state of awareness is immediate as a dream. Ursula does not have to look at the horses: they materialize in all their horror and splendor in her psyche. The vision is non-natural in focus, with enlargement and illumination of the most terrifying detail (the hoofs). Ursula obviously fears destruction by the forces unleashed upon, or within, her. Since the expressionist style renders a subjective response, it is impossible to measure the degree, if any, of objective menace. The horses exist, but they are also a traumatic objectification of all the social and sexual pressures on Ursula (now pregnant), and a vengeful reflex of her own apocalpytic yearnings. The expressionist style emphasizes force, mass, weight, speed, and chiaroscuro to convey emotion that springs from the unconscious. There is a clash of concentrating and dissolving wills, and of the elements of fire and water. Only by a desperate effort does Ursula finally evade the horses that seem to have her trapped. But the shock is cathartic, and she reaches the ground of her being, beyond all change.

The final apocalyptic vision of the Rainbow is a superb piece of rhetoric, but it carries the full onus of Lawrence's biblical, psychological, and social prophecy, and thus expressionism is subordinated to more explicit symbolism. Ursula's religious quest, however, can be related to the expressionist quest for dynamic spiritual experience: "In everything she saw she grasped and groped to find the creation of the living God, instead of the old, hard barren form of bygone living" (494). This, too, is Lawrence's quest in that "one bright book of life," the novel.[67] It was his development of a form of expressionism — not borrowed from any outer source, but painfully evolved from his own inner needs and visions — that led him to exult in *The Rainbow* as a "voyage of discovery towards the real and eternal and unknown land" (*L*, 240).

Notes

1. In *Paintings of D. H. Lawrence*, ed. Mervyn Levy (London: Cory, Adams & Mackay, 1964), pp. 63, 64.

2. "The Poetry of D. H. Lawrence — with a Glance at Shelley," in *D. H. Lawrence: Novelist, Poet, Prophet*, ed. Stephen Spender (New York: Harper & Row, 1973), p. 227.

3. *Oedipus in Nottingham: D. H. Lawrence* (Seattle: University of Washington Press, 1962). The reproductions in this book prove that "Munch's subjects lend themselves to D. H. Lawrence's vision with a fidelity that is almost illustration" (p. x).

4. R. S. Furness, *Expressionism* (London: Methuen, 1973), p. 45. Furness (p. 94) identifies expressionist elements in *Women in Love*, and notes Lawrence's "openness" to the milieu of German Expressionism. Max Wildi, "The Birth of Expressionism in the Work of D. H. Lawrence," *English Studies*, 19, 6 (December 1937), 241–59, compares Lawrence's writing with lyric and dramatic (rather than visual) forms of expressionism.

5. See Walter H. Sokel, *The Writer in Extremis: Expressionism in Twentieth-Century German Literature* (1959; rpt. New York: McGraw-Hill, 1964).

6. Quoted in J. P. Hodin, *Oskar Kokoschka: The Artist and his Time* (Greenwich, Conn.: New York Graphic Society, 1966), p. 104.

7. *Expressionism and Fauvism*, trans. Richard Rickett (New York: McGraw-Hill, 1972), p. 5.

8. Quoted in Sotriffer, p. 6.

9. Quoted in Bernard S. Myers, *The German Expressionists: A Generation in Revolt*, Concise Edition (New York: McGraw-Hill, n.d.), p. 208.

10. *Women in Love* (1920; rpt. New York: Viking Compass, 1964), p. viii. Subsequent references in my text are based on this edition.

11. *The Rainbow* (1915; rpt. New York: Viking Compass, 1971). Subsequent references in my text are based on this edition.

12. *The Von Richthofen Sisters: The Triumphant and the Tragic Modes of Love* (New York: Basic Books, 1974), p. 370. Subsequent references in my text are based on this edition.

13. *The Letters of D. H. Lawrence*, ed. Aldous Huxley (London: Heinemann, 1932), p 190. Subsequent references in my text are based on this edition, abbreviated as *L*.

14. Cf. Lawrence, "Morality and the Novel" (1925), *Phoenix*, ed. Edward D. McDonald (1936; rpt. New York: Viking, 1964), p. 527: "When Van Gogh paints sunflowers, he reveals, or achieves, the vivid relation between himself, as man, and the sunflower, as sunflower, at that quick moment of time." The resultant vision is neither an image of man nor of sunflower, but "a third thing," that exists in a "fourth dimension." Here Lawrence comes close to defining expressionist art.

15. Introduction to These Paintings," *Phoenix*, p. 574.

16. Maurice Tuchman, Introduction, *Van Gogh and Expressionism* (New York: Guggenheim Foundation, 1964), n.pag.

17. See *Futurist Manifestos*, ed. Umbro Apollonio (London: Thames & Hudson, 1973).

18. Lawrence (*L*, p. 368) praises Mark Gertler for giving radical expression to social chaos in his painting "The Merry-Go-Round": "I *do* think that in this combination of blaze, and violent mechanized rotation and complete involution, and ghastly, utterly mindless human intensity of sensational extremity, you have made a real and ultimate revelation." Here Lawrence fuses essential features of futurism with the process of reduction he was currently describing in *Women in Love*.

19. See Lothar-Gunther Buchheim, *The Graphic Art of German Expressionism* (New York: Universe Books, 1960), p. 27.

20. Max Beckmann, quoted in Peter Selz, *German Expressionist Painting* (Berkeley: University of California Press, 1974), p. 51. Cf. Fromentin, quoted in Leone Vivante, *A Philosophy of Potentiality* (London: Routledge & Kegan Paul, 1955), p. 4: "Painting is but the art of expressing the invisible through the visible." Paul Klee, *The Thinking Eye*, ed. Jurg Spiller, trans. Ralph Manheim, 2nd rev. ed. (New York: Wittenborn, 1964), writes: "Art does not reproduce the visible but makes visible" (p. 76).

21. Quoted in *The Imagist Poem*, ed. William Pratt (New York: Dutton, 1963), p. 18.

Michael Hamburger, *Reason and Energy: Studies in German Literature* (London: Routledge & Kegan Paul, 1957), p. 214, points to a possible link between Imagism and Expressionism.

22. See *Van Gogh's "Diary": The Artist's Life in His Own Words*, ed. Jan Hulsker (New York: Morrow, 1971), p. 109: "Behind the head, instead of painting the ordinary wall of the mean room, I paint infinity, a plain background of the richest, intensest blue that I can contrive, and by this simple combination of the bright head against the rich blue background, I get a mysterious effect, like a star in the depths of an azure sky." Similarly, young Will Brangwen is seen as pure potentiality isolated in space, "with the stars in heaven whirling fiercely about the blackness of his head . . ." (*Rainbow*, p. 111).

23. See J.-B. de la Faille, *The Works of Vincent Van Gogh: His Paintings and Drawings* (New York: Reynal, 1970), p. 428, F612.

24. See Werner Timm, *The Graphic Art of Edvard Munch*, trans. Ruth Michaelis-Jena with Patrick Murray (Greenwich, Conn.: New York Graphic Society, 1972), Pls. 25, 67.

25. Timm, Pl. 31.

26. Timm, Pls. 35, 47, 80. See also Franz von Stuck's "The Sphinx's Kiss," reproduced in Archie K. Loss, "The Pre-Raphaelite Woman, the Symbolist *Femme-Enfant*, and the Girl with Long Flowing Hair in the Earlier Work of Joyce," *JML*, 3, 1 (February 1973), 20, Fig. 7.

27. "The Novel," *Phoenix II*, ed. Warren Roberts and Harry T. Moore (New York: Viking Compass, 1970), p. 419.

28. See A. M. Brandabur, "The Ritual Corn Harvest Scene in *The Rainbow*," *DHLR*, 6, 3 (Fall 1973), 284–302.

29. See J. P. Hodin, *Edvard Munch* (London: Thames & Hudson, 1974), p. 104.

30. See "Foreword" to *Women in Love*, p. viii.

31. A. M. Hammacher, *Genius and Disaster: The Ten Creative Years of Vincent Van Gogh* (New York: Abrams, n.d.), p. 83.

32. De la Faille, p. 427, F612; Hammacher, p. 135.

33. Hammacher says that "the spiral is a primeval symbol of movement, which does not belong to sun-worshiping but to the sphere of the moon. It is the eternal cycle, which reveals itself in the fertility of woman, in agrarian life, and in the four seasons" (p. 160).

34. E. T., *D. H. Lawrence: A Personal Record* (London: Cape, 1935), p. 127.

35. Alois Riegel, cited in Hodin, *Kokoschka*, p. 205.

36. See *Edvard Munch: The Major Graphic*, Catalog of the Munch Museum, Oslo, p. 58, Pl. 35.

37. Quoted in Wolf-Dieter Dube, *Expressionism*, trans. Mary Whittall (New York: Praeger, 1973), p. 132.

38. Werner Haftmann, *Emil Nolde*, trans. Norbert Guterman (New York: Abrams, n.d.), on Pl. 12, "Candle Dancers." Subsequent references in my text are based on this edition.

39. Quoted in Will Grohmann, *E. L. Kirchner*, trans. Ilse Falk (New York: Arts, 1961), p. 24.

40. *Phoenix*, p. 144.

41. Mary Wigman was a student of Jacques-Dalcroze, whose eurhythmic dance movements are performed by Gudrun in a highly expressionist scene in *Women in Love* (pp. 157–58).

42. Quoted in A. M. Hammacher, "Van Gogh and the Words," in de la Faille, p. 23.

43. Kirchner, quoted in Dube, p. 38, writes: "I needed to invent a technique of grasping everything while it was in motion."

44. Monet's "Haystacks in the Snow," at the National Gallery of Scotland, Edinburgh, is the painting I have in mind here.

45. Hodin, *Munch*, p. 69, Pl. 49; p. 104, Pl. 74. See also Kirchner's "Moonlit Night," in

Ernst Ludwig Kirchner: A Retrospective Exhibition, Catalogue, ed. Donald E. Gordon (Boston: Museum of Fine Arts, 1968), Pl. 97.

46. Haftmann, *Nolde*, on Pl. 37, "Flowers and Clouds."

47. Sokel finds "in Expressionism the Dionysian roots of vitalism . . ." (p. 87).

48. Cf. Myers, p. 98.

49. Paul Klee, in *Thinking Eye*, writes: "The chosen artists are those who dig down close to the secret source where the primal law feeds the forces of development. What artist would not like to live where the central organ of all space-time motion . . . activates all functions? In the womb of nature, in the primal ground of creation, where the secret key to all things lies hidden?" (p. 93). One such artist is Nolde, of whose work Haftmann says: "It is an art at the mercy of a dark stream of images, whose sources remain lost in an altogether unverifiable domain, deep underground. . . . It is rooted in the depths of the unconscious mind, and is at home in regions where myth is born in the whisper of primeval memories" (p. 38).

50. See Munch, "Ashes II," in Timm, Pl. 76.

51. Quoted in Selz, p. 201.

52. *Phoenix*, pp. 22–31.

53. Haftmann, *Nolde*, p. 10.

54. On the primitive, see Marc, quoted in Myers, p. 177; August Macke, in Selz, p. 220; and Nolde, ibid., p. 290. Wilhelm Worringer's *Abstraction and Empathy* (1908) encouraged those artists who distorted the natural to fit the subjective forms of their imagination. Lawrence relates to the empathic phase of expressionism, rather than to the abstractionist phase pioneered by Kandinsky. Yet he would have endorsed Kandinsky's "*principle of internal necessity*" (*Concerning the Spiritual in Art* [1912; rpt. New York: Wittenborn, Schultz, 1947], p. 47).

55. In "The Novel" (*Phoenix II*, p. 420), he says the quick of life "seems to consist in an odd sort of fluid, changing, grotesque or beautiful relatedness."

56. Quoted in Fritjof Capra, "The Tao of Physics: Reflections on the Cosmic Dance," *Saturday Review*, 10 December 1977, p. 23. See also Capra, *The Tao of Physics* (London: Fontana/Collins, 1976), p. 205.

57. Sheldon Cheney, *Expressionism in Art* (1934; rpt. New York: Liveright, 1958), p. 132.

58. "The Tao of Physics," p. 23. Cf. Lawrence, *Fantasia of the Unconscious*, in "*Psychoanalysis and the Unconscious*" and "*Fantasia of the Unconscious*" (192, 1922; rpt. New York: Viking Compass, 1965): "The supreme lesson of human consciousness is . . . how to live dynamically, from the great Source, and not statically . . ." (p. 112).

59. *Concerning the Spiritual in Art*, p. 29. Myers says of the Blue Rider group: "their work struggles between . . . the material and the spiritual . . ." (p. 161).

60. Cf. the art of James Ensor and George Grosz, as well as Nolde's "Masks" (1911).

61. J. Middleton Murry, reviewing *Women in Love*, in *D. H. Lawrence: A Critical Anthology*, ed. H. Coombes (Harmondsworth, Middlesex: Penguin, 1973), unjustly complains that "man and woman are indistinguishable as octopods in an aquarium tank" (p. 140).

62. Quoted in *The World of Van Gogh, 1853–1890* (New York: Time-Life Books, n.d.) p. 100.

63. Ibid., p. 101 (detail); de la Faille, p. 234, F422.

64. Frank Elgar, *Van Gogh: A Study of His Life and Work*, trans. James Cleugh (New York: Praeger, 1966), p. 121.

65. In *Apocalypse* (1931; rpt. New York: Viking Compass, 1966), Lawrence says that "the sun has a great blazing consciousness" microcosmically reflected in "[my] little blazing consciousness" (p. 43).

66. Cf. Henry Fuseli's "The Nightmare" (c. 1782, and 1790–91) (an early example of symbolist art) and Franz Marc's "Tower of Blue Horses" (1913) — which shows a rainbow in the background.

67. "Why the Novel Matters," *Phoenix*, p. 535.

Lawrence's *Götterdämmerung*: The Apocalyptic Vision of *Women in Love*
Joyce Carol Oates*

And was he fated to pass away in this knowledge, this one process of frost-knowledge, death by perfect cold? Was he a messenger, an omen of the universal dissolution into whiteness and snow?
Birkin thinking of Gerald, *Women in Love*

In a little-known story of Lawrence's called "The Christening" an elderly wreck of a man contemplates his illegitimate grandchild and attempts to lead his embarrassed and impatient household in a prayer in "the special language of fatherhood." No one listens, no one wishes to hear. He is rambling, incoherent, bullying even in his confession and self-abnegation, yet his prayer is an extraordinary one: he implores God to shield the newborn child from the conceit of family life, from the burden of being a *son* with a specific *father*. It was his own interference with his children, his imposition of his personal will, that damaged them as human beings; and he prays that his grandson will be spared this violation of the spirit. Half-senile he insists upon his prayer though his grown-up children are present and resentful:

> "Lord, what father has a man but Thee? Lord, when a man says he is a father, he is wrong from the first word. For Thou art the Father, Lord. Lord, take away from us the conceit that our children are ours. . . . For I have stood between Thee and my children; I've had *my* way with them, Lord; I've stood between Thee and my children; I've cut 'em off from Thee because they were mine. And they've grown twisted, because of me. . . . Lord, if it hadn't been for me, they might ha' been trees in the sunshine. Let me own it, Lord, I've done 'em mischief. It would ha' been better if they'd never known no father."

Between the individual and the cosmos there falls the deathly shadow of the ego: the disheveled old man utters a truth central to Lawrence's work. Where the human will is active there is always injury to the spirit, always a perversion, a "twisting"; that human beings are compelled not only to assert their greedy claims upon others but to manipulate their own

*Reprinted from *Contraries: Essays* (New York: Oxford University Press, 1981), 141–70, by permission of Oxford University Press and the author.

lives in accord with an absolute that has little to do with their deeper yearnings constitutes our tragedy. Is it a tragedy of the modern era; is it inevitably bound up with the rise of industry and mechanization? Lawrence would say that it is, for the "material interests" of which Conrad spoke so ironically are all that remain of spiritual hopes; God being dead, God being unmasked as a fraud, nothing so suits man's ambition as a transvaluing of values, the reinterpretation of religious experience in gross, obscene terms. Here is Gerald Crich, one of Lawrence's most deeply realized and sympathetic characters, surely an alter ego of his — "In his travels, and in his accompanying readings, he had come to the conclusion that the essential secret of life was harmony. . . . And he proceeded to put his philosophy into practice by forcing order into the established world, translating the mystic word harmony into the practical word organisation."[1] *Harmony* becomes *organization*. And Gerald dedicates himself to work, to feverish, totally absorbing work, inspired with an almost religious exaltation in his fight with matter. The world is split in two: on one side matter (the mines, the miners), on the other side his own isolated will. He wants to create on earth a perfect machine, "an activity of pure order, pure mechanical repetition"; a man of the twentieth century with no nostalgia for the superannuated ideals of Christianity or democracy, he wishes to found his eternity, his infinity, in the machine. So inchoate and mysterious is the imaginative world Lawrence creates for *Women in Love* that we find no difficulty in reading Gerald Crich as an allegorical figure in certain chapters and as a quite human, even fluid personality in others. As Gudrun's frenzied lover, as Birkin's elusive beloved, he seems a substantially different person from the Gerald Crich who is a ruthless god of the machine; yet as his cultural role demands extinction (for Lawrence had little doubt that civilization was breaking down rapidly, and Gerald is the very personification of a "civilized" man), so does his private emotional life, his confusion of the individual will with that of the cosmos, demand death — death by perfect cold. He is Lawrence's only tragic figure, a remarkable creation in a remarkable novel, and though it is a commonplace to say that Birkin represents Lawrence, it seems equally likely that Gerald Crich represents Lawrence — in his deepest, most aggrieved, most nihilistic soul.

Women in Love is an inadequate title. The novel concerns itself with far more than simply *women* in love; far more than simply women *in love*. Two violent love affairs are the plot's focus, but the drama of the novel has clearly to do with every sort of emotion, and with every sort of spiritual inanition. Gerald and Birkin and Ursula and Gudrun are immense figures, monstrous creations out of legend, out of mythology; they are unable to alter their fates, like tragic heroes and heroines of old. The mark of Cain has been on Gerald since early childhood, when he accidentally killed his brother; and Gudrun is named for a heroine out of Germanic legend who slew her first husband. The pace of the novel is often frenetic. Time is running out, history is coming to an end, the Apocalypse is at hand. *Dies Irae* and *The Latter Days* (as well as *The Sisters* and *The Wedding Ring*) were titles Lawrence considered for the novel, and though both are too explicit, too shrill, they are more suggestive of the chiliastic mood of the work (which even surprised Lawrence when he read it through after completion in November of 1916: it struck him as "end-of-the-world" and as "purely destructive, not like *The Rainbow*, destructive-consummating").[2]

Women in Love is a strangely ceremonial, even ritualistic work. In very simple terms it celebrates love and marriage as the only possible salvation for twentieth-century man and dramatizes the fate of those who resist the abandonment of the ego demanded by love: a sacrificial rite, an ancient necessity. Yet those who "come through"—Birkin and Ursula—are hardly harmonious; the novel ends with their arguing about Birkin's thwarted desire for an "eternal union with a man," and one is given to feel that the shadow of the dead man will fall across their marriage. And though the structure of the novel is ceremonial, its texture is rich, lush, fanciful, and, since each chapter is organized around a dominant image, rather self-consciously symbolic or imagistic; action is subordinate to theme. The perversity of the novel is such that its great subject of mankind's tragically split nature is demonstrated in the art-work itself, which is sometimes a fairly conventional novel with a forward-moving plot, sometimes a gorgeous, even outrageous prose poem on the order of the work Aloysius Bertrand and Charles Baudelaire were doing in the previous century. Birkin is sometimes a prophetic figure, and sometimes merely garrulous and silly; Ursula is sometimes a mesmerizing archetypal female, at other times shrill and possessive and dismayingly obtuse. In one of Lawrence's most powerful love scenes Gerald Crich comes by night to Gudrun's bedroom after his father's death and is profoundly revitalized by her physical love, but Gudrun cannot help looking upon him with a devastating cynicism, noting his ridiculous trousers and braces and boots, and she is filled with nausea of him despite her fascination. Gudrun herself takes on in Gerald's obsessive imagination certain of the more destructive qualities of the Magna Mater or the devouring female, and she attains an almost mythic power over him; but when we last see her she has become shallow and cheaply ironic, merely a vulgar young woman. It is a measure of Lawrence's genius that every part of his immensely ambitious novel works (with the possible exception of the strained chapter "In The Pompadour") and that the proliferating images coalesce into fairly stable leitmotifs: water, moon, darkness, light, the organic and the sterile.

Our own era is one in which prophetic eschatological art has as great a significance as it did in 1916; Lawrence's despairing conviction that civilization was in the latter days is one shared by a number of our most serious writers, even if there is little belief in the Apocalypse in its classical sense. The notion of antichrist is an archaic one, a sentiment that posits unqualified belief in Christ; and the ushering in of a violent new era, a millennium, necessitates faith in the transcendental properties of the world, or the universe, which contrast sharply with scientific speculations about the fate we are likely to share. Even in his most despairing moments Lawrence remained curiously "religious." It is a tragedy that Western civilization may be doomed, that a man like Gerald Crich must be destroyed, and yet—does it really matter? Lawrence through Birkin debates the paradox endlessly. He cannot come to any conclusion. Gerald is beloved, yet Gerald is deathly. Gerald is a brilliant young man, yet he is a murderer, he is suicidal, he is rotten at the core. It is a possibility that Birkin's passionate love for him is as foully motivated as Gudrun's and would do no good for either of them. *Can* human beings alter their fates? Though his pessimism would seem to undercut and even negate his art, Lawrence is explicit in this novel about his feelings for mankind; the vituperation expressed is perhaps unequaled in serious literature. Surely it is at the very heart of the work, in Birkin's strident ranting voice:

> "I detest what I am, outwardly. I loathe myself as a human being. Humanity is a huge aggregate lie, and a huge lie is less than a small truth. Humanity is less, far less than the individual, because the individual may sometimes be capable of truth, and humanity is a tree of lies. . . ."

> ". . . I abhor humanity, I wish it was swept away. It could go, and there would be no *absolute* loss, if every human being perished to-morrow."

But Ursula also perceives in her lover a contradictory desire to "save" this doomed world, and characteristically judges this desire a weakness, an insidious form of prostitution. Birkin's perverse attachment to the world he hates is not admirable in Ursula's eyes, for Ursula is no ordinary woman but a fiercely intolerant creature who detests all forms of insincerity. She is Birkin's conscience, in a sense; his foil, his gadfly; a taunting form of himself. Yet later, immediately after Birkin declares that he loves her, she is rather disturbed by the starkly nihilistic vision he sets before her; and indeed it strikes us as more tragic than that of Shakespeare:

> "We always consider the silver river of life, rolling on and quickening all the world to a brightness, on and on to heaven, flowing into a bright eternal sea, a heaven of angels thronging. But the other is our real reality . . . that dark river of dissolution. You see it rolls in us just as the other rolls—the black river of corruption. And our flowers are of this— our sea-born Aphrodite, all our white phosphoresent flowers of sensuous perfection, all our reality, nowadays."

Aphrodite herself is symptomatic of the death-process, born in what Lawrence calls the "first spasm of universal dissolution." The process cannot be halted. It is beyond the individual, beyond choice. It ends in a universal nothing, a new cycle in which humanity will play no role. The prospect is a chilling one and yet — *does* it really matter? Humanity in the aggregate is contemptible, and many people (like Diana Crich) are better off dead since their living has somehow gone wrong. No, Birkin thinks, it can't *really* matter. His mood shifts, he is no longer frustrated and despairing, he is stoical, almost mystical, like one who has given up all hope. For he has said earlier to Gerald, after their talk of the death of God and the possible necessity of the salvation through love, that reality lies outside the human sphere:

> "Well, if mankind is destroyed, if our race is destroyed like Sodom, and there is this beautiful evening with the luminous land and trees, I am satisfied. That which informs it all is there, and can never be lost. After all, what is mankind but just one expression of the incomprehensible. And if mankind passes away, it will only mean that this particular expression is completed and done. . . . Humanity doesn't embody the utterance of the incomprehensible any more. Humanity is a dead letter. There will be a new embodiment, in a new way. Let humanity disappear as quick as possible."

Lawrence's shifts in mood and conviction are passionate, even unsettling. One feels that he writes to discover what he thinks, what is thinking in him, on an unconscious level. Love is an ecstatic experience. Or is it, perhaps, a delusion? Erotic love is a way of salvation — or is it a distraction, a burden? Is it something to be gone through in order that one's deepest self may be stirred to life? Or is it a very simple, utterly natural emotion . . . ? (In *Sons and Lovers* Paul Morel is impatient with Miriam's near-hysterical exaggeration of ordinary emotions; he resents her intensity, her penchant for mythologizing, and finds solace in Clara's far less complex attitude toward sexual love.) Lawrence does not really know, regardless of his dogmatic remarks about "mind-consciousness" and "blood-consciousness." He cannot *know*; he must continually strive to know, and accept continual frustration.[3]

Tragedy for Lawrence arises out of the fatal split between the demands of the ego and those of the larger, less personal consciousness: we are crippled by the shadow of the finite personality as it falls across our souls, as the children of the old man in "The Christening" are crippled by his *particular* fatherliness. If at one point in history — during the great civilization of the Etruscans, for instance — there was a unity of being, a mythic harmony between man and his community and nature, it is lost to us now; the blighted landscapes in Beldover through which Lawrence's people walk give evidence that humanity is no longer evolving but devolving, degenerating. ("It is like a country in an underworld," says Gudrun, repulsed but fascinated. "The people are all ghouls, and everything is ghostly. Everything is a ghoulish replica of the real world . . . all soiled, everything sordid. It's like being mad, Ursula.") One England blots out another England, as Lawrence observes in *Lady Chatterley's Lover* some years later.

In Lawrence's work one is struck repeatedly by the total absence of concern for community. In the novels after *Sons and Lovers* his most fully developed and self-contained characters express an indifference toward their neighbors that is almost aristocratic. Both Anna and Will Brangwen of *The Rainbow* are oblivious to the world outside their household: the nation does not exist to them; there is no war in South Africa; they are in a "private retreat" that has no nationality. Even as a child Ursula is proudly contemptuous of her classmates, knowing herself set apart from them and, as a Brangwen, superior. She is fated to reject her unimaginative lover Skrebensky who has subordinated his individuality to the nation and who would gladly give up his life to it. ("I belong to the nation," he says solemnly, "and must do my duty by the nation.") Some years later she and Gudrun express a loathing for their parents' home that is astonishing, and even the less passionate Alvina Houghton of *The Lost Girl* surrenders to outbursts of mad, hilarious jeering, so frustrated is she by the limitations of her father's household and of the mining town of Woodhouse in general. (She is a "lost" girl only in terms of England. Though her life in a primitive mountain village in Italy is not a very comfortable one, it is nevertheless superior to her former, virginal life back in provincial England.)

Lawrence might have dramatized the tragedy of his people's rootlessness, especially as it compels them to attempt desperate and often quixotic relationships as a surrogate for social and political involvement (as in *The Plumed Serpent* and *Kangaroo*); but of course he could not give life to convictions he did not feel. The human instinct for something larger than an intense, intimate bond, the instinct for community, is entirely absent in Lawrence, and this absence helps to account for the wildness of his characters' emotions. (Their passionate narrowness is especially evident when contrasted with the tolerance of a character like Leopold Bloom of *Ulysses*. Leopold thinks wistfully of his wife, but he thinks also of innumerable other people, men and women both, the living and the dead; he is a man of the city who is stirred by the myriad trivial excitements of Dublin — an adventurer writ small, but not contemptible in Joyce's eyes. His obsessions are comically perverse, his stratagems pathetic. Acceptance by Simon Dedalus and his friends would mean a great deal to poor Bloom, but of course this acceptance will be withheld; he yearns for community but is denied it.)

For the sake of argument Gudrun challenges Ursula's conviction that one can achieve a new space to be in, apart from the old: "But don't you think you'll *want* the old connection with the world — father and the rest of us, and all that it means, England and the world of thought — don't you think you'll *need* that, really to make a world?" But Ursula speaks for Lawrence in denying all inevitable social and familial connections. "One has a sort of other self, that belongs to a new planet, not to this," she says. The disagreement marks the sisters' break with each other; after this heated discussion they are no longer friends. Gudrun mocks the lovers with her false enthusiasm and deeply insults Ursula. "Go and find your new world, dear. . . . After all, the happiest voyage is the quest of Rupert's Blessed Isles."

Lawrence's utopian plans for Rananim aside, it seems obvious that he could not have been truly interested in establishing a community of any permanence, for such a community would have necessitated a connection between one generation and the next. It would have demanded that faith in a reality beyond the individual and the individual's impulses which is absent in Lawrence—not undeveloped so much as simply absent, undiscovered. For this reason alone he seems to us distinctly un-English in any traditional sense. Fielding and Thackeray and Trollope and Dickens and Eliot and Hardy and Bennett belong to another world, another consciousness entirely. (Lawrence's kinship with Pater and Wilde, his predilection for the intensity of the moment, may have stimulated him to a vigorous glorification of Nietzschean instinct and will to power as a means of resisting aestheticism: for there is a languid cynicism about Birkin not unlike that of Wilde's prematurely weary heroes.)

Halfway around the world, in Australia, Richard Somers discovers that he misses England, for it isn't freedom but mere *vacancy* he finds in this new, disturbingly beautiful world: the absence of civilization, of culture, of inner meaning; the absence of spirit.[4] But so long as Lawrence is in England he evokes the idea of his nation only to do battle with it, to refute it, to be nauseated by it. The upper classes are sterile and worthless, the working classes are stunted aborigines who stare after the Brangwen sisters in the street. Halliday and his London friends are self-consciously decadent—"the most pettifogging calculating Bohemia that ever reckoned its pennies." Only in the mythical structure of a fabulist work like *The Escaped Cock* can Lawrence imagine a harmonious relationship between male and female, yet even here in this Mediterranean setting the individual cannot tolerate other people, nor they him: "the little life of jealousy and property" resumes its sway and forces the man who died to flee. There is, however, no possibility of a tragic awareness in these terms; it is not tragic that the individual is compelled to break with his nation and his community because any unit larger than the individual is tainted and suspect, caught in the downward process of corruption.[5] The community almost by definition is degraded. About this everyone is in agreement— Clifford Chatterley as well as Mellors, Hermione as well as Ursula and Gudrun. Community in the old sense is based on property and possessions and must be rejected, and all human relationships not founded upon an immediate emotional rapport must be broken. "The old ideals are dead as nails—nothing there," Birkin says early in *Women in Love*. "It seems to me there remains only this perfect union with a woman—sort of ultimate marriage—and there isn't anything else." Gerald, however, finds it difficult to agree. Making one's life up out of a woman, one woman only, seems to him impossible, just as the forging of an intense love-connection with another man — which in Lawrence's cosmology would have saved his life — is impossible.

"I only feel what I feel," Gerald says.

The core of our human tragedy has very little to do with society, then, and everything to do with the individual: with the curious self-destructive condition of the human spirit. Having rejected the theological dogma of original sin, Lawrence develops a rather similar psychological dogma to account for the diabolic split within the individual between the dictates of "mind-consciousness" and the impulses of "blood-consciousness." In his essay on Nathaniel Hawthorne in *Studies in Classic American Literature*, he interprets *The Scarlet Letter* as an allegory, a typically American allegory, of the consequences of the violent antagonism between the two ways of being. His explicitness is helpful in terms of *Women in Love*, where a rich verbal texture masks a tragically simple paradox. The cross itself is the symbol of mankind's self-division, as it is the symbol, the final haunting image, in Gerald's Crich's life. (Fleeing into the snow, exhausted and broken after his ignoble attempt to strangle Gudrun, Gerald comes upon a half-buried crucifix at the top of a pole. He fears that someone is going to murder him. In terror he realizes "This was the moment when the death was uplifted, and there was no escape. Lord Jesus, was it then bound to be — Lord Jesus! He could feel the blow descending, he knew he was murdered.")

Christ's agony on the cross symbolizes our human agony at having acquired, or having been poisoned by, the "sin" of knowledge and self-consciousness. In the Hawthorne essay Lawrence says:

> Nowadays men do hate the idea of dualism. It's no good, dual we are. The cross. If we accept the symbol, then, virtually we accept the fact. We are divided against ourselves.
>
> For instance, the blood *hates* being KNOWN by the mind. It feels itself destroyed when it is KNOWN. Hence the profound instinct of privacy.
>
> And on the other hand, the mind and the spiritual consciousness of man simply *hates* the dark potency of blood-acts: hates the genuine dark sensual orgasms, which do, for the time being, actually obliterate the mind and the spiritual consciousness, plunge them in a suffocating flood of darkness.
>
> You can't get away from this.
>
> Blood-consciousness overwhelms, obliterates, and annuls mind-consciousness.
>
> Mind-consciousness extinguishes blood-consciousness, and consumes the blood.

> We are all of us conscious in both ways. And the two ways are antagonistic in us.
>
> They will always remain so.
>
> That is our cross.

It is obvious that Lawrence identifies with the instinct toward formal allegory and subterfuge in American literature. He understands Hawthorne, Melville, and Poe from the inside; it is himself he speaks of when he says of Poe that he adventured into the vaults and cellars and horrible underground passages of the human soul, desperate to experience the "prismatic ecstasy" of heightened consciousness and of love. And Poe knew himself to be doomed, necessarily — as Lawrence so frequently thought himself (and his race). Indeed, Poe is far closer to Lawrence than Hawthorne or Melville:

> He died wanting more love, and love killed him. A ghastly disease, love. Poe telling us of his disease: trying even to make his disease fair and attractive. Even succeeding.
>
> Which is the inevitable falseness, duplicity of art, American art in particular.

The inevitable duplicity of art: an eccentric statement from the man who says, elsewhere (in an essay on Walt Whitman), that the essential function of art is moral. "Not aesthetic, not decorative, not pastime and recreation. But moral." Yet it is possible to see that the artist too suffers from a tragic self-division, that he is forced to dramatize the radically new shifting over of consciousness primarily in covert, even occult and deathly terms: wanting to write a novel of consummate health and triumph whose controlling symbol is the rainbow, writing in fact a despairing, floridly tragic and rather mad work that resembles poetry and music (Wagnerian music) far more than it resembles the clearly "moral" bright book of life that is the novel, Lawrence finds himself surprised and disturbed by the apocalyptic nature of this greatest effort, as if he had imagined he had written something quite different. The rhythm of Lawrence's writing is that of the American works he analyzes so irreverently and so brilliantly, a "disintegrating and sloughing of the old consciousness" and "the forming of a new consciousness underneath." Such apocalyptic books must be written because old things need to die, because the "old white psyche has to be gradually broken down before anything else can come to pass" (in the essay on Poe). Such art must be violent, it must be outlandish and diabolic at its core because it is revolutionary in the truest sense of the word. It is subversive, even traitorous; but though it seeks to overturn empires, its primary concerns are prophetic, even religious. As Lawrence says in the poem "Nemesis" (from *Pansies*), "If we do not rapidly open all the doors of consciousness / and freshen the putrid little space in which we are cribbed / the sky-blue walls of our unventilated heaven / will be bright red with blood." In any case the true artist does not determine the direction of his art; he surrenders his ego so that his deeper self may be heard. There is no freedom except in compliance with the spirit within, what Lawrence calls the Holy Ghost.

The suppressed Prologue to *Women in Love* sets forth the terms of Birkin's torment with dramatic economy.[6] "Mind-consciousness" and "blood-consciousness" are not mere abstractions, pseudo-philosophical notions, but bitterly existential ways of perceiving and of being. When Birkin and Gerald Crich first meet they experience a subtle bond between each other, a "sudden connection" that is intensified during a mountain-climbing trip in the Tyrol. In the isolation of the rocks and snow they and their companion attain a rare sort of intimacy that is to be denied and consciously rejected when they descend again into their unusual lives. (The parallel with Gerald's death in the snow is obvious; by suppressing the Prologue and beginning with the chapter we have, "Sisters," in which Ursula and Gudrun discuss marriage and the home and the mining town and venture out to watch the wedding, Lawrence sacrificed a great deal. "Sisters" is an entirely satisfactory opening, brilliant in its own lavish way; but the Prologue with its shrill, tender, almost crazed language is far more moving.)

Preliminary to the action of *Women in Love*, and unaccountable in terms of *The Rainbow*, which centers so exclusively upon Ursula, is the passionate and undeclared relationship between Birkin and Gerald, and the tortured split between Birkin's spiritual and "sisterly" love for Hermione and his "passion of desire" for Gerald. Birkin is sickened by his obsession with Gerald; he is repulsed by his overwrought, exclusively mental relationship with Hermione (which is, incidentally, very close to the relationship of sheer nerves Lawrence discusses in his essay on Poe: the obscene love that is the "intensest nervous vibration of unison" without any erotic consummation). That Birkin's dilemma is emblematic of society's confusion in general is made clear, and convincing, by his immersion in educational theory. What is education except the gradual and deliberate building up of consciousness, unit by unit? Each unit of consciousness is the "living unit of that great social, religious, philosophic idea towards which mankind, like an organism seeking its final form, is laboriously growing," but the tragic paradox is that there *is* no great unifying idea at the present time; there is simply aimless, futile activity. For we are in the autumn of civilization, and decay, as such, cannot be acknowledged. As Birkin suffers in his awareness of his own deceitful, frustrated life, he tries to forget himself in work; but he cannot escape a sense of the futility to all attempts at "social constructiveness." The tone of the Prologue is dark indeed, and one hears Lawrence's undisguised despair in every line:

> How to get away from this process of reduction, how escape this phosphorescent passage into the tomb, which was universal though unacknowledged, this was the unconscious problem which tortured Birkin day and night. He came to Hermione, and found with her the

pure, translucent regions of death itself, of ecstasy. In the world the autumn itself was setting in. What should a man add himself on to? — to science, to social reform, to aestheticism, to sensationalism? The whole world's constructive activity was a fiction, a lie, to hide the great process of decomposition, which had set in. What then to adhere to?

He attempts a physical relationship with Hermione which is a cruel failure, humiliating to them both. He goes in desperation to prostitutes. Like Paul Morel he suffers a familiar split between the "spiritual" woman and the "physical" woman, but his deeper anxiety lies in his unacknowledged passion for Gerald Crich. Surely homoerotic yearning has never been so vividly and so sympathetically presented as it is in Lawrence's Prologue, where Birkin's intelligent complexity, his half-serious desire to rid himself of his soul in order to escape his predicament, and his fear of madness and dissolution as a consequence of his lovelessness give him a tragic depth comparable to Hamlet's. He *wants* to love women, just as he wants to believe in the world's constructive activity; but how can a man create his own feelings? Birkin knows that he cannot: he can only suppress them by an act of sheer will. In danger of going mad or of dying — of possibly killing himself — Birkin continues his deathly relationship with Hermione, keeping his homoerotic feelings to himself and even, in a sense, secret from himself. With keen insight Lawrence analyzes Birkin's own analysis of the situation. "He knew what he felt, but always kept the knowledge at bay. His a priori were: 'I *should not* feel like this,' and 'It is the ultimate mark of my own deficiency, that I feel like this.' Therefore, though he admitted everything, he never really faced the question. He never accepted the desire, and received it as part of himself. He always tried to keep it expelled from him." Not only does Birkin attempt to dissociate himself from an impulse that *is* himself, he attempts to deny the femaleness in his own nature by objectifying (and degrading) it in his treatment of Hermione and of the "slightly bestial" prostitutes. It maddens him that he should feel sexual attraction for the male physique while for the female he is capable of feeling only a kind of fondness, a sacred love, as if for a sister. "The women he seemed to be kin to, he looked for the soul in them." By the age of thirty he is sickly and dissolute, attached to Hermione in a loveless, sadistic relationship, terrified of breaking with her for fear of falling into the abyss. Yet the break is imminent, inevitable — so the action of *Women in Love* begins.

A tragedy, then, of an informal nature, experimental in its gropings toward a resolution of the central crisis: how to integrate the male and female principles, how to integrate the organic and the "civilized," the relentlessly progressive condition of the modern world. It is not enough to be a child of nature, to cling to one's ignorance as if it were a form of blessedness; one cannot deny the reality of the external world, its gradual transformation from the Old England into the New, into an enthusiastic acceptance of the individual as an instrument in the great machine of society. When Hermione goes into her rhapsody about spontaneity and the instincts, echoing Birkin in saying that the mind is death, he contradicts her brutally by claiming that the problem is not that people have too much mind, but too little. As for Hermione herself, she is merely making words because knowledge means everything to her: "Even your animalism, you want it in your head. You don't want to *be* an animal, you want to observe your own animal functions, to get a mental thrill out of them. . . . What is it but the worst and last form of intellectualism, this love of yours for passion and the animal instincts?" But it is really himself he is attacking: Hermione is a ghastly form of himself he would like to destroy, a parody of a woman, a sister of his soul.

Women in Love must have originally been imagined as Birkin's tragedy rather than Gerald's, for though Gerald feels an attraction for Birkin, he is not so obsessed with it as Birkin is; in the Prologue he is characterized as rather less intelligent, less shrewd, than he turns out to be in subsequent chapters. Ursula's role in saving Birkin from dissolution is, then, far greater than she can know. Not only must she arouse and satisfy his spiritual yearnings, she must answer to his physical desire as well: she must, in a sense, take on the active, masculine role in their relationship. (Significantly, it is Ursula who presses them into an erotic relationship after the death of Diana Crich and her young man. It is she who embraces Birkin tightly, wanting to show him that she is no shallow prude, and though he whimpers to himself, "Not this, not this," he nevertheless succumbs to desire for her and they become lovers. Had Ursula not sensed the need to force Birkin into a physical relationship, it is possible their love would have become as spiritualized, and consequently as poisoned, as Birkin's and Hermione's.) Ursula's role in saving Birkin from destruction is comparable to Sonia's fairly magical redemption of Raskolnikov in *Crime and Punishment*, just as Gerald's suicide is comparable to Svidrigaylov's when both men are denied salvation through women by whom they are obsessed. Though the feminine principle is not sufficient to guarantee eternal happiness, it is nevertheless the way through which salvation is attained: sex is an initiation in Lawrence, a necessary and even ritualistic *event* in the process of psychic wholeness. Where in more traditional tragedy — Shakespeare's *King Lear* comes immediately to mind — it is the feminine, irrational, "dark and vicious" elements that must be resisted, since they disturb the status quo, the patriarchal cosmos, in Lawrence it is precisely the darkness, the passion, the mind-obliterating, terrible, and even vicious experience of erotic love that is necessary for salvation. The individual is split and wars futilely against himself, civilization is split and must fall into chaos if male and female principles are opposed. Lawrence's is the sounder psychology, but it does not follow that his world view is more optimistic, for to recognize a truth does not inevitably bring with it the moral strength to realize that truth in one's life.

Birkin's desire for an eternal union with another man is thwarted in

Women in Love, and his failure leads indirectly to Gerald's death. At least this is Birkin's conviction. "He should have loved me," he says to Ursula and she, frightened, replies without sympathy, "What difference would it have made!" It is only in a symbolic dimension that the men are lovers; consciously, in the daylight world, they are never anything more than friends. In the chapter "Gladiatorial" the men wrestle together in order to stir Gerald from his boredom, and they seem to "drive their white flesh deeper and deeper against each other, as if they would break into a oneness." The effort is such that both men lose consciousness and Birkin falls over Gerald, involuntarily. When their minds are gone their opposition to each other is gone and they can become united — but only temporarily, only until Birkin regains his consciousness and moves away. At the novel's conclusion Birkin is "happily" married, yet incomplete. He will be a reasonably content and normal man, a husband to the passionate Ursula, yet unfulfilled; and one cannot quite believe that his frustrated love for Gerald will not surface in another form. His failure is not merely his own but civilization's as well: male and female are inexorably opposed, the integration of the two halves of the human soul is an impossibility in our time.[7]

Hence the cruel frost-knowledge of *Women in Love*, the death by perfect cold Lawrence has delineated. Long before Gerald's actual death in the mountains Birkin speculates on him as a strange white wonderful demon from the north, fated like his civilization to pass away into the universal dissolution, the day of "creative life" being finished. In *Apocalypse* Lawrence speaks of the long slow death of the human being in our time, the victory of repressive and mechanical forces over the organic, the pagan. The mystery religions of antiquity have been destroyed by the systematic, dissecting principle; the artist is driven as a consequence to think in deliberately mythical, archaic, chiliastic terms. How to express the inexpressible? Those poems in *Pansies* that address themselves to the problem — poems like "Wellsian Futures," "Dead People," "Ego-Bound," "Climb Down, O Lordly Mind," "Peace and War" — are rhetorical and strident and rather flat; it is in images that Lawrence *thinks* most clearly. He is too brilliant an artist not to breathe life even into those characters who are in opposition to his own principles. In a statement that resembles Yeats's (that the occult spirits of *A Vision* came to bring him images for his poetry) Lawrence indicates a surprising indifference to the very concept of the Apocalypse itself: "We do not care, vitally, about theories of the Apocalypse. . . . What we care about is the release of the imagination. . . . What does the Apocalypse matter, unless in so far as it gives us imaginative release into another vital world?"[8]

This jaunty attitude is qualified by the images that are called forth by the imagination, however: the wolfishness of Gerald and his mother; the ghoulishness of the Beldover miners; the African totems (one has a face that is void and terrible in its mindlessness; the other has a long, elegant body with a tiny head, a face crushed small like a beetle's); Hermione striking her lover with a paperweight of lapis lazuli and fairly swooning with ecstasy; Gerald digging his spurs into his mare's sides, into wounds that are already bleeding; the drowned Diana Crich with her arms still wrapped tightly about the neck of her young man; the demonic energy of Winifred's rabbit, and Gudrun's slashed, bleeding arm which seems to tear across Gerald's brain; the uncanny, terrifying soullessness of Innsbruck; the stunted figure of the artist Loerke; the final vision of Gerald as the frozen carcass of a dead male. These are fearful images, and what has Lawrence to set against them but the embrace of a man and a woman, a visionary transfiguration of the individual by love? — and even the experience of love, of passion and unity, is seen as ephemeral.

Birkin sees Gerald and Gudrun as flowers of dissolution, locked in the death-process; he cannot help but see Gerald as Cain, who killed his brother. Though in one way *Women in Love* is a naturalistic work populated with realistic characters and set in altogether probable environments, in another way it is inflexible and even rather austerely classical: Gerald is Cain from the very first and his fate is settled. Birkin considers his friend's accidental killing of his brother and wonders if it is proper to think in terms of *accident* at all. Has everything that happens a universal significance? Ultimately he does not believe that there is anything accidental in life: "it all hung together, in the deepest sense." (And it follows that no one is murdered accidentally: ". . . a man who is murderable is a man who in a profound if hidden lust desires to be murdered.") Gerald plainly chooses his murderer in Gudrun, and it is in the curious, misshapen form of Loerke that certain of Gerald's inclinations are given their ultimate realization. Gerald's glorification of the machine and of himself as a god of the machine is parodied by Loerke's inhuman willfulness: Gudrun sees him as the rock-bottom of all life. Unfeeling, stoic, he cares about nothing except his work, he makes not the slightest attempt to be at one with anything, he exists a "pure, unconnected will" in a stunted body. His very being excites Gerald to disgusted fury because he is finally all that Gerald has imagined for himself — the subordination of all spontaneity, the triumph of "harmony" in industrial organization.

Of the bizarre nightmare images stirred in Lawrence's imagination by the idea of the Apocalypse, Loerke is perhaps the most powerful. He is at once very human, and quite inhuman. He is reasonable, even rather charming, and at the same time deathly — a "mud-child," a creature of the underworld. His name suggests that of Loki, the Norse god of discord and mischief, the very principle of dissolution. A repulsive and fascinating character, he is described by Lawrence as a gnome, a bat, a rabbit, a troll, a chatterer, a magpie, a maker of disturbing jokes, with the blank look of inorganic misery behind his buffoonery. That he is an artist, and a homosexual as well, cannot be an accident. He is in Lawrence's imagination the diabolic alter ego who rises up to mock all that Lawrence takes to be sacred. Hence his uncanny power, his parodistic talent: he accepts the hypothesis that industry has replaced religion and he accepts his role as artist in terms of industry, without sentimental qualms. Art should interpret industry; the artist fulfills himself in acquiescence to the machine. Is there nothing apart from work, mechanical work? — Gudrun asks. And he says without hesitation, "Nothing but work!"

Loerke disgusts Birkin and Gerald precisely because he embodies certain of their own traits. He is marvelously self-sufficient; he wishes to ingratiate himself with no one; he is an artist who completely understands and controls his art; he excites the admiration of the beautiful Gudrun, and even Ursula is interested in him for a while. Most painful, perhaps, is his homosexuality. He is not divided against himself, not at all tortured by remorse or conscience. In the Prologue to the novel Birkin half-wishes he might rid himself of his soul, and Loerke is presented as a creature without a soul, one of the "little people" who finds his mate in a human being. It is interesting to note that the rat-like qualities in Loerke are those that have attracted Birkin in other men: Birkin has felt an extraordinary desire to come close to and to know and "as it were to eat" a certain type of Cornish man with dark, fine, stiff hair and dark eyes like holes in his head or like the eyes of a rat (see the Prologue); and he has felt the queer, subterranean, repulsive beauty of a young man with an indomitable manner "like a quick, vital rat" (see the chapter "A Chair"). The Nietzschean quality of Loerke's haughtiness and his loathing of other people, particularly women, remind us of the aristocratic contempt expressed by the middle-aged foreigner whom Tom Brangwen admires so much in the first chapter of *The Rainbow*: the man has a queer monkeyish face that is in its way almost beautiful, he is sardonic, dry-skinned, coldly intelligent, mockingly courteous to the women in his company (one of whom has made love with Tom previously), a creature who strangely rouses Tom's blood and who, in the form of Anna Lensky, will be his mate. There is no doubt but that Lawrence, a very different physical type, and temperamentally quite opposed to the cold, life-denying principle these men embody, was nevertheless powerfully attracted by them. There is an irresistible *life* to Loerke that makes us feel the strength of his nihilistic charm.

Surely not accidental is the fact that Loerke is an artist. He expresses a view of art that all artists share, to some extent, despite their protestations to the contrary. It is Flaubert speaking in Loerke, declaring art supreme and the artist's life of little consequence; when Loerke claims that his statuette of a girl on a horse is no more than an artistic composition, a certain form without relation to anything outside itself, he is echoing Flaubert's contention that there is no such thing as a subject, there is only style. ("What seems beautiful to me, what I should like to write," Flaubert said, in a remark now famous, "is a book about nothing, a book dependent on nothing external. . . .") Loerke angers Ursula by declaring that his art pictures nothing, "absolutely nothing," there is no connection between his art and the everyday world, they are two different and distinct planes of existence, and she must not confuse them. In his disdainful proclamation of an art that refers only to itself, he speaks for the aesthetes of the nineteenth century against whom Lawrence had to redefine himself as a creator of vital, moral, life-enhancing art. Though Lawrence shared certain of their beliefs — that bourgeois civilization was bankrupt, that the mass of human beings was hopelessly ignorant and contemptible — he did not want to align himself with their extreme rejection of "ordinary" life and of nature itself. (Too unbridled a revulsion against the world would lead one to the sinister self-indulgent fantasies of certain of the decadent poets and artists — the bizarre creations of Oscar Wilde and Huysmans and Baudelaire, and of Gustave Moreau and Odilon Redon and Jan Toorop among others.) Loerke's almost supernatural presence drives Ursula and Birkin away, and brings to the surface the destructive elements in the love of Gudrun and Gerald. He is an artist of decay: his effect upon Gudrun is like that of a subtle poison.

"Life doesn't *really* matter," Gudrun says. "It is one's art which is central."[9]

Symbolically, then, Gerald witnesses the destruction of his love, or of a part of his own soul, by those beliefs that had been a kind of religion to him in his operating of the mines. Lawrence himself plays with certain of his worst fears by giving them over to Loerke and Gudrun, who toy with them, inventing for their amusement a mocking dream of the destruction of the world: humanity invents a perfect explosive that blows up the world, perhaps; or the climate shifts and the world goes cold and snow falls everywhere and "only white creatures, polar-bears, white foxes, and men like awful white snow-birds, persisted in ice cruelty." It is Lawrence's nightmare, the Apocalypse without resurrection, without meaning; a vision as bleak and as tragically unsentimental as Shakespeare's.

Only in parable, in myth, can tragedy be transcended. In that beautiful novella *The Escaped Cock*, written while Lawrence was dying, the Christian and the pagan mate, the male and the female come together in a perfect union, and the process of dissolution is halted. The man who had died awakes in his tomb, sickened and despairing, knowing himself mortal, not the Son of God but no more than a son of man — and in this realization is his hope, his true salvation. He is resurrected to the flesh of his own body; through the warm, healing flesh of the priestess of Isis he is healed of his fraudulent divinity. "Father!" he cries in his rapture, "Why did you hide this from me?"

Poetic, Biblical in its rhythms, *The Escaped Cock* is an extraordinary work in that it dramatizes Lawrence's own sense of resurrection from near death (he had come close to dying several times) and that it repudiates his passion for changing the world. The man who had died realizes that his teaching is finished and that it had been a mistake to interfere in the souls of others; he knows now that his reach ends in his fingertips. His love for mankind had been no more than a form of egotism, a madness that would devour multitudes while leaving his own being untouched and virginal. What is crucified in him is his passion for "saving" others. Lawrence has explored the near dissolution of the personality in earlier works — in Ursula's illness near the end of *The Rainbow*, and in her reaction to Birkin's love-making in *Women in Love*; and in Connie Chatterley's deepening sense of nothingness before her meeting with Mellors — but never with such powerful economy as in *The Escaped Cock*. The man who had died wakes slowly and reluctantly to life, overcome with a sense of nausea, dreading consciousness but compelled to return to it and to his fulfillment as a human being. The passage back to life is a terrible one; his injured body is repulsive to him, as is the memory of his suffering. The analogy between the colorful cock and the gradually healing flesh of the man who had died is unabashedly direct and even rather witty. In this idyllic Mediterranean world a cock and a man are kin, all of nature is related, the dead Osiris is resurrected in the dead Christ, and the phenomenal world is revealed as the transcendental world, the world of eternity. Simply to live in a body, to live as a mortal human being — this is enough, and this is everything. Only a man who had come close to dying himself and who had despaired of his efforts to transform the human world could have written a passage like this, in awed celebration of the wonders of the existential world:

> The man who had died looked nakedly onto life, and saw a vast resoluteness everywhere flinging itself up in stormy or subtle wave-crests, foam-tips emerging out of the blue invisible, a black-and-orange cock, or the green flame tongues out of the extremes of the fig-tree. They came forth, these things and creatures of spring, glowing with desire and with assertion. . . . The man who had died looked on the great swing into existence of things that had not died, but he saw no longer their tremulous desire to exist and to be. He heard instead their ringing, defiant challenge to all other things existing. . . . And always, the man who had died saw not the bird alone, but the short, sharp wave of life of which the bird was the crest. He watched the queer, beaky motion of the creature.
>
> . . . . . .
>
> And the destiny of life seemed more fierce and compulsive to him even than the destiny of death.

The man who had died asks himself this final question: *From what, and to what, could this infinite whirl be saved?*

The mystic certitude of *The Escaped Cock*, like the serenity of "The Ship of Death" and "Bavarian Gentians," belongs to a consciousness that has transcended the dualism of tragedy. The split has not been healed, it has simply been transcended; nearing death, Lawrence turns instinctively to the allegorical mode, the most primitive and the most sophisticated of all visionary expressions. *Women in Love* is, by contrast, irresolute and contradictory; it offers only the finite, tentative "resurrection" of marriage between two very incomplete people. Like Connie Chatterley and her lover Mellors, the surviving couple of *Women in Love* must fashion their lives in a distinctly unmythic, unidyllic landscape, their fates to be bound up closely with that of their civilization. How are we to escape history? — defy the death-process of our culture? With difficulty. In sorrow. So long as we live, even strengthened as we are by the "mystic conjunction," the "ultimate unison" between men and women, our lives are tempered by the ungovernable contingencies of the world that is no metaphor, but our only home.

Notes

1. All quotations from *Women in Love* are taken from the Modern Library edition.

2. *Collected Letters*, ed. Harry T. Moore (New York, 1962), pp. 482 and 519.

3. As Lawrence says in an essay about the writer's relationship to his own work: "Morality in the novel is the trembling instability of the balance. When the novelist puts his thumb in the scale, to pull down the balance to his own predilection, that is immorality. . . . And of all the art forms, the novel most of all demands the trembling and oscillating of the balance," *Phoenix: The Posthumous Papers of D. H. Lawrence* (London, 1936), p. 529.

4. Richard Somers is fascinated and disturbed by Australia, into which he has projected the struggle of his own soul. The bush has frightened him with its emptiness and stillness; he cannot penetrate its secret. At one point it seems to him that a presence of some sort lurks in the wilderness, an actual spirit of the place that terrifies him. As for the social and political conditions of Australia — what is more hopelessly uninteresting than accomplished liberty? (See *Kangaroo*, London, 1968, p. 33.)

5. That Lawrence might have dealt with the tragic implications of the individual's failure to find a home for himself in his own nation is indicated by remarks he makes elsewhere, for instance in the introductory essay, "The Spirit of Place," to *Studies in Classic American Literature*: "Men are free when they are in a living homeland, not when they are straying and breaking away. Men are free when they are obeying some deep, inward voice of religious belief. Obeying from within. Men are free when they belong to a living, organic, *believing* community, active in fulfilling some unfulfilled, perhaps unrealized purpose." The *Studies* were written between 1917 and 1923.

6. The Prologue is available in *Phoenix II* (New York, 1968) and in a recently published anthology, *The Other Persuasion*, ed. Seymour Kleinberg (New York, 1977).

7. It is interesting to note Lawrence's intense dislike of the very idea of homosexuality in women. Miss Inger of *The Rainbow* is revealed as a poisonous, corrupt woman who makes an ideal mate for Ursula's cynical uncle Tom Brangwen. Ursula had loved them both but when she realizes that they are in the "service of the machine," she is repulsed by them. "Their marshy, bitter-sweet corruption came sick and unwholesome in her nostrils. . . . She would leave them both forever, leave forever their strange, soft, half-corrupt element" (*The Rainbow*, London, 1971, p. 351). In *Lady Chatterley's Lover* Mellors begins to rant about women he has known who have disappointed him sexually, and the quality of his rage — which must be, in part, Lawrence's — is rather alarming. He goes through a brief catalogue of unacceptable women, then says, "It's astonishing how Lesbian woman are, consciously or

unconsciously. Seems to me they're nearly all Lesbian." In the presence of such a woman, Mellors tells Connie, he fairly howls in his soul, "wanting to kill her" (*Lady Chatterley's Lover*, New York, 1962, p. 190).

8. *Phoenix*, pp. 293–94.

9. Gudrun is an artist of considerable talent herself, one who works in miniatures, as if wishing to see the world "through the wrong end of the opera glasses." It is significant that she expresses a passionate wish to have been born a man, and that she feels an unaccountable lust for deep brutality against Gerald, whom in another sense she loves. Far more interesting a character than her sister Ursula, Gudrun is fatally locked into her own willful instinct for making herself the measure of all things: her vision is anthropomorphic and solipsistic, finally inhuman. We know from certain of Lawrence's poems, particularly "New Heaven and Earth," that the "maniacal horror" of such solipsism was his own. He seems to have been driven nearly to suicide, or to a nervous breakdown, by the terrifying conviction that nothing existed beyond his own consciousness. Unlike Lawrence, who sickened of being the measure of all things, Gudrun rejoices in her cruel talent for reducing everyone and everything — robins as well as people — to size. Her love affair with Gerald is really a contest of wills; in her soul she is a man, a rival. Like one of the seductive chimeras or vampires in decadent art — in the paintings of Munch and in the writings of Strindberg — Gudrun sees her lover as an "unutterable enemy," whom she wishes to kiss and stroke and embrace until she has him "all in her hands, till she [has] strained him into her knowledge. Ah, if she could have precious *knowledge* of him, she would be filled . . ." (379). At the novel's end she has become so dissociated from her own feelings and so nauseated by life that she seems to be on the brink of insanity. It strikes her that she has never really lived, only worked, she is in fact a kind of clock, her face is like a clock's face, a twelve-hour clock dial — an image that fills her with terror, yet pleases her strangely.

"Reading Out" a "New Novel": Lawrence's Experiments with Story and Discourse in *Mr Noon*   Lydia Blanchard*

When the Cambridge edition of D. H. Lawrence's *Mr Noon* appeared in September 1984, it made front-page news and was an instant best-seller. Early reviews of *Mr Noon* did not live up to initial billing, however, and early reviewers, less than enthusiastic, generally agreed that Lawrence showed remarkable good sense when he left the work unfinished; *Mr Noon* parts 1 and 2 seemed little more successful than part 1 had been in 1934.[1] Even reviewers who liked *Mr Noon* agreed that it was interesting primarily for the insights it offered into Lawrence's own turbulent life — the novel is closely autobiographical — and faulted Lawrence for his lack of a clear artistic vision. In particular, early reviewers found little connection between parts 1 and 2 of *Mr Noon*. In trying to place *Mr Noon* within Lawrence's canon, Raymond Williams voiced a typical concern about the novel's structure: "Why [are] the two sections of the novel . . . so different

*This essay was written specifically for this volume and appears here for the first time by permission of the author.

from each other, with only the nominal continuity of the title character, who is himself substantially altered?"[2]

Although Williams warned against answering that question with what he called "biographical displacement," critics again, almost without exception, agreed that the cause for the break was, in fact, biographical. Their argument basically was this: part 1 is about Lawrence's friends in the Midlands, with Gilbert Noon modeled after Lawrence's friend George Henry Neville, and Emmie (Noon's partner in spooning) after another Eastwood acquaintance. Part 2 is about Lawrence and Frieda after their elopement to Germany, Noon turning—like Woody Allen's Zelig—into Lawrence himself, with Frieda the model for Johanna, Noon's new partner.[3] With such a radical change in model for the central character and the women with whom he is involved, could the parts be coherently connected? Most reviewers answered "no."

In fact, however, a closer look at parts 1 and 2 reveals a remarkably tight coherence, for the two parts are bound together through a repetition of deep narrative structures that links *Mr Noon* to experiments with rhythm and repetition—and creation of character—that Lawrence began in *The Rainbow* and *Women in Love*, making the difference in character model only a surface change. In the Foreword to *Women in Love*, Lawrence acknowledges the "continual, slightly modified repetition" of his work, and explains, "It is natural to the author; . . . every natural crisis in emotion or passion or understanding comes from this pulsing, frictional to-and-fro which works up to culmination."[4] For Lawrence, such a movement represented the "struggle for verbal consciousness, . . . the passionate struggle into conscious being." In *The Rainbow*, such repetition is found primarily on the sentence level, although as Lawrence moves from one generation of Brangwens to the next, he does repeat certain key scenes. In *Women in Love*, the narrative also moves forward in a repetitive way, as each chapter, often as independent as a short story, is built on frictional to-and-fro. With *Mr Noon*, Lawrence again visualized his work in terms of repetition, repetition effected on a very large scale. Although this repetition was apparently not part of the original plan, Lawrence strengthened its role through the revision process once the novel began to develop.

Mr Noon was conceived apparently in 1920. Lawrence first refers to it in his letters two days after he finished *The Lost Girl*. He stopped work on *Mr Noon* in 1921, when he was also having difficulty finishing other long fiction, finally abandoning it altogether in October 1922. Initially he did not divide the manuscript into sections, creating the division only after he hoped to publish the first part separately. In January 1921 he wrote to Robert Mountsier that "the first 200 pages of *Mr Noon* might make a rather funny serial. It is an episode all by itself: a little book all to itself,"[5] and in April, Martin Secker did agree to publish the first part of *Mr Noon* separately. Secker wrote about this first part to Curtis Brown, "It is certainly excellent, and I fully share your enthusiasm for it. It is quite clear from the last page that it is complete as it stands, and that the author intends it to be published in a book by itself, with one sequel, possibly more, to follow later."[6] Nevertheless, no part of *Mr Noon* was published during Lawrence's lifetime.

Seen finally in its entirety, *Mr Noon* can be read as an experimental reworking, in part 2, of the various narrative elements of story and discourse in the "complete" creation of part 1. In both parts of the novel, the story events are essentially identical, with what Seymour Chatman would call the *kernels* (after Roland Barthes's *noyau*) being virtually the same. Story existents (that is, characters and setting) do change, but only in a limited way. It is on the level of discourse (the structure of narrative transmission and manifestation) that there is significant difference, for Lawrence uses the second part of *Mr Noon* for a full-scale attack on fiction's "gentle reader," examining the influence of the reader in shaping elements of the narrative and in thus becoming, as narratee, part of the creative process.

To achieve repetition on a broad story level is unusual in Lawrence (although in *Sons and Lovers*, Paul's story to some extent repeats William's), and yet to "read out" *Mr Noon* (that is, to decode "from surface to deep narrative structures")[7] is to uncover remarkable similarities. The stories of parts 1 and 2 basically advance the plot by "raising and satisfying" similar questions in a series of similar kernels, "narrative moments that give rise to cruxes in the direction taken by events, . . . branching points which force a movement into one of two (or more) possible paths."[8] For Chatman, working out of a plot is "a process of declining or narrowing possibility; . . . choices become more and more limited," with the final choice an "inevitability"[9] — although here *Mr Noon* presents, in its final kernel and satellites, Noon making a different choice in part 2 than he does in part 1.

Basically the story with which Lawrence is concerned is this: a woman with an allegiance to one man (through engagement or marriage) finds herself attracted to another. In pursuing this attraction, she reveals a free spirit — love of rebellion and adventure, refusal to make a secret of her desire for sex. The attraction for her of the young man (Noon) is based to a very great extent on sexual compatibility. However, the couple are frequently thwarted in their efforts to consummate their attraction. They are interrupted in lovemaking by family; they meet with disapproval, particularly from the woman's father who fears social sanctions, but also from friends who fear the union consists of two opposites; they have their choices limited to some extent by authorities. The man tries to precipitate action to resolve their uncertain status by making decisive breaks with the past (in part 1 by resigning his job; in part 2 by writing a letter to the woman's husband, revealing himself as her lover). The woman turns to another man (men in part 2), helping her partner clarify a decision about the future. In developing the key blocking events and agents in both parts, the narrator becomes increasingly involved, as if to explain why, in the outcome of part 2, the man comes to a decision different from that reached in part 1.

Chatman acknowledges the difficulty of identifying and naming "kernel" moments in the narrative, moments when the agent makes a choice (or is acted upon in a decisive way), but surely any listing of the kernels of *Mr Noon* would include those cited; they are the events that lead to the point in both sections when Noon, knowing the woman has an alternative lover, must decide to stay with her or leave. Such an emphasis on what the characters *do* rather than on what the characters *are* makes appropriate for *Mr Noon* Vladimir Propp's observation that characters are simply the products of what the story requires of them: according to Chatman, "It is as if the differences in appearance, age, sex, life concerns, status, and so on were *mere* differences, and the similarity of function were the only important thing."[10]

Now Lawrence was surely open to such an attitude about character, not only understanding the Aristotelian distinction between agent (*pratton*) and character (*ethos*), but also believing with Aristotle in the primacy of *pratton* (Chatman quotes O. B. Hardison as pointing out that while agents are essential to a drama, "character in the technical Aristotelian sense is something that is added later and, in fact, is not even essential"[11]). As early as June 1914, Lawrence wrote to Edward Garnett about Marinetti's interest in the physiology of matter and the consequences for Lawrence's fiction. Lawrence told Garnett: "[The] non-human, in humanity, is more interesting to me than the old-fashioned human element — which causes one to conceive a character in a certain moral scheme and make him consistent. The certain moral scheme is what I object to."[12] Lawrence went on, "I don't so much care about what the woman *feels* — in the ordinary usage of the word. That presumes an *ego* to feel with. I only care about what the woman *is* — what she *is* — inhumanly, physiologicallly, materially — according to the use of the word: but for me, what she *is* as a phenomenon (or as representing some greater, inhuman will), instead of what she feels according to the human conception."[13] The differences between the women of parts 1 and 2 of *Mr Noon* — that is, the differences between Emmie and Johanna (the Frieda figure) — are basically what Propp sees as *mere* differences (appearance, age, life concerns, status), for the function of the women — that is, what the women *do* — is basically the same. In at least this sense (by repeating function), Lawrence seems to have achieved his desire to create character as "phenomenon."

The opening of part 2 suggests that Lawrence had at least some awareness that his repetitive structure was based on this view of character as "phenomenon," for at the beginning of part 2, Noon appears newborn, to start his story over again in a setting of higher status, up the social scale. "We have gone up a peg or two," the narrator tells us, and then he admonishes, "be prepared for the re-incarnation of Mr. Now [a play on Noon's name in German]."[14] This reincarnation upward is presented as an arbitrary choice by the narrator, who argues that by changing the setting the reader expected (a brothel or someplace similarly "shady"), he has—with much pleasure—thwarted the reader's expectations, suggesting the ease with which a narrator can change story existents and discourse, building on similar story events. A great many plots can be made from the same story, Chatman maintains, and *Mr Noon* can be read as Lawrence's demonstration of such an idea.

What determines the elements of existents and discourse, at least in *Mr Noon*, is the reader's expectations, and these the narrator of *Mr Noon* is prepared to battle: "Oh, I know you, gentle reader. In your silent way you would like to browbeat me into [placing Noon in a setting like a brothel]. But I've kicked over the traces at last, and I shall kick out the splashboard of this apple-cart if I have any more expectations to put up with" (98). Instead, Noon wakes "in a very nice bedroom with a parquet floor and very nice Biedermeier furniture of golden-coloured satin-wood or something of that sort, with a couple of handsome dark-red-and-dark-blue oriental rugs lying on the lustrous amber polish of the parquet floor." The narrator refuses to tell his reader how Noon got there ("Eat the sop I've given you, and don't ask for more"), but does give the reader time to readjust to the change in expectations, making the reader/narratee a visible character in the story ("You [the narratee] had better go upstairs and change your dress and above all, your house shoes" [97, 99]—because, presumably, the narratee has also moved up scale).

In fact, when the narrator says, "We have gone up a peg or two," he refers not only to Noon (and himself and the reader), but also to the other characters in the novel: key characters in part 1 have their counterparts, up a peg or two, in part 2. For example, whatever their social backgrounds (Emmie is working class, Johanna aristocracy), the two women with whom Noon is involved share similar character traits. As already indicated, they are rebellious, irreverent, exuberant, sensual, undaunted by outside "blocking agents" like parents or the weather, independent, resourceful, easily forgetful or dismissive of their engagement/marriage. Emmie's father may be a railwayman, Johanna's a Baron, but they are also both womanizers (Alf Bostock living on memories, the Baron able to support a separate household), hypocritical in their objections to their daughter's behavior and knowing it, anxious to maintain appearances.

Both young women have sisters who are married to academics—Fanny Bostock Wagstaff to the schoolmaster of a small (forty-five-student) school; Louise (Johanna's school-sister) to Herr Professor Alfred Kramer, who holds a university chair. Whatever the differences in status, however, both react similarly to their sisters' involvement with Noon: they are sympathetic and helpful, but believe their sisters would be better off with the person to whom they had a prior attachment (Emmie's fiancé,

Johanna's husband). These men are surprisingly similar as well: both Walter George Whiffen and Dr. Everhard Keighley are eminently respectable citizens but willing to tolerate Emmie and Johanna in their experiences with other men as long as these experiences do not have to be acknowledged. The women's mothers follow a pattern similar to that of the sisters, providing some support for their daughters but at the same time wanting a compromise with the father's expectations — to keep family peace and to insure some financial stability for their daughters.

Moreover, many of the minor characters of part 2 of *Mr Noon* are simply specific examples of a phenomenon established in a general way in part 1. For example, we are told that Noon was not the first man with whom Emmie had "spooned" — indeed, both have reputations as spooners and sports, and in part 2, the same point is made about Johanna by showing her involvement with a succession of men besides Noon: the Japanese on the train, Rudolf, Berry, Stanley. Essential story kernels, that is, are simply expanded through repetition, affecting discourse time but not story.

Lawrence's revisions also help to reinforce the distinction between the two parts as one of social scale. Of Whiffen, for example, the narrator writes: "And indubitably he was gone on Emmie. We prefer the slang, as having finer shades than the cant though correct phrase *in love with*" (77). Lawrence originally wrote "vulgar" for "cant though correct"; the change, the stress that *in love with* is *correct*, allows him to prefer "love" and "lover" when he turns to Noon with Johanna. The narrator, however, is anxious to caution the reader not to therefore look down on the characters in part 1. After the initial spooning between Noon and Emmie, for example, the narrator comments:

> Ah, dear reader, I hope you are not feeling horribly superior. You would never call an umbrella a brolly, much less a gamp. And you have never so much as seen a Co-op. entry. But don't on this small account sniff at Emmie. No, in that notorious hour when a woman is alone with her own heart, really enjoying herself, ask yourself if your spoon is brighter than Emmie's, if your spooner is better than Gilbert. Nay, if you prefer *love* and *lover*, say love and lover to yourself. It all amounts to the same. But in communion with your naked heart, say whether you have reached Gilbertian heights and Emmelian profundities of the human kiss — or whether you have something to learn even from our poor pair.
>
> (24)

Emmie writes about Noon, "He's the best spoon out" (46), while Johanna prefers to talk about her lovemaking in the language of Freud and Otto Gross, but this is not a structural difference between the two parts, and the narrator constantly stresses that these obvious, observable surface differences are not significant. The narrator simply shows the reader how he is able to retell in part 2 the story of part 1, preferring *love* and *lover*: "It all amounts to the same."

To strive for such balance in the stories of parts 1 and 2 is, of course, perfectly consistent with Lawrence's understanding of balance in relation-ships in life, a formal equivalent for the philosophy that Lawrence articulated in *The Rainbow* and *Women in Love*. Birkin may be Law-rence's most famous advocate for these ideas, but the narrator in *Mr Noon* presents similar views.

> Ultimately, a woman wants a man who, by entering into complete relationship with her, will keep her in her own polarity and equipoise, true to herself. The man wants the same of a woman. It is the eternal oscillating balance of the universe. It is the timeless inter-related duality of fire and water. Let life overbalance in either direction, and there is a fight, a terrific struggle to get back the balance. And let the mechanistic intervention of some fixed ideal neutralise the incalculable ebb-and-flow of the two principles, and a raging madness will supervene in the world. A madness which is pleasantly accumulating in mankind today.
>
> (212)

Since in *Mr Noon* the stories of parts 1 and 2 are essentially the same, the reader can call the first *vulgar* and *common* only by applying the same adjectives to the second (Noon does indeed feel shabby, at times, with Johanna) or by openly acknowledging that the differences between Emmie and Johanna (and Noon's attraction to Johanna rather than Emmie) are based on money and aristocratic background: Emmie and Noon feel "the eternal oscillating balance of the universe" as much as do Johanna and Noon. What we have then is a two-part novel in which the second part repeats the story of the first, repeats kernel events and key characters as they are manifested in what they do and in the traits that subsequently emerge. Structurally the novel is an interesting experiment, reinforcing through form Lawrence's interest in the underlying repetitive rhythms of life; since the surface manifestations are so clearly autobiographical, the experiment is particularly arresting, as if Lawrence were challenging the reader to separate his art from his life. Such a self-consciousness about the fictionality of his work, and his challenge to the reader, are particularly evident on the discourse level, in Lawrence's ongoing construction of an audience.

The two parts of *Mr Noon*, brought together and read intertextually, resonate against each other, the long form of the two parts together clarifying and enriching the short forms, the two parts read as separate units. In *Mr Noon*, Lawrence enters into what Robert Alter has called the *other* great tradition, the tradition of self-conscious fiction.[15] He develops the interest he articulated, while writing *The Rainbow*, in the nonhuman in humanity, in what the woman is "inhumanly, physiologically, materi-ally"; he creates characters that are the product of what the story requires of them; he uses *Mr Noon* to create the fictional reader who eluded him in

The Rainbow and *Women in Love*; he plays with narrative structure, with story and discourse, in new and exciting ways. The question about *Mr Noon* is not, as early reviews asked, why the two sections seem so different from each other, but why, given how well they play against each other, Lawrence did not continue the work. The answer for that question may finally have to come from "biographical displacement," for as aesthetic experiment, *Mr Noon* is rich in possibility.

Notes

1. Although the new edition received some kind words, dismissal was more common. For example, James Fenton called *Mr Noon* "tiresome junk" ("Bing, Bang, Bump Factions," *Times* [London], 13 September 1984, p. 13); Paul Gray wrote that the novel "is not very good" ("Men and Women in Love," *Time* 15 October 1984, p. 101); and John Ezard reported that it contained "too much undigested essay-style material" ("Lawrence Late Entry Already Best Seller," *Manchester Guardian Weekly*, 23 September 1984, p. 21). Even in a generally enthusiastic review, V. S. Pritchett said *Mr Noon* "may not be great prose" ("His Angry Way," *New York Review*, 25 October 1984, p. 18). For a discussion of the 1934 response to part 1 of *Mr Noon* (appearing in *A Modern Lover*), see Lindeth Vasey's Introduction to the Cambridge edition, pp. xxxvi–xxxviii.

2. Similarly, Graham Hough commented on the "preposterous abruptness of [the] transitions" ("From Spooning to the Real Thing," *Times Literary Supplement*, 14 September 1984, p. 1028); Diana Trilling called the sections "loosely connected" ("Lawrence in Love," *New York Times Book Review*, 16 December 1984, pp. 3, 24–25); Gray saw "significant change" from part 1 to part 2 (*Time*, p. 101). An important exception is Anthony Heilbut, who commented on the relationship between the two sections: "The young Noon's life provides a text that the other Noon must then re-write" ("All Mixed Up," *Nation*, 9 February 1985, p. 154).

3. Evelyn J. Hinz and John J. Teunissen, on the other hand, saw Noon "as a portrait of H. G. Wells" ("War, Love and Industrialism: The Ares / Aphrodite / Hephaestus Complex in *Lady Chatterley's Lover*," in *D. H. Lawrence's "Lady": A New Look at "Lady Chatterley's Lover"*, ed. Michael Squires and Dennis Jackson [Athens: University of Georgia Press, 1985], p. 220). Such are the dangers of "biographical displacement" and the underlying reason why *Mr Noon*, like any work of fiction, is best studied as artistic creation. Like Hinz and Teunissen, however, I agree that *Mr Noon* anticipates *Lady Chatterley's Lover*.

4. *Women in Love* (New York: Viking Press, 1960), p. viii.

5. Letter from Lawrence to Robert Mountsier, 25 January 1921, in *The Letters of D. H. Lawrence, Volume III: October 1916–June 1921*, ed. James T. Boulton and Andrew Robertson (Cambridge: Cambridge University Press, 1984), p. 653.

6. Ibid., 717*n*.

7. Seymour Chatman, *Story and Discourse: Narrative Structure in Fiction and Film* (Ithaca, N.Y.: Cornell University Press, 1978), p. 42.

8. Ibid., p. 53.

9. Ibid., p. 46.

10. Ibid., p. 111.

11. Ibid., p. 109.

12. Letter from Lawrence to Edward Garnett, 5 June 1914, in *The Letters of D. H. Lawrence, Volume II: June 1913–October 1916*, ed. George J. Zytaruk and James T. Boulton (Cambridge: Cambridge University Press, 1981), p. 182.

13. Ibid., p. 183.

14. *Mr Noon*, ed. Lindeth Vasey (Cambridge: Cambridge University Press, 1984), p. 99. Page numbers are hereafter cited in the text.

15. Robert Alter, *Partial Magic: The Novel as a Self-Conscious Genre* (Berkeley: University of California Press, 1975).

[Reading Lawrence's American Novel: *The Plumed Serpent*]

L. D. Clark*

About 1914, Lawrence came to believe that true consciousness was ultra-human and universal, and that the individual received his portion of it, his soul, through the blood, not the mind.[1] In time he formed a conviction that this pristine spirit of the universe still beat closer to the surface in America than anywhere else, and that the greatest hope for reviving its power lay in atonement between the white race and the red on the American continent. He prepared himself to approach this spirit through intense study and lengthy interpretation of early American literature, in which he believed he had found a new and original understanding of human psychology.[2] From 1920 on, he endeavored to put his discoveries into his poetry and fiction.[3] Analysis of the results, in conjunction with Lawrence's ongoing experience with the New World, which led him to New Mexico in 1922, to Mexico in 1923, and to a more complex if less tangible involvement with "America" until the publication of *The Plumed Serpent* in 1926, leaves no doubt that this novel is the key to understanding his American quest, probably the most important one of his lifetime. The substance of this novel relies on the symbology Lawrence had elaborated out of his thought on American literature, a symbology formed out of the necessity to control and articulate the rhythmic cycle of tormenting and life-giving forces in his own nature. He saw the application of this symbology as authentic prophecy, moved by the conviction that his struggles with self-knowledge entitled him to offer true utterance on race-knowledge. Whatever the achievement of *The Plumed Serpent* itself, the task of imagination that produced it was probably the greatest creative ordeal of Lawrence's life, fully as arduous as the *Rainbow-Women in Love* struggle, and longer in maturing in his work.

None of which makes *The Plumed Serpent* an easy novel to assess. The reader may object to some of its elements on both moral and esthetic grounds — at least, a number of readers[4] have done so — and the objections may be so strong as to discourage any real effort to understand what Law-

*Excerpted, with revisions by the author, from "D. H. Lawrence and the American Indian," *D. H. Lawrence Review*, 9 (Fall 1976):305–72, by permission of the journal and the author.

rence intended, let alone discover whether his intentions were realized. His direct comments outside the novel are not of much help: they have more often proved to be misleading. Responding to a question passed on by his British publisher just before the novel appeared, Lawrence asserted that he did mean "what Ramón means — for all of us."[5] But since we do not know whether Lawrence was referring to the character of Ramón in general, or to one certain action or statement of his, nor even what the specific question was, the remark has little exact significance: which has not prevented some critics from using it as evidence that the novel as a whole conveys a "message" in the most literal sense, and that Lawrence accomplishes little beyond this message.[6] He made other statements which have a greater bearing on his intentions in the novel, revealing an ambitious purpose indeed, but the connection between these statements and *The Plumed Serpent* has been largely overlooked. They are contained chiefly in five short essays on the modern novel in general, the only ones Lawrence ever wrote on that subject, one dating from just before he began and the rest from just after he finished *The Plumed Serpent*.[7] In one of these essays he calls for a new mating of "philosophy and fiction," the two having once been united "right from the days of myth" until Aristotle wrenched them apart (*P* 520). Any novelist of today who could reintegrate these in a single endeavor would demonstrate that "the novel is the highest example of subtle inter-relatedness that man has discovered" (*P* 528). We find also in these essays Lawrence's attacks on didacticism in fiction and such often-quoted assertions — almost never in context — as "the novel is the one bright book of life" (*P* 535). Condemning the experiments of contemporaries like Joyce and Proust as absorption in a morbid self-consciousness, Lawrence infers that he has set out in a totally different direction, into "the innermost primeval place in man, where God is, if He is anywhere," there to restore the whole consciousness of man to the realm of fiction (*P* 759). What the essays really come to is an extended argument at one remove from *The Plumed Serpent* in support of Lawrence's declaration that this was the most significant piece of work he had ever done.[8] It may be tempting to assume that he was exercising his powers of persuasion to overcome a fear that he had failed in the novel, but there is no convincing evidence to call his sincerity into question. We might then go ahead two-and-a-half years, as commentators frequently do, to point out that Lawrence had by this time changed his mind about certain elements of the novel, and to conclude from this change that he had repudiated the work altogether.[9] Deeply absorbed in *Lady Chatterley's Lover*, with Mellors in view as the great man of the future, Lawrence now saw a hero like Don Ramón as "obsolete, . . . [a] militant ideal: and the militant ideal, or the ideal militant" now seemed "a cold egg." The new responsiveness — "a pure relationship, a pure relatedness, the only thing that matters," as he put it in one of the 1926 essays — would have to be "some sort of tenderness, sensitive, between men and men and men and women."[10] But then as late as 1929, when *The Plumed Serpent* was characterized by a friend as "*satanisch*," Lawrence defended it as celebrating the restoration of Lucifer, "the Son of the Morning, . . . who is really the Morning Star" — which certainly does not suggest a repudiation of the fundamental power-urge of the novel.[11]

Even if Lawrence's views of *The Plumed Serpent* did not contain such contradictions, to grant them authority in judging the book would still be unjustifiable; it would be committing the elementary error of taking what an author says about his book for what the book itself says. We are left then where we ought to be left, with the novel as such on our hands. But not quite that alone, for no single work of Lawrence's can be taken in isolation. His writing was too much a part of his day-to-day conflicts over a lifetime to be read at its most meaningful in the separate segments in which it was necessarily published. After *Women in Love*, at least, Lawrence saw his novels as a continuing engagement with "the writer's own desires, aspirations, struggles; in a word, a record of the profoundest experiences in the self" (*PII* 275–76). He had a particular talent, too, in the transference of these experiences to the written word, for laying hold of them closer to the source than most novelists do, and transferring them to the page with a minimum of conscious interference. The immediacy and the indivisibility of life and art that go into the making of a Lawrence novel do not permit it to be read by any traditional "art of the novel" approach. It must be seen in accord with structural and thematic principles to which Lawrence's own genius will respond. His words about *Women in Love* and related remarks elsewhere embody his refusal to pursue formal perfection and a complete resolution of themes in a novel.[12] The endings of his longer fiction, for instance, are never rounded out, because the battle to reconcile life and art was unceasing, and a respite at the close of a novel was not a conclusion. Our criteria must accordingly look beyond to the acceptance of gropings that reveal fantastic corners of experience which may never be brought fully to light but which carry a conviction of psychological reality in the realm of fiction for all their lack of form and clarity. The compelling strangeness of the experience generates its own significance, in great part because of Lawrence's genius for achieving an almost unmediated transformation of autobiography into fiction.

Lawrence's total commitment to producing a "record of the profoundest experiences in the self" brought his vision to the verge of hallucination in *The Plumed Serpent*. Even so, whatever the thematic and structural faults caused by this hyperintensity, the novel carries the conviction of that prophecy which Lawrence's "records" always reach for. Our difficulty in grasping his meaning does not stem altogether from any impossibility of reconciling the faults with other elements of the novel but to a great extent from our failure to comprehend the American Indian traditions Lawrence chose for conveying his vision, most of them a mystery to European and white American readers in any other sense than as folkloric and interesting but not to be taken seriously as real forces in modern human psychology. All in all, as Ronald Walker has suggested, it may be simply that we have not yet learned how to read *The Plumed Serpent*.[13]

As stated above, a resurgence of the primordial spirit in America had meant to Lawrence for many years the bringing about of a new fusion between the white invader and the dark native. During his sojourn in America the fusion came to require also a restoration of the native gods, together with the old ways of communicating with them. The experiences of the woman and the two men at the center of *The Plumed Serpent* are Lawrence's supreme effort to achieve a "yearning myth" — as he designated Cooper's search for an imagined America, but it was also his own.[14] Kate of *The Plumed Serpent* is the final American personification of the rare feminine spirit in rebellion against a greedy and dying society, who seeks new birth in the New World through submission to the great power from beyond. In the three shorter pieces of fiction that preceded *The Plumed Serpent*, Lawrence had confined the effort to attain harmony with the spirit of America to this sort of female persona. In his final confrontation with the New World, he could no longer limit himself to working out the salvation of the female side of his nature. The male identity demanded also to be heard. In the shorter works several roughly hewn shapes of the dark stranger had already appeared, descendants of Ciccio of *The Lost Girl*: the young cacique of "The Woman Who Rode Away," Phoenix of *St. Mawr*, and Romero of "The Princess" — none of them similar, however, to the questing white male in the lineage of Richard Somers and Aaron Sisson, nor of the cross between savior and self-healer like Birkin, Lilly, and Kangaroo. Attributes of all these types of seekers, some originating as early as 1917, are evident in the two male protagonists of *The Plumed Serpent*. Having also gotten rid of the debilitated male in Rico of *St. Mawr* and the husband of the woman who rode away, and having consigned the princess to an elderly member of that species, Lawrence was ready to attempt fulfillment of an old ideal: to create, in balance with the American continent and a redeemed woman, a pair of blood brothers like Natty Bumppo and Chingachgook, the white man and the Indian in a new and mystical concord.[15] In the first and still unpublished version of his American novel, Lawrence betrayed some indecision as to which race was to dominate, whether indeed the whole white mystique was not to be repudiated in favor of a reawakened native American spirit — analogous to what he soon afterwards created in "The Woman Who Rode Away." The first Ramón and the first Cipriano both possess a large strain of American Indian blood, and both identify strongly with the aboriginal America.[16] In the definitive *Plumed Serpent* Lawrence took his final stand: the European must lead. Don Ramón Carrasco has scarcely any Indian blood — in Kate's eyes, he belongs to aboriginal

Europe—while Don Cipriano Viedma is nearly pure Indian, and Ramón is unquestionably the leader.[17] But Ramón has done what Lawrence recommended in his essay on Melville's *Typee* and *Omoo*: he has taken his great curve in the direction of the aboriginal.[18] His ambition now, beginning with Mexico, is to show the way to revival of the ancient gods and their rites in all countries, each land according to its own pagan antiquity, while at the same time each will retain such other enlightenment as has been achieved in its history since the old gods disappeared.

Lawrence chose to set forth his restoration of a strange and ancient American religion in a realistic context. The effect of this procedure on readers has had one distinct advantage. Nearly all agree that the setting is vivid, almost magically so, and this quality serves to attract those who fail to see any other significant accomplishment in the novel. Paradoxically, the fascination of the setting has sometimes provided justification for dismissing the rest of the novel, as though this were a book like *The Lost Girl*, a realistic story with unreal pageantry attached. On the contrary, the Mexico of *The Plumed Serpent* is far different from the Woodhouse of *The Lost Girl*. In this Mexico the mysterious is constantly imminent. Darkness, exoticism, and danger emanate even from the reporter-like narration of the bull-fight chapter and from Kate's daily routines at Lake Sayula. A young emissary of the gods swimming up to a commonplace rowboat in an actual lake may be taken as a scene reflecting many of its kind. The lake and the mountains shine like mythical places through the description, with storms prowling or boats edging across, or quiet morning coming to light, the filmy water drawing a whole land in a magic circle around it. All around, too, are the native faces of dark strength or of gloomy lethargy. A profusion reigns everywhere: flowers, birds, dirt, and lurking demons. And in this setting nothing is left to such vagueness as the reason why the Natcha-Kee-Tawara troupe of *The Lost Girl* see their stage act as the essence of their lives. Everyone in *The Plumed Serpent*, indeed the whole of Mexico, is swept into the Quetzalcoatl movement, and the men behind it are powerful if fantastic figures.

At least some of this power of the men and the movement reaches those who respond to the setting. The first insurmountable difficulty, for many, arises when they are asked to render fictional belief to the ceremonialism of the novel: the invented costumes, the dances, the chants, the myths. Yet a person who has witnessed real Indian ceremonies for any length of time can see that quite a few of the rituals, especially in the earlier part of the book, are true to the tone and spirit of their originals. Lawrence was not wrong in his estimate of Indian dancers and white onlookers—or of Indian-like rituals and white readers.[19] Indian dance is ordinarily a simple cadence of stamping hour after hour. Any pattern of movement is also simple: a little lining up, turning in place, or circling. The Indian's purpose is to communicate with powers that give life, not to perform, which is what Europeans and Americans almost inevitably expect. These powers may be reached verbally, but more important than words is rhythm: the rhythm of chanting, drumming, and dancing, on and on past the point of monotony to the uninitiated white observer, to whom words bearing mental concepts have long since become the chief if not the only vehicle for communicating with deities. But even with this problem of communication, if Lawrence had not gone beyond such ceremonies as the first dance in the book, in the "Plaza" chapter, he would never have been accused of the preposterous fabrication that critics of his novel charge him with.

The dance in the plaza is modeled on the Taos Round Dance, with certain features emphasized.[20] The absorption of the dancers is certainly natural to the scene, and Kate's sense of merging with a greater reality is credible and convincing under the circumstances. Only in the chants that Lawrence invents is there a real difference from what might be part of an actual Indian ritual. The appeal, in these as in most Indian chants, is to the great mute powers like sun and earth, and Lawrence's chants are also authentic in that the rhythm is more important than the words. What Lawrence does differently in building on borrowed actuality is not excessive by any reasonable imaginative standards either. The introduction of his Quetzalcoatl-Christ cycle takes a poetic form natural to his tradition: symbols presented by metaphor and other analogy, not the Indian's direct personification of the elements with symbolism implied. The idea of a replacement of old gods by new, even a cycle of departure and return, is not far-fetched by either Old or New World standards. Indeed, that Christ was victorious over Quetzalcoatl is a historical fact, and a reverse development at some time in the future is not beyond imagining. The avatar recounted here is appealing simply as a story, if as nothing else. Quetzalcoatl emerges from a cave called Dark Eye and descends to claim his bride, Mexico. Lawrence does not forget that he is telling an "Indian" tale, for what happens has many Indian-like twists: the lake and the fish calling for men; the god who brings them forth and finds them helpless, not knowing even how much water to drink; his teaching them how to plant and build; the religious instruction he gives them. It may be added here, simply as an example of how suggestion worked for Lawrence, that the cave which is called Dark Eye no doubt owes its name to the same cavern that furnished a model of the sacrificial cave in "The Woman Who Rode Away": the Arroyo Seco cave formerly of great importance to the Taos Indians, who may have looked on it as the Place of Emergence through which the Black Eyes, the Taos version of the Pueblo Indian clowns better known as Koshare, led the people into this world.[21] Much the same can be said of nearly every ceremony in the novel up through the rain vigil in Chapter XIII, and even the marriage ceremony in Chapter XX: that they bear a general similarity to real-life origins and that no real violence need be done to our precepts of fiction to make them ring true within the framework of the novel.

A number of the later rituals of *The Plumed Serpent* do unfortunately become pretentious with sermons and involved in apotheoses that strain suspension of disbelief, with the further complication of a ceremonial execution. Lawrence becomes entangled in a series of contradictions and circumventions as the novel draws toward its close. For one thing, he never quite makes up his mind about how much divinity to attribute to his heroes. After Ramón has declared to the bishop, and to his sons and others, that he is only a prophet and forerunner of Quetzalcoatl, he then has himself declared the living Quetzalcoatl, Cipriano the living Huitzilopochtli, Kate the living Malintzi. A worse flaw appears in Lawrence's indecision about what to do with Cipriano. It may easily seem that his intention is merely to gloss over that character's tendencies to savagery. Ramón speaks of peace and beatific vision, and he does restrain Cipriano from beginning a holy war either to convert or wipe out. But when murderers and bandits are executed for attempting to assassinate Ramón, he seems hardly aware that in allowing these executions to be carried out as ritual human sacrifice he all but guarantees a reversion to the old blood lust of the Aztecs which he has condemned. Lawrence appears to be evading issues when in the final chapters he turns to building vivid scenes of description and triumphant action to affirm that the animistic spirit and the new race are established in all their reawakened glory. Cipriano and his warriors dance and fight like the old-time Red Indians. Ramón has done away with clock hours and substituted days that pass to drum-beats. And going about the nation he leads a host of men to the Morning Star — the world of Lake Sayula has turned again to awareness of the "greater mystery," with Lawrence's prose realizing his old anticipation of a pristine world in America.[22] But after all is said and done, the ideal of men like gods and a land like Eden has not transformed itself into a perfected actuality. Still, we ought not to expect this. A transcendental success unalloyed by failures would spoil this or any similar story. But at least the idyllic, the savage, and the exalted should have been moving, through the pages, toward a greater coherence, whereas in fact they move away from it, and at last Lawrence can no longer avoid the dilemma by multiplying ceremonies and illuminating his scenes with powerful prose.

Lawrence might well attempt to evade the problems the two male protagonists give rise to, but he could not fail to deal directly with that of his female persona, Kate, the most important character in the book. For one thing, it is clear all through the narrative that Kate bears more of her creator's concerns than any other character — reflecting those "profoundest experiences in the self" pursued in the novel. Her uncertainties directly reflect his own as to the nature of the primitive in America. And it is here, if we look at the novel within the whole framework of Lawrence's experiences with America, that the prophetic tone begins to ring true, and toward the end assists the novel in redeeming itself from some of the flaws apparent in earlier pages.

From the start Kate has had her moments of rebellion against the Quetzalcoatl movement, times when she decided to return to Europe and forget about America. The closer Ramón comes to final victory the more urgent the necessity for Kate to make a firm decision. Her wavering leads her more than once to extremes. At one point she decides to separate the warrior in Cipriano from the man who is her husband, to be content to overlook the killer and live in harmony with the man and husband — which is surely a dangerous moral contradiction, in the novel's own terms, if nothing else, for here she approaches the harem mentality that she so mistrusts in Ramón's second wife, Teresa. At the level of conscious choice, Kate in fact never ceases to waver. In the final pages of the book she has not totally committed herself to the new religion and the new aristocratic politics. Still, when she considers going home to Europe, only to grow old and catty in a London apartment, she recoils. She reasons with herself that a future in Mexico is far more desirable. Better to press on than to regress. Yet, even as she is about to concede, to throw her lot with Ramón and Cipriano, she resists: "I will make my submission; as far as I need, and no further." And when she faces them she surrenders to a contradictory feeling that she is being compelled — "You won't let me go!" — and permits this impulse to make the decision that she cannot consciously bring herself to make. However, in a novel that relies so heavily on subliminal forces, this is a fitting conclusion, balancing Kate's extended history of attractions and repulsions in this strange land as probably nothing else could, a reconciliation that encompasses Ramón and Cipriano and Mexico itself, and maybe even where she will stand in relation to the kind of womanhood represented by Teresa. The ending does not encompass the political dimension of the novel. The best that Lawrence could do here was to state his doubts, a few pages before the end, and let them go unresolved: "The whole country was thrilling with a new thing, with a release of new energy. But there was a sense of violence and crudity in it all, a touch of horror."

To turn away from politics in a "political" novel is an unfortunate divergence, no doubt, but we would do well to remember that Lawrence thought he was reaching into forgotten depths of the human soul and writing his novel at the quick of unfolding events. To impose a plot resolution in such circumstances would be unthinkable. He could only acknowledge that the revival of the primitive in America, which he had held to be inevitable since early in his study of American literature, might well be accompanied by cruelty and violence. Knowing the course of history since 1926 and observing from the turmoil of our own times, we may find it natural to ponder the conclusions and implications of a novel that laid claim to such a prophecy several decades ago. What is the real likelihood of a resurgence of the primitive in America, and what would it be like? In answer to these questions the happenings of *The Plumed Serpent* appear to me, in spite of the shortcomings of the latter part of the book, to offer certain historical insights, even though they may be wrapped in all the obscurity of a Delphic utterance.

It is at least symptomatic, though no astonishing case of prophecy come true, that movements to resuscitate the pre-Conquest gods have flourished in Mexico for some time, ever since the Revolution, near the end of which Lawrence wrote his novel. These movements are reported now and again in isolated regions and have been heard of even in university circles.[23] More revealing yet, if Lawrence had been writing *The Plumed Serpent* in the 1960s, he could easily have laid the scene in the United States, if not with Aztec gods then with others equally primitive, and with cult adherents decked out in serapes, beads, headbands, feathers and so on, pounding drums to clear the blood of the pollutions of industrialized civilization. This development in American society, curious if we pause to think of it, might also make us consider what Lawrence said about the United States from a new standpoint: that the nation was moving on toward the last stages of machine culture faster than other nations, hence would be ripe for the breakdown of that culture sooner than others. We had all around us in the Sixties not only many examples of youth renouncing the culture of the machine and the consumer, and making gestures toward rousing the primitive body, but we saw that in some ways their activities were surprisingly analogous to what goes on in *The Plumed Serpent*.

There are modern instances, as well, that bring to mind Lawrence's quandary over how to solve the problem of the violence that so often goes with reform. His apocalyptic predilections, like those of many of our contemporaries, prevented him from believing in improvement without revolution. And destroying the system means, willy-nilly, destroying the most powerful of those who uphold it. This violence is frequently seen by its proponents as a form of sacrifice, the spilling of blood necessary for the regeneration of man. No need to look far to discover cases of violence performed in a sacrificial, almost ritual vein by those who in our decades live under the spell of some revolutionary fervor. Clearly the violence that Lawrence saw latent in the American character is more in evidence now than it was when he sensed its presence. But *The Plumed Serpent* goes much further in posing questions about the nature of violence in America. If some kind of return to the primitive lies in the future of the continent, does the concomitant violence belong to a temporary, restorative phase, or would it be permanent and crippling to a revived primitivism, even one inspired by the best of human instincts? If men confess that the blood as well as the spirit belongs to the gods, then how does a blood-worshipping society avoid the brutal excesses to which such societies have been prone in the past? Recognizing that the Aztecs had made this fatal error and drowned in their own gory rites, Lawrence foresaw a recurrence, and he often blamed this disaster of the Aztecs on the inability of man to cope with the fierce spirit of the continent itself. The direction in which

Cipriano is drifting, late in *The Plumed Serpent*, is already drawing the Quetzalcoatl movement into that danger; the new race of Americans that Lawrence had hailed in the American essays does not, unhappily, appear headed for so magical a future after all; and by the end of the novel Lawrence has gone part of the way, himself, toward rejecting the animistic reconstruction of society that Ramón and Cipriano have undertaken.

So *The Plumed Serpent* ends in a manner typical of Lawrence's longer works: with an incarnation of the author standing between two worlds, attracted and repelled by the future, where the fear of imminent peril is tempered by expectation of newness of life beyond the ordeal, his projected self determined not to revert to the past, which is dead beyond hope of resurrection. If this ending appears to suffer from a greater indecision and incompleteness than those of the other major novels, the reason is that Lawrence undertook more in this novel than in any other. The most important consideration may be that he succeeded as well as he did, and that the accomplishment may appear greater at some future date than it ever has in the nearly sixty years since the book was written.

Notes

1. *The Letters of D. H. Lawrence, Volume II: June 1913–October 1916*, ed. George J. Zytaruk and James T. Boulton (Cambridge: Cambridge University Press, 1981), 182–83, 218.

2. Lawrence's discovery of American literature began when he happened upon a copy of *Moby-Dick* in early 1916 (*Letters II*, ed. Zytaruk and Boulton, 528). He was soon delving into Cooper, Dana, Crevècoeur, and others. In August 1917 he began his American literature essays, which he saw as a continuation of the symbology that had occupied him since 1914, and which evolved through several revisions before appearing in book form as *Studies in Classic American Literature* (1923); see *The Letters of D. H. Lawrence*, ed. Aldous Huxley (New York: Viking Press, 1932), 414. For Lawrence's claim that his new psychology was superior to Freud's "windy theory of the unconscious," see *Collected Letters*, ed. Harry T. Moore (New York: Viking Press, 1962), 596.

3. See "Cypresses" and "Turkey-Cock," *Complete Poems of D. H. Lawrence*, ed. Vivian de Sola Pinto and Warren Roberts (New York: Viking Press, 1964), 296–98, 369–72. While *The Lost Girl* (1920) is Lawrence's first identifiable use of aboriginal American themes in fiction, the few American elements in *Aaron's Rod* (1921) may date from as early as 1917, when he began this book. See *The Quest for Rananim: D. H. Lawrence's Letters to S. S. Koteliansky, 1914–1930*, ed. George J. Zytaruk (Montreal: McGill-Queen's University Press, 1970), 219.

4. For example, F. R. Leavis in *D. H. Lawrence: Novelist* (London: Chatto & Windus, 1955) and Eliseo Vivas, *D. H. Lawrence: The Failure and the Triumph of Art* (Evanston, Ill.: Northwestern University Press, 1960). For one of the few balanced views, see Keith Sagar, *The Art of D. H. Lawrence* (Cambridge: Cambridge University Press, 1966).

5. *Collected Letters*, ed. Moore, 859.

6. Vivas, *D. H. Lawrence: The Failure and the Triumph of Art*, 73. For a similar argument about the dangers of the "ideal" as message, see Mark Spilka, *The Love Ethic of D. H. Lawrence* (Bloomington: Indiana University Press, 1955).

7. See *Phoenix: The Posthumous Papers of D. H. Lawrence*, ed. with introduction by Edward D. McDonald (London: William Heinemann, 1936), 517–20, 527–38, 755–60

(*Phoenix* hereafter cited parenthetically in the text as *P*); and *Phoenix II: Uncollected, Unpublished, and Other Prose Works by D. H. Lawrence*, ed. Warren Roberts and Harry T. Moore (London: William Heinemann, 1968), pp. 416–26 (*Phoenix II* hereafter cited parenthetically in the text as *PII*).

8. *Letters*, ed. Moore, p. 845; *The Centaur Letters*, introduction by Edward D. McDonald (Austin, Texas: Humanities Research Center, 1970), p. 20.

9. For example, Spilka, *Love Ethic*, 210.

10. *Letters*, ed. Moore, 1045.

11. Frieda Lawrence, *Not I, But the Wind . . .* (New York: Viking Press, 1934), 272.

12. Lawrence's first declaration of independence from principles of fiction widely accepted in his day came about through disagreement with his then editor, Edward Garnett, in 1914. See *Letters*, ed. Moore, 281–83.

13. Introduction to *The Plumed Serpent* (Harmondsworth, England: Penguin, 1983), 24.

14. In "Fenimore Cooper's Leatherstocking Novels," *Studies in Classic American Literature*.

15. *Ibid.*

16. The typescript of the first version of *The Plumed Serpent* is in the Houghton Library, Harvard University. For a lengthier discussion see L. D. Clark, *Dark Night of the Body* (Austin: Texas University Press, 1964), 98–101, 119–20.

17. *The Plumed Serpent* (Harmondsworth, England: Penguin, 1983), 275.

18. In "Herman Melville's *Typee* and *Omoo*," *Studies in Classic American Literature*.

19. See "The Hopi Snake Dance," *Mornings in Mexico* (1927).

20. *Dark Night of the Body*, 110.

21. *Dark Night of the Body*, 38.

22. In an early version of "Fenimore Cooper's Leatherstocking Novels," published in the *English Review* (March 1919), collected in *The Symbolic Meaning*, ed. Armin Arnold (Centaur Press Ltd. of Fontwell, 1962).

23. See "Laurentiana," *D. H. Lawrence Review*, 5 (Spring 1972): 94–95.

The "Old Pagan Vision": Myth and Ritual in *Lady Chatterley's Lover*

Dennis Jackson*

Though Lawrence's suggestions of ancient myth and ritual are not so explicit in *Lady Chatterley's Lover* as those in *The Plumed Serpent* or *The Escaped Cock*, they nonetheless yield a comparable connotative richness through their intimations of a magic pagan world underlying and fused with the story's realistic surface. While the human level of the narrative focuses on the themes of Connie's and Mellors's need for personal regeneration, England's need for social revitalization, and the whole modern

*This essay was extensively revised and expanded for publication in this volume. It is reprinted from the *D. H. Lawrence Review* 11 (Fall 1978):260–71, by permission of the journal and the author.

world's need for renewal, the mythic level bodies forth such archetypes as those of the underworld descent, the dying-reviving god, the restoration of the powers of fertility, and the hierogamy of sun and earth.

Lawrence's knowledge of such mythic patterns came largely from his reading, first in 1915 and again in 1922, of Sir James George Frazer's anthropological classic, *The Golden Bough*.[1] Writing to Bertrand Russell in 1915, Lawrence indicated that his recent reading of *The Golden Bough* and another of Frazer's books, *Totemism and Exogamy*, had confirmed his own belief that "there is another seat of consciousness than the brain and the nerve system," "a blood-consciousness which exists in us independently of the ordinary mental consciousness." The "tragedy of this our life," he continued, is that this mental consciousness "exerts a tyranny" over the blood-consciousness, and he traced the blame for this back to Plato (*CL* 393–94).[2] In Frazer, then, Lawrence had found support for his own dualistic philosophy, for his belief that man has two ways of *knowing* the universe. This epistemological interest is manifested in much of Lawrence's later writing, and it certainly informs *Lady Chatterley's Lover*, where he so determinedly juxtaposes the symbolic worlds of Wragby Hall, where reason and the "life of the mind" prevail, and Wragby Wood, where intuition and the "life of the body" are paramount. One of Lawrence's spokesmen in the novel, Tommy Dukes, echoes the 1915 letter to Russell as he declares: "Real knowledge comes out of the whole corpus of the consciousness, out of your belly and your penis as much as out of your brain and mind. Set the mind and the reason to cock it over the rest, and all they can do is . . . make a deadness. . . . [W]hile you *live* your life, you are in some way an organic whole with all life. But once you start the mental life you pluck the apple. You've severed the connection between the apple and the tree, the organic connection" (*LCL* 41). As had Lawrence in the 1915 letter, Dukes attributes this deadening tyranny of the "mental life" to the Greek philosophers: "Socrates started it" (*LCL* 44). In his essay "A Propos of *Lady Chatterley's Lover*," Lawrence again stresses the "two ways" man has for knowing the universe—"knowing in terms of apartness, which is mental, rational, scientific, and knowing in terms of togetherness, which is religious and poetic," and he repeatedly asserts that an over-reliance on the former has caused man to lose the sense of "togetherness with the universe, . . . togetherness of the body, the sex, the emotions, the passions, with the earth and sun and stars" (*PII* 512). Such statements suggest clearly why Lawrence had been fascinated by *The Golden Bough* with its delineation of myths and rituals of primitive peoples who had still felt such "togetherness" with their external world, and why he had found such interest in Frazer's speculations on the mental structures of these savages in whom the "two ways of knowing" had not been separated by Platonic rationalism.

Several writers, most notably John B. Vickery, have traced the influence of Frazer's work on Lawrence's fictions,[3] but nothing has been done along those lines with *Lady Chatterley's Lover*, a novel that embraces, on page after page, in its images, similes, allusions, characters, scenes, and actions, many of the major notions concerning myth and ritual to be found in *The Golden Bough*. Many actions of Lawrence's two main figures in the story bear marked resemblance to primitive seasonal rituals. This is especially evident in chapters 11 and 12, wherein Connie emerges from an "underworld" to plant flowers and to become "new-born" in spring, and in chapters 13 through 15, wherein the lovers bear the scapegoat villain Clifford out of the forest, pay homage to the newly risen phallus, and bring branches of springtime greenery and flowers into the hut preparatory to the staging of their own personalized May Rites and the mock "wedding" of their genital parts, "John Thomas" and "Lady Jane." To illustrate how ancient myth and ritual elements reinforce Lawrence's themes and motifs in *Lady Chatterley's Lover*, and to show how these elements help give the novel its form, I shall focus primarily on these chapters, 11 through 15, where I find the pagan forms most prevalent and most expressive. Especially in these chapters the experiences of the lovers form a pattern of mythic regeneration analogous in many ways to the death-and-resurrection archetype found in the vegetative myths in *The Golden Bough*.

ii

Connie's car trip through the "mining and iron Midlands" in chapter 11 becomes, through Lawrence's graphic and suggestive imagery and diction, a mythic voyage through a ghastly underworld, a descent precedent to her becoming a "new-born thing" while making love with Mellors in the next chapter. This underworld visit/rebirth pattern parallels the myth of the Greek vegetative goddess Persephone, whose annual wintertime descent and springtime rebirth Frazer discusses in *The Golden Bough*.[4] Persephone, so the tale runs, was gathering flowers in a meadow when the earth opened and Pluto, lord of the Dead, issued from the abyss and carried her off to be his bride in a gloomy subterranean world (known in Greek myth as "Hades" or "Dis"). Her bereaved mother, the goddess Demeter, subsequently vowed not to let seeds grow in the earth until Persephone was restored to her. The land lay bare, nothing grew, and mankind was in danger of perishing until Zeus stipulated that Persephone would henceforth spend only one third of every year in the netherworld— each spring she would emerge into the sunshine to spend two thirds of the year in the upper world. A joyful Demeter consequently made the earth heavy with leaves and blossoms each time her daughter returned. Lawrence clearly had this myth of Persephone in mind as he described his heroine's experiences in *Lady Chatterley*. As the story begins, Connie is taken to live at her husband's ancestral home, Wragby Hall, which sits amid a gruesome industrial landscape filled with smoke and steam and burning pit-banks. (Like Pluto, known in Greek mythology as the God of Wealth, Sir Clifford takes his ample riches from under the earth, as owner of the Tevershall coal mines.) Connie finds that the air at Wragby always smells "of something under-earth," and begins to feel that she is "living underground" (*LCL* 12). Wragby is even more clearly identified with Pluto's underworld realm by Tommy Dukes, who laments that the "mental-lifers" gathered at the hall are not "alive in all the parts" of their bodies, and "can only talk"—"Another torture added to Hades!" (*LCL* 44). When on a March day Connie ventures away from this Hades and enters the nearby wood, she is said to be thinking about the "resurrection of the body" and about two of Swinburne's poems on Proserpine (as Pluto's mate is called in Roman myth),[5] and she explicitly parallels herself on that occasion with "Persephone . . . out of hell on a cold morning" (*LCL* 98). She descends in chapter 11 into a smoky, hellish Midlands industrial district directly designated by Lawrence as "an underworld" (*LCL* 181). In the myth as recounted by Frazer, Persephone's emergence from the underworld each year marked the death of winter and the advent of spring and a newly burgeoning vegetal life on earth. During Connie's own "underworld" travels she visits a gentleman named "Winter," who dies soon after her trip ends (*LCL* 188). Further, on her return from this industrial underworld, Lawrence's heroine exhibits her own beneficent effect on floral life as she plants carnations in her garden, and a dozen flower references fill the next chapter's opening paragraph, which describes the wonderfully renascent floral life that greets her return to Wragby Wood (she finds dandelions "making suns," celandines "pressed back in urgency, and the yellow glitter of themselves," primroses "thick-clustered," hyacinth buds "rising like pale corn," forget-me-nots "fluffing up," columbines "unfolding"—"Everywhere the bud-knots and the leap of life!" [*LCL* 196]). It is in that twelfth chapter, while at the hut in the wood, that Connie experiences symbolic rebirth during lovemaking with Mellors, as she feels herself becoming a "new-born thing" (*LCL* 208). Subsequent chapters show further rites of passage that mark her continued development toward wholesomeness of being. But in the next three chapters, 13 through 15, the emphasis is much less on Connie than on Mellors and the process of his own sexual and psychic revitalization.

In *The Golden Bough* Frazer details the Succession to the Kingdom of the ancient Sacred Kings who represented to their communities the spirit of vegetation (*GB* 176–84), and he also recounts other analogous primitive rituals—the annual killing of the Tree-Spirit, the companion ceremonies of Carrying Out Death and Bringing in Summer, the ritual May Day battles between representatives of summer and winter (*GB* 334–69), and the corollary action of bearing out the village scapegoat each year (*GB*

624–86). Each of these rituals features a struggle between the two opposed forces of nature (those of barrenness and fecundity), the subsequent expulsion of maleficent influences on nature, and the rebirth of the vegetative spirit in the person of a more youthful and fertile tanist, or successor. In the scene in *Lady Chatterley* wherein the keeper pushes his employer's wheelchair out of the wood, Sir Clifford suffers a symbolic death while Mellors is being "revived," and their experiences form a symbolic reenactment of this ritual combat of the anthropomorphic representatives of winter and spring depicted by Frazer. In that scene in chapter 13, Mellors becomes the tanist to Clifford and in effect succeeds to the "kingdom."

These two chief male figures of *Lady Chatterley* are, through Lawrence's imagery and through certain symbolic associations, paralleled to the dying-reviving year gods or to the dying-reviving anthropomorphic representatives of the vegetative spirit in ancient spring rites. Like the King of the Wood at Nemi, Mellors guards an oak wood, his job being that of "rear[ing] the pheasants" and protecting rabbits during their "breeding season." His affinity with vegetation is suggested by the literal way he is almost always surrounded by fresh plants and towering trees and by the numerous figurative comparisons drawn between his body and botanical specimens. In varying ways and degrees he is frequently associated with fruition—the forest he protects buds, the birds he tends hatch chicks, the woman he loves becomes pregnant. In that and in his wearing of green clothes he bears resemblances to the tree-spirits or to fertility figures such as the Green George and Summer figures described by Frazer.

While the keeper represents the beneficient qualities of the vegetative spirit, Sir Clifford projects a maleficent influence on all human and natural life around him. While Mellors nourishes and protects the woodland creatures, the baronet kills pheasants for sport, blasts cooing woodpigeons into silence with his horn, and yearns to destroy "unpleasant" little moles in the forest. In Clifford's presence in Wragby Hall violets hang over "limp on their stalks" (*LCL* 105); in the forest his wheelchair squashes flowers, replicating on a small scale what his giant machines are doing to the wood, to all nature, on a vaster scale. He is frequently associated with dead or dying vegetation, with "fallen" leaves, "lifeless" stumps, "leaning" saplings, and he is linked consistently with images of "coldness" and with Winter. Because he cannot give his wife the sensuality she needs, her body is metaphorically a greyish, "unripe" pear tree lacking the "sun and warmth" (*LCL* 80) needed to revivify it. Among ancient peoples, Frazer reports, a sacred king found similarly unable to satisfy the sexual passion of his wives was killed or deposed, for it was believed that the general course of nature depended sympathetically on his generative power. The king's removal was meant to open the way for a more vigorous successor. Clifford, like those dying kings, cannot perform the deed of strength necessary to maintain his position, and especially after the events of chapter 13, he is succeeded as Connie's mate by the more potent game-keeper.

The myth and ritual pattern of the Ancient Near East originally featured a combat to the death between the representatives of the vegetative deity and the one who wanted to succeed him, but in its later development it featured merely an annual symbolic death and rebirth of the Sacred King. The kings often had to prove, by strong hand in combat or by fleet foot in a race, that they still had the power to rule. Such a contest for the kingship, connected as it was with the ushering in of new life, long remained a regular feature of ancient spring rites. Significantly, Connie views the clash between her two men in the forest in chapter 13 as a contest for power, for the right to *rule*. She and Clifford lengthily discuss the opposition of "ruling classes" and "serving classes," and later, when he sits a helpless "prisoner" in his stalled wheelchair, waiting for his game-keeper to give him a push, Connie considers with disgust her husband's earlier arrogant declaration that "I can do my share of ruling," and she subsequently tells him, "You, and *rule*! . . . You don't rule. . . . Rule! What do you give forth of rule? . . . You only bully with your money" (*LCL* 232). During the scene of conflict in Wragby Wood, Clifford pits his fierce willpower against the chair while Mellors pits his bodily power against the same object. Clifford tries to move the chair with the power of his mind; in the end, it is the body of the keeper that propels the chair out of the entangling bluebells. (In Mellors's act of pushing Clifford's wheel-chair through Wragby Wood there is strong suggestion of the other, more meaningful way he is supplementing his employer's power—as a sexual mate to Connie.) His engine dead, Clifford acknowledges defeat by asking the keeper to push him home. Joining with Connie to push the chair, Mellors feels his "limbs revive," feels a "flame of strength" going down his back and into his loins, "reviving him" (*LCL* 230). Clifford conversely experiences symbolic death: Connie rejects him, wishing suddenly that he might be "obliterated from the face of the earth" (*LCL* 230), and she thinks of him as a "dead fish," a cold "skeleton," "very dead, really" (*LCL* 232–33).

This wheelchair scene suggests, in several important ways, the archetypal chasing away of the scapegoat villain. Upon the sacrificial scapegoat or dying year god were laid the accumulated evils afflicting the whole people, and he supposedly became the vehicle that bore these evils away from the community forever. Chatterley bears, both in his physical deficiencies and in his mental attitudes, the evils of the intellectualized and mechanistic world, and Mellors and Connie, in their act of pushing Clifford out of the wood, are in effect making an effort to rid themselves and the wood of such evils, if ever so temporarily. The regeneration of Lawrence's heroine comes as much through her rejection of Clifford and his sterile attitudes as through her concomitant acceptance of Mellors and of "phallic reality."[6]

The vegetative cults portrayed in *The Golden Bough* appealed to Lawrence particularly because they celebrated the vital phallic relation of man and woman, and, as *Lady Chatterley* evidences, it was in such that he envisioned the psychic and physical revitalization of what he viewed as modern impotence. The novel is as much a story of a man's psychic and physical renewal through the traditional healing powers of a woman as it is that of a woman's rebirth through phallic awareness, and this is evident especially in the scenes in chapter 14 when Connie stays overnight at the cottage. On that occasion Mellors rehearses his "awful experiences of women" (*LCL* 245), noting particularly his sexual failure with his former mate Bertha Coutts. Connie, too, has come to this new union from a marriage in which the husband has experienced sexual failure, though, of course, Clifford's problem is very different from that of the keeper. Clifford has, like the dying gods of the ancient myths, suffered a sexual wound; but unlike Attis, Adonis, and Osiris, he has no real hope for subsequent restoration. In a significant symbolic way Mellors, too, has incurred such a wound, but as in the case of the dying gods, his phallic power is not irredeemably lost. He initially shies away from Connie because "he had a big wound from old contacts" (*LCL* 102), a wound the nature of which[7] becomes very clear during his recollection of how his first two lovers "had nearly taken all the balls out of me" and of how Bertha's genitals had "torn at me down there, as if it was a beak tearing me" (*LCL* 241–42). Images of destruction — of tearing, rubbing, grinding — fill his description of his wife's genitals, and the "beak" image he uses is a variant of the *vagina dentata* or "toothed vagina" image which in myth and folklore symbolizes men's universal fear of castration and impotence. Erich Neumann comments on this image in his exposition of the Archetypal Feminine Character in *The Great Mother*: "The destructive side of the Feminine, the destructive and deathly womb, appears most frequently in the archetypal form of a mouth bristling with teeth."[8] In her "beakishness" Bertha Coutts is seen as a type of the "destructive female" or "Terrible Mother" that Neumann characterizes. "She had to let herself go, and tear, tear, tear," Mellors continues. "Well, in the end I couldn't stand it. We slept apart." Because of his phallic mistrust of women, he had for many years thereafter "wanted to have nothing to do with any woman any more" (*LCL* 242, 244). To Connie he describes himself as a "broken-backed snake that's been trodden on," obviously referring to the phallic impotence he had experienced because of Bertha's "beak," and as he says this, Connie senses in him the continuing despair, "the death of all desire, the death of all love" (*LCL* 247). This "death" motif crops up again in the next chapter, when in apparent reference to his previous failures in love he tells Connie, "It seems to me I've died once or twice already" (*LCL* 260).

Throughout chapters 14 and 15, an emasculation motif is sounded in Mellors's speeches with meaningful frequency. He blames the world of "mechanized greed" for taking the workers' "manhood" away, and complains: "The world is all alike: . . . Pay 'em money to cut off the world's cock . . . and take spunk out of mankind" (*LCL* 261). Such talk as this, coupled with his more personal references to the "beak" and "broken-backed snake" images, relate his story to that of the dying-reviving vegetation gods, whose death myths frequently included a castration or wounded genitals motif. The year gods all die violently, by castration or dismemberment, and severed genitals figure prominently in the stories of Attis, Dionysus, Osiris, and other of the dying gods. But an implied or implicit part of these vegetative myths had to do with the restoration of the fertilizing powers of nature and, more specifically, of the hero's potency, and in most cases, a goddess was instrumental in restoring the dead hero to life. Isis, for example, revived Osiris by fanning his cold clay with her wings, and the Babylonian goddess Ishtar brought Tammuz back from the underworld so that nature could be revived. Connie similarly plays the role of *restorer* to Mellors. While Bertha's "tearing" vagina had meant "the death of all desire" to his genitals, Connie's body has had a salutary effect on his wounded phallic nature: "It heals it all up, that I can go into thee," he tells her (*LCL* 211). Similarly, the "man who had died" in *The Escaped Cock* experiences the Priestess like a "tender flame of healing" (*EC* 46), and as he feels in his "slain penis" a new "manhood and . . . power," he announces, "I am risen!" (*EC* 56–57). That story follows the archetypal pattern wherein the goddess restores vitality and potency to the dead god who subsequently renews her own womb — such a pattern as I find replicated in *Lady Chatterley's Lover.*

It is replicated not only in the relationship of Lady Chatterley and her lover but also, in a parodical, sharply ironic way, in the union of Clifford and Mrs. Bolton. Wounded in Flanders in 1917, Chatterley has been shipped home from the war "smashed," his body, like that of Osiris in the Egyptian myth, "more or less in bits" (*LCL* 1). After Osiris had been killed and dismembered, bits of his body were buried at various locales, but Isis recovered and reconstituted the pieces, and revived him. One body part not recovered, Osiris's genital member, she replaced with a wax image, and thus her mate's resurrection was completed (*GB* 420–27). As with Osiris, Clifford's "bits seemed to grow together again." But he, too, has a part missing — "the lower half" of his body remains "paralyzed for ever" (*LCL* 1), and in his case, obviously, no genuine restoration is possible. Connie tries to give her husband support and strength, but only "Mrs. Bolton's talk . . . really put a new fight into Clifford" (*LCL* 124). Connie makes him "sensitive and conscious of himself," and this just saps his energy, while Mrs. Bolton makes him "aware only of outside things," for example of business and the need for improved mining technology — and these are areas where he still has potential to "win a man's victory" (*LCL*

125, 127). It is thus the nurse who ultimately is to play Isis to his Osiris, acting as agent for his restoration to a weird sort of "potency." Mrs. Bolton sparks in him a new interest in mining when she announces that Te**v**ershall pit is thought to be "finished . . . a sinking ship"; if such is so, she suggests, "it'll be like the end of the world," since a "dead colliery" is "like death itself." She consequently urges him to give the collieries a "new lease on life," to help resurrect this dying colliery world, and in such an effort to "[pull] Teversgall out of the hole," he goes "down in a tub" into the workings of the mines — literally descending into the underworld. In an ironic way this descent forms a symbolic burial, a return to the womb of the Earth-Mother to be reborn: "And he seemed verily to be re-born. *Now* life came into him. He had been gradually dying, with Connie." It is also suggested that he emerges from this descent restored to a strange new sort of potency — "Somehow he got his pecker up. In one way, Mrs. Bolton made a man of him, as Connie never did" (*LCL* 123–26). And further: "He really felt, when he had his periods of energy and worked so hard at the question of the mines, as if his sexual potency were returning" (*LCL* 174). His relationship with Mrs. Bolton seems a strangely sexual one — there is "growing voluptuousness" in their union, she is "thrilled to a weird passion" by their contact, and they gamble at cards with "strange lust" (*LCL* 114, 116, 257). Ultimately, they fall into "an intimacy of perversity" as he becomes a "child-man" fondling and kissing the breasts of the "Magna Mater" (*LCL* 352), and she — like the Ancient Near East goddesses who ministered to their reborn mates — becomes "half-mistress, half foster-mother" to him (*LCL* 130). Like Ishtar and Isis, she has a lover under-ground: her husband Ted Bolton had descended into the pit, but, unlike Clifford, he had never returned from that underworld "re-born," and Mrs. Bolton cannot Isis-like fan his cold clay back to life. Only to Clifford can she play the role of restorer. When Ishtar's Tammuz returned to upper earth, all the natural world was regenerated; when Clifford returns from underground, only the mechanical world, that of the dying collieries, is revitalized. Thus his relationship with the nurse perversely parallels that of the vegetative gods and their goddesses, as well as that of Connie and the keeper, and his "rebirth" into "potency" forms an obviously ironic commentary on the phallic rites scene and on the theme of Mellors's own regeneration in the story.

The keeper's restoration is effected gradually throughout the whole last half of the novel, but it is confirmed most forcefully in the symbolic scene that concludes chapter 14, when Connie worships his phallus. As it towers up before her, she marvels because it seems "so lordly . . . like another being," and she crawls on her knees on the bed towards him, drawing him to her so that her "hanging, swinging breasts [touch] the tip of the stirring, erect phallus and [catch] the drop of moisture" there, in a gesture of homage (*LCL* 252). Earlier Mellors had admitted that he had erred by being "very mistrustful" with Bertha. When Connie had asked, "You don't mistrust with your body, when your blood comes up . . . do you?", he had answered, "No" (*LCL* 245), but his old castration anxiety, his old fear of the *vagina dentata*, crops up again even in the middle of the phallic rites scene, when he says of his phallus: "I wouldn't have him killed." Significantly, his very next statement to Connie — "There! Take him then! He's thine!" (*LCL* 253) — suggests that her worshipful acceptance of his phallus in the scene has helped him overcome his lingering fear of the tearing "beak" of woman. The scene constitutes important Rites of Transition for both lovers, for Connie as she worships the man's erection in ritual signification of her acceptance of "phallic reality," and for Mellors as he has his wounded phallic life and his phallic trust restored.

Like Osiris and other of the vegetative gods, Mellors is closely identified with the reborn sun, particularly in this scene of the phallic rites. The lovers awaken as the sun rises over the wood at daybreak, and sunshine subsequently penetrates the cottage window lighting up the keeper's "erect phallus rising . . . hot-looking from the little cloud of vivid gold-red hair" (*LCL* 251). Lawrence emphasizes the sun-like attributes of the phallus, the way it "rises" from a "cloud," "hot-looking," amidst "gold-red" colors. Earlier in the novel Connie's naked body had seemed "unripe," "greyish and sapless," "as if it had not had enough sun" (*LCL* 80). Later, after she had become pregnant, she had felt "a quiver in her womb . . . as if the sunshine had touched it" (*LCL* 193). Like the sun a genial bringer of life, the man's phallus had "ripened" her body. All through the novel Connie is linked through imagery and metaphor with botanical specimens in need of sun and also with *earth*, and her union with Mellors is evocatively rendered in metaphorical terms of the bright and vital sun coming to reawaken the brown, dormant earth. Further, Mellors in his final letter directly relates his and Connie's union to that "between the sun and the earth" (*LCL* 364). The importance of such associations is indicated in "A Propos of *Lady Chatterley's Lover*," where Lawrence affirms that "sex goes through the rhythm of the year, in man and woman, ceaselessly changing: the rhythm of the sun in his relation to the earth." But, he laments, modern men have turned love, the "inward rhythm" of a couple in marriage, into a "merely personal feeling . . . cut off" from any sort of sympathetic correspondence with the larger rhythms of nature. And he concludes: "marriage is no marriage that is not basically and permanently phallic, and that is not linked up with the sun and the earth, . . . in the rhythm of days, in the rhythm of months, in the rhythm of . . . years" (*PII* 504–05).

In chapter 15 of *Lady Chatterley* the lovers celebrate their own May rites, dancing dithyrambically in the green rain of Wragby Wood, copulating on the forest floor, and ceremonially adorning their naked bodies with flowers before they stage the "wedding" (*LCL* 274) of "John Thomas" and

"Lady Jane." These flowery nuptials set amid the newly blossoming forest emulate in many ways the archetypal Sacred Marriage ceremonies which involved a male demi-god representing the sun or generative force in nature being married to a priestess who personified the Earth or Mother-Goddess, a union intended to ensure the revival of nature by means of homeopathic magic (*GB* 161–69). The Sacred Marriage, the *hieros gamos*, of opposites is memorialized in many of the myths delineated in *The Golden Bough*, and Frazer discerns a faded image of this Sacred Marriage lingering in pagan May Day festivals wherein leaf-clad or flower-decked mummers — the King and Queen of May — joined in a mock marriage (*GB* 175). Mellors and Connie, as they decorate each other's body with oak-sprays, bluebells, hyacinths, forget-me-nots, and other flora, bear obvious resemblance to those ancient flower-clad mummers of the vegetative spirits, and their playful wedding of John Thomas and Lady Jane clearly mimes the ceremonial marriages of the reciprocal powers of nature that formed part of the old fertility rituals.

Lawrence's complaint that post-Socratic men have lost their "magic connection" with "the wheeling sun and the nodding earth" (*PII* 504) is answered, in a fashion, in the action of the lovers in *Lady Chatterley*. Mellors's final letter strongly suggests that at least he and Connie have reestablished their own connection with the natural fertility cycle. Their affair had begun in February and had extended through late summer, the period of cyclic rebirth, growth and fruition in nature, and now, at the time Mellors writes his September 29 letter to Connie, he is engaged in harvesting hay and oats on a Midlands farm, and his mistress is in Scotland, pregnant. They will remain separated "till spring [is] in, till the baby [is] born," but he promises her, "we'll be together next year" (*LCL* 360, 364). He relates their union to the generative duality of Sun-god and Earth-Mother when he writes: "We fucked a flame into being. Even the flowers are fucked into being between the sun and the earth. But it's a delicate thing, and takes patience and the long pause" (*LCL* 364). This "long pause" between conception and birth is noted in the dying god myth. Adonis, Attis, Tammuz, Osiris all die in winter; the female principle survives dormant and waiting to be renewed in the spring by the revived male. During the period of gestation, the male principle is unnecessary to the female and to the new life within her. This same archetype is expressed at the close of *The Escaped Cock*, where the man animates new life in the priestess and then bids her goodbye, promising as he does to "come again" in spring even as "the suns come back in their seasons" (*EC* 61). In the end, Lawrence's story of new life and resurrection in *Lady Chatterley's Lover* follows the archetypal pattern, as his protagonists are submersed finally into the vast, mysterious rhythm of nature's eternal cycle of the seasons. Their union thus exemplifies the "true phallic marriage . . . set again in relationship to . . . the old pagan rhythm of cosmic ritual" that he speaks of in the "A Propos" essay (*PII* 509), and it is in such that he envisions the regeneration not only of his two lovers in *Lady Chatterley* but of all England.

iii

Several of Lawrence's most interesting late nonfiction works — "Pan in America" (1924), *Etruscan Places* (1927), "A Propos of *Lady Chatterley's Lover*" (1929), *Apocalypse* (1929), and the introduction to Frederick Carter's *The Dragon of the Apocalypse* (1930) — bear importantly on *Lady Chatterley*, in the way they give Lawrence's "emotional beliefs which perhaps are necessary as a background" to the novel (*PII* 514), and particularly in the way they illuminate his use in the story of primitive myth and ritual elements. There is, for example, the following passage from "A Propos" which expresses Lawrence's interest in the myths of the year gods, and, in so doing, provides strong support for my belief that he had the oriental nature cults in mind as he wrote the novel:

> "Knowledge" has killed the sun, making it a ball of gas, with spots: "knowledge" has killed the moon, it is a dead little earth . . . ; the machine has killed the earth for us. . . . How, out of all this, are we to get back the grand orbs of the soul's heavens, that fill us with unspeakable joy? How are we to get back Apollo, and Attis, Demeter, Persephone, and the halls of Dis? . . .
>
> We've got to get them back, for they are the world our soul, our greater consciousness, lives in.
>
> [*PII* 511].

Because the "world of reason and science" has so caused men to perceive nature only in terms of its "*apartness*" from their own lives, Lawrence asserts, the world has come to seem "dry and sterile," and he consequently argues that men must change, "*must* get back into . . . vivid and nourishing relation to the . . . universe," and this "means a return to ancient forms," forms from "a long way" back, "before Plato," before man's three-thousand-year "excursion into ideals, bodilessness, and tragedy," before men had "abstracted the universe into Matter and Force" (*PII* 511–12, 516). In all the late essays I have mentioned, Lawrence praises the way ancient peoples had led their lives untainted by the sort of "thought-forms" proposed in the *Dialogues*, the way primitive men had perceived the wonder of life directly through their senses. But neither in these essays nor in *Lady Chatterley* does the author mean to suggest that ancient fertility cults somehow hold the clue to the salvation of the modern Western world, or that men should revert to the practice of pagan rituals. As Lawrence states in one of his Melville essays, "We can't go back to the savages[,] . . . back towards their . . . uncreate mind." Yet, he does urge his contemporaries to make "a great swerve in our onward-going life-course now, to gather up again the savage mysteries" (*SCAL* 137–38) — by which he means man's incorporating primitive modes of perception into the modern consciousness.

In his introduction to *The Dragon of the Apocalypse* Lawrence praises the Chaldeans for the direct, intuitive way they had "*experienced*" the sun, moon, stars, and planets, for the way they had projected themselves sympathetically into "the life of the heavens." Acknowledging that modern men cannot "*experience*" the same Babylonian cosmos, he argues that they can "discover a new vision in harmony with the memories of old. . . . far-off experiences that lie within us. So long as we are not deadened or drossy, memories of Chaldean experience still live within us, at great depths, and can vivify our impulses in a new direction, once we awaken them" (*P* 298, 301). Such an awakening will come, he insists, through "imaginative experience" — a phrase that figures importantly not only in this essay on *The Dragon of the Apocalypse* but also in relation to Lawrence's theme in *Lady Chatterley*.[9] Discussing Carter's book, Lawrence again delineates man's "two ways of knowing," as he contrasts *astronomy* — man's calculated scientific measuring of space, with *astrology* — a more intuitive reading of celestial dynamics. Predictably, he comes down hard in favor of the latter. The "astronomist," he contends, diminishes the bodies of the universe by rendering them into mere "thought-forms that have no sensual reality" for man, while the astrologer's interpretation of the ancient zodiacal heavens contrastingly allows man to fantasize a correspondence between his own life and that of the Macrocosm, and affords "a real release of the imagination [which] renews our strength and our vitality" (*P* 298–300, 294). Such a "fantasy" of our direct relation to the sun, moon, stars, and various heavenly bodies "enhances our life" and affords a valuable "extension of [our] being," and it is this that Lawrence has in mind when in "A Propos" he urges men "to get back the grand orbs of the soul's heavens" by again seeking the sun-god Apollo, the year gods Attis, Demeter, and Persephone, and "the halls of Dis" (referring to Pluto's realm). By seeking these old nature gods through the *imagination*, ancient men had established a vital sense of rapport with the turning year, and Lawrence seeks to have modern men make a similar sort of sympathetic extension to nature, to recapture through "imaginative experience" their own magic correspondence with nature and thereby achieve a needed psychic rebirth.

Clifford Chatterley will never experience any such imaginative "extension of . . . [his] being" to the circumambient natural world, and, consequently, neither can he experience the genuine sort of psychic revitalization that Connie and her lover achieve. Like the "mechanized human being" mentioned at the end of "Pan in America," Clifford has "his windows nailed up, or bricked in," as he limits his perception to what his eyes and mind alone register and denies by strength of will what his other senses or intuitive knowledge could bring to his consciousness. His enthusiasm for Plato, Racine, Alfred North Whitehead,[10] and the "technical science of industry" (*LCL* 126) marks him as an exemplar of that "world of reason and science" condemned in "A Propos"; his is clearly the modern "mechanical conquered universe" (*P* 31) wherein the individual suffers severe "*apartness*" from all nature. He never touches what Lawrence calls "the spirit of the wood" (*LCL* 21) — to the baronet, the forest is mere "property" to be protected from trespass, and like others among his English ruling class, he views a coal-mine and its attendant machinery as a bit of "first-rate landscape gardening" (*LCL* 187). As the story progresses, he insulates himself more and more into mechanisms — industrial engines, his motorized wheelchair, his typewriter, his mechanical horn, his radio. He comes at last to prefer the wireless to having his cronies visit Wragby. His lone tie with those "mental-lifers," at any rate, is a certain "mental friction" (*LCL* 40), and he is "cut off" as well from the miners he employs. Further, and most significantly, "the sex part" of marriage "did not mean much to him" even in the short time he and his wife were physically intimate, before he left for the war (thus his sterility and lack of vital life thereafter are not simply the inevitable result of his war wound), and he and Connie remain "utterly out of touch" (*LCL* 10, 18). Like those "plucked apples" Dukes mentions when condemning the "mental life," Clifford lacks all "organic connection" with life.

Connie establishes her own connection with "the spirit of the wood," with "the substantial and vital world," by leaving Clifford, "the most modern of modern voices," and uniting with the gamekeeper, recognized on his initial appearance in the story as a man of "the old style" (*LCL* 20, 57, 51). He proves to be "old style" in more than just his green velveteens and gaiters. Writing to Connie, Mellors argues that "the mass" of men should "be forever pagan" — that they should "learn to be naked and handsome" and to "dance the old group dances" again; that they should acknowledge "the great god Pan" as their "only god . . . forever" (*LCL* 363). And while Clifford professes his faith in scientific materialism, in a world where Wellsian "men . . . like gods" (*LCL* 126)[11] can subjugate Matter to mankind's great benefit, Mellors damns "the industrial epoch" as a "black mistake" and longs to "wipe the machines off the face of the earth again" so that men could "go back" to a simpler, more primitive existence (*LCL* 263–65).

Unlike Clifford, Mellors and Connie remain receptive to the forces by which they can be "broken open again" to "Life" (*LCL* 138), and consequently experience through the "life of the body" (*LCL* 282) that "release of the imagination" through which Lawrence believed men could gain "extension of . . . being" and communion with "another vital world" (*P* 294). By daring to "let go everything . . . and be gone in the flood" (*LCL* 207) of sensuality, in the flow of that "blood consciousness"

Lawrence had first championed after reading *The Golden Bough*, the two lovers discover a new sense of connection with the natural phenomena of the forest and with the numinous world beyond (Mellors imagines a "pentecost flame" they have created between them, and Connie imagines the awakening in her "guts" of "whatever God there is" [*LCL* 364, 282]).

Such a transcendent sense of man's "live relatedness" to god and nature, to "the Oversoul, the Allness of everything," was commonplace among men in the ancient "Pan-world," Lawrence observes in "Pan in America" (*P* 22–31). In those "old days," before human beings had "got too much separated off from the universe," men had known "with a pantheistic sensuality that the tree has its own life." Such ancient sensibility Lawrence illustrates directly in *Lady Chatterley*, notably in the scene in which Connie experiences the "erect, alive" pine tree that rises up and sways against her with its "curious life" on the March day when she has ventured, like "Persephone . . . out of hell," away from Wragby Hall. Sitting with her back against that phallic pine, she seems "to get into the current of her own proper destiny" (*LCL* 99). Like men in the old Pan-world who knew that "the vast trees hummed with energy" (*P* 23), Connie later stands amid the dark trees of Wragby Wood, just before her second sexual encounter with Mellors, and perceives that "the green things on earth seemed to hum with greenness" (*LCL* 144). During the ensuing lovemaking, she feels "a new nakedness emerging," as do the "half-open buds, half-unsheathed flowers" (*LCL* 148, 144) which surround her there, and later, after her third sexual union with the keeper, she rapturously perceives herself to be "like a forest . . . [in] spring, moving into bud" (*LCL* 163). On these and other occasions, Connie seems to be in some obvious sort of primal sympathy with the wild things of the wood, and often nature itself seems to respond animistically to the two lovers' actions. For instance, as Connie runs home in the twilight after the sex act during which she has been "born: a woman," it is said that "the world seemed a dream; the trees in the park seemed bulging and surging at anchor on a tide, and the heave of the slope to the house was alive" (*LCL* 208, 213). Some sort of living vibration seems to pass here between Connie and nature, a vibration that is at the heart of Lawrence's theme in *Lady Chatterley*. Clearly Lawrence means in the novel, in the later scenes set in Wragby Wood, to recreate the ancient sort of "living universe of Pan" which he had earlier described in "Pan in America."

iv

Writing to Frederick Carter in 1929, Lawrence declared, "I very much want to put into the world again the big old pagan vision" (*CL* 1205), and it is obvious that he is, with *Lady Chatterley*, making an effort to do that, to restore that vision, and to suggest something about those "ancient forms" that he felt needed retrieving in order for men to reestablish what Dukes calls "the organic connection" with life. Through the story of the two woodland lovers, Lawrence is making an effort to illustrate the sort of reaccommodation with the spirit of the ancients— with their animistic conception of an earth that was alive and sacred, and especially with their attitude toward sexuality—that he so often advocates in the essays written over the last half dozen years of his life. The many echoes of a pagan past in the novel serve as indices of Lawrence's meaning as they create suggestions of a magic, vital ancient world starkly and ironically contrasted to the profane and meaningless life of modern man depicted in many parts of the novel. Despite Mellors's warning that "there's a bad time coming" for mankind (*LCL* 363), *Lady Chatterley's Lover* is not a chronicle of despair; more than anything else, what saves it from being such are those very resonances of ancient myth and ritual that I have been tracing here. Lawrence clearly saw, in the "old pagan vision," viable possibilities for a reborn world.

I wish to thank the University of Delaware for giving me a General University Research Grant that allowed me to spend time working on this and several related essays.

Notes

1. Lawrence's first reading of *The Golden Bough* is acknowledged in a December 1915 letter to Bertrand Russell—see *The Collected Letters of D. H. Lawrence*, ed. Harry T. Moore (New York: Viking Press, 1962), 1:393. His 1922 re-reading of *The Golden Bough* is noted in Edward Nehls, *D. H. Lawrence: A Composite Biography* (Madison: University of Wisconsin Press, 1958), 2:345.

2. Lawrence's works are cited parenthetically in my text by abbreviated title and page numbers in the following editions:

CL   *The Collected Letters of D. H. Lawrence*, 2 vols., ed. Harry T. Moore (New York: Viking Press, 1962).

EC   *The Escaped Cock*, ed. Gerald M. Lacy (Los Angeles: Black Sparrow Press, 1978).

LCL   *Lady Chatterley's Lover* (New York: Grove Press, 1959).

P   *Phoenix: The Posthumous Papers of D. H. Lawrence*, ed. Edward D. McDonald (New York: Penguin Books, 1978).

PII   *Phoenix II: Uncollected, Unpublished, and Other Prose Works by D. H. Lawrence*, ed. Warren Roberts and Harry T. Moore (New York: Penguin Books, 1978).

SCAL   *Studies in Classic American Literature* (New York: Viking Press, 1971).

3. "Frazer's drama of the dying and reviving god and his wife-mother-lover" is "one of Lawrence's major leit-motivs" in his short stories, Vickery argues in "Myth and Ritual in the Shorter Fiction of D. H. Lawrence," *Modern Fiction Studies* 5 (Spring 1959):65. Vickery similarly traces influences of *The Golden Bough* on one of Lawrence's longer fictions in "*The Plumed Serpent* and the Reviving God," *Journal of Modern Literature*, 2 (November 1972):505–32.

4. Sir James George Frazer, *The Golden Bough: A Study in Magic and Religion*,

"Abridged Edition" (New York: Macmillan Company, 1951), 456–62. Subsequent references to this one-volume edition of *The Golden Bough* are cited parenthetically in my text by the abbreviation *GB* and the pertinent page number(s).

5. On that occasion (in chapter 8), Connie first thinks of the phrase "Pale beyond porch and portal," which forms part of line 49 of Swinburne's "The Garden of Proserpine"; shortly thereafter she recalls the line "the world has grown pale with thy breath," as Lawrence has her misquote part of line 35 of Swinburne's "Hymn to Proserpine," which should read: "the world has grown *gray from* thy breath."

6. In a March 1928 letter to Witter Bynner, Lawrence contrasts "the phallic reality" against "the non-phallic cerebration unrealities" (*CL* 1046).

7. In the novel's second version, published in 1972 as *John Thomas and Lady Jane* (New York: Viking Press), the suggestion of the keeper's being "wounded" sexually is even more explicit: he is there described as a "maimed human being" (87) whose "phallic nature . . . had been hurt" (232) and whose phallus "had always been wounded" (233).

8. Erich Neumann, *The Great Mother: An Analysis of the Archetype*, tr. Ralph Manheim (Princeton, N.J.: Princeton University Press, 1974), 168.

9. In " 'The Big Old Pagan Vision': The Letters of D. H. Lawrence to Frederick Carter," *Library Chronicle of the University of Texas at Austin*, n.s. 34 (1986):39–51, Leonora Woodman describes the strong interests—especially those concerning astrology, the value of primitive man's spiritual vision, and the great need for an imaginative "reintegration of microcosm and macrocosm" that would revivify modern life—shared by Lawrence and the British mystic and artist. Lawrence's letters to Carter, Woodman observes, "present a number of ideas that form the thematic center of *The Plumed Serpent*, *Etruscan Places*, *The Escaped Cock*, and *Apocalypse*—important works of Lawrence's later years" (51), but she fails to mention how the same ideas just as profoundly inform *Lady Chatterley's Lover*.

10. I have commented on Lawrence's allusions to Plato, Racine, and Whitehead in "Literary Allusions in *Lady Chatterley's Lover*," in *D. H. Lawrence's "Lady": A New Look at "Lady Chatterley's Lover*," ed. Michael Squires and Dennis Jackson (Athens, Ga.: University of Georgia Press, 1985), 170–96.

11. Lawrence's allusions to H. G. Wells's utopian romance *Men Like Gods* are noted in my article, "Literary Allusions in *Lady Chatterley's Lover*," 190–91, 196n.20.

On the Short Fiction

D. H. Lawrence's "Odour
of Chrysanthemums":
The Three Endings   Mara Kalnins*

"I have just finished getting together a book of short stories. Lord, how I've worked again at these stories — most of them — forging them up. They're good, I think"[1] wrote Lawrence in July 1914 about his revision of *The Prussian Officer* tales, and "it's great — so new, so really a stratum deeper than I think anybody has ever gone"[2] of his novel writing in the crucial period after *Sons and Lovers*. As the *Collected Letters* and other sources reveal,[3] this was a period of intense creative activity, when Lawrence was experimenting with language and style and feeling his imaginative vision, his insight into human nature, and his artistic powers unfolding with great rapidity. *The Prussian Officer* came out in December 1914, only a few months before the completion of *The Rainbow*,[4] and as J. C. F. Littlewood has shown in his article[5] many of the tales that were revised between the summers of 1913 and 1914 are much closer to the style and *Weltanschauung* of *The Rainbow* than to the work of Lawrence's youth. A comparative study of the original and revised versions of the tales offers insight into the development of Lawrence's writing at this time and yields important critical information about that development. This is particularly true of one of the earliest tales, "Odour of Chrysanthemums," which underwent several revisions between 1910 and 1914.[6]

The writing of this tale, and the mutations it passed through, have been fully described in an article by J. T. Boulton[7] but it is an article that contains a fundamental critical misconception about the ending of the tale and the nature of Elizabeth Bates' tragedy. Professor Boulton describes the stages of the story's composition, pointing out the superiority of the 1911 version (published in *The English Review* for June 1911)[8] over the early 1910 text (the proof sheets of which are published after his article) and argues that the corrections and changes reveal Lawrence's growing critical discrimination in the more idiomatic language of the later version, its greater economy of description and dialogue, and the paring away of superfluous detail in the early part of the tale to focus more sharply on the

*Reprinted from *Studies in Short Fiction* 13 (1976):471–79, by permission of the journal and the author.

central tragedy of the miner's death. But his evaluation of the revisions sees them as progressive stages "to embodying the adult emotion of maternal love as a unifying principle for the entire action"[9] and this surely is to misunderstand the central idea behind the story. A comparison of the three very different endings to the 1910, 1911 and 1914 "Chrysanthemums" stories reveals, on the contrary, the striking advances in Lawrence's understanding of Elizabeth's reaction to her husband's death, from the brief statement of her newly awakened and essentially maternal love for him in the first text to the profound and complex analysis in the third of her recognition of the meaning of death, her realisation of her husband's alienation from her even in life and her acute sense of isolation, presented through a close imaginative following of her train of thought and feeling in language significantly similar to that of *The Rainbow*. It is worth quoting extensively from the conclusions to the three texts for the purposes of discussing these endings and of showing how Lawrence's growing understanding of and identification with Elizabeth's experience altered his approach and style as he sought to express that understanding with greater precision in each succeeding version.

The feeling of maternal love for the miner is certainly strong in the 1910 version where old Mrs. Bates and Elizabeth jealously seek to establish their respective claims on the dead man as they lay out his body — "so heavy, and helpless, more helpless than a baby, poor dear" (1910, p. 44) — and in their rivalry the victory is old Mrs. Bates': "He's my lad again now, Lizzie" (1910, p. 43).

> When they rose and looked at him lying naked in the beauty of death, the women experienced suddenly the same feeling; that of motherhood, mixed with some primeval awe. But the pitiful mother-feeling prevailed. Elizabeth knelt down and put her arms round him, and laid her cheek on his breast. His mother had his face between her hands again and was murmuring and sobbing. Elizabeth touched him and kissed him with her cheek and her lips. Then suddenly she felt jealous that the old woman had his face.
>
> (1910, p. 42)

Although the corresponding passage in the 1911 version is virtually identical, the element of maternal love in the story is much diminished; for example, only the miner's dead inertness is compared to that of "a baby fallen heavily asleep" (p. 433). The focus has shifted to the wife in Lawrence's analysis of Elizabeth's marriage, and in Elizabeth's recognition that "The great episode of her life was closed with him" the role of the mother is further reduced.

> She saw the great episode of her life closed with him, and grief was a passion. The old mother was hushed in awe. She, the elder, less honourable woman, had said: "She drives him to it, she makes him ten thousand times worse." But now the old mother bowed down in respect

for the wife. As the passion of Elizabeth's grief grew more, the old woman shrank and tried to avoid it.

(1911, p. 433)

"I can only write what I feel pretty strongly about: and that, at present, is the relation between men and women."[10] Lawrence's letter to Edward Garnett in 1913 points to the changing direction of his interest in his fiction, and the final version of "Chrysanthemums" centres firmly on the failed marriage relationship of the miner and his wife, and surely reveals no trace of maternal pity for her husband in Elizabeth as she confronts death, recognises its finality and acknowledges her separation from the dead man.

> When they arose, saw him lying in the naïve dignity of death, the women stood arrested in fear and respect. For a few moments they remained still, looking down, the old mother whimpering. Elizabeth felt countermanded. She saw him, how utterly inviolable he lay in himself. She had nothing to do with him. She could not accept it. Stooping, she laid her hand on him, in claim. He was still warm, for the mine was hot where he had died. His mother had his face between her hands, and was murmuring incoherently. The old tears fell in succession as drops from wet leaves; the mother was not weeping, merely her tears flowed. Elizabeth embraced the body of her husband, with cheek and lips. She seemed to be listening, inquiring, trying to get some connexion. But she could not. She was driven away. He was impregnable. (1914, p. 221. Page numbers refer to *The Prussian Officer*, Penguin edition)

There is a remarkable resemblance between this paragraph and the passage in *The Rainbow* where Tom Brangwen has been brought home drowned. In the story, as in the novel, Lawrence has sought to describe the fact of experiencing something beyond the rational understanding of the individual human consciousness and his profound insight into the effect of death on both Elizabeth and Lydia is conveyed in the unusual and idiosyncratic language characteristic of his mature writing, of the style we recognise as "Laurentian" and which this article will discuss later.

> There, it looked still and grand. He was perfectly calm in death, and, now he was laid in line, inviolable, unapproachable. To Anna, he was the majesty of the inaccessible male, the majesty of death. It made her still and awe-stricken, almost glad.
>
> Lydia Brangwen, the mother, also came and saw the impressive, inviolable body of the dead man. She went pale, seeing death. He was beyond change or knowledge, absolute, laid in line with the infinite. What had she to do with him? He was a majestic Abstraction, made visible now for a moment, inviolate, absolute. And who could lay claim to him, who could speak of him, of the him who was revealed in the stripped moment of transit from life into death? Neither the living nor

the dead could claim him, he was both the one and the other, inviolable, inaccessibly himself.

(*The Rainbow*, pp. 250–251, Penguin)

The three "Chrysanthemums" endings, beginning with the sentence "Elizabeth looked up" reveal Lawrence's progressively surer and more complete knowledge of Elizabeth's experience as well as his growing command over the resources of style and language. The 1910 proof sheets end with this paragraph presenting Elizabeth's idealisation of her dead husband as the pure young lover of her early marriage.

> Elizabeth, who had sobbed herself weary, looked up. Then she put her arms round him, and kissed him again on the smooth ripples below the breasts, and held him to her. She loved him very much now — so beautiful, and gentle, and helpless. He must have suffered! What must he have suffered! Her tears started hot again. Ah, she was so sorry, sorrier than she could ever tell. She was sorry for him, that he had suffered so, and got lost in the dark places of death. But the poignancy of her grief was that she loved him again — ah, so much! She did not want him to wake up, she did not want him to speak. She had him again, now, and it was Death which had brought him. She kissed him, so that she might kiss Death which had taken the ugly things from him. Think how he might have come home — not white and beautiful, gently smiling . . . Ugly, befouled, with hateful words on an evil breath, reeking with disgust. She loved him so much now; her life was mended again, and her faith looked up with a smile; he had come home to her, beautiful. How she had loathed him! It was strange he could have been such as he had been. How wise of death to be so silent! If he spoke, even now, her anger and her scorn would lift their heads like fire. He would not speak — no, just gently smile, with wide eyes. She was sorry to have to disturb him to put on his shirt — but she must, he could not lie like that. The shirt was aired by now. But it would be cruel hard work to get him into it. He was so heavy, and helpless, more helpless than a baby, poor dear! — and so beautiful.

(1910, p. 44)

Lawrence attempts to convey the only half-articulate thoughts in Elizabeth's consciousness to give the reader the valuable illusion of close access to her mind — "Think how he might have come home — not white and beautiful, gently smiling . . . Ugly, befouled, with hateful words on an evil breath, reeking with disgust" — but the passage is flawed by the stilted personifications of death, the unidiomatic quality of much of the writing — "her anger and her scorn would lift their heads like fire" — and the sentimental tone — "her faith looked up with a smile" — which brings the conclusion dangerously close to bathos. Lawrence does not analyse the failure of Elizabeth's marriage which gives depth to the later story's tragedy. When he revised the proof sheets for the 1911 publication (possibly at the suggestion of Austin Harrison, then editor of *The English Review*),[11] he condensed the story, extensively revised it for the better, and completely rewrote the ending in accordance with his changing notions of character presentation, as explained to his fiancé Louie Burrows: "It has taken me such a long long time to write these last two pages of the story. You have no idea how much delving it requires to get that deep into cause and effect."[12] But in his wish to establish the "cause and effect" of the failed marriage and perhaps in his anxiety that the reading public should not miss the moral in the story's tragedy, Lawrence inserted a long homily on the evils of the public house in a speech which destroys what might have been a successful piece of objective narrative by forcing the writer's own beliefs on the reader.

Elizabeth looked up. The man's mouth was fallen back, slightly open under the cover of the moustache. The eyes, half shut, did not show glazed by the small candlelight. His wife looked at him. He seemed to be dreaming back, half awake. Life with its smoky burning gone from him, had left a purity and a candour like an adolescent's moulded upon his reverie. His intrinsic beauty was evident now. She had not been mistaken in him, as often she had bitterly confessed to herself she was. The beauty of his youth, of his eighteen years, of the time when life had settled on him, as in adolescence it settles on youth, bringing a mission to fulfill and equipment therefor, this beauty shone almost unstained again. It was this adolescent "he," the young man looking round to see which way, that Elizabeth had loved. He had come from the discipleship of youth, through the Pentecost of adolescence, pledged to keep with honour his own individuality, to be steadily and unquench-ably himself, electing his own masters and serving them till the wages were won. He betrayed himself in his search for amusement. Let Education teach us to amuse ourselves, necessity will train us to work. Once out of the pit, there was nothing to interest this man. He sought the public-house, where, by paying the price of his own integrity, he found amusement; destroying the clamours for activity, because he knew not what form the activities might take. The miner turned miscreant to himself, easing the ache of dissatisfaction by destroying the part of him which ached. Little by little the recreant maimed and destroyed himself.

It was this recreant his wife had hated so bitterly, had fought against so strenuously. She had strove, all the years of his falling off, had strove with all her force to save the man she had known new-bucklered with beauty and strength. In a wild and bloody passion she fought the recreant. Now this lay killed, the clean young knight was brought home to her. Elizabeth bowed her head upon the body and wept.

She put her arms round him, kissed the smooth ripples below his breasts, bowed her forehead on him in submission. Faithful to her deeper sense of honour, she uttered no word of sorrow in her heart. Upright in soul are women, however they bow the swerving body. She owned the beauty of the blow.

And all the while her heart was bursting with grief and pity for him. What had he suffered? What stretch of horror for this helpless man! She wept herself almost in agony. She had not been able to help him. Never again would she be able to help him. It was grief unutterable to think that now all was over between them. Even if it were a case of meeting in the next world, he would not need her there; it would be different. She saw the great episode of her life closed with him and grief was a passion.

(1911, pp. 431–432).

Lawrence has avoided the sentimentality of the 1910 ending but this passage is trite, weak and didactic with its strained and laboured biblical similes, the unconvincing comparisons of the collier to a pure young knight, and the painfully smug, sweeping judgment "Upright in soul are women, however they bow the swerving body." The second ending then returns to Elizabeth's thoughts — "What had he suffered!" — but the wife does not submit herself to the experience of death nor to the self-knowledge it would have brought her. Lawrence must have been aware of the disunity of his second ending, for although he retained the rest of the 1911 text basically unchanged for *The Prussian Officer* volume, he completely re-wrote the conclusion, greatly expanding it, and grafted it onto the existing story. And it is this ending, with its remarkably intense and complex portrayal of Elizabeth's response to death and of what Lawrence later believed to be the importance of the individual's "passionate struggle into conscious being,"[13] that illustrates the immense advance in imaginative insight and the ability to transmit that insight in his fiction, to go as he did in the next phase of his *Rainbow* writing "so really a stratum deeper than I think anybody has ever gone."

If the reader will turn to the last three pages of this third version beginning with "Elizabeth looked up" (pp. 222–224) the nature and extent of Lawrence's development from the earlier endings will be clear. Here the deep and penetrating analysis of the disintegration of Elizabeth's normal consciousness in a moment of crisis exemplifies Lawrence's changing notions of "character" and his fascination with unexplored states of being, as he explained to Edward Garnett in the summer of 1914: "I don't so much care about what the woman *feels* — in the ordinary usage of the word . . . I only care about what the woman *is* — what she *is* — inhumanly, physiologically, materially — according to the use of the word: but for me, what she *is* as a phenomenon (or as presenting some greater, inhuman will), instead of what she feels according to the human conception."[14] The language of the "Chrysanthemums" passage foreshadows the original and idiosyncratic style of *The Rainbow*, the style that Lawrence created to describe sensations and emotions that the language of prose fiction had not previously evolved a vocabulary for describing. Consider such unusual formulations as "her soul died in her for fear" and "Her soul was torn from her body and stood apart" and how Elizabeth's pregnancy, only briefly mentioned in the earlier versions, becomes an integral part of her sense of dislocation: "the child within her was a weight apart from her," "In her womb was ice of fear" and "The child was like ice in her womb." The repetitive nature of the writing, merging Elizabeth's thoughts with the author's analysis, mirrors the incoherent workings of a mind under emotional stress — "How does one think when one is thinking passionately and with suffering? Not in words at all but in strange surges and cross-currents of emotion which are only half-rendered by words"[15] — and the organic, growing quality of the prose, reminiscent of the language of scripture, uses a balanced repetition and antithesis — "for his look was other than hers, his way was not her way" — to convey the essence of an experience that is indescribable, the shock of revelation in a woman's soul as she perceives and understands at last the meaning of death and of life ("The horror of the distance between them was almost too much for her — it was so infinite a gap she must look across"). Lawrence recognized this repetitive feature of his writing and later defended it as natural and appropriate, believing that "every natural crisis in emotion or passion or understanding comes from this pulsing, frictional to-and-fro, which works up to culmination"[16]; but the young writer of the 1910 and 1911 "Chrysan-themums" stories probably did not possess this insight and certainly did not reveal it in his early writing.

"My great religion is a belief in the blood, the flesh, as being wiser than the intellect"[17] stated Lawrence in the well-known letter to Ernest Collings in 1913. And it is against this new vision of and belief in marriage as the creative means to fulfillment that we must see the importance of Elizabeth's recognition of her failure: "She was a mother — but how awful she knew it now to have been a wife." The notion of separateness, what Lawrence called each person's "intrinsic otherness," the paradox of a physical relationship between a man and a woman in "such intimacy of embrace and such utter foreigness of contact" (*The Rainbow*, p. 48) and yet the "strange, inviolable completeness of the two of them" (*The Rainbow*, p. 47) in a creative and fulfilling relationship, are ideas which he first explored in *The Rainbow*. But the origin of these ideas, and the philosophy of life arising out of them, can also be seen in the revised stories of *The Prussian Officer* though, significantly, not in their early versions. The crucial response, or the failure to respond, to this otherness of being is central to many of the revised tales: to Emilie in "The Thorn in the Flesh" — "More than that, the man, the lover, Bachmann, who was he, what was he?" — to Louisa in "Daughters of the Vicar" — "What was he as he sat there in his pit-dirt?" — and to Elizabeth Bates — "What was that I have been living with?" And consider the striking similarity of theme and style between these passages which convey Elizabeth's full recognition of her failure and Lydia's recollection of her unsatisfactory first marriage with Lensky:

> Now he was dead, she knew how eternally he was apart from her, how eternally he had nothing more to do with her. She saw this episode of

her life closed. They had denied each other in life. Now he had withdrawn. An anguish came over her. It was finished then: it had become hopeless between them long before he died. Yet he had been her husband. But how little!

(1914, pp. 223–224)

She, Lydia Brangwen, was sorry for him now. He was dead — he had scarcely lived. He had never known her. He had lain with her, but he had never known her. He had never received what she could give him. He had gone away from her empty. So, he had never lived. So, he had died and passed away. Yet there had been strength and power in him.

(*The Rainbow*, p. 258)

After the completion of *Sons and Lovers* in 1912 when he began work on *The Sisters*, the novel that was to become *The Rainbow*, Lawrence recognized that his writing was changing: "I shall not write quite in that style any more. It's the end of my youthful period" and "I have to write differently . . . I am going through a transition stage myself."[18] The nature and direction of this "transition stage" is revealed in Lawrence's deeper perception of Elizabeth's experience and the greater artistic unity of the third "Chrysanthemums" ending as against those of the early versions. In its vision of the primacy of the marriage relationship and of each individual's "otherness," in its style and use of language to describe the critical states through which not only the mind but also the body pass in the conscious and unconscious interplay of emotions, perceptions and thoughts, the third ending belongs to the next stage of Lawrence's "struggle for verbal consciousness"[19] as he called it, to the exploration he was to make in *The Rainbow* of the human soul in the relations between men and women.

Notes

1. *Collected Letters*, ed. H. T. Moore (hereafter cited as *CL*), (London: Heineman, 1965) p. 287. See also pp. 213–215.

2. Ibid., p. 193.

3. Ibid., p. 183, p. 189, p. 200, p. 203.

4. Ibid., p. 327.

5. J. C. F. Littlewood, "D. H. Lawrence's Early Tales," *The Cambridge Quarterly*, 1 (Spring 1966), 107–124.

6. For the purposes of this article only the 1910 proof sheets, the 1911 story and the final version as it appeared in the 1914 volume of *The Prussian Officer* are discussed. For the various stages of the tale's revision see J. T. Boulton, *Lawrence in Love* (Nottingham, 1968), p. 52, p. 87, pp. 90–91, p. 93, and footnote (7) below.

7. J. T. Boulton, "D. H. Lawrence's *Odour of Chrysanthemums*: An Early Version," *Renaissance and Modern Studies*, 13 (1969) 4–48.

8. *The English Review*, 8 (June 1911), 415–433.

9. J. T. Boulton, "D. H. Lawrence's *Odour of Chrysanthemums*: An Early Version," p. 11.

10. *CL*, p. 200.

11. Cf. Boulton, *Lawrence in Love*, p. 87.

12. Ibid., p. 91.

13. "Foreword to Women in Love," *Phoenix II* (London: Heinemann, 1968), p. 276.

14. *CL*, p. 282.

15. *The First Lady Chatterley* (New York: Dial Press, 1944), p. 194.

16. *Phoenix II*, p. 276.

17. *CL*, p. 180.

18. Ibid., p. 205 and p. 263.

19. *Phoenix II*, p. 276.

D. H. Lawrence's "The Horse Dealer's Daughter": An Interpretation

Clyde de L. Ryals*

At first glance "The Horse Dealer's Daughter" seems not entirely satisfying: a doctor's rescue of a young lady from a murky pond and their subsequent realization of love for one another does not appear sufficiently motivated. Indeed, upon cursory reading the story, which dispenses with much of the realistic machinery employed in Lawrence's longer works of fiction, seems contrived. Yet when one studies the story closely one sees at work certain poetic devices which carry the story along obliquely and which force the realization that the characters and situations stand for more than themselves. The reader, in other words, becomes aware of the symbolic nature of the story, and ultimately it is to the symbolism — of psychic death and rebirth through love — that he responds. For "The Horse Dealer's Daughter" is, *inter alia*, a vivid presentation of what Jung calls the rebirth archetype.

The story opens with a family conclave: the three brothers are met to learn the fate of their sister, to ask, "Well, Mabel, and what are you going to do with yourself?" But we learn immediately that they, like jesting Pilate, aren't really interested in the answer, because each is interested only in himself. They are like animals concerned only with their own personal physical welfare. Each, in fact, is described as an animal: Joe, "sensual," stupid," "horsey," as "a subject animal"; Fred Henry, with a "coarse" mustache, as "an animal which controls"; and Malcolm, the baby of the family, as a young man "with a fresh, jaunty *museau*." They are like

*Reprinted from *Literature and Psychology* 12 (Spring 1962):39–43, by permission of the journal and the author.

the horses outside, whose movement shows "a massive, slumbrous strength, and a stupidity which held them in subjection."

Bestial by nature, they treat their sister as an animal. They characterize her visage as "bull-dog," and Fred Henry calls her the "sulkiest bitch that ever trod." She means no more to the three brothers than the bitch-terrier which lies on the hearth and to which Joe throws a bacon-rind, as a casual kindness; she is noticed from time to time simply because she is there.

As for Mabel herself, she is "impassive," "alone," and she takes no notice of them or what goes on around her. "They had talked at her and round her for so many years, that she hardly heard them at all." Her isolation is complete. The only love which had ever entered into her life was that for her father before he remarried and for her mother who had died when Mabel was fourteen. At twenty-seven she has nothing left, no one with whom she can communicate. Formerly, life was bearable because of her pride—"curious, sullen, animal pride," made possible by money: "Then, however brutal and coarse everything was, the sense of money had kept her proud, confident. The men might be foul-mouthed, the women in the kitchen might have bad reputations, her brothers might have illegitimate children. But so long as there was money, the girl felt herself established, and brutally proud, reserved." Now, however, there was an end to even that; for her "the end had come": "Mindless and persistent, she endured from day to day. Why should she think? Why should she answer anybody? It was enough that this was the end, and there was no way out. . . . This was at an end. She thought of nobody, not even of herself. Mindless and persistent, she seemed in a sort of ecstasy to be coming nearer to her fulfilment, her own glorification, approaching her dead mother, who was glorified." There can be no question that Mabel is dead, spiritually dead. Differing from her brothers (who too lack "inner freedom") only in knowing that she is dead, she exists in a living hell.

Lawrence's description of external detail in the first part of the story underscores this sense of defeat, sterility, and death. The family, seated around the "desolate" table, are gathered in a "dreary" room which "looked as if it were waiting to be done away with." The house itself appears almost uninhabited, and outside "sloping, dank, winter-dark fields stretched away on all sides." This is the landscape of hell, a psychological hell which is not allegorical but existential, the perfect setting for the human cut off from all sources of joy.

Into this situation comes Dr. Fergusson, who, because he is not part of the family and also because he is a doctor, seems at first an instrument of salvation. But we learn that he too is spiritually exhausted. A "mere hired assistant," he is "slave to the country-side," his life "nothing but work, drudgery." Like Mabel, he is almost completely isolated within himself; and the loss of the Pervins adds to his sense of aloneness: "Another resource would be lost to him, another place gone: the only company he cared for in the alien, ugly little town he was losing."

Dr. Fergusson is also physically ill, but his condition goes unregarded. Joe, in fact, jokes about his sickness, treating him almost in the same way that he treats his sister. The Pervins thus are a "resource" to him only in that they provide company of the same condition. It is as though the author were saying that hell is bad enough, but that hell in total isolation is unendurable. Appropriately, Fergusson speaks in terms of hell: "this is the devil's own," he says to Fred. Further he exclaims, "The devil" and "Miss you like hell," and characterizes the town as a "hellish hole." The infernal landscape is fully realized.

When we next meet Mabel she is in the churchyard at the grave of her mother. Here she felt "secure," "immune from the world," for "the life she followed here in the world was far less real than the world of death she inherited from her mother." Mabel takes great pains in cleaning and beautifying her mother's grave, performing this ritual "in a state bordering on pure happiness, as if in performing this task she came into a subtle, intimate connection with her mother." Here is an almost classic case of regression in the Freudian sense. Feeling herself rejected by her father in favor of his second wife, she retreats to the memory of her mother, to the time when she felt secure and perfectly adapted to her environment. Her only wish now is to regain that state of bliss — "her fulfilment, her own glorification" — which means that she must join her mother in death.

Passing along the churchyard, Fergusson sees her in this almost beatific state, and "it was like looking into another world," touching some "mystical element in him." Seeing her and meeting her eyes assume a strange power over him; for where previously he had felt weak and done for, life now comes back to him: "he felt delivered from his own fretted, daily self." The sense of escape from self is, however, but momentary. Too long has he lived in "this hellish hole," unable to feel or to think. Like Mabel, "why should he think or notice?" — the same question that Mabel only a few paragraphs prior had asked herself. Transport from this living death must attend some greater psychic shock, something, in Coleridge's words, to "startle this dull pain, and make it move and live."

Mabel's attempted suicide which follows and Fergusson's rescue of her are symbolic actions which have meaning on several different levels of significance. First of all, this part of the story is a careful working out of the rebirth archetype, embodying the rite of baptism, the purification and revivification by water. The descent into the pool is an example of the myth of the night-journey under the sea as described by Jung. The pond in which she seeks to drown herself contains "foul earthy water" smelling of "cold, rotten clay," which is repugnant to both the man and the woman, and which is symbolic of the repressed contents of the mind of neurotic persons. Jung calls such contents "slime out of the depths," using the same symbolism as Lawrence's story; but, says Jung, this slime contains not only "objectionable animal tendencies, but also germs of new possibilities of life."[1] Indeed, this ambivalent character in slimy things Lawrence seems to have felt when he wrote this story, for out of the slime comes for Mabel and Fergusson the possibility of a new life.

Secondly, this action is a mythological enactment of the desire to return to the maternal depths. It is well-known that the image of water is often fused with that of the mother. Freud, speaking of the symbolism of dreams, writes: "Birth is almost invariably represented by some reference to water: either we are falling into water or clambering out of it, saving someone from it or being saved by them; i.e., the relation between mother and child is symbolized."[2] In the case of "The Horse Dealer's Daughter" there is little need to consult Freud, for the author explicitly says that by drowning herself in the pond Mabel seeks to reunite herself with her mother.

Thirdly—and this point is closely related to the second—the drowning episode is a parody, probably conscious on Lawrence's part, of the birth of a child. It is indicative of this that Fergusson is made a doctor. He goes about "spreading his hands under the water and moving them round, trying to feel for her." He finally grasps her and pulls her to shore, where, like a doctor delivering a child, making the water come from her mouth, he works to restore her: "He did not have to work very long before he could feel the breathing begin again in her; she was breathing naturally. He worked a little longer. He could feel her live beneath his hands. . . . He wiped her face, wrapped her in his overcoat." Like a new-born baby, Mabel "was conscious in herself, but unconscious of her surroundings."

The last part of the story is concerned with the characters' responses to their experience. By drowning, Mabel had sought to quiet her frustration; but instead of physical death her descent into the pool had provided her with the germs of a new life. She is now willing to forget the self which had been so oppressive by recognizing the worth of something quite independent of self; in other words, she is ready for the acceptance of rebirth, by which her former condition is transcended, to use Jung's term, or glorified, to use Lawrence's. Realizing that she had been saved by Fergusson, an act which she recognizes as love, she looks at him "with flaring, humble eyes of transfiguration, triumphant in first possession," and she speaks to him "in strong transport, yearning and triumphant." Fergusson, on the other hand, had not entered the pool voluntarily; immersing himself in the cold water had been fearful and repellent, and the process of "glorification" is for him far more difficult at this point than it is for Mabel. He was "mortally afraid," began "to shudder like one sick," seemed "to be going dark in his mind"; "something stubborn in him could not give way." The process of birth is seemingly too painful. Here the roles become switched: from the delivered Mabel becomes the deliverer. Looking at her, he becomes quieter, "life came back in him, dark and unknowing." Her hands, like his formerly, draw him out of the darkness of self:

> Her hands were drawing him, drawing him down to her. He was afraid, even a little horrified . . . : his whole will was against his yielding. It was horrible. . . . He had a horror of yielding to her. Yet something in him ached also. . . . He could not bear the touch of her eye's question upon him, and the look of death behind the question.

And so, lifted by her out of the frustrated self, he now (like the Ancient Mariner who blesses the water-snakes which he had formerly found repellent) yields to that which was previously repugnant: "his heart seemed to burn and melt away in his breast"; Fergusson "had crossed over the gulf to her, and all that he had left behind had shrivelled and become void."

At the end we find the two characters brought back to the real world, where he must go to surgery and she must make tea. Shy of each other, they are not quite adapted to their new roles and their new situation. But one thing they are certain of: they know that something of transcendent importance has happened to them and that they will never be the same again.

Structurally the story employs the "frame effect" which F. R. Leavis has spoken of in connection with another of Lawrence's stories.[3] It begins in the everyday world of common things and it ends in the same way; but the essential drama of the story is contained in the middle section, which leaves the world of external reality for the world of inner consciousness. The frame-effect thus emphasizes the shift from an outer circle of things, or non-self, to a shrunken core of ego, which, transformed and enlarged by its sympathies, grows once again to participate in a larger circle of experience.

The movement of the story from periphery to center back to periphery is underscored by the light imagery. At the beginning the predominant image is darkness and this is increasingly intensified until Mabel is submerged in the pool. When Fergusson enters the water, the light imagery is momentarily suspended: from the point where he enters the pool until he drags her out to land there is no image of light or darkness for three paragraphs. Upon their return to the house a new image is introduced with the sentence "But the fire was burning in the grate," and this image is further expanded in the words "burning" and "flame." The unmeaningful phenomenal world is thus symbolized by darkness, which is finally cancelled out by the dissolution of the isolated ego into pure abstractedness; and the return of the transformed self to reality is indicated by the image of fire, suggestive of purification and the establishment of organic bonds.

The whole rhythm of the story, indeed its poetic texture, directs the attention away from conventional characterization to concern with a special state of being and awareness. As Lawrence wrote to Edward Garnett in reference to *The Rainbow*, one must not look for "the old stable ego of the character" in his fiction: "There is another *ego*, according to whose action the individual is unrecognisable, and passes through, as it were, allotropic states which it needs a deeper sense than any we've been used to exercise, to discover are the states of the same single radically unchanged element."[4] Clearly Lawrence's concern in "The Horse Dealer's Daughter" is with substitution of a new way of feeling and thinking for an old one. Regarded as a presentation of the rebirth archetype, the story sums up everything Lawrence had to say about love as the vital spark of life. For what happens when the doctor saves Mabel from "death by water" is a psychic rebirth for both of them — a rebirth, Lawrence seems to say throughout his fiction, which must come to all men and women unless they are to dry up in a living death.

Notes

1. *Contributions to Analytical Psychology*, trans. H. G. and C. F. Baynes (London, 1928), pp. 39–40. I do not discuss the rebirth archetype at greater length since its application to literature has been made so well-known by Maud Bodkin in her *Archetypal Patterns in Poetry* (London, 1934).

2. *A General Introduction to Psychoanalysis*, trans. Joan Riviere (Garden City, N.Y., 1943), p. 137.

3. *D. H. Lawrence: Novelist* (London, 1955), p. 56.

4. D. H. Lawrence, *Selected Literary Criticism*, ed. Anthony Beal (New York, 1956), p. 18.

The Defeat of Feminism: D. H. Lawrence's *The Fox* and "The Woman Who Rode Away"

R. P. Draper*

The Fox and "The Woman Who Rode Away," tales about the defeat of woman's independence, are part of Lawrence's answer to the suffragettes. Already in *Sons and Lovers* he had shown a militant feminist, Clara Dawes, up in arms against the tyranny of man when what she really wants, as Paul Morel conveniently discovers, is to be reunited with her husband. More seriously, the histories of Mrs. Morel and Miriam reflect the influence of strong-willed, high-minded women who think they know as well as a man himself what is good for him. What Lawrence thought of such women in later life, when his sympathy for his mother had almost

*Reprinted from *Studies in Short Fiction* 3 (Winter 1966):186–98, by permission of the journal and the author.

turned sour, is summed up in the essay "Women Are So Cocksure": "As sure as a woman has the whip-hand over her destiny and the destinies of those near her, so sure will she make a mess of her own destiny, and a muddle of the others."

In *The Rainbow* and *Women in Love* his theme is similar—"woman becoming individual, self-responsible, taking her own initiative" (letter of 22 April 1914)—although the treatment is far more sympathetic and intelligently balanced. Despite his anti-feminist attitude, Lawrence possessed a markedly feminine temperament; and this, aided by a quite considerable amount of self-identification with the character of Ursula, gives a quality of inwardness and sympathetic understanding to his presentation of the modern, independent-minded woman in these two novels. *The Fox* and "The Woman Who Rode Away" are undeniably inferior in this respect. They come much nearer to exemplifying the cruder attitude of "Women Are So Cocksure." But they also have two very important compensating qualities. Firstly, we see the defeat of woman as a recovery of her lost self, which, even though it is associated with a distorting simplification of the roles of male and female, releases Lawrence's own feminine awareness in passages of great visionary power. Secondly, the reactionary view of woman which informs these two stories is pushed to an unacceptable extreme, and in the process the extravagances and vindictive motivation which such a view implies are brought out into the open. This has unpleasant consequences but is a valuable, and fundamentally healthy, process. It is an immersion in the destructive element from which self-knowledge becomes at least a possibility.

The Fox, started in 1918 and finished in Taormina in 1921, belongs to the period at the end of the First World War. During the war the suffragette movement was in abeyance, but the shortage of men on the home front was giving far more effective support to the feminist cause than any of the previous agitations had done. The government called upon more and more women to work like men in factories and on the land, to dress like men, to behave like men. Other stories besides *The Fox* show Lawrence's interest in all this. "Tickets, Please," which first appeared in the *Strand* (April 1919), is a story about girls who replaced men tram-conductors and their relationship with a philandering ticket inspector, aptly named John Thomas Raynor—"always called John Thomas, except sometimes in malice, Coddy." His sexual conceit is given a rough tumble when the girls with whom he has played around once too often corner him in their lounge and beat him up. [Harry T. Moore suggests that there might have been a personal experience behind this story. The girls in the surgical firm where Lawrence worked as a young man are said to have "pounced on him, and tried to expose his sex." (*The Intelligent Heart*)]. In another tale, "Monkey Nuts," first published in 1922 but completed before the summer of 1919, Lawrence writes satirically about a land-girl who reverses the customary roles of the sexes and becomes the wooer of a shy young soldier. This story has the same Berkshire setting as *The Fox*, and its land-girl may very well be based on the same person as became March. The war is also an important part of the background of *The Fox*. Lawrence refers to the Daylight Saving Bill, to the food shortage, to soldiering in France and Salonika, and at one point to the specific year 1918. And he describes March, if not Banford, as wearing puttees and breeches, belted coat and loose cap — the semi-military uniform of the land-girl, in which she looks "almost like some graceful, loose-balanced young man."

March and Banford, though not specifically replacing men who have gone to the war, are putting into practice the notion of female independence and equality with the male. They form a "couple" of their own, Banford the woman, March the man. But the union is barren. Their farming is not a success because the two girls cannot put really creative energy into their work. Their hens prove infertile, and they panic when one of the heifers is about to calve. They lack the single-mindedness of men; the cultural frills are as important to them as the business of farming. Above all, ". . . they seemed to have to live too much off themselves." Their feminist self-sufficiency excludes them from the main stream of life.

March, however, is not the "man" that her clothes and her work proclaim her. "But her face was not a man's face ever"; and the false part that she is playing brings an unconsciously "satirical flicker" into her eyes. This is a weakness in the Lesbian ménage that the coming of the fox exploits. March's failure to shoot when she has the opportunity is part of her own vulnerability, merely disguised by the masculine pose she has adopted. The very effort that she has to make to be on the lookout for the fox reveals her unfulfilled condition: she lapses into an "odd, rapt state, her mouth rather screwed up. It was a question whether she was there, actually consciously present, or not." The fox holds her "spellbound" (the word is one that Lawrence insists upon), against her will, and yet without an effect of arbitrary magic. It is an actual beast out there in the natural world, charged, however, with a poetic aura and conveying a hint of mockery that makes it a creature of special significance for March. Its mesmeric influence does not affect Banford or Henry because its power to influence is dependent upon, and even to some extent created by, the frustration unconsciously existing within March herself. The *mana* is also transferable. When Henry appears on the scene, closely resembling the fox in several physical details, this mesmeric influence becomes his — superficially because of the resemblance, but fundamentally because it is he who can fulfill the unconscious need, the resemblance being more in the nature of an effect than a cause. Not that he is essentially a glamorous person, any more than March is. For all the false ideas that have grown up about the Lawrentian hero — fed, it must be admitted, by Lawrence himself through the creation of such spurious figures as Count Psanek and Don Cipriano — the man who comes to satisfy the unfulfilled woman does not have to be some incredible exotic. If the assumptions involved are romantic, Lawrence is not guilty of a fairy tale, or in its debased form a women's magazine romanticism. Henry exists in the story as a rather ordinary, even vulgar, young man, nothing remotely resembling a Prince Charming. But where Lawrence parts company with other realists is in accepting the transforming glow of sexual desire as an aspect of reality. He even sets up a deliberate opposition between the realism of the enlightened Banford, who sees no more than the vulgarity of Henry, and the kind of vision that descends upon March when she feels the pull of the unconscious "bond" with Henry. And the opposition expresses itself within March as a conflict between the needs of her real self and the false demands and protests of her modern woman's independent self.

The story also involves a reevaluation of realism. Lawrence is careful to preserve a convincingly naturalistic surface. Henry's reason for suddenly turning up at the farm is plausible; the dialogue between the three main characters is prosaically matter-of-fact; and Lawrence keeps the growth of events—Henry's slow winning of March's confidence, for example, counterpointed with rising hostility between him and Banford—from violating the reader's sense of probability. But concurrently with this, the reader feels Henry's presence at a different, and more compelling, level of reality. If we could view the events independently of Lawrence's narrative, it might seem that Henry's power was merely hallucinatory. Within the story, which is the only place where we can in fact view the events, the power is far more real than the commonplace world that the "realism" of the story presents. Lawrence does not belittle the surface, either intentionally or by failure to give it appropriate substance; but as in Wordsworth's "Resolution and Independence," where the old leech-gatherer's voice becomes "like a stream / Scarce heard," a visionary awareness supervenes upon the commonplace reality for which in some way it is a source of strength. March struggles against the spell of Henry, her modern feminism being in conflict with the visionary awareness; and this makes an important difference between the experiences recorded in the tale and in the poem. She has to undergo the Wordsworthian experience in spite of herself:

> March was busy in the kitchen preparing another meal. It was about seven o'clock. All the time, while she was active, she was attending to the youth in the sitting-room, not so much listening to what he said as feeling the soft run of his voice. She primmed up her mouth tighter and tighter, puckering it as if it were sewed, in her effort to keep her will uppermost. Yet her large eyes dilated and glowed in spite of her; she lost herself.

As a "lost girl," March has many sisters among Lawrence's stories and novels, and like them she loses contact with the world of commonplace reality as the price of finding herself at a deeper level.

In the passage just quoted, Lawrence sets March's strain "to keep her will uppermost" against the dilation and glowing of her eyes. Julian Moynahan has drawn attention (in *The Deed of Life*) to the significance of eye-references in *The Fox*. The responsiveness betrayed in March's eyes, the sharpness and "fixed attention" in Henry's, and the weakness of Banford's sight are details that at once belong to the naturalistic surface of the tale and that also through varied repetition acquire a symbolic status. The purpose of the symbolism thus built up within the story is to give the reader imaginative access to the deeper level of reality where, in spite of their seeming incompatibilities, March and Henry meet. The eye is a symbol traditionally associated in works as various as *King Lear* and "The Hollow Men" with the reevaluation of reality, and it has similar associations in *The Fox*. A striking example occurs in a passage following a more than usually banal conversation among March, Banford, and Henry:

> "Do you get so tired, then?" he asked.
> "So bored," said Banford.
> "Oh!" he said gravely. "But why should you be bored?"
> "Who wouldn't be bored?" said Banford.
> "I'm sorry to hear that," he said gravely.
> "You must be, if you were hoping to have a lively time here," said Banford.
> He looked at her long and gravely.
> "Well," he said, with his odd, young seriousness, "it's quite lively enough for me."
> "I'm glad to hear it," said Banford.
> And she returned to her book. In her thin, frail hair were already many threads of grey, though she was not yet thirty. The boy did not look down, but turned his eyes to March, who was sitting with pursed mouth laboriously crocheting, her eyes wide and absent. She had a warm, pale, fine skin, and a delicate nose. Her pursed mouth looked shrewish. But the shrewish look was contradicted by the curious lifted arch of her dark brows, and the wideness of her eyes; a look of startled wonder and vagueness. She was listening again for the fox, who seemed to have wandered farther off into the night.

The repetition of *bored* recalls the "I'd be bored. You'd be bored" exchange between Sweeney and Doris in "Sweeney Agonistes." It is symptomatic of a life lived only on the surface level of reality, and there are accompanying suggestions in Banford's premature aging and March's pursed mouth and shrewish look of a withering from within. But these suggestions are "contradicted" in March by her complexion, her dark brows and especially her eyes, which reveal how far she has withdrawn from this surface world and is yielding to the more compelling reality of Henry and the fox.

We can make another comparison between Lawrence and Eliot in their treatment of the deeper level of reality. For both of them it is initially painful. In "Burnt Norton" the vision of the pool "filled with water out of sunlight" is momentary only: "human kind / Cannot bear very much reality." The Birth at last found by the wise men in "Journey of the Magi" was "Hard and bitter agony for us, like Death, our death." There is a similarly double-edged quality in March's dream of the fox:

> That night March dreamed vividly. She dreamed she heard a singing outside which she could not understand, a singing that roamed round the house, in the fields, and in the darkness. It moved her so that she felt she must weep. She went out, and suddenly she knew it was the fox singing. He was very yellow and bright, like corn. She went nearer to him, but he ran away and ceased singing. He seemed near, and she wanted to touch him. She stretched out her hand, but suddenly he bit her wrist, and at the same instant, as she drew back, the fox, turning round to bound away, whisked his brush across her face, and it seemed his brush was on fire, for it seared and burned her mouth with a great pain. She awoke with the pain of it, and lay trembling as if she were really seared.

The fox is sweet, desirable, and, through the image of the corn, associated with natural fertility—an intentional contrast with the barrenness of March and Banford's farming. But it is also savage and terribly hurtful. By making this not simply a beautiful, but also an extremely painful, vision, Lawrence hints that the reality that attracts March contains the agony of destruction as well as the joy of creative release. The paradox of the dream is realized in Henry, who not only hurts March by destroying her friendship with Banford, but also has an effect upon her that is more like paralysis, or the cauterizing of a wound, than the ecstasy of romantic love. This is, of course, part of a healing process; the pain and destruction that come with Henry and the fox are counterbalanced by a regenerative process that restores March to her true self and brings appearance and reality into accord. March, for example, puts on a dress one evening instead of her land-girl's uniform, and Henry notices that "Through the crape her woman's form seemed soft and womanly." Passivity and a longing for sleep—appearance and feeling alike indicating the emergence of true femininity as feminist assertion gives way—replaced the feeling of responsibility that had been a "great stimulant" for March, but also a deadly strain. Yet there is something harsh even here, a quality almost of violation in the "helplessness and submission" that is imposed upon March, and Lawrence admits at the end: "Something was missing. Instead of her soul swaying with new life, it seemed to droop, to bleed, as if it were wounded."

The destruction-creation theme is tainted by a strain of vindictiveness in Henry's triumph over Banford, about which Lawrence himself is ambiguous. When Henry announces that he is going to marry March, we read that he is a "bright and gloating youth," the second adjective seeming to evoke a feeling that Lawrence approves rather than condemns. This is unpleasantly confirmed by the later scene in which Henry watches Banford struggle back from the station with her arms full of parcels, and mutters: "You're a nasty little thing, you are." The ambiguity stretches to his wooing of March as well. The paragraph describing his decision to hunt her down like a deer is powerful and psychologically convincing but also repellent in its reduction of March to the status of mere quarry. And because of the symbolic identity of Henry and the fox, it is impossible to isolate from Henry himself the sadistic element in the presentation of the fox. Lawrence may here be attempting to communicate the cruelty inevitable in the Dionysian mixture of savagery and vitality, but Henry's sulkiness and resentment when not getting his own way are not so easily explained. There is some truth in Banford's view of him: "Oh, Nellie, he'll despise you, he'll despise you, like the awful little beast he is, if you give way to him. I'd no more trust him than I'd trust a cat not to steal. He's deep, he's deep, and he's bossy, and he's selfish through and through, as cold as ice. All he wants is to make use of you. And when you're no more use to him, then I pity you." As March says, he is not as bad as all that; but it is an old rhetorical trick to undermine a potentially embarrassing view by exaggerating it and putting it in the mouth of a discredited opponent. Something of what Banford says sticks. Henry is, after all, willful and bullying, and the fact that Lawrence is honest enough to present him so is an important piece of authorial self-criticism.

At the end of the story—the "longer tail" that was added, significantly, during the Sicily revision—the domineering insistency of Henry becomes more evident. At the same time he becomes more of a mouthpiece for Lawrence's own theory of the utter separateness of the sexes. (Parts of this last section read almost like an extract from the roughly contemporary *Fantasia of the Unconscious.*) March, too, loses her individuality and becomes an abstraction representing all women who try to usurp male responsibility and imagine that they can find happiness. In all this Lawrence is his worst, tiresomely jeering, self.

The one passage in which he recovers his power to write evocatively and compellingly is a description of the state of mind that Henry demands from the unwilling March:

> No, she had to be passive, to acquiesce, and to be submerged under the surface of love. She had to be like the seaweeds she saw as she peered down from the boat, swaying forever delicately under water, with all their delicate fibrils put tenderly out upon the flood, sensitive, utterly sensitive and receptive within the shadowy sea, and never, never rising and looking forth above water while they lived. Never. Never looking forth from the water until they died, only then washing, corpses, upon the surface. But while they lived, always submerged, always beneath the wave. Beneath the wave they might have powerful roots, stronger than iron; they might be tenacious and dangerous in their soft waving within the flood. Beneath the water they might be stronger, more indestructible

than resistant oak trees are on land. But it was always under-water,
always under-water. And she, being a woman, must be like that.

This is feminine, but not restrictively female; not so much a statement
about the nature of woman as a quality of mind akin to Keats's negative
capability or a "Consider the lilies of the field" *insouciance*. ("Insouciance" is the revised title of a relevant essay by Lawrence, originally
called "Over-earnest Ladies.") It is a condition of creative relaxation in
which consciousness of self — for Lawrence the peculiarly modern dis-
ease — gives way to immersion in the flux of life. The hyper-conscious and
strenuously competitive nature of modern life is something that we might
metaphorically call "masculine," and then by comparison this "sensitive
and receptive" state would be "feminine." Particular men and women,
however, are complex beings in whom both active and passive principles
exist and need to exist. To simplify them into wholly masculine males and
wholly feminine females in accordance with Lawrentian theory would be
to destroy them as living human beings. From this point of view March's
reluctance to abandon herself unquestioningly to her husband is a sign of
health. Lawrence does not explode the theory — and, as later work,
including "The Woman Who Rode Away," shows, he continued to be
addicted to it — but at least implies a scepticism by the conclusion in which
nothing is concluded. Not only March, but also Lawrence "can't tell what
it will be like over there."

"The Woman Who Rode Away" repeats on a larger, mythical scale the
contradictions and confusions of *The Fox*. What Lawrence muted in the
earlier tale, in this story he gives extreme development — though he still
balks at the final translation of theory into imagined action. In particular,
his attack on modern feminism receives its sharpest and most explicit
expression in the woman's thoughts on her own impending death: "Her
kind of womanhood, intensely personal and individual, was to be obliterated again, and the great primeval symbols were to tower once more over
the fallen individual independence of woman. The sharpness and the
quivering nervous consciousness of the highly-bred white woman was to
be destroyed again, womanhood was to be cast once more into the great
stream of impersonal sex and impersonal passion."

Lawrence gives greater emphasis to self-consciousness here than in
The Fox and the theme of the tale is correspondingly more generalized.
The annihilation of the entire mode of Western intellectual civilization is
at stake, for the sacrifice of the woman will enable the blood-consciousness
of the Indians to triumph over the mind-consciousness of the white man.
But as in *The Fox*, the fate of the independent modern woman remains the
central concern of the tale. And again as in *The Fox* we feel the woman to
be the object of compassionate rescue and of vindictive outrage.

The sterility that Lawrence obliquely shows to be the result of the
Banford-March relationship is starkly presented at the beginning of "The

Woman Who Rode Away" in the surrealistic setting of the woman's home. Lawrence's insistence on its deadness anticipates his description of Tevershall in *Lady Chatterley's Lover*; and Lederman, the woman's husband, is equally an anticipation of Sir Clifford Chatterley. He and the scientists who make an expedition to the Chilchui Indians, but see "nothing extraordinary," are representative of modern indifference to all that evokes mystery and wonder. For Lederman "Savages are savages, and all savages behave more or less alike: rather low-down and dirty, insanitary, with a few cunning tricks, and struggling to get enough to eat." To be able to see the Indians, as the woman does, in a more romantic light is a sign of grace. Though at first she feels it to be a "foolish romanticism more unreal than a girl's," when the woman sets out in search of the Chilchuis, she falls increasingly under its influence. Eventually, like March, she becomes "spell-bound, and as if drugged"; and in this condition she achieves a visionary awareness that is the very opposite of the denial of wonder from which she has fled.

Lawrence, however, makes no simple antithesis between the woman and the deadness she seeks to escape. She is, or has been, as much a meaningless "dynamo of energy" as her husband. As a "rather dazzling Californian girl from Berkeley" she represents an egalitarian, yet intensely competitive, society and a more advanced stage of feminism than we find in *The Fox*. The failure of her marriage has undermined her confidence, but the details of her behaviour show that she is still a woman of the world. She insists on having a horse of her own and dreams of "being free as she had been as a girl, among the hills of California." Her voice is an "assured, American woman's voice," and in her eyes there is "a half-childish, half-arrogant confidence in her own female power" (though balanced by "a curious look of trance"). Her ride to the Chilchuis is itself an expression of her independence. From the Indians who guide her she expects as a matter of course both social and sexual recognition, and when they rebuff her, "All the passionate anger of the spoilt white woman rose in her." But these are in a sense the twitches of the corpse, evidence that the woman is part of the sterility of her civilization. On her journey she seems to hear "a great crash at the centre of herself, which was the crash of her own death." The whole of the first section of the tale, not only the opening, is thus a prolonged death movement, culminating in a symbolic night of coldness, numbness, and death: "All was silent, mountain-silent, cold, deathly. She slept and woke and slept in a semi-conscious numbness of cold and fatigue. A long, long night, icy and eternal, and she was aware that she had died."

Section II, a life-movement counterpoising the death-movement of Section I, opens with the striking of flint and "a red splutter of fire." With the dawn comes heat, and then "in the full blaze of the mid-morning sun" the woman has her first sight of the Indian village. It is an idealized place, in some ways suggestive of the Utopian Eastwood of Lawrence's "Autobiographical Fragment," neat, glittering with white houses and having gardens "full of flowers and herbs and fruit-trees"; and as against the crude, dehumanized squalor of the mining town this has "a soft narrow track between leaves and grass, a path worn smooth by centuries of human feet, no hoof of horse nor any wheel to disfigure it." The Indians themselves wear the flame colors of red, orange, yellow, and black; their steps are "soft and heavy and swift" and they move rhythmically. Their old chief has the dignity and visionary splendor (he "roused himself like a vision") of an Old Testament prophet. It is astonishing how much of this, inspired as it is by Mexico and the American Southwest, recalls the idealized countryside and chapel-going fervor of Lawrence's youth. The world to which the woman has come is a recovered Eden of warmth and natural human dignity.

But the longing which gives rise to this idyllic, yet vigorous, pastoral is also in Lawrence something bitterly frustrated. As a result, what might have been a simple Golden Age fantasy turns into a weird complex of idealism and vindictiveness. Having persuaded himself that Western civilization is responsible for the strangulation of this ideal, and that the independent-minded white woman is the epitome of the strained con-sciousness on which Western civilization is based, Lawrence exults in the subjugation of the woman by the Indians and craves the satisfaction of her sacrifice. The matter is further complicated, however, for Lawrence is not content that the woman should die—she must also be converted. Her physical death followed a spiritual death that has reduced her to the passivity demanded of woman by the Lawrentian theory. Accordingly, despite her remaining a victim who cannot be said to give more than hallucinated consent to her fate, the woman receives the reward of the "feminine" vision proposed for March at the end of *The Fox*:

> Afterwards she felt a great soothing languor steal over her, her limbs felt strong and loose and full of languor, and she lay on her couch listening to the sounds of the village, watching the yellowing sky, smelling the scent of burning cedar-wood, or pine-wood. So distinctly she heard the yapping of tiny dogs, the shuffle of far-off feet, the murmur of voices, so keenly she detected the smell of smoke, and flowers, and evening falling, so vividly she saw the one bright star infinitely remote, stirring above the sunset, that she felt as if all her senses were diffused on the air, that she could distinguish the sound of evening flowers unfolding, and the actual crystal sound of the heavens, as the vast belts of the world-atmosphere slid past one another, and as if the moisture ascending and the moisture descending in the air re-sounded like some harp in the cosmos.

The heightened sensitivity described in this passage is matched by other moving descriptions of a state of mind that annihilates self-con-sciousness, the woman's senses being released "into a sort of heightened, mystic acuteness and a feeling as if she were diffusing out deliciously into the harmony of things." Through such passages Lawrence communicates a feeling of relaxation and renewal that succeeds in making the woman's experience seem the satisfaction of a deep human need. But, as the context reasserts itself, he reminds us, inevitably, and even with something like malevolent purpose, that the woman is a prisoner, that her visions are drug-induced, and that she is being deliberately conditioned to accept the part of victim in a ritual sacrifice. The resulting impression is that Lawrence is wresting his own vision to suit some incompatible end that is more like vengeance than regeneration.

Lawrence's treatment of the Indians involves similar contradictions. When he is describing their dancing in long rhythmic periods of hypnotic repetition, he makes completely convincing their symbolic identification with the sources of natural power. The language vibrates on the mind as immediately as a physical sensation; the Indians seem the very embodiment of vital energy. In this respect they are a mythopoeic extension of the wild regenerative force associated with Henry in *The Fox*. But like Henry, only again on a grander scale, they are also vindictive and treacherous in a peculiarly human way. Lawrence may well have intended the opposite effect — something to be compared with the distinctively animal slyness and bloodthirstiness of the fox. But it is purely human dishonesty that is suggested by the ambiguity in the question ". . . do you bring your heart to the god of the Chilchui?" and again in the answer given to the woman's question about her fate: "Have I got to die and be given to the sun?" she asked.

"Some time," he said, laughing evasively. "Some time we all die." There is more of the animal power that can be represented as inextricably destructive-creative in the description of the priests who watch over the woman just before she is to be sacrificed: ". . . their eyes, with that strange glitter, and their dark, shut mouths that would open to the very broad jaw, the small, strong, white teeth, had something very primitively male and cruel." This is strongly reminiscent of the description of the fox in the earlier tale. But even here the phrase "primitively male and cruel" attaches an ideological animus to what we might otherwise take for a healthy instinctive ferocity.

What distorts Lawrence's treatment both of the woman and of the Indians is the intrusion, as in *The Fox*, of his sexual theory and its accompanying enmity towards the independence of woman. He insists upon the same doctrine of the separateness of the sexes. The Chilchui men have all the colorful glamor and activity — phrases like "darkly and powerfully male" and "storm-like sound of male singing" become almost a cliché. Their women, on the other hand, dress in black and look on passively. And Lawrence invents a somewhat spurious symbolism in which "men are the fire and the daytime" and "women are the spaces between the stars at night," or, alternatively, men are guardians of the sun and women of the moon. Resentment of the woman, not as an individual, but as a representative of her kind, permeates the tale and reveals itself in words like *derision* and *malignancy*, used to describe the Indians' attitude towards her — derogatory, yet seeming to carry Lawrence's approval. This, too, is incorporated in the symbolism as the anger of the moon at being kept in the white woman's cave. And what looks like a reference to cancer (the disease from which Lawrence's mother died) is also incorporated: " 'The moon, she bites white women — here inside,' and he pressed his side."

Unpleasant as this element is, it remains in balance with the genuinely visionary element until the time for the ritual sacrifice arrives. Then, in Section III, it dominates the narrative. Lawrence builds up a sickening climax, from the "long, strange, hypnotic massage" that is like a parody of love-making, through the mass-hysteria of the crowd when the woman is shown to them, to the final horrific scene, made the more appalling by the emotions of "glittering eagerness, and awe, and craving" attributed to the Indians. The whole section reads, paradoxical though it may be, like an experiment in deliberate abandonment to the vindictiveness that has been gnawing at the tale throughout.

In *Fantasia of the Unconscious* Lawrence writes of sexual consummation as a thunderstorm that clears the atmosphere, giving release to the "inevitable electric accumulation in the nerves and the blood, an accumulation which weighs there and broods there with intolerable pressure." There is an analogously orgasmic effect in this last section of "The Woman Who Rode Away." Its mounting tension drives towards a final act that is also a consummation, though the real release that can be hoped for is not from the tyranny of mental consciousness, as Lawrence would have us believe, but from the "accumulation in the nerves and the blood" that has manifested itself in the persistent vindictiveness of the tale. The climax, however, remains a suspended one — possibly because the release is there in the writing, and vicariously in the reading, of it; more probably because the clearing of the atmosphere that succeeds it is the subject for a different kind of art. And, as a final speculation, we may find the sequel towards which "The Woman Who Rode Away" points in *Lady Chatterley's Lover* and "The Man Who Died," where Lawrence, though still an opponent of the feminists, is no longer pursued by the demon of his own animosity towards them.

Realism and Romance in Lawrence's *The Virgin and the Gipsy*

Barnett Guttenberg*

The few critics who have concerned themselves with Lawrence's *The Virgin and the Gipsy* have found its structure troubling. R. P. Draper comments: "The surface of the tale suggests a novel, recording accurate impressions of people, place, and tone of voice; but the sharp distinction between good and evil is that of a moral fable."[1] Kingsley Widmer remarks on the "odd combination of harsh realism and lyrical fairy tale"; noting the incongruence of the gypsy as mythic figure and "the gypsy as he appears to the ordinary world," he concludes, "Perhaps Lawrence's desire to mythicize the primitive figure in terms of his mysterious desirability works at loggerheads with his own intellectual perceptions."[2] *The Virgin and the Gipsy* does indeed show a contradiction in modes. That contradiction makes the story pivotal in Lawrence's canon, for it represents a theoretical and formal impasse which in turn reflects a critical juncture in Lawrence's development.

One of the contradictory modes in the story is that of realism: a number of scenes seem drawn from the novel of manners. The setting for these scenes is the rectory, the dancehall, the automobile. Central characters are the rector and his mother, both servants of appearance — "I wish you would take a message from me to Lady Louth," says Granny, flaunting her connections with aristocracy — together with the young circle of Framwells and available beaux, who, although professed rebels, find Granny to their liking. A concern with mores seems to shape these scenes. Thus, Leo's ludicrous proposal of marriage to Yvette: "when she was eating her pistachio ice, he said to her, 'Why don't you and me get engaged, Yvette? I'm absolutely sure it's the right thing for us both.' "[3] Even closer to the world of Jane Austen is the episode of Yvette's tea-cake transgression, in which she sins against decorum by absent-mindedly winding up with two cakes on her plate.

The mode interwoven with that of manners involves the displacement of myth into romance, as defined by Northrop Frye.[4] The drawing-room setting of marriage proposals and tea-cakes dissolves into a pastoral scene of country life. The romance involves an intensification of good and evil: a godly hero (in undisplaced myth, an actual god) sets out to overcome a villain. The comic romance involves, in addition, an erotic intrigue between a young man and woman which is temporarily blocked, usually by paternal opposition. Yvette, as Lady of Shalott imprisoned in the rectory, waits for the noble Lancelot to "come along singing 'tirra-lirra!' "

*Reprinted from *Studies in Short Fiction* 17 (1980):99–103, by permission of the journal and the author.

(p. 51). Her knight-errant proves to be the wandering gypsy-hero, who is pitted against the Granny-dragon and oversees its slaying.

Lawrence uses the two modes of myth and realism ironically. He regards social mores, which of course in the novel of manners afford ultimate sanction, from a rather jaundiced perspective, subverting the normative view. As the tea-cake episode demonstrates by drawing sympathies away from the custodians of morality and toward the erring Yvette, decorum has no value within the scheme of the story. Leo's offhand proposal of marriage violates the emotional verities rather than the proprieties. To the extent that Yvette is infatuated with appearances, as in her concern with clothing, her life remains the farce which she has charge of, *Mary in the Mirror*; like the Lady of Shalott, she remains imprisoned in a mirror-structure and sees only shadowy facades.

Just as he inverts the normative vision of the novel of manners, Lawrence inverts the conventions of romance. His hero comes not from the upper world, but from the lower: the quarry where he resides with his troop is a "sudden lair, almost like a cave" (p. 28). The villain of the piece, correspondingly, is God's representative, a writer and a rector, a man of the word and the Word, a "Saywell." The gypsy dispatches the dragon, but despite the conventional discovery of the hero's inherent worthiness through his rescue of the princess ("I think that gipsy deserves a medal!"), he does not claim the princess and take his true place in society, for his true place remains peripheral.

Lawrence, it would seem, introduces the formal elements of manners and romance in order to frustrate the expectations which these elements arouse. Yvette does not marry a Mr. Knightley, the stalwart embodiment of the community; Leo, the appropriate counterpart, is an effeminate representative of a defunct society. Neither does Yvette run off with the gypsy. Their relationship clearly falls short, and this quite apart from the question of just where their bedroom scene ends: a question which has troubled the story's critics.[5] The point here would seem to be that Lawrence contrives to have his young couple in bed together, and then, instead of fleshing out the scene, says nothing. With an uncharacteristic fadeout, he carefully frustrates the expectations aroused by his reputation, by the situation, by the very title of his story. Those expectations, for all of their unconventionality in terms of propriety, are the conventional expectations of romance, and, in Lawrence's view, they are as unreal as the conventions of the rectory.

Lacking a sense of Lawrence's ironic perspective toward the conventions of romance, critics have tended to be misled by the Eastwoods, the unmarried honeymooners: perhaps because, in Meyers' words, they "are living together, like Lawrence and Frieda, in an isolated cottage where they do their own housework, until the woman can get her divorce."[6] Meyers views their relationship as vital; to Moynahan, the Major is "a Gerald [Crich] reborn to wholesome desire."[7] The Eastwoods, nonetheless, are figures of death. The Jewess wears a coat "of many dead little animals" (p. 71); Yvette, attracted to the couple, "followed the fur coat of the Jewess, which seemed to walk on little legs of its own" (p. 77). The Major has been reborn from ice unregenerate, as his description makes clear: he is blue-eyed, abstract, northern. He spends his time in housewifely tasks, sacrificing his manhood to move in a female orbit. His only outside activity seems to involve his car, and this preoccupation is also damning. The gypsy is a man of horses; Yvette visits him on a bicycle; the Eastwoods interrupt the liaison and take her off in their car, which is clearly one of Lawrence's symbols of modern mechanism. In his surrender to the female sphere, in his mechanical unmanning, the Major is a more prepossessing version of Clifford Chatterley in his wheelchair.

What has proved most confusing about the Eastwoods is that they say the right things about the gypsy's fire. She says "Don't you love fire! Oh, I love it" (p. 73), while he remarks, "Desire is the most wonderful thing in life. Anybody who can really feel it is a king" (p. 87). Her glaring insincerity is matched by his mechanical abstraction, which is suggested by his removing the pipe from his mouth to comment on desire, and returning the pipe upon concluding. The Eastwoods are not alone among Lawrence's characters in saying the right thing while being the wrong ones. (Hermione in the schoolroom scene of *Women in Love* comes instantly to mind.) Their system of stoves reveals their actual feelings toward fire; within their hothouse cottage, fire has been abstracted, domesticated, intellectualized. "Perhaps," Yvette reflects upon the Jewess, "her honesty was *too* rational" (p. 74). The Eastwoods, with their outspoken adultery, belong completely to the conventions of romance. In their honeymoon haven, they self-consciously inhabit their own romantic dream, and serve as a warning, in opposition to the reader's romantic expectations, that the adulterous flight of Yvette's mother may or may not prove an adequate alternative to the rectory.

Yvette must discover that the dream of the gypsy which she has conceived, like the dream which the Eastwoods inhabit, is as abstract, artificial, and unreal as the moral code of the rectory: the romance and the code of manners both finely wrought illusions. Yvette comes to understand the rectory through two confrontations with her father. When he humiliates her for her mishandling of the Window Fund money, mishandling which is careless but certainly not malicious, she sees "what an utter unbeliever he was, at the heart . . . a heart which has no core of warm belief in it, no pride in life" (p. 37). In a second clash over the Eastwoods, she turns from her father and all he represents: "She lost her illusions in the collapse of her sympathies" (p. 95).

Yvette moves toward a similar devaluing of the gypsy and his romantic mode after she nearly becomes part of it. As mythic figure of salvation, he dashes dramatically to her rescue, saving her from Granny, the bloated embodiment of propriety, and from the water, the flood-tide of the repressed unconscious. In a heavily symbolic scene, he insists on her removing her wet clothes and warms her beside the chimney, which, he assures her, will remain standing. Lawrence thwarts all expectations here because Yvette's communion with the gypsy, though revivifying, resembles the Jungian state of introversion, in which the individual is potentially lost in himself. Even after the rescue, Yvette lies in bed enthralled by the conventional formulas of her own romance, moaning, "Oh, I love him! I love him! I love him!"

Yvette must come down from her dream. The gypsy's letter proves that dream untenable, forcing her to recognize the disparity between man and myth. The romantic gypsy is the illiterate Joe Boswell, and the mundane nature of his being, evident in his name, is underscored by Yvette's response — which concludes the story — to his signature: "only then she realised that he had a name." With that realization, the bubble of romance bursts. The loss of virginity portrayed in the story is Yvette's loss of illusion, which finally involves her fall from romance into knowledge. The gypsy, warming her, rekindles her pride and bravery in order that she might endure the fall, which, thus cushioned, is rendered as her graceful descent down the ladder. If she faints "appropriately" into her father's arms, it is because her vulnerability to convention is finally shattered only with the gypsy's letter, which, arriving a day or two later, is the bottom rung of her descent. The Lady of Shalott, touched by the sensuality of Sir Lancelot, leaves her tower of artifice. For Yvette, that tower is sensual as well as spiritual: hence the bedroom scene in the rectory. The Lady of Shalott comes down to seek her death; Yvette, on the other hand, comes down to begin her real life.

Yet the Lady of Shalott's fate is not wholly irrelevant; although Yvette's fall is graceful, leaving her intact and ready for a new beginning, it is not altogether a fortunate fall. As early as *Twilight in Italy*, Lawrence advocated the twin consummations of spirit and flesh: "When both are there, they are like a superb bridge, on which one can stand and know the whole world."[8] With a slight metaphorical shift, Lawrence transformed that "superb bridge" into the rainbow, providing one of his novels with its title, an overarching symbol of hope. The title *The Virgin and the Gipsy*, however, is ironic; the title characters, controverting expectation, fail to come together, for "the bridge was gone" (p. 115). The path leads not across, but down. Instead of finding the rainbow and knowing the world, instead of achieving either heavenly or earthly consummation, Yvette is ready to begin her search knowing that the arenas of each consummation accessible in the wasteland — a rectory of spiritual artifice and a gypsy-caravan of illiterate vagrancy — are alternate realms of impossibility.

Lawrence uses these realms, first, to represent antithetical patterns of existence: Yvette can remain with her father in a stasis of spiritual corruption, or follow the gypsy in derelict vitality. Lawrence also uses these realms to represent patterns of artistic performance, modes of fiction with their associated conventions: the realistic mode of the novel of manners and the mythic mode of the romance. Each realm is appropriately developed in the mode it represents. And each realm, both as potential fulfilment for the individual and as possible form for the novel, is, the story suggests, bankrupt.

Lawrence wrote *The Virgin and the Gipsy* in Italy, bloody, and, as the story indicates, somewhat bowed after his dispiriting quest and debilitating illness in Mexico. The escape into romance, like the evasion of manners, was inadequate: old and new forms equally exhausted. At the close of the story, Lawrence stands with Yvette at a threshold which is formal as well as metaphysical. Where does the rainbow begin and end, and what is the new novel that will bridge the void? In 1925, while Lawrence worked on *The Virgin and the Gipsy*, *Lady Chatterley's Lover* was slouching toward Italy to be born.

Notes

1. R. P. Draper, *D. H. Lawrence* (New York: Twayne, 1964), p. 142.

2. Kingsley Widmer, *The Art of Perversity: D. H. Lawrence's Shorter Fictions* (Seattle: University of Washington Press, 1962), pp. 181, 184.

3. D. H. Lawrence, *The Virgin and the Gipsy* (1930; rpt. New York: Bantam, 1968), p. 60. All page references in the text are to this edition.

4. Northrop Frye, *Anatomy of Criticism* (1957; rpt. New York: Atheneum, 1966), pp. 33–34, 43–44.

5. Does she or doesn't she? Moynahan says she doesn't; Widmer and Meyers claim she does.

6. Jeffrey Meyers, " 'The Voice of Water': Lawrence's 'The Virgin and the Gipsy,' " *English Miscellany* (Rome), 21 (1970), 202. Apparently it does not quite go without saying that the Major and the Jewess need hardly be Lawrence and Frieda, the superficial similarity of situation notwithstanding.

7. Julian Moynahan, *The Deed of Life* (New Jersey: Princeton University Press, 1963), p. 211.

8. D. H. Lawrence, *Twilight in Italy* (1916; rpt. New York: Viking, 1958), p. 95.

Allusions and Symbols in D. H. Lawrence's *The Escaped Cock*   James C. Cowan*

Always concerned with the problems of religion and sexual love, D. H. Lawrence sought in the last years of his life to revitalize what he considered to be the sterile and misdirected religious experience of modern

*This essay was revised and expanded for publication in this volume. It first appeared as "The Function of Allusions and Symbols in D. H. Lawrence's *The Man Who Died*," in *The American Imago* 17 (Fall 1960):241–53, and is reprinted by permission of the journal and the author.

man by re-establishing contact with pagan mythology. Christianity, he felt, "had misunderstood love throughout its history." In Christian society, love — even sexual love — had been abstracted as an intellectual ideal. The pale concept of Christian love was without realistic basis in the deep well-springs of being. Lawrence pleaded for balancing the intellect by "reasserting . . . 'the blood' as a source of religious experience."[1] As early as 1912, he wrote to Ernest Collings: "My great religion is a belief in the blood, the flesh, as being wiser than the intellect. We can go wrong in our minds. But what our blood feels and believes and says, is always true" (*Letters* I, 503).[2] In three of his later works, *The Plumed Serpent* (1926), *The Escaped Cock* (1929), and *Apocalypse* (1931), Lawrence censured Christianity and championed the vitalistic paganism of the "religion of the blood."

In the short novel *The Escaped Cock*, published in England and America under the title *The Man Who Died*, Lawrence presents an imagined version of the revitalizing experiences of Jesus after the resurrection, a version vastly different from Biblical accounts of Christ's appearances after death.[3] Although numerous parallels to the gospels establish clearly the life and death from which the man who died has been liberated, Lawrence never calls the character "Jesus" but presents him as a universal figure for the risen lord. His body has been taken down from the cross and laid in the tomb, but the man's death had been spiritual rather than physical. His old missionary life as teacher and savior is dead within him, and he is free to seek the true sources of human happiness in a more vital life than he has lived before. He realizes that he has been saved from his own salvation, that he has neglected the needs of his own body to pursue a spiritual mission. Forsaking that mission, he decides to use his healing powers as a physician and to follow a life in which his own wounds will be healed. Leaving his former followers, he finds, in a temple of Isis, the fulfillment for which he has been searching. Although it is more difficult to love sexually than it had been to die, he learns, through his relationship with the priestess, what human love is, and recognizes that he has offered and asked for only "the corpse of love" before. In telling his story of the resurrection in *The Escaped Cock*, Lawrence employs both traditional symbols and Biblical and mythic allusions, which I should like to examine in an effort to determine their function as structural and thematic devices in the novella.

The central symbol in Part I is a young gamecock owned by a poor peasant. The cock "[looks] a shabby little thing, but . . . [puts] on brave feathers as spring [advances], and [is] resplendent with arched and orange neck, by the time the fig-trees are putting out leaves. Cutting a splendid figure in that dirty yard the cock learns to arch his neck and crow shrill answers to the faraway, unseen cocks crowing beyond the wall. The peasant, fearing that his prized bird will fly away, ties him to a post. But one day, with a mighty burst of strength, the rooster snaps the string that holds him and flies over the wall. At the same moment, a man awakens "from a long sleep in which he [has been] tied up" (*EC* 13–15).

In these few opening paragraphs, Lawrence, through the metaphor of the gamecock, both foreshadows the nature of the new life to which the man is awakening and refers back to the old life he has left behind. The gamecock is a fitting thematic image; it heralds both Jesus's death and the man's rebirth, both Peter's denial of Christ (John 18:15–27) and the risen man's self-affirmation through instinctual experience. Thematically, the idea of male sexuality is effectively presented in the image of the cock, which, besides being the male of its species, suggests the phallic connotations of its name in slang usage. From the moment when both the man and the cock break the fetters that bind them (the bandages wound around the buried man and the string attached to the cock's spur), the man is identified with the cock. It is clear that the man will break not only the physical bonds of death but also the metaphorical fetters of sexual repression that have prevented his living so vital a life as the cock.

Lawrence graphically illustrates the aggressive gamecock's sexuality as both dominant and tender. Even when he is again fettered, the young cock crows with a voice "stronger than chagrin" out of "the necessity to live, and even to cry out the triumph of life." Watching him the man sees "not the bird alone, but the short, sharp wave of life of which the bird [is] the crest" (*EC* 21). When he throws "a bit of bread to the cock, it [calls] with an extraordinary cooing tenderness, tousling and saving the morsel for the hens." But when his favorite hen comes near him, "emitting the lure," he pounces "on her with all his feathers vibrating." Watching "the unsteady, rocking vibration of the bent bird," the man who had died sees "not the bird . . . , but one wave-tip of life overlapping for a minute another, in the tide of the swaying ocean of life" (*EC* 22). The man sees in the life of the gamecock a more vital existence than he has known before in the life of the spirit. "Surely," he says, "thou art risen to the Father, among birds" (*EC* 28). But it is clear that he uses the phrase to denote an earthly, instinctual life which he himself has not yet learned to live rather than the heavenly, spiritual life denoted by the phrase in Biblical usage (see John 20:17). When he decides to go out in search of the new vital life, he buys the cock from the peasant. But there is a difference between this purchase and the one by which Jesus had been betrayed (see Matthew 26:14–16), for the man who had been sold into imprisonment and death buys freedom and life for the bird. By this time the cock has become a symbol of virtue for him, and the life of the cock, the good life.

When the risen man meets two of his followers along the way (in Lawrence's version of Jesus's appearance after resurrection to Cleopas and another follower on the road to Emmaus [Luke 24:13–35]), this conversation ensues:

> "Why do you carry a cock?"
> "I am a healer," he says, "and the bird hath virtue."

"You are not a believer?"
"Yea! I believe the bird is full of life and virtue."

(*EC* 33)

This dialogue has no parallel in the gospel source, which aims at verifying the resurrection as a warrant of belief and reveals the presence of Christ through his celebration of the communion. According to Evelyn J. Hinz and John J. Teunissen, Lawrence here identifies the risen man with Asclepius, the god of healing and patron of medicine, who was associated with both serpent and cock and to whom cocks were sacrificed by those who had been healed. "The conversion of the man who died from his mission as 'savior' to his role as 'healer' consists largely of . . . a movement away from the Christian and plebeian toward a pagan and elitist attitude to regeneration and away from an ego-centric to a self-sufficient concept of deity."[4]

The man's disposition of the gamecock illustrates the shift from salvation to self-sufficiency. When he comes to an inn, where the cock engages in a fight with the innkeeper's cock, the man, indicating his growing willingness to risk all for life, prevents the innkeeper from stopping the fight by promising that he may have the gamecock to eat if he loses or keep him for his hens if he wins. When the gamecock wins, the man who has died says to it, "Thou at least hast found thy kingdom, and the females to thy body" (*EC* 33). The speech, which parallels Jesus's words to Pilate, "My kingdom is not of this world" (John 18:36), illustrates again the change in the risen man's attitude toward life: no longer looking to be more than human, he now wishes to be what is even more difficult for him to be — an integrated man.

The gamecock, of course, is the central symbol in Part I of *The Escaped Cock*, but there are other symbols and other allusions in this section of the novella which serve to point up the contrast between the old life and the new, and to illustrate the risen man's changing attitude as he emerges into the rich, vital life of the blood.

After arising from the tomb, the man is taken to the humble cottage of a peasant. Still numb with pain and "the great void nausea of utter disillusion" (*EC* 18), he has no desire, even for food and drink. Nevertheless, he moistens a bit of bread in water and eats it. At his "last supper" Jesus had had his twelve disciples with him; but at what might be called his "first breakfast" the risen man has with him only a poor peasant and his wife. But whereas three of the disciples had fallen asleep as Jesus prayed in the Garden of Gethsemane and one had thrice denied him (see Matthew 26:36–75), these peasants, though "limited, meagre in their life, without any splendour of gesture and of courage," offer the man shelter at the risk of their own lives. "They [have] no nobility, but fear [makes] them willing to serve" (*EC* 19).

When the peasant departs for work in the vineyard of his master, the man who had died asks to lie in the yard in the sun. This he does again for the following two days. In its suspension in the sky the sun has phallic significance, thus foreshadowing the risen man's subsequent identification with Osiris, who is often represented as a sun-god.[5] More importantly, the sun appears here in its function as a health-renewing, life-giving force. According to Hinz and Teunissen, in Asclepian medicine, "health was not merely physical well-being, but the condition of harmony between the body and the mind." Hence, "the cock and the sun work together to heal the psychic and physical 'scars' of the man," a cure symbolized thematically "in his assumption of the Asclepian role as the 'healer' associated with the cock."[6] This means inevitably a revisionist view of his former role as savior. Looking at the stupid, dirty peasant, the man thinks to himself: "Why then should he be lifted up? Clods of earth are turned over for refreshment; they are not to be lifted up. Let the earth remain earthy, and hold its own against the sky. I was wrong to seek to lift it up. It was wrong to try to interfere. . . . No man can save the earth from tillage. It is tillage, not salvation . . ." (*EC* 22–23). The allusion to Jesus's statement about his own crucifixion and glorification, "And I, if I be lifted up from earth, will draw all men unto me" (John 12:32), illustrates the man's changing attitude toward all humanity, including himself.

Lawrence's version of the conversation between the risen man and Madeleine in *The Escaped Cock* differs in several ways from Biblical accounts of the encounter between the risen Jesus and Mary Magdalene at the sepulchre (see Matthew 28:9–10, Mark 16:9, and John 20:14–18). In John's account, Jesus says to Mary Magdalene, "Touch me not; for I am not yet ascended to my Father: but go to my brethren, and say unto them, I ascend to my Father and your Father; and to my God, and your God" (John 20:17). But in Lawrence's version, the man says, "Don't touch me, Madeleine. . . . Not yet! I am not yet healed and in touch with men" (*EC* 23). The change of phrase from "ascended to my Father" to "in touch with men" indicates a shift in allegiance on the part of the risen man from the spiritual forces of heaven to the physical forces of earth. Later in the conversation, Madeleine asks him, "And will you come back to us?" And he answers, "What is finished is finished. . . . For me that life is over" (*EC* 24). This part of the conversation has no parallel in the gospel accounts, but the man's statement recalls Jesus's final words on the cross as recorded by John: "When Jesus therefore had received the vinegar, he said, It is finished: and he bowed his head, and gave up the ghost" (John 19:30). In Lawrence's version, what is "finished" is the man's spiritual mission. As he goes on to explain, "The teacher and saviour are dead in me; now I can go about my business, into my own single life" (*EC* 24). Once Jesus's parents had found him, at the age of twelve, teaching the elders of the temple: "And he said unto them, How is it that ye sought me? wist ye not that I must be about my Father's business?" (Luke 2:49). The radical change in regard to whose "business" he is concerned with makes any reference to

Lawrence's character as "the Christ"[7] inappropriate: he has clearly rejected his former messianic mission.

Obtaining a little money from Madeleine, the man who had died returns to the cottage and gives it to the peasant's wife. "Take it!" he says. "It buys bread, and bread brings life" (*EC* 27). Once when Jesus had fasted for forty days and forty nights in the wilderness, the devil had tempted him: "If thou be the Son of God, command this stone that it be made bread. And Jesus answered him, saying, It is written, That man shall not live by bread alone, but by every word of God" (Luke 4:2–4). Since Christ's rejection of the temptation of the bread reverses Adam's yielding to the temptation of the forbidden fruit, it therefore reverses the effect of the Fall. Hence, the risen man's act of offering money to the peasant woman for non-sacramental bread suggests an acceptance of the fallen, that is, the human, world as natural and appropriate to earthly life.

Thinking over the changes that have been wrought in him by death, he says to himself, "Now I belong to no one, and have no connection, and my mission or gospel is gone from me. Lo! I cannot make even my own life, and what have I to save? I can learn to be alone" (*EC* 29). In effect, he admits the truth of the mocking words of the chief priests as Jesus hung on the cross: "He saved others; himself he cannot save" (Mark 15:31).

Aware of the vital forces of life going on around him, the man who had died reconsiders another of his old ideas: "The Word is but the midge that bites at evening. Man is tormented with words like midges, and they follow him right into the tomb. But beyond the tomb they cannot go. Now I have passed the place where words can bite, and the air is clear, and there is nothing to say, and I am alone within my own skin, which is the walls of all my domain" (*EC* 30). Jesus had told a parable about the sower and the word (Mark 4:14–20). And once when many of his followers had deserted him, he had said to his twelve disciples, "Will ye also go away," and Simon Peter had answered him, "Lord, to whom shall we go? thou hast the words of eternal life" (John 6:67–68). Now the man thinks that these "words" lead not to "eternal life" but to "the tomb," beyond which "they cannot go." By this change Lawrence revises the Christian tradition that he had criticized as early as the unpublished "Foreword to *Sons and Lovers*" (1913), in his rejection of St. John's doctrine that "The Word was made Flesh" (John 1:1): "For what was Christ? He was Word, or He became Word. What remains of Him? No flesh remains on earth, from Christ . . . He is Word. And the Father was Flesh. For even if it were by the Holy Ghost His spirit were begotten, yet flesh cometh only out of flesh" (*FSL* 22). In *The Escaped Cock* Lawrence attempts to restore the natural order that he thinks John had reversed.

The man who had died also has a new definition of immortality. The Apostle Paul wrote to Timothy that "our Saviour Jesus Christ . . . hath abolished death, and hath brought life and immortality to light through the gospel" (II Timothy 1:10). But the risen man, Lawrence says, "healed of his wounds, and enjoyed his immortality of being alive without fret. . . . For in the tomb he had left his striving self . . ." (*EC* 30). Now for the first time, in the interest of preserving his self inviolate, he elevates phenomenology above spirituality as he decides to venture forth "among the stirring of the phenomenal world": "Strange is the phenomenal world, dirty and clean together! . . . And life bubbles everywhere, in me, in them, in this, in that. But it bubbles variously. Why should I ever have wanted it to bubble all alike?" (*EC* 30–31). From this new perspective he arrives at the insight that he had been executed because his preaching had closed the fountains of the phenomenal world.

In Part II of *The Escaped Cock*, Lawrence introduces the Osiris-Isis myth as a thematic device. The section opens at the temple of Isis in Search, which stands on a peninsula "a little, tree-covered tongue of land between two bays," facing southwest toward Egypt, toward "the splendid sun of winter as he [curves] down toward the sea" (*EC* 35). As the man watches, two half-naked slaves, a boy of about seventeen and a girl, dress pigeons for the evening meal, making of the process the ritual of a sacrifice. When the girl lets one of the pigeons escape and fly away, the boy beats her with his fist until she slips to the ground, "passive and quivering": "He twisted her over, intent and unconscious, and pushed his hands between her thighs, to push them apart. And in an instant he was in to her, covering her in the blind, frightened frenzy of a boy's first coition. Quick and frenzied his young body quivered naked on hers, blind, for a minute. Then it lay quite still, as if dead" (*EC* 36–37).

An aura of eroticism pervades the entire passage. Sexuality emanates not only from the detailed description of the sex act but also from the carefully chosen phallic symbols (the peninsula, the sun, the trees, the pigeons) and yonic symbols (the temple, the two bays, the sea), indeed, from the sensuous phrasing itself: "radiance flooded in between the pillars of painted wood," "the light stood erect and magnificent off the invisible sea, filling the hills of the coast," "on the rocks under which the sea smote and sucked," "a high wall, inside which was a garden" (*EC* 35), and from the presentation of orgasm as the "little death." From the perspective of an enlightened modern consciousness, Janice Hubbard Harris offers some well-taken objections to the scene, and to the elitist reaction of the priestess.[8] But the naturalistic description of naïve primitive sexual behavior modulates into the sexual symbolism, which Lawrence employs effectively to introduce the pagan religious consciousness embodied in the myth of Isis and Osiris.

The priestess serves the goddess Isis — not Isis, Mother of Horus, or Isis Bereaved, Lawrence makes clear, but Isis in Search. After the evil brother Set had torn Osiris's body into fourteen pieces and scattered them abroad, the goddess sailed throughout the marshes in search of the pieces, burying each one as she found it, although she never found the genitals.[9] A few obvious parallels between Christ and Osiris make the Osiris myth a particularly appropriate choice to hold in balance with the Christ myth. Both performed seeming miracles, Osiris introducing the treading of grapes and Christ turning water into wine. Both were betrayed by men who called themselves brothers. Both were slain. And both were deified: Osiris, like Christ, was "a god of the dead, assuring personal resurrection to man."[10] One essential difference between them, of course, is that Christ was celibate and Osiris was not. Lawrence's purpose in establishing the parallel is to introduce to modern Christianity a vitalism lacking in the Christ myth, or more specifically, through the risen man's at least temporary assumption of the role of Osiris, to view the spiritual message of Christianity from the critical perspective of the pre-Socratic vitalism of the Osiris myth.

In *The Escaped Cock*, Christianity and the Osiris myth are brought together when the risen man asks shelter at the temple of Isis in Search. Continuing the reversal of Christian tradition, Lawrence here takes up the plan first proposed to Satan by Belial, "the dissolutest Spirit that fell, / The sensualist," in John Milton's *Paradise Regained*:

> "Set women in his eye and in his walk,
> Among daughters of men the fairest found;
> Many are in each Region passing fair
> As the noon Sky; more like to Goddesses
> Than Mortal Creatures, graceful and discreet,
> Expert in amorous Arts, enchanting tongues,
> Persuasive, Virgin majesty with mild
> And sweet allay'd, yet terrible to approach,
> Skill'd to retire, and in retiring draw
> Hearts after them tangl'd in Amorous Nets."
> (Bk.II, ll. 153–62)[11]

In Milton's sexual pun, women have such power to "Enerve," "Draw out with credulous desire, . . . / As the Magnetic hardest Iron draws," that they beguiled even Solomon "And made him bow to the Gods of his Wives." In his reply, Satan, cautioning that Belial ever judges others by his own fabled lechery, rejects the proposal: "But he whom we attempt is wiser far / Than *Solomon*"; no woman can be found, "Though of this Age the wonder and the fame," on whom a man of such "exalted mind" would cast "an eye / Of fond desire" (Bk. II, ll. 205–11). The difference is that in Milton Belial proposes to use woman as a means of tempting Christ to his downfall, whereas in Lawrence woman becomes the means of consummation and fulfillment for the man who had died. Although I have found no specific references to *Paradise Regained*, Lawrence, who was familiar with Milton, may have had this passage in mind in his description of the risen man's mating with the priestess of Isis, who, it may be said, is "more like to Goddesses / Than Mortal Creatures," "Expert in amorous Arts," "yet terrible to approach," and able to "Enerve," "Draw out with credulous desire" and lead the risen man to bow to her god.

The priestess gives the man a place to sleep in the cave of the goats, which becomes a place of rebirth for him, as the stable of Jesus's nativity (Luke 2:1–20), with its association with sheep and shepherds, is ironically replaced by one of the haunts of Pan associated with satyr-like goats, which Christ at the Judgment will metaphorically separate from the faithful sheep (Matthew 25:32). The cave also compares with the tomb from which the man arose at the beginning of the novella. Both the sepulchre, "the rocky cavity from which he had emerged" (*EC* 16), and the cave, a dark place, "absolutely silent from the wind," in which there is "a little basin of rock where the maidenhair fern [fringes] a dripping mouthful of water" (*EC* 41), are, in context, womb symbols. But whereas his emergence from the sepulchre marks a physical rebirth, his emergence from the cave, as the satyr-image of the goats indicates, marks the rebirth of long repressed sexuality.

The priestess, who has seen the man's nail-scarred hands and feet as he slept, believes, on the basis of his "beauty of much suffering" (*EC* 43), that he is the lost Osiris. Greatly attracted to him sexually, she invites him to the temple, detaining him for a second night. As "The all-tolerant Pan [watches] over them" (*EC* 48), their coming together enacts a ritual whereby Lawrence brings into creative balance the myths of Christ and Osiris. Pan's influence is apparent in the man's saying to himself, "Unless we encompass it in the greater day, and set the little life in the circle of the greater life, all is disaster" (*EC* 50). He agrees to come to the priestess again, but before he goes, he meditates on the "destinies of splendour" which await him, admitting to himself, "I am almost more afraid of this touch than I was of death. For I am more nakedly exposed to it" (*EC* 52). (Compare with Matthew 26:39.) When he goes to her, wanting now desperately to be healed in flesh and spirit, he is still afraid, still repressed and inhibited sexually. "It has hurt so much!" he says. "You must forgive me if I am still held back." But at her gentle suggestion, he removes his clothes and walks naked towards the idol, where, like Solomon (I Kings 11:1–8), he prays to the woman's God, in this case Isis: "Ah, Goddess, . . . I would be so glad to live, if you would give me my clue again" (*EC* 54).

The sexual union is presented as an act of sacramental healing. "Let me anoint you!" the woman says to him softly. "Let me anoint the scars!" As the priestess chafes the risen man's feet "with oil and tender healing" (*EC* 54), he remembers another woman, a former prostitute (Mary Magdalene), who had washed his feet with her tears, dried them with her hair, and poured precious ointment on them (Luke 7:36–38). Suddenly it dawns on him why he was put to death: "I asked them all to serve me with the corpse of their love. And in the end I offered them only the corpse of my love. This is my body—take and eat—my corpse—" (*EC* 55). This revisionist view of the Last Supper (see Matthew 26:26–28, Mark 14:22–23, Luke 22:19–20) is followed by a radical psychoanalytic interpretation of Judas's kiss of betrayal: "I wanted them to love with dead bodies. If I had kissed Judas with live love, perhaps he would never have kissed me with death. Perhaps he loved me in the flesh, and I willed that he should love me bodilessly, with the corpse of love—" (*EC* 55).[12]

With this new self-knowledge, "a new sun [is] coming up in him" under the woman's tender ministrations. The healing ritual also alludes to both myths: "Having chafed all his lower body with oil, his belly, his buttocks, even the slain penis and the sad stones, having worked with her slow intensity of a priestess, . . . suddenly she put her breast against the wound in his right side, and she pressed him to her, in a power of living warmth . . ." (*EC* 56). The Christian allusion is to the disciple Thomas's insistence on empirical evidence of Jesus's resurrection: "Except I shall see in his hands the print of the nails, and put my finger into the print of the nails, and thrust my hand into his side, I will not believe" (John 20:25). When Jesus later appears in their midst in a closed room, "Then saith he to Thomas, Reach hither thy finger, and behold my hands; and reach hither thy hand, and thrust *it* into my side, and be not faithless, but believing" (John 20:27). The structural repetition of the action in the priestess's pressing her breast against the wound in the risen man's side shifts the meaning from empirical evidence of his overcoming mortality to the means of his healing. According to Larry V. LeDoux, "The image of the priestess as a healing girdle around his body is a direct representation of bas-relief pictures of Osiris rising from the dead from between the outstretched wings of Isis."[13]

Touching the woman, the man says, "On this rock I build my life!" (*EC* 57). The allusion to Jesus's words to Simon Peter—"And I say also unto thee, That thou art Peter, and upon this rock I will build my church; and, the gates of hell shall not prevail against it" (Matthew 16:18)— emphasizes the contrast between the old life and the new. No longer interested in the spiritual world or its human institutions, he now wants only to build a solid life for himself and the woman he loves in the sacramental communion of flesh with flesh. Crouching to her, he feels "the blaze of his manhood and his power rise up in his loins, magnificent," and he declares: "I am risen!" (*EC* 57). (See Luke 24:6.) Lawrence's multileveled pun presents erection as the metaphorical equivalent of resurrection, but it also has a more general phallic significance: he is "risen" with the "new sun" of the vital life of the blood.

"Father! he [says]—Why did you hide this from me?" Responding for the first time to "the deep, interfolded warmth, warmth living and penetrable, the woman, the heart of the rose," he says to himself, "My mansion is the intricate warm rose, my joy is this blossom!" (*EC* 57). The phrasing recalls Jesus's words to his disciples: "In my Father's house are many mansions: if it were not so, I would have told you" (John 14:2). The risen man recognizes that there is one "mansion" that the "Father" has hidden from him! "My hour is upon me, I am taken unawares—" (*EC* 58), he thinks. The allusion to Jesus's words to his mother, "mine hour is not yet come" (John 2:4), and, on another occasion, to Andrew and Philip, "The hour is come that the Son of man should be glorified" (John 12:23), Lawrence places at the exact moment of the first sexual experience of the man who had died, thus altering the meaning from "hour of death" to "hour of life."

After the sexual union, Lawrence signals the nature of the contact accomplished between the two myths in the responses of the two principal figures: the priestess: "I am full of Osiris. I am full of the risen Osiris!" and the man: "This is the great atonement, the being in touch" (*EC* 58). For her, the risen man has supplied the missing phallus of Osiris; for him, the priestess of Isis, through the sexual relation, has given new meaning to the Christian concept of atonement. The contrast with St. Paul's view that atonement with God is mediated by Christ's sacrifice (Romans 5:11) reveals Lawrence's opposition to the Pauline direction taken by Christianity since the time of Christ.

A short time later, the priestess discovers that she is pregnant, and she is afraid that her mother and her mother's slaves will make trouble for her and her lover. "Let not your heart be troubled!" he says. "I have died the death once" (*EC* 60). The quotation of Jesus's words to his disciples, "Let not your heart be troubled: ye believe in God, believe also in me" (John 14:1), is here given a new dimension: he wants the woman to believe in him not as a savior but as a lover and a man committed to life. Then he tells her, "I must go now soon. Trouble is coming to me from the slaves. But I am a man, and the world is open. But what is between us is good, and is established. Be at peace. And when the nightingale calls again from your valley-bed, I shall come again, sure as spring" (*EC* 60). The "trembling balance" between Christianity and the Osiris myth is now established. This passage contains allusions to both religions. The Biblical reference is to Christ's words to his disciples: "I will come again, and receive you unto myself; that where I am, there ye may be also" (John 14:3) and "Peace I leave with you, my peace I give unto you: not as the world giveth, give I unto you. Let not your heart be troubled, neither let it be afraid" (John 14:27). The promise and the benediction are both enhanced by the references to the Osiris myth: Osiris, who "travelled over the world, diffusing the blessings of civilisation and agriculture wherever he went," is, in his aspect as a corn god, closely identified with the cycle of the seasons and the subject of popular rites of the Egyptian harvest in the spring.[14] In addition, the sexual connotations of such words as "nightingale," "valley-bed," and "I shall come again" invest the passage with the phallic significance of Lawrence's "religion of the blood."

As I have tried to show, the Biblical allusions in *The Escaped Cock* serve as reference points in the dialectic which Lawrence sets up between the self-denying life of the spirit and the self-affirming life of the blood. Words which in their Biblical context state basic tenets of orthodox Christianity are made applicable to the "religion of the blood" in the unorthodox meanings which the context of Lawrence's novella gives them. Lawrence's ultimate thematic purpose must be further explored.

As Janice Harris notes, criticism of the novella is "divided not on the issue of quality but on the 'heretical' nature of the work."[15] The question, then, is whether Lawrence seeks to revitalize the established Christian religion or to substitute in its place a pre-Socratic religion founded on pagan vitalism. The answer is not a simple one. In Hinz and Teunissen's view: "What is revitalized in the story is pre-Christian symbolism." Since "there is no possible way of reconciling" the opposites, "the healing of the man who died is essentially a healing of the duality that is the Platonic and Christian inheritance."[16] But in Lawrencean terms, the healing of the duality does not lie in the triumph of either side but in the polarity between them. In rejecting spiritual interference with the peasants' souls, the risen man says, "Let the earth remain earthy, and hold its own against the sky" (*EC* 22). But does not the reverse, in principle, also apply? What if the lion really annihilated the unicorn? Lawrence asks in "The Crown." "Would not the lion at once expire, as if he had created a vacuum around himself? Is not the unicorn necessary to the very existence of the lion, is not each opposite kept in stable equilibrium by the opposition of the other?" (*P II* 366). In Lawrence's controlling metaphor, "The crown is upon the perfect balance of the fight, it is not the fruit of either victory" (*P II* 373).

On the other hand, to speak of the relation that Lawrence establishes between the two myths as a "fusion," as I did in an earlier version of this study, is equally inexact. On reconsideration, I want to retract that wording, although it is common in criticism of the novella.[17] There is, undeniably, a coming together, a touching, a creative balance of the two myths; but the merger is purposefully incomplete. LeDoux is surely correct in his observation that although the priestess of Isis three times "identifies him as the embodiment of Osiris, . . . the man who died never questions his own identity and never credits her identification," even when he acquiesces, by his conditional "If you will" (*EC* 53), in "ritualistically supplying the missing part of the god."[18] Lawrence's ridicule of "merging" in the "Whitman" essay (*SCAL* 169–70) provides clear evidence of his attitude on "fusion." In his discussions of dualism, he repeatedly insists that there be no confusion of the opposites. His comments in *Twilight in Italy* are still applicable to *The Escaped Cock*:

[There] are two Infinites, twofold approach to God. And man must know both.

> But he must never confuse them. They are eternally separate. The
> lion shall never lie down with the lamb. The lion eternally shall devour
> the lamb, the lamb eternally shall be devoured. Man knows the great
> consummation in the flesh, the sensual ecstasy, and that is eternal. Also
> the spiritual ecstasy of unanimity, that is eternal. But the two are
> separate and never to be confused. To neutralize the one with the other
> is unthinkable, an abomination.
>
> (*TI* 58)

Lawrence suggests in "The Crown" that any revelation of God is
manifested only in the physical, temporal world: "The revelation is a
condition in the whole flux of time. When this condition has passed away,
the revelation is no more revealed." It exists only in memory as the
"perpetuation of a momentary cohesion in the flux." Because modern man
hates the "imprisoning memory," he seeks war to annihilate it, preferring
to destroy the old revelation rather than "to create a new revelation of
God" (*P II* 414).

Christ's passion was a revelation imprisoned in the memory of
orthodox Christianity. As Lawrence says in his review of Tolstoy's *Resurrection*, "We have all this time been worshipping a dead Christ: or a
dying." But the mystery of the resurrection is an on-going revelation: "the
Cross was only the first step into achievement. The second step was the
tomb. And the third step, whither?" In western Christianity as represented by Tolstoy, "the stone was rolled upon him" (*P* 737), leaving Christ a
God of death and spirit, not of life and flesh. In "The Risen Lord," Lawrence declares: "the Churches insist on Christ Crucified, and rob us of the
fruit of the year," for in the liturgical calendar, all the months from Easter
to Advent belong to "the risen Lord" (*P II* 571):

> If Jesus rose from the dead in triumph, a man on earth triumphant in
> renewed flesh, triumphant over the mechanical anti-life convention of
> Jewish priests, Roman despotism, and universal money-lust; triumphant
> above all over His own self-absorption, self-consciousness, self-impor-
> tance; triumphant and free as a man in full flesh and full, final
> experience, even the accomplished acceptance of His own death; a man
> at last full and free in flesh and soul, a man at one with death: then He
> rose to become at one with life, to live the great life of the flesh and the
> soul together, as peonies or foxes do, in their lesser way. If Jesus rose as a
> full man, in full flesh and soul, then He rose to take a woman to
> Himself, to live with her, and to know the tenderness and blossoming of
> the twoness with her; He who had been hitherto so limited to His
> oneness, or His universality, which is the same thing.
>
> (*P II* 575)

In *The Escaped Cock*, Lawrence brings modern Christianity, which
he finds to be overintellectualized and therefore sterile, into contact with
the instinctual experience of flesh-and-blood sexuality through allusions to

the Osiris-Isis myth. For it is modern, western civilization, not historical, primitive Christianity, to which Lawrence addresses himself. Through the vehicle of the risen man's relationship with the priestess of Isis, he attempts to reconcile the Christian religion in which he was brought up with an imagined religion of the blood based on pre-Socratic vitalism.

In his review of *Georgian Poetry: 1911–1912*, Lawrence wrote:

> I worship Christ, I worship Jehovah, I worship Pan, I worship Aphrodite. But I do not worship hands nailed and running with blood upon a cross, nor licentiousness, nor lust. I want them all, all the gods. They are all God. But I must serve in real love. If I take my whole, passionate, spiritual and physical love to the woman who in return loves me, that is how I serve God. And my hymn and my game of joy is my work.
>
> (*P* 307)

The Escaped Cock is a hymn to the resurrection of the body, not the glorified body of Christianity but the instinctual body of physical being. The symbolism in the novella often has phallic significance, but if it is carnal, it is never licentious. It is, rather, the religious imagery through which Lawrence evokes the sacramental mystery of sex. "Rare women," the philosopher tells the priestess of Isis in Search, "wait for the re-born man" (*EC* 39). And through sexual union with her, the man who died, in an entirely different sense than Jesus intended in his words to Nicodemus (John 3:3), is "born again." Written as a parable for contemporary Christian society, the novella sets forth one of D.H. Lawrence's major themes: rebirth of the whole man through tenderness in the sexual relationship.

Notes

1. Frederick J. Hoffman, "Lawrence's Quarrel with Freud," *Freudianism and the Literary Mind*, 2nd ed. (Baton Rouge: Louisiana State University Press, 1957), 159, 168. In my view, Hoffman errs in his opinion that Lawrence called for a "denial of the intellect."

2. Lawrence's works are cited parenthetically in the text by abbreviated title and page numbers as follows:

EC   *The Escaped Cock*, ed. with a commentary by Gerald M. Lacy (Los Angeles: Black Sparrow Press, 1972).

FSL   "Foreword to *Sons and Lovers*," in *D. H. Lawrence and "Sons and Lovers": Sources and Criticism*, ed. E. W. Tedlock, Jr. (New York: New York University Press, 1965), 22–29.

Letters I   *The Letters of D. H. Lawrence, Volume I: September 1901–May 1913*, ed. James T. Boulton (Cambridge: Cambridge University Press, 1979).

P   *Phoenix: The Posthumous Papers of D. H. Lawrence*, ed. Edward D. McDonald (New York: Viking Press, 1936; rptd 1968).

P II   *Phoenix II: Uncollected, Unpublished, and Other Prose Works by D. H. Lawrence*, ed. Warren Roberts and Harry T. Moore (New York: Viking Press, 1968).

SCAL   *Studies in Classic American Literature* (New York: Viking Press, Compass Book, 1961).

TI   *Twilight in Italy* (New York: Viking Press, 1958).

3. See Matthew 28, Mark 16, Luke 24, and John 20 and 21. All references to The Holy Bible in my text are to the Authorized King James version. Additional literary analogues are discussed in Leslie M. Thompson, "The Christ Who Didn't Die: Analogues to D. H. Lawrence's *The Man Who Died*," *The D. H. Lawrence Review* 8 (Spring 1975):19–30.

4. Evelyn J. Hinz and John J. Teunissen, "Savior and Cock: Allusion and Icon in Lawrence's *The Man Who Died*," *Journal of Modern Literature* 5 (April 1976):287.

5. Sir James George Frazer, *The Golden Bough*, 1 vol. abridged ed. (New York: Macmillan and Co., 1951), 446–47.

6. Hinz and Teunissen, "Savior and Cock," 284, 289.

7. See, for example, Larry V. LeDoux, 'Christ and Isis: The Function of the Dying and Reviving God in *The Man Who Died*," *The D. H. Lawrence Review* 5 (Summer 1972): 133. Most critics have referred to the man as Christ or Jesus, but Lawrence's text, though it employs many reverse parallels to the Gospels, provides no authority for the name.

8. Janice Hubbard Harris, *The Short Fiction of D. H. Lawrence* (New Brunswick, N.J.: Rutgers University Press, 1984), 242, 305, notes 62, 63.

9. Frazer, *The Golden Bough*, 421–24.

10. LeDoux, "Christ and Isis," 146, 10.

11. John Milton, *Paradise Regained*, in *John Milton: Complete Poems and Major Prose*, ed. Merritt Y. Hughes (New York: Odyssey Press, 1957), 497–98. Subsequent references will be cited parenthetically in the text by book and line numbers.

12. Lawrence's ambivalent attitude toward Judas is examined in detail in Leslie M. Thompson, "D. H. Lawrence and Judas," *The D. H. Lawrence Review* 4 (Spring 1971):1–19.

13. LeDoux, "Christ and Isis," 138. LeDoux cites a reproduction in Joseph Campbell, *The Hero with a Thousand Faces*, 2nd ed. (Princeton, N.J.: Princeton University Press, 1968), 209.

14. Frazer, *The Golden Bough*, 421, 431.

15. Harris, *Short Fiction*, 302, n. 55.

16. Hinz and Teunissen, "Savior and Cock," 279, 296. The duality is embodied for them in the opposites of Christ as Savior and a bronze icon in the Vatican museum, "a composite of a phallus, a cock, and the head and shoulders of a man," entitled "The Saviour of the World" (p. 293).

17. See James C. Cowan, "The Function of Allusions and Symbols in D. H. Lawrence's *The Man Who Died*," *The American Imago* 17 (Fall 1960):251; Gerald Fiderer, "D. H. Lawrence's *The Man Who Died*: The Phallic Christ," *The American Imago* 25 (1968):95–96; and Gerald M. Lacy, "Commentary," in *The Escaped Cock*, by D. H. Lawrence, ed. Gerald M. Lacy (Los Angeles: Black Sparrow Press, 1973), p. 124.

18. LeDoux, "Christ and Isis," 138–39.

On the Poetry

The Genesis of D. H. Lawrence's Poetic Form

Hebe R. Mace[*]

I

The problem in reading Lawrence's poetry seems to lie not so much in what he says but in how he says it: how does one respond to a poet who is given to excess in language and experiment in form, with the two at times clearly engaged in open warfare? A prudent resolution might dictate one of two alternatives: either deny that the poetry succeeds as poetry, as many of the earlier critics did, or stringently control the reading process by deflecting it to other purposes, such as thematic investigations, as most of the later studies have done.[1] As useful as the thematic studies have been, however, it seems to me that a great deal is lost by refusing to take Lawrence seriously as a poet. He certainly took his poetry seriously and devoted considerable effort to it, as the 1,000 or so titles in *The Complete Poems* attest, and a careful look at that volume reveals not only the development of thematic statement but also the persistent working out of appropriate poetic forms for it. Since most critics generally agree that Lawrence produced some successful poems in his later work ("Snake," for example, and "The Ship of Death"), it might be more useful here to map a reading of one of his earliest attempts to fit what he wanted to say into the shape of a poem, so that we can watch him as he tries to work past the traditional meters of "the poetry of the past" toward the freer forms of a "poetry of the sheer present."[2]

"Cherry Robbers" (*CP* 36–37), first published in 1913, provides a useful example. Since its testing of formal limits is still cautious and tentative, enough of the conventional rhymed quatrain remains to prevent the runaway thematic statement that plagued some of his first attempts at free verse. Because the content of the poem is presented in a relatively straightforward manner, we should be able to see more clearly the points of departure in its form. An attempt to scan the poem using traditional English meter does indeed highlight the problem spots:

[*]This essay was written specifically for this volume and appears here for the first time by permission of the author.

Únder/the lóng/dárk boúghs,/líke jew/els réd

In the haír/of an Eást/ern girl

Hang stríngs/of crím/son cher/ries, as if/had bléd

Blóod-drops/beneáth/each cúrl.

Únder/the glíste/ning chér/ries, with fóld/ed wings

Thrëe deád/biřds lie:

Pále-breásted/throstles/and a/bláckbird,/robberlings

Staíned with/réd dýe.

Agaínst/the háy/stack a gírl/stánds laúgh/ing at mé,

Chérries/hung round/her eařs.

Offers mé/her scar/let frúit:/I will sée

If she/has án/y teárs.

Lines 3 and 5 are troublesome; in each the major image, cherries, is divided by a foot boundary, with the result that each line also contains an anapest broken by a caesura. Line 6 is impossible to scan with any certainty: an iamb followed by a trochee interrupts another major image, dead birds; uniting that image under a spondee leaves a weak stress hanging forlornly on either side. Line 7 could be scanned in a dactylic-trochaic pattern or turned around to become mostly iambic; either way, the line ends limply in two weak stresses, the latter of which must also carry the rhyme. The penultimate line of the poem is scannable, but if it begins and ends with anapests, the key and single action of the girl, as well as the first direct expression of the persona, receive curiously evasive weak stress. The last line presents an unassertive sequence of three iambs, its sing-song meter certainly inappropriate for the threat its words express. The meter so works against the poem that its dominant rhythmic pattern is established more by syntactic parallelism, in the three prepositional phrases of place that open each stanza, than it is by metric arrangement. This repeated emphasis on the straightforward images of boughs, cherries, and haystack so call attention to the realism of the scene that the reader may not notice the subtle shift in metaphor, in the first stanza, in which dark boughs become curls, clearly not an ordinary sight. Using the methods of scansion that many of us learned under the banner of New Criticism, in fact, demonstrates that the poem is more of a failure than it first appeared to be in its unanalyzed state.

What are we to make of this collapse: that a young Lawrence had not yet caught on to the English quatrain? Or, forgiving the poet, that formalist analysis destroys the poetic voice? We can make the first assertion only if we assume that the nearly infinite range of English stress can arrange itself only into iambs, trochees, anapests, dactyls, spondees, and pyrrhic feet, and the second only if we wish to state that poetic form has nothing to do with poetry. We might try saying that "Cherry Robbers" is free verse and therefore has no need to conform to English meter; but the poem clearly is not fully realized free verse because of its consistent pattern of stanza and end rhyme. The only way out of this dilemma is to give Lawrence the benefit of the doubt and to assume that he did hear a different rhythm in his lines as he tried to catch the moment's experience; to hear what he heard, however, requires that we abandon our "habitu-ated ears,"[3] and reexamine the nature of English stress, meter, and poetic line.

II

Elsewhere I have made a preliminary argument for a theory of English poetic form: its main points were that any line of English poetry can hardly avoid establishing some patterning of stress, since the language itself is stressed; therefore, that any English poetic line can attain meter by arranging the language in the line to correspond to various combinations of weak/strong stress (whether or not the line does or even should attain meter is another question); that the establishment of such meter depends on the degree to which the poet controls the length of the line, regardless of what that line length is, since the line sets the outer boundaries within which meter can be formed; and, consequently, that metric pattern and line break are distinctive markers of English poetic form.[4] I now wish to add that the levels of metric stress are not relative to their context in the line, as levels of linguistic stress (the degrees of stress inherent in the language) are relative to their context in the word or word group, but absolute binary oppositions of weak and strong stress. In order to clarify the last assertion, it will be helpful at this point to digress, for a moment, to consider the nature of English stress.

In our language, stress exists in a dense system of almost infinite range in which precise degrees of accent are not readily apparent.[5] In the context of the word or word group, however, the ear can distinguish gross differences of more or less stress relative to surrounding degrees of stress. In other words, in such a context the attachment of stress to phoneme schematizes the dense system into one in which levels of stress become relatively discrete. More importantly, in any utterance the language code matches phonemes (units of sound) to sememes (units of meaning); consequently, stress is also attached to meaning. Moreover, although the relation of stress to phoneme and sememe is definitive, it is not fixed; by shifting primary stress from one place to another in a word sequence, meaning can be changed. In any utterance, therefore, stress can function as far more than a rhythmic marker.

In addition to its relationship to meaning, stress along with pitch can also mark various rhetorical maneuvers such as question, command, or exclamation. Because the linguistic stress patterns that necessarily arise in English word groups are further delineated by the junctures or pauses that mark their boundaries, patterns of stress supported by juncture also mark the boundaries of any syntactically and semantically coherent sequence of words.[6] This last function of linguistic stress explains why syntactic parallelism is a favorite device of speech-makers and poets (including Lawrence): such parallelism not only establishes a rhythmic pattern but also correlates that pattern with a particular kind of statement that most native speakers, with no specialized knowledge of syntax, can immediately recognize as part of the language code they have assimilated. Any number of people, Pound and Jakobson among them, have speculated about how these rhythmic patterns, or intonation contours, might operate within a poetic form, but few have gone as far as to say that intonation patterns can become the basis for poetic meter. Anthony Easthope, however, notes that since intonation contours tend to recur, they can establish patterns of repetition and variation. Therefore, "intonation can provide the basis of a meter, a principle for line organization through 'parallelism of the signifier.'"[7]

Eco defines a code as the process that correlates expression and content: the code produces the rules that generate signs (or sign-functions) that, in turn, establish the specific correlations between the abstract units of expression and content.[8] Since any such system is at once recursive and open to change, Eco comments that "a code as *'langue'*" might be better understood as a "complex network of subcodes which goes far beyond such categories as 'grammar,' however comprehensive they may be."[9] Following this model, it seems reasonable to suppose that stress, pitch, and juncture could be thought of as units of expression that operate as adjuncts to the phoneme and that, in their multiple interactions, constitute at least part of that "network of subcodes" in the language.

In relation to poetic meter, however, Eco is most helpful when he discusses invention, the special kind of sign production that occurs in aesthetic texts. An aesthetic text is ambiguous, he says, meaning that the language breaks the normal codes of both the expression and content planes so that the reader must "reconsider their correlation"; the text becomes "self-focusing: it directs the attention of the addressee primarily to its own shape" — that is, to "the lower levels" of expression which made up the network of subcodes.[10] Unless these subcodes are joined with a sign-function, they are "mere signals." In an aesthetic text, however, such signals become important:

> Using the everyday rules of a language I can utter a word in many ways, changing the pronunciation, stressing certain syllables differently, or altering intonation patterns; yet the word remains the same. But in aesthetic discourse every free variation introduced in 'uttering' the sign-

vehicle has a 'formal' value. This means that even those features that usually pertain to the [expression] continuum and that a semiotic approach does not need to consider . . . here become semiotically relevant.[11]

Theoretically, then, pitch and juncture could function as well as stress as a basis for poetic meter. In certain languages they do: Chinese poetry is organized around the opposition of high and low tones; traditional French poetry takes into account the intonation patterns of phrases with an equal number of syllables; Anglo-Saxon poetry depends on the strong junctures that mark the mid-line caesura and line end to identify word groups otherwise not clearly marked by repeated stress patterns. But in modern English, the variation of pitch and juncture is not altogether free: if either were placed in a binary system in which the opposed values were discernible, they would distort utterance beyond acceptable limits. Stress, however, can be so arranged and without negative effect; because of the subcodes that generate units of expression, it is the most easily perceived and the most consistently attached to meaning.

English poetic meter can now be defined as a pattern of stress that has been abstracted from linguistic stress and restructured in a binary system of absolute weak and strong values. It functions exactly to call attention "to its own shape," always assuming the limitation of the line. The line does not make meter, but it is the necessary condition for it, because no pattern of any kind can exist apart from the boundaries which define it. Once established within the limits of the line, poetic meter becomes "semiotically relevant" because it permits stress to operate as the dominant subcode which generates the poem's text. Its new coding ability lies in its taking on the power to order the sequence of correlations performed by the language code: meter influences the choices of word and word sequence and therefore influences, or in-forms, the meaning of the poem.

III

Eco comments that a semiotic theory should be "able to explain every case of sign-function in terms of the underlying systems of elements mutually correlated by one or more codes."[12] Although our ambitions here are far less than Eco's attempt to explain all signs, using a semiotic approach to a theory of English poetic form nevertheless permits us to concentrate on the function of stress in the aesthetic text we call poetry. Consequently we can ignore, for the moment, both the long tradition of English poetry as well as the apparently random proliferation of new forms which refuse to follow that tradition, since a theory of poetic form should be able to accommodate all kinds of poetry that is written in English and in which the limitation of the line is a key marker. Since nothing in the theory so far indicates that English metric stress is arbitrarily limited to six patterns, we are now in a position to hear (as well as to see) Lawrence's poem anew without privileging either traditional prosody or the idea that "free" verse cannot be metered:

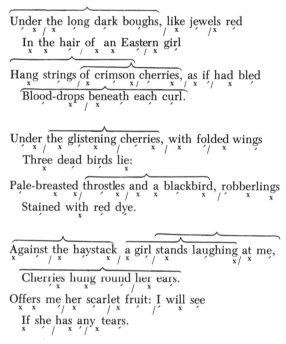

Since we both see and hear a poem printed on the page, and since we often use a vertical metaphor to indicate relative positions and functions, I have placed the weak/strong symbols beneath the line of verse in order to make visible the generative function of poetic meter. Brackets above the line mark various combinations of metric patterns. But these matters of typography aside, what does this new scansion tell us that the old one did not?

For one thing, it tells us that admitting new metric patterns to English prosody does not result in chaos; the new meters in the poem seem clearly derivative from traditional prosody, extending its meters by a controlled addition of weak and strong stress. For another, these extended meters seem to function in relation to the English word group, rather than in relation to the syllable as the conventional feet do.[13] The bracketed patterns, in this poem resulting from the combination of traditional and extended meters, indicate that what we see and hear, when we read a poem, is more complex than a standard scansion might indicate; the combinations, which also function in relation to the word group in such a way as to extend its boundaries, establish metric patterns of five and six stresses which are then repeated and varied throughout the poem. Those familiar with Lawrence's poetry will also see that the stability of these metric patterns depends on the control of the line; in his early attempts at free verse, Lawrence abandoned the line with the result that meter, or indeed any formal device other than syntax, collapses. Finally, it is apparent that the new scansion has not solved all problems, since some stress patterns are still ambiguous; the question remains, however, as to whether or not this metrical undecidability is necessarily a flaw in the poem's structure.

In any case, it is interesting at this point to let the eye see what the ear hears — that is, to remember that the unhabituated ear need not be a prisoner of the horizontal and linear logic of reading. We can play this game, paradoxically, by relieving the eye of its customary context: separating both statement and the stress pattern that organizes it from the body of the poem, and each from the other, reveals how both content and meter are overlaid with an embroidery of metrical repetition and variation. For example, the emphatic combinations — those beginning and ending with strong stress — in the first and fourth lines now foreground that shift in metaphor in which boughs become curls, and then unite dark images, via variation, with the cherries in line 10:

Under the long dark boughs	′ x x ′ ′ ′
Blood-drops beneath each curl	′ x x ′ ′ ′
Cherries hung round her ears	′ x x′ x′

The effect is to compromise those innocent cherries. Other vertical connections are made through a series of combined meters which begin and end in less emphatic weak stress:

Hang strings of crimson	x ′ x ′ x
of crimson cherries	x ′ x ′ x
the glistening cherries	x ′ x ′ x

In line 3, it is impossible to decide which of the two coherent sequences of words should be gathered under the umbrella of a combined metric pattern. The ear, however, can accept the doubled rhythm; its effect is to produce a metrical echo of "crimson," calling attention twice over to the color that glistens.

This series of meters continues in line 9 at the beginning of the third stanza in which the "real" girl first appears, unattached to any metaphor:

Against the haystack	x ′ x ′ x
a girl stands laughing	x ′ x ′ x
stands laughing at me	x ′ x x ′

Again the overlapping echo, here foregrounding the girl's laughter rather than the girl herself who, if we assume a formal context that permits no indistinct boundaries between meters, at first glance seems to stand metrically isolated in the middle of the line. The slight variation of the third pattern, in which the combination ends with a strong stress on the word *me* now becomes significant. The meter here seems to be trying to conceal, and in the act of concealing to reveal, a contradictory focus of the poem's statement, one not on the girl herself but on her act of "laughing at me."

In the middle stanza, another pairing takes place in lines 6 and 8 with the occurrence of a single extended meter and its reversal:

| Three dead birds lie | x ´ ´ x |
| Stained with red dye | ´ x ´ ´ |

But there the metrical thread breaks. In line 7, the birds are now splendidly united in a fluid combination in the center of the line, balanced by dactyls on either side. But its ambivalent stress pattern

| throstles and a blackbird | ´ x x x ´ x |

which begins with a strong stress but ends in weak stress, could place it in either series of combined meters. I also might hope to discover a stronger metrical connection between blood-drops, red dye, and the tears in the last line, but no clear link exists. That I am disappointed makes the placid iambs in line 12 seem all the more noticeable. And the metric pattern of line 6 remains ambiguous; the only advantage I have gained in this scansion is that I am not compelled to break the extended meter in half.

The game of seeing the meter has not been disappointing, however. Its most obvious lesson has been that neither seeing nor hearing is necessarily confined to the left-right, horizontal logic of the line; we can read or listen to the patterns of meter, and therefore make connections between the word groups organized by meter, vertically — up and down as well as left to right. The wonderful paradox here is that while the line is the essential condition for the formation of meter, meter once formed can de-lineate the poem. Far from objectifying the poem as a dead artifact, the metered and controlled line makes possible the transcendence of formal limits by calling our attention, again paraphrasing Eco, to the new coding possibilities offered by the aesthetic text.[14] The next step is to see what kinds of interpretive play these codes can offer the writer/reader.

IV

I am not making the claim that the reader of a poem cannot understand it, or receive whatever message it communicates, without also analyzing its form. What I am saying is that its form, in this case an unconventional meter within the conventional lineation of the English quatrain, is an inseparable part of that message. In a sense, the metric structure of "Cherry Robbers" has left a trail of clues which, as we have seen, transcends the poetic form it helped make possible; it should not be unreasonable, then, to suppose that these same clues will work to transcend the poem's language, in that they will qualify or subvert any unilateral interpretation.

It therefore seems significant that the syntactic insistence on the poem's setting, made by the parallel prepositional phrases that open each stanza, is not supported by a similar repetition in each stanza's initial meters. In the first stanza, the meter calls attention instead to the pairing of the opening phrase in line 1 with line 4, as well as the metrical doubling of "crimson." The context has suddenly shifted, so that the union of "the long dark boughs" with "beneath each curl" makes those curls less innocent than lifeless, as the dark boughs are perhaps leafless. The explicit connection between "crimson" and "cherries" now qualified, the implicit connection between "crimson" and "blood-drops" is promoted, the ambiguous meter pointing the way around the cherries and the simile which follows it. The surface of the poem does not dissipate so much as become transparent; the metrical detour around a major image and the figure which follows it suggests a way of looking through, rather than at the pastoral scene established in the first stanza. Place has been displaced; the poem's metrical structure, which has subverted the pastoral and revealed the poetic *topos* of the tree in the garden, has transferred the images to another system of signification. The cherries can now take on the added power of the deceiving fruit in Eden, or the imitation of fruitfulness in a Bower of Bliss; the girl, potentially both Eve and Duessa, can figure now as mythic Woman — the killing kind, Medusa.

At this point, it might be well to heed Paul de Man's warning about a too-quick interpretation of poetic scene as a symbolic landscape in which the representational level of language disappears. De Man notes that the operation of a symbol is synecdochal, rather than analogical, since it "is always a part of the totality that it represents."[15] In the interaction between subject and object, the consequence of symbolization is that "the relationship with nature has been superseded by an intersubjective, interpersonal relationship that, in the last analysis, is a relationship of the subject toward itself," resulting in a "radical idealism."[16] One way lyric poetry deals with this "enigma of language," de Man suggests, is through allegory which operates by analogy and thus preserves the distinction between self and non-self, since the language of allegory is "representational and nonrepresentational at the same time."[17]

Lawrence was also acutely aware of this risk, and much of his work can be taken as a struggle to preserve the distinction between self and other. Thus in the first stanza of "Cherry Robbers," even though pastoral scene has been displaced by the mythic tree and garden, the representational function of the language remains; the mythic symbols can produce allusions to Eve and Duessa, but only the mimetic or representational combination of dark boughs, blood-drops, and curls can embody the shadowy Medusa that the language, on another level of mimesis, tried to suppress by evasive figuration: "like jewels red / in the hair of an Eastern girl" and "as if had bled" cannot substitute the blandness of deceptively straightforward similes for the powerful allegory the meter reveals.

The pastoral scene reasserts its presence in the second stanza, the birds named as if to validate their real presence, dead or alive, in this real place. But the meter in line 6, which announces the birds' presence, is reversed in line 8, emphasizing the strong stress on "stained"; metric pattern again subverts context and invites interpretation: with the addition of sin to death, pastoral landscape becomes the fallen world. But metrical scene stealing is not so successful in this stanza as it was in the first. Since the girl is not present, either by mythic symbol or figure of speech, no concrete image exists as the basis for allegory. Absent an Eve, the dead birds are the only petty sinners left. I cannot refuse to remember that the cherry robbers scene in *Sons and Lovers* is the prelude to the "test on Miriam," a sexual initiation which she fails,[18] but the metrical conversion, which also fails, does not convince me that a similar situation exists in the text of the poem. I therefore resist seeing the (implied) girl as one of those oft celebrated ladies whose spiritualized flesh is chaste. In that reading, the girl becomes a pallid imitation of the mythic goddess in the first stanza, a petty thief who stains and is stained by the timidity of her denial of the life of the body. She kills by pretense. In this interpretation of poem and novel as single intertext, the birds are served up as a ready-made symbol for the death of the disembodied soul. However, the false falsity of the absent girl calls attention to the word play possible in line 6: the birds lie. But about what? The meter in this line also lies, or at least remains ambiguous.

The final stanza presents another attempt, more successful this time, to preserve place against metrical displacement. The scene here is concerned with the commonplaces of haystacks and human laughter. At last a fully-realized presence, the girl stands metrically protected in the center of line 9. But again undecidable combined meters suggest a shift in emphasis from the girl's action to the object of it, the "me" at whom her laughter is directed. The metrical ambiguity suggests that the laughter may be her real "stain." Although the remaining lines continue to urge normalcy, both syntax and meter suffer from the strain of keeping up appearances. The subject of the sentence which begins line 11 is suppressed so that the focus again shifts from actor to the act of offering. The caesura, marked by the colon after "fruit," asks for the strong stress on "I" so that both syntax and meter are rigged to assert the persona's presence and the girl's absence. But the rigging comes at some cost: the metric pattern of the subject-less "offers me" is uncertain; without the interaction between the girl and the persona, which should have been the thematic climax of the poem, the forced stress on "I" is mere bravura. Line 12, which could have made a strong statement, can only arrange itself in docile iambs.

Michael Riffaterre claims that the semiotic process which transforms ordinary language into poetic discourse begins when the reader discovers that the "ungrammaticalities," the apparent disjunctures in the representational language of the text, can be integrated into another system in which they do "signify as components of a different network of relationship."[19] The reader then discovers the hypogram, a preexisting system of signs — a word, a phrase, a text — that lies outside the poem's text. The hypogram establishes the matrix, the abstract form of the poem, which then "becomes visible only in its variants, the ungrammaticalities" it generates in the text.[20] But in "Cherry Robbers," disjunctures in the representational level of language are not apparent; rather, it seems clear that the metric subcode, or hypocode in Riffaterrean terminology, has mapped the semiotic transformation, leading the reader back and forth through the text, first identifying the major images, then urging their reinterpretation by shifting the context from pastoral, to the ancient myth of the Magna Mater, to the fallen world of sin, and finally to the real world of the laughing girl.

This function of meter suggests that in English poetry, with its long tradition of metrical practice, there might be metric ungrammaticalities as well, which derive from metric as well as textual hypograms. The traditional scansion of "Cherry Robbers" revealed awkward tangles of meter in almost every line, so many that none could, with any confidence, be labelled "ungrammatical" as opposed to simply inept. Hearing the poem again in Lawrence's meters, however, solved most of these problems, at least to some degree, with one notable exception: line 6, at the center of the poem, is still ambiguous, refusing to settle into any certain meter. In this case, the undecidability in the meter is not an error but another invitation to interpretation, our attention called again to the second stanza.

Taking a clue from the absent Eve in this stanza, we can note other absences: the persona himself is excluded, functioning only as an observer outside the scene; if the novelistic intertext is considered, one of the novel's four birds is also missing. And there is one presence, almost overlooked because its power is disguised by a diminutive: the robbers of the title are here demoted to mere robberlings. The substitution of the three birds, the robbers, for the presence of the girl, the possible victim of the robbery, suggests a displacement in the persona's vision in which he sees the birds as emblems of himself. The result is that the observer and the observed are momentarily united, the separation of self and other lost. In this symbolic landscape, the number three takes on added significance: the tree perhaps becomes the cross, the blackbird Christ, the pale throstles the robbers who also suffer crucifixion. Or, and at the same time, the three birds could become the three women the Gospels describe at the foot of the cross, variously configured but always including Mary Magdalene, the sinful woman purified. In either case, the ruined Eden of the allegorized scene in the first stanza, which never stabilizes in the second, becomes a symbolic Golgotha.

Lawrence may have had something like this in mind, since the theme of crucifixion is a strong one in his work. In any case, the transformation of persona into victim, betrayed by Woman (mother / lover / virgin) who would rob him of his soul, his separate identity, prepares the way for the cruelty of his last statement in the poem. The poem's hypogram would thus be some pre-text based on revenge against the Magna Mater in all women, perhaps a version of the biblical quotations Lawrence uses at times in similar contexts: "Noli me tangere," and "Woman, what have thou to do with me?"

A reader of English poetry, however, might sense that the rhythm of "three dead birds lie" is a metrical echo of "And no birds sing." Keats's poem, in a dream vision more like a nightmare, expresses chilling fear of Woman as mysterious Other. The meeting of the knight and the beautiful lady also takes place at harvest time, in a pastoral setting, in which the knight makes "a garland for her head." But after their sexual union, the knight awakes to see a company of "pale warriors, death-pale were they all," who warn him that he too is "in thrall," that he will be as they are, "starved lips" agape, their souls driven out. It may be that such a vision was too close to the nerves for Lawrence to confront directly in 1913; in the preceding year he had abandoned all, eloped with Frieda, and worked through the last revisions in *Sons and Lovers*. In both the novel and the poem, the persona in the cherry robbers scene clearly feels more sinned against than sinning, although Paul Morel does admit some guilt. However, since Keats's poetic concerns so strikingly prefigure Lawrence's, it may also be that Keats is the strong precursor, in Harold Bloom's terms, whom the younger poet must repress or be condemned to futile imitation. Either way, Lawrence adroitly manages to keep yet conceal the metrical echo of Keats's poem by beginning his line with the word "three" which at once renders the meter uncertain and deflects the textual path of allegory to symbolic crucifixion and thus to revenge. But the meter discovers the lie: the pretext of revenge fades and "La Belle Dame sans Merci" takes its place; we glimpse the persona, himself enthralled, on the brink of becoming merely the pale throstles, foolish and accidental victims, driven by hunger.

Hence the sad little final stanza with its docile meter and syntactic manipulations; the girl's laughter, the stain of the human condition, is keenly felt. In terms of the poetic text, the dilemma in which the poet finds himself is described by de Man as the opposition between the symbolic and allegorical modes: while symbolism offers the possibility of identification, allegory, controlled by the typology of a tradition, is necessarily distanced from its origins, so that it "establishes its language in the void of this temporal difference."[21] Language, and especially the language in a poem, also establishes itself in spatial differences, the rhythmic tracks of its meter played out across a linear space. But difference implies the existence of an Other; the very act of utterance subverts the assertion of symbolic union, forcing the poet's painful recognition that the non-self is forever beyond his grasp. It is worth noting that although the persona in "Cherry Robbers" retreats from the brink of this dilemma in the poem's final stanza, the dilemma itself is left unresolved.

Far from erecting a barrier between poem and reader, the metrical organization of this short lyric leads us into and through the poem's surface; instead of preventing interpretation, the meter once recognized always invites us to new ways of reading, new coding possibilities. In the end, in spite of Lawrence's assertion of closure, we are made to see that the defenses erected by language and meter also uncover the poet's vulnerability and the poem's irresolution. Eco speaks about the encyclopedic nature of the sememe in which "every marker is in its turn the origin of a new sememic analysis."[22] In this sense, "Cherry Robbers" is itself a sign which contains an encyclopedia of Lawrence's poetic oeuvre: as a poem, it enacts the powerful dilemma which prefigures part of the major thematic material of his later poetry, as well as the metrical practice to express it; as intertext, it embodies the lyric tradition within which it must inevitably both have and lose its identity.

Notes

1. See, for example, Tom Marshall, *The Psychic Mariner: A Reading of the Poems of D. H. Lawrence* (New York: Viking Press, 1970); Sandra Gilbert, *Acts of Attention: The Poems of D. H. Lawrence* (Ithaca, N.Y.: Cornell University Press, 1972); Ross Murfin, *The Poetry of D. H. Lawrence: Texts and Contexts* (Lincoln: University of Nebraska Press, 1983); and Gail Porter Mandell, *The Phoenix Paradox: A Study of Renewal Through Change in the "Collected Poems" and "Last Poems" of D. H. Lawrence* (Carbondale: Southern Illinois University Press, 1984). None of these studies, although valuable in other respects, pays more than passing attention to the specifics of poetic form. Mandell's analysis of the revisions Lawrence made of previously published poetry for the 1928 *Collected Poems* does attend to the details of language changes within the line. However, in demonstrating how revisions in the language change a given poem, she does not consider that the opposite process might have occurred: Lawrence's ability to control the line and thus the rhythmic patterns within it may have precipitated changes in the wording.

2. *The Complete Poems of D. H. Lawrence*, ed. Vivian de Sola Pinto and F. Warren Roberts (New York: Viking Press, 1971), p. 183. Hereafter cited as *CP* and appropriate page number.

3. *The Letters of D. H. Lawrence, Volume II: June 1913–October 1916*, ed. George J. Zytaruk and James T. Boulton (Cambridge: Cambridge University Press, 1981), p. 104.

4. See "The Achievement of Poetic Form: D. H. Lawrence's *Last Poems*," *The D. H. Lawrence Review*, 12 (Fall 1979): 275–88. In that essay and this, I am obviously not concerned with the mixed form called a prose poem. See Michael Riffaterre, *Semiotics of Poetry* (Bloomington and London: Indiana University Press, 1978), pp. 116–24, for an analysis of the semiotic elements producing the text of a prose poem.

5. By dense system, I do not mean that linguistic stress is without structure, but that the boundaries between specific levels of stress within its structure are not clearly defined. See Umberto Eco, *A Theory of Semiotics*, on "Discretedness and gradated continua" (Bloomington and London: Indiana University Press, 1976), pp. 176–77.

6. The relation of stress pattern to English word groups has been amply demonstrated by Morris Halle and Samuel J. Keyser in *English Stress: Its Form, Its Growth, and Its Role in Verse* (New York: Harper & Row, 1971).

7. Anthony Easthope, *Poetry as Discourse* (London and New York: Methuen, 1983), p. 155.

8. Eco, *A Theory of Semiotics*, p. 50.

9. Ibid., p. 125.

10. Ibid., p. 264.

11. Ibid., p. 266.

12. Ibid., p. 3.

13. See Halle and Keyser, *English Stress*.

14. Eco, A Theory of Semiotics, p. 272.

15. Paul de Man, *Blindness and Insight: Essays in the Rhetoric of Contemporary Criticism*, 2d. rev. ed. (Minneapolis: University of Minnesota Press, 1983), p. 191.

16. Ibid., p. 196.

17. Ibid., p. 185.

18. *Sons and Lovers* (New York: Viking Press, 1958), pp. 285–92.

19. Riffaterre, *Semiotics of Poetry*, p. 4.

20. Ibid., p. 13.

21. De Man, *Blindness and Insight*, p. 207.

22. Eco, *A Theory of Semiotics*, p. 100.

On the Plays

Heroic Theater in *David*

Holly Laird*

Drama, D. H. Lawrence thought, should never Hamletize. Heroes should not brood about themselves. In a letter of 1914, he expressed his typical complaint:

> . . . the moderns today prefer to end insisting on the sad plight. It is characteristic of us that we have preserved, of a trilogy which was really *Prometheus Unbound*, only the *Prometheus Bound* and terribly suffering on the rock of his own egotism.
> But the great souls in all time did not end there.[1]

A great soul, Lawrence elsewhere wrote, needed fertilizing by relationship with another; and only such fertilized souls could produce great "dramatic" literature (*Letters II*, 115). But did Lawrence free Prometheus from his bonds, or crack the rock of his egotism? There is no more common Lawrentian theme, but like it or not, his theme had everything to do with the suffering of a modern ego. When he attempted epic drama in 1925, his play *David* hung on the suffering of heroes. Yet the heroes of *David* did not endure their torment in solitude; theirs was suffering undergone for the sake of glimpsing something or someone beyond the ego. Lawrence reenacted not the drama of Prometheus bound to his rock, and not Prometheus unbound, but the full spectacle of Prometheus in strife with Zeus: the titanic man breaking under the hands of another.

David was Lawrence's last play and one of his most experimental works; in it he attempted to innovate in the theater with an epic form comparable, as Sylvia Sklar has suggested, to the drama of Bertolt Brecht.[2] There should be no better place than this to uncover Lawrence's notion of the heroic. But his drama has fallen victim to the belief that a writer cannot do more than one or two things seriously or well—an opinion which ignores the tradition of the man of letters from which Lawrence arose. Contrary to the common belief, he took both his drama and its performance seriously, as Sklar demonstrates in *The Plays of D. H. Law-*

*This essay was written specifically for this volume and appears here for the first time by permission of the author.

rence (pp. 223–48). He associated the verbal with the performative in his fictional writings, turning the language of the novel into a vehicle for bodily action and gesture. Among his friends, he was an adept actor of charades and a ham. While the success of his drama cannot bear comparison with his fiction, the plays have yet to be appreciated for what they offer as theater. I propose to consider how *David* embodies Lawrence's ideas of the heroic by taking the measure of this play as a theatrical event and by examining its place in Lawrence's life and career.

There are two heroes in *David*: a shepherd and his king. Lawrence named his play after a heroic figure who is better known for his relationships with others (with Goliath and with Jonathan) than for his individualism. While Saul plays the villain to the upstart David, Saul does not appear the lesser man. The play focuses with a special intensity on the dilemma of a hero who must make his way by undoing another great man. The two heroes divide the characteristics of Prometheus between them, for Saul is challenged by a younger Olympian, who is the more clever man. Moreover, these heroes are presented as necessary complements: Saul, the active and arrogant warrior, requires aid and solace from the humble songwriter, David. The man of action is bound to his ingenious alter ego. At one point while composing *David* (in a manuscript notebook containing a text of the play, held in the collection of George Lazarus), Lawrence effaced the title "David" and wrote over it "Saul."[3]

This easy trade of names counts as only one of many exchanges between characters in the play. Jonathan, first son and successor to Saul, must also suffer replacement by David, though he goes willingly. When Saul breaks the promise of his first daughter as a bride for David, Michal is readily engaged as a substitute. Eventually (as we are told in the final speech of the play) David too will be swapped for someone else. He is far from securing Saul's place. In this speech by Jonathan, Lawrence closes his play with the keenest irony of all: "Take thou the kingdom, and the days to come. In the flames of death where Strength is, I will wait and watch till the day of David at last shall be finished, and wisdom no more be fox-faced, and the blood gets back its flame."[4] This is a world in which every soul must give way to another—where a soul is created by the sacrifice of its soulmate.

Behind all these conflicts, including that between David and Saul, looms the larger tension between man and his God. Saul and David are stricken by their God. Even the prophet Samuel agonizes at the will of the Lord: "I am sore for Saul, and my old bones are weary for the king. . . . My heart opens its mouth with vain cries, weak and meaningless, and the Mover of the deeps will not stoop to me. My bowels are twisted in a knot of grief" (*Complete Plays*, 74). From its first scene, this play exposes us to a frightening, only occasionally ennobling process of reduction before the Unknown. The first image we see is that of the Amalekite leader, Agag, bound in stage center and surrounded by spearmen. By the end of the first scene, Agag has been dragged out of sight, to be murdered downstage behind a wall. Meanwhile, we have witnessed a clash between king and prophet, between the Sword and the Voice. Because Saul has hesitated, Samuel must fulfill his God's command to destroy Agag. Samuel acts to unbind the Israelites from the Amalekites, to finish freeing an imprisoned people, even if that coincides with unravelling the nation of Israel itself, as Saul becomes displaced by David. At the end of scene 1, we see instead of Agag a prophet with a bloody sword. This final image—Agag absent and a prophet in his stead—completes the exchange foredoomed at the curtain's raising: Agag has been terribly unbound.

Sklar's primarily thematic analysis reveals only the most basic functions of imagery in this play, as it enlivens, structures, and prompts the actor through long monologues.[5] But images of the bound man and the sword, or of hands, trees, and flame, shuttle in and out of speech *and* action to extend our sight beyond the proscenium. In scene 1 the sword is established as a vital stage prop that is placed in conflict with something only the actor can make palpable on stage—the voice of prophecy. That conflict ends in divorcing a man from his sword, and in marrying the sword with the unseen power of the Word.

Half of *David*'s sixteen scenes (Lawrence's text indicates no "acts") begin with the image of a single man or woman, alone and awaiting the doom conveyed by a greater man or a voice. In nearly every other episode, a chorus stretches to see beyond the appointed scene, straining toward something yet to arrive. The one exception is the central scene 8 where David, Saul and Jonathan are joined, momentarily, in celebration over Goliath. Exits and entrances, too, become opportunities for a continual process of visitation, for the encounter of the actors with something beyond anything they or we can witness on stage. Such visitations echo the encounter between David and Goliath, the most legendary event in the biblical story of David, when the monstrously visible Goliath is brought down by a man and a god past his reckoning. In Lawrence's *David*, this event occurs offstage, so that while our knowledge of the legend informs our experience of all other events in the play, this crucial moment is staged as yet another episode in which, as we watch Saul watching, we too are kept waiting for an impending doom.

David possesses a triangular development and might easily have been worked into a five-act tragedy. But Lawrence deliberately broke it into sixteen parts of various lengths, fracturing our sense of the larger development, to string out a chain of potentially innumerable, isolated events. Why should his epic play have taken an episodic form? It may be tempting to see this effect as a crude adaptation of Biblical chapters into drama. Since Lawrence made few glaring alterations in the sequence of events narrated in Sam. I:15–20—bringing the women into the limelight, enlarging prayers into long monologues, keeping Goliath offstage—it could be argued that he was dominated by his source. But the scripture ran in Lawrence's blood, transfusing the themes and style in much of his writing; so that it would also be reasonable to describe his source more modestly as having acquired the status of a prior draft for his play. The episodic structure might then be viewed as a reapplication of a picaresque effect from his earlier "leadership" novels to his drama. The theatrical problem was this: a triangular development would have subjected this play to the convention of a teleological progress, which Lawrence had learned to avoid, and which is absent from the story of Saul and David. Instead his play, like the devolving legend, wanders along the path of exile — not drifting, but facing a steady series of obstacles to its desire. There is no climax, no calculated catharsis, instead a staggered rain of blows. The story became a Lawrencean book of days, in which at every point another crisis occurs, a submission of the seen to the unseen, an imposition of forms and a Promethean exertion to break them.

This is a play above all about exile. Any effort to "come home" must lead in *David* to greater distance.[6] In the first scene, as we watch a bound man awaiting his unbinding, we must find equal irony in the first line that we hear, sung by Saul's daughter Merab: "Saul came home with the spoil of the Amalekite" (*Complete Plays*, 67). At face value this is a bare and undramatic record of fact. But the opening line is haunted by doublings. Although Saul "comes home" triumphantly from performing the commands of his God, he is now transgressing those same commands because God had ordered the Israelites to torch every vestige of the Amalekite. The first line announces Saul's doom; in coming home with spoils, he spoils himself. The line, furthermore, is expressed in the historical past; while we await the coming of Saul and the doom of Agag, the narrative past tense reminds us that we already know from the Bible what happened, that this first event determined Saul's doom. It is an opening which submits the audience to the double pressure of seeing in the present the process of following one's fate, and at the same time suffering with the knowledge of a doom already completed. While seeking the future, the play *David* is located at a point where it is both bound by the past and refused reentry. In this first line, we also discover a spine for the play, an ambiguous directive: to come home with spoils is to spoil for home.

Why did Lawrence choose to write an epic play in 1925? and why did he engage himself with the story of his namesake? In her memoir, Dorothy Brett suggested that, as often in the past, a woman was the catalyst, that he conceived *David* for the actress Ida Rauh.[7] When asked her opinion, she declared her taste for plays based on Bible stories; in response, he suggested the part of Michal, who refused to live with her husband "after David came back from the wars." It was a teasing remark, meant half-seriously, and the scene mentioned did not appear in the play — at the end, David is still yearning to come back. Yet it is possible that Lawrence had his actress in mind before he thought of *David*, and if so, he wanted someone whose answering role would be as restless and as provocative as that of the leading males. The theatrical possibilities were, clearly, foremost as he imagined his play. At the same time, he must have grasped at the idea of drama and its superhuman energies for other, more personal reasons. In retrospect, the conception itself of this immense play seems extraordinary, rising out of defeating circumstances.

Frieda described *David* as the arena in which "he worked off his struggle for life,"[8] for he began the play as he was recovering from the terrible illness of 1925. He felt himself escaping, just barely, from death. Like his Israelites, he survived by surrendering his healthier, more virile self. *David* emerged with his loss of potency with Frieda, his loss of fascination in America (hence his defeat as a messiah), and the loss of his father. With the death of the elder, the son might take his place, but this prospect accentuated their differences, their different types: the weakness of the pale younger man contrasting with the ruddy health of his father, and Lawrence's wanderings in exile far from the settled provinciality of his parent. At the same time, his father's failures as a man seemed to enforce on Lawrence his outcast state, much like David at the play's end. *David* is one more autobiographical fiction, charting a resurrection of a self which must first be crucified on the back of another, dying man.

The illness of 1925 also marks a transition in Lawrence's career. The composition of *David* registers his return after 1925 to European culture and his creation, in most of the last works, of a newly devotional language with its source in the Bible. In "The Novel," written after *David*, he argued that the Books of the Old Testament must be counted among the greatest novels.[9] The writing of *David* records a corresponding shift in theme from the overtly political to the personal. Lawrence had completed *The Plumed Serpent* just before his illness and during convalescence turned from it, temporarily at least, with revulsion. This novel was his last effort to draw up a blueprint for social revolution. *The Plumed Serpent* (a "leadership" novel) is a chevalresque fable, charting the mythic resurgence of a primeval nobility. Lawrence had also begun a play, *Noah's Flood*, before his illness but never completed it. Reworking a theme from the novel, three rebels seek to undermine Noah by stealing fire — thus altering the story of Prometheus to dramatize the clash between a petty people and the power of a more ancient, greater man. As a sequel to both this play and the novel, *David* represents a less political and more problematic exploration of Promethean struggles. Whether masterful or cunning, every ego in this play suffers submission to another, or is broken. *David* admits us to a time of imaginative crisis for Lawrence, the death of his dream of himself as an American savior, and the birth of a struggle with his own gods.

Yet while Lawrence's decision to write a play should not be seen primarily as an attempt to create another political fable, it does represent an effort at envisaging communal change. Lawrence had for too long seen himself (and been seen by others) as a potential messiah, not to see any change he underwent as symbolic of, or affecting social change. In this play of long trials of suffering by mutually dependent individuals, each endures alteration by the others. The tribe is wrenched from within.

Lawrence had definite views too, in 1925, on the proper relationship between a play and its audience. He was sick of the traditional view of the theater as mere entertainment where the spectator feels an easy sympathy with characters on stage, while reposing safely in his "plush seat," like a little god "lording it" over the spectacle.[10] Like Brecht, Lawrence insisted on redesigning this experience of the drama to provoke the audience. Unlike Brecht, as Sklar adds, Lawrence wanted a theater in which there would be "no division between actor and audience," rather a continuous ritualistic participation.[11] Brecht's concept of "Verfremdungseffekt," or the "Alienation-effect," has no direct application to the theater of *David* because it entailed the foregrounding of theatrical devices. Brecht's audience was forced to consciousness by actors performing as if they knew they were acting, or by the exposure of machinery backstage, from scene drops to lightbulbs, disrupting any vicarious pleasure in a realistic illusion.[12] Lawrence by contrast meant to waken passion, not thought. Even so, I would argue against Sklar that while inviting us to participate in its moods of passion and suspense, this play also distances us. The Old Testament narrative, the scriptural rhetoric, the episodic progress, combine to make this play strange and estranging. It urges us to hear, alongside the heroes of his play, an Other power of alien, godly utterance. Shaped from archaic sources, *David* recreates a community of ancient sufferers, while staging their grief at distance enough to exclude its audience from identification or conversion.

The achievement of *David* as innovative theater derives finally from its movement out of the parlor and marketplace (most of Lawrence's plays had been set in mining towns) into the primitive huts and *terra deserta* of a pre-Christian age. Lawrence placed his social action in a legendary arena, so that the social must be evaluated not by conventional modern manners, but from two skewed perspectives: we sympathize with a proud David, yet see him dwarfed in a rock-strewn open space. Lawrence was responding to the same impulse which motivated Yeats and Eliot, Beckett and Brecht, to rediscover the mythic dimensions of man. T. S. Eliot found a subject for his drama in the experience, as Michael Goldman has expressed this, of a "calamitous loss of self and imprisonment in self that haunts our era, a dis-ease that may drive the fortunate man to glimpse transcendence, but which even those glimpses cannot cure."[13] Lawrence took Eliot's imprisoned man outside and projected him into a religious context which precedes, even preempts, a Christian viewpoint, but while his Prometheus was one of those fortunate enough to "glimpse transcendence," he found it—as Hamlet did—a withering vision.

Notes

1. *The Letters of D. H. Lawrence, Volume II: June 1913–October 1916*, ed. George J. Zytaruk and James T. Boulton (Cambridge: Cambridge University Press, 1981), p. 248.

2. Sylvia Sklar, *The Plays of D. H. Lawrence* (London: Vision Press, 1975), pp. 219–20.

3. E. W. Tedlock, Jr., *The Frieda Lawrence Collection of D. H. Lawrence Manuscripts: A Descriptive Bibliography* (Albuquerque: University of New Mexico Press, 1948), p. 123.

4. *The Complete Plays of D. H. Lawrence* (London: Heinemann, 1965), p. 154.

5. Sklar, *Plays*, pp. 225, 231–33.

6. While convalescing and before beginning to write *David*, Lawrence worked on a fictional piece, "The Flying Fish," which he never finished, but which told a parallel story of exile. A man named Day, upon notice of the death of his last relative, ends his extensive wandering to return home. The first two words of his cablegram become the first two words of the story: "Come Home" (*Phoenix: The Posthumous Papers of D. H. Lawrence*, ed. Edward D. McDonald [New York: Penguin Books, 1978], p. 780).

7. Dorothy Brett, *Lawrence and Brett* (Philadelphia: J. B. Lippincott, 1933), p. 60.

8. Frieda Lawrence, *"Not I, But the Wind . . ."* (New York: Viking Press, 1934), p. 151.

9. *Phoenix II: Uncollected, Unpublished, and Other Prose Works by D. H. Lawrence*, ed. F. Warren Roberts and Harry T. Moore (New York: Penguin Books, 1978), p. 418.

10. *Mornings in Mexico and Etruscan Places* (New York: Penguin Books, 1967), p. 53.

11. Sklar, *Plays*, pp. 219–20.

12. Bertolt Brecht, *Brecht on Theater*, ed. John Willett (New York: Hill and Wang, 1964), pp. 91–99.

13. Michael Goldman, "Fear in the Way: The Design of Eliot's Drama," in *Eliot in His Time*, ed. A. Walton Litz (Princeton, N.J.: Princeton University Press, 1973), p. 179.

A Miner's Dream of Home   Sean O'Casey*

Mr Garnett in his introduction tells us that D. H. Lawrence pencilled a note on the MS., saying that he was but twenty-one when he wrote the play, and that it was "Most horribly green." It is green, certainly, but only in contrast to the withered things that clutter the English stage and wait for a righteous judgment and a general burning. It is not a great play, not even a fine play, but it is a work which plainly shows the makings of a fine dramatist in Lawrence. There is in the work the three-coloured bud of force, humour, and dramatic feeling. There is, as Mr Garnett points out in his introduction, a strong delineation of character, and the " 'greenness'

*Review of *A Collier's Friday Night*, with preface by Edward Garnett (Secker, 1934). Reprinted from *Blasts and Benedictions* (London: Macmillan, 1967), 222–25, by permission of Macmillan, London and Basingstoke. The review first appeared in the *New Statesman & Nation*, 28 July 1934.

lies rather in the cocksureness of the author." But this "cocksureness" is only the undisciplined confidence of a young writer who knows too much and hasn't learned enough. It is a confidence that every young dramatist ought to have, must have, if he wants to put anything better than popular successes on to the stage. This cocksureness of Lawrence—childlike at times—is saturated with an intense and accurate feeling in the vision of the life of the family he seeks to set upon the stage. It isn't a play that the English managers would rush out to meet, though many of them are ever in the market place crying out for plays so that they may make hay while the sun shines or the rain falls; but the moment they get a play with the touch and go of life in it, they start to gibber like jays, close their eyes, shake their heads, and say, how long, oh Lord, how long! They are dead with a play, and dead without one.

Here is a play that was worth production when it was first written, and it is worth production now. Had Lawrence got the encouragement the play called for and deserved, England might have had a great dramatist. It's no use saying that the play was hid, and no one knew about it; the point is that even had everyone known about it the play would not have been produced, for the play is too good in essence to ensure a shower of gold into a manager's lap. Life has vanished, and art has vanished off the English stage. The pomp and circumstance of glorious life has been degraded down to the inglorious pomp and circumstance of a bed.

The play gives us, in the description of its scene even, a fine and lively idea of an English miner's home. It gives us a fine and sharp representation of a clash between a tired-out workman and his tired-out wife, and the clash between these two and their children. It gives us, too, an acute scene of a clash between woman and man, and woman and woman. Not as a cocktail-nourished dramatist gives them gives he them unto us, but as an earnest and young man, surprised and perplexed, sees them and feels them for the first time. The play is weak in dramatic action; it is not graceful, neither is there in it the sound of silken garments moving, but there is the sweat of life in it, and that is something. Some part of the play sinks to softness; a lot of it is hard and even brutal, and it ends on a note of puzzling, strange, and striking pathos. He shows us that the miner thinks more of the Miner's Arms than he thinks of the Miner's Dream of Home, which isn't a pleasant thing to the huge leaven of the sentimentally diseased among the great gang of theatre-goers.

There is a fine picture in the play when Lambert, the father, first enters. He is, the directions say, "a man of middling stature, a miner, and black from the pit. . . . He wears a grey-and-black neckerchief, and, being coatless, his arms are bare to the elbows, where end the loose dirty sleeves of his flannel singlet." He gets hold of the table, and pulls it nearer the fire, away from his daughter.

> The Daughter: Why can't you leave the table where it was. We don't
> *want* it stuck on top of the fire.

Father: Ah dun, if you dunna.

Here, in a few chosen words, is sharply and closely depicted the irritated selfishness of the old man, and the corresponding irritated selfishness of the young daughter. It is very clever and very good.

There is humour at the edge and in the core of the play. Humour over the old man's damp breeches, when he ejaculates a naughty expression that sets his wife and his daughter's friend laughing, and flashes a flush of shame on to his daughter's cheeks; humour in the washing of his back by his wife who claps an ice-cold flannel on it and makes him yell resentment; humour in the visiting miner pounding "The Maiden's Prayer" out of the piano; and humour over the baking of the bread when Ernest, deep in his puzzling and shrinking battle with the girls, forgets what he ought to do, and lets the loaves be burned to a cinder.

There is a gleam of poetry in the play when Ernest, after reading from a French book, says: "That's what they can do in France. It's so heavy and full and voluptuous: like oranges falling and rolling a little way along a dark-blue carpet: like twilight outside when the lamp's lighted."

Vivid flashes of anger and rage light up the quarrel between the old man and the young boy, and, later on, like sad summer lightning, the softer anger of the mother lightens the scene in which the woman's jealousy rebukes her son for allowing a girl to gather attentions from him that she wistfully and foolishly thinks to be still due to her.

It is maddening to think of the stillness that lay around the evident possibilities in Lawrence to create drama. A little more experience, a little more encouragement, and, in Lawrence, England might have had a great dramatist. It is no use saying that with more experience he wrote additional plays, plays deeper and greater than this effort of twenty-one. There never was a chance of him moving behind the curtain, and so getting into intimate touch with the hidden life of the theatre. The bugs and the bears of the theatre gave him the back of their hand. He came into the theatre, and the theatre received him not. Even today there isn't a theatre in England in which a writer like Lawrence would be certain to get a chance. Millions of money spent on football; millions of money spent on cricket; football grounds and cricket pitches everywhere, but ne'er a theatre to make a new-born dramatist sure of himself. And the community singers still sing Land of Hope and Glory. A great dramatist might have come from the ready acceptance of *A Collier's Friday Night*. Many and many a far worse play has been put on by the Abbey Theatre. There were the makings of a fine dramatist in D. H. Lawrence, but he is gone now, and the chance is gone forever with him.

Novelist on Stage

Anaïs Nin*

D. H. Lawrence's complete dramaturgic output—eight full-length plays and two fragments, written at various points in his literary career, from 1909 onward—has now been published in a single volume. While the book mysteriously lacks introductory comment of any sort, and while Lawrence is not widely recognized for his stagecraft (only a few of the plays ever having been produced), the collection is interesting for the light it sheds on Lawrence's efforts to express his ideas in a different medium.

The plays will appeal to those who were mystified by Lawrence's daring and unique attempt to crack the surface of naturalism in his novels, to find a way to release emotions, instincts, intuitions, to find a special language of the senses. For the dramatic form, with its severe limitations on lyric expression, would not seem suited to Lawrence's aims.

In his plays, which range from situation comedy to realism, Lawrence respected the need for action and dialogue—faithfulness to what is manifested on the surface and directly expressed. Absent are deep exploration of motivations and emotional ambivalences. Direct, simple, almost classical, and free of admixture, these plays remind one of the perfect rendering of the illusion of reality by the Moscow Art Theater. Lawrence does not strive for denouements, for tension: he is content to present a lifelike portrait of instants. He makes no attempt to break with conventions of the theater, as he did with those of the novel.

His favorite themes, similar to the themes of his novels, are reduced to extreme artlessness. At times his faithfulness to ordinary dialogue is extreme, as in *The Daughter-in-Law*, where he supplies a short-hand colloquialism for the spoken dialect which is to me almost unreadable. He records the atmosphere of poverty. He is concerned with the simple patterns of daily life which help to contain outbreaks of emotion. He endows these patterns with ritualistic meaning that conveys inner states of mind. The serving of food, the very descriptions of food itself, laundering, ironing, folding sheets, baking bread, making beds, lighting lamps or candles are anchors and roots to prevent emotional explosions.

His poetic moments are sensitive and unadorned. In *The Widowing of Mrs Holroyd*, Mrs Holroyd, while her husband is drinking at the pub, is visited by Blackmore, the electrician working around a mine who describes himself as a "gentleman": "ours is gentlemen's work."

> *She puts her two palms on the table and leans back. He draws near to her, dropping his head.*
> Blackmore: Look here!
> *He has put his hand on the table near hers.*

*Review of *The Complete Plays of D. H. Lawrence* (New York: Viking, 1966). Reprinted from the *New York Times Book Review*, 10 April 1966, pp. 4, 33, by permission of the periodical.

Mrs Holroyd: Yes, I know you've got nice hands — but you needn't be vain of them.
Blackmore: No — it's not that — But don't they seem — (*he glances swiftly at her; she turns her head aside; he laughs nervously*) — they sort of go well with one another. (*He laughs again.*)
Mrs Holroyd: They *do*, rather — .

This is a key moment in the play, for the attraction between them dramatized by this quiet scene has its preparation and consequences. Blackmore is aware that Mrs Holroyd suffers from her husband's drinking — that he brutalizes the family when he returns from his drinking sprees, and has humiliated her by bringing prostitutes to his home. Mrs Holroyd has wished for his death, to be free of him. She confesses this to Blackmore. But when her husband dies in a mine accident she is distraught; she feels that it is her wish which caused his death. She says despairingly: "I never loved you enough."

In *The Married Man* Lawrence attempts light comedy and is less successful. He deals with complicated philandering, but adds little touches typical of his writing: "I should think it would be the easiest thing in life to write a poem about a couch. I never see a couch but my heart moves to poetry. The very buttons must be full of echoes."

All the plays foreshadow the series of films made so much later about working classes in England: the moods for Tony Richardson's *The Loneliness of the Long Distance Runner* and Karel Reisz's *Saturday Night and Sunday Morning*, inarticulate tenderness; frustrated ambitions; atmospheres of limitation and greyness.

In *Daughter-in-Law* a husband is unfaithful, the wife leaves him, but then returns to find her husband has been wounded in a strike. They rediscover the depth of their love for each other.

In *Touch and Go* Lawrence tackles a social theme, and shows that he was able as early as 1920 to foresee that the struggle of labor against capital would be thwarted not by objective factors (whether or not the demands were fair) but by the personal, irrational, subjective resistance of individuals.

A Collier's Friday Night, which parallels *Sons and Lovers*, is probably the most moving of all the plays. The father drinks, and is brutal, the mother feels superior to him and has transferred her love to her son. She is jealous of her son's interest in a young girl, Maggie, and when he goes to visit her she cannot sleep until he returns safely home. When her son tries to explain that there are different kinds of love, that there are things he can talk about with Maggie which he cannot talk about with her, she can only reproach him for not loving her more than anyone else. The play ends with a full expression of their love, an overwhelming tenderness. "There is in their tone a dangerous gentleness — so much gentleness that the safe reserve of their soul is broken."

It is this reserve (which is rarely broken in the plays) which makes them less revealing of other dimensions than are the novels, where Lawrence proved himself a speleologist of the unconscious. He penetrated realms people feared and did not acknowledge. He portrayed ambivalences, dualities, and instinctive, intuitive states. He allowed his characters moments of desperation, loss of control, blind impulsiveness. Those who were not at ease with these explorations, who do not wish to witness any outbreaks of the irrational in the pattern of harmonious tradition, will prefer the plays, with their detachment and linear organization.

A Major Miner Dramatist   Philip French*

When D. H. Lawrence's collected plays were belatedly published three years ago there was no introduction making significant claims on their behalf, merely a dust-jacket note that the book "makes a valuable addition to the understanding of Lawrence's complete work." Nor had his splendid biographer, Harry T. Moore, suggested that we revise the contemporary judgment that Lawrence wasn't a playwright; and F. R. Leavis's admirable critical study ignored the plays altogether. (In retrospect one is astonished that Dr. Leavis didn't seize the opportunity at one of the twenty-odd points where he belaboured T. S. Eliot to argue that Lawrence was also a superior playwright.) Lawrence himself was disappointed at the response to his dramatic work, especially to his biblical piece *David*, which is however the only one of the eight completed plays I shouldn't care to see staged. After the failure of *David*, Lawrence denounced the critics (in a 1927 letter to Earl Brewster) as "eunuchs." "It is a fight," he declared, in which "I want subtly, but tremendously, to kick the backsides of the ball-less." These words closely anticipated the reaction of a later playwright who also owes his reputation—as Lawrence now does—to the English Stage Company at the Royal Court. For the revaluation of Lawrence the dramatist has almost wholly been brought about by Peter Gill. In August 1965 Gill directed *A Collier's Friday Night* as a Sunday evening production without decor, and followed it up with *The Daughter-in-Law* early last year. Now he has added *The Widowing of Mrs Holroyd*, and the three plays running in repertory at the Court constitute one of the outstanding theatrical events in recent years. There is little likelihood of Lawrence's plays coming to be regarded as highly as his fiction (this would make him at the very least the peer of Shaw or O'Neill), but Gill has established beyond doubt that he is a major dramatist in the

*Review of the 1968 Royal Court Theatre (London) production of *A Collier's Friday Night*, *The Daughter-in-Law*, and *The Widowing of Mrs Holroyd*. Reprinted from *New Statesman*, 22 March 1968, p. 390, by permission of the periodical.

naturalistic tradition, unrivalled in his ear for working-class speech. And in proving this Gill has provided what must be considered the highwater-mark of naturalistic presentation in the country.

The Court trilogy comprises Lawrence's three best plays, each closely related to his fiction without being eclipsed by it and to each other through common themes and Midland settings. *A Collier's Friday Night* (1909) is just that, an evening in a miner's home with a possessive mother, who despises her drunken husband, and a student son growing away from his family; this clearly pre-figures the relationships of *Sons and Lovers*. *The Daughter-in-Law* (1912), set against the background of a pit strike, concerns the threat to a six-week-old marriage between a mother-domi-nated miner and his superior wife (who's returned from service in Manchester to marry him) by the news that a local girl is with child by the husband; some years later Lawrence used the same situation in a slightly different form in the superb story "Fanny and Annie." *The Widowing of Mrs Holroyd* (1914) is a dramatisation of the early story "Odour of Chrysanthemums," where the neglected wife of a hard-drinking miner copes with his death in the pits; in the play Lawrence has added an appearance by the husband and introduced a sensitive young colliery electrician who wants Mrs Holroyd to desert her husband.

Seventeen actors appear in the plays, most in two productions and only Anne Dyson in the three. But there is never any question of them duplicating parts even where there are certain resemblances — as there are between the husbands and wives that Michael Coles and Judy Parfitt so beautifully realise in *The Daughter-in-Law* and *Mrs Holroyd*. The same is true of John Gunter's four sets; all four are kitchens in miner's cottages, but each is very precisely the home of the people who very precisely inhabit it. The house in *A Collier's Friday Night* is where a middle-aged miner and his wife have brought up their family, just as the spruce living room with its racks of shiny plates in *The Daughter-in-Law* is the new home of the house-proud, disdainful Minnie. Into the first comes a defeated, brutalised man who sits down unwashed to suck his tea from a saucer; into the second shuffles an insecure youngster who hesitates to hang his jacket over a chair. The actors are so sunk in their roles that every unemphasised gesture is part of a personal history, a network of relation-ships, and a contribution to creating a portrait of a way of life that extends beyond these tiny rooms. Washing off the coal dust after a day's exhausting work, baking a pie, preparing a meal, shoving a stubbed cigarette into a pocket, and a hundred other activities are performed with an exact, unobtrusive veracity that, with the carefully spoken dialect speech, convinces us that the world outside created by our imagination is as real as the smell of the stew that wafts over the footlights. Despite the persistent humour, the warmth and depth of the way these characters feel for each other, this is a grim hard life they live, and to embody it as totally as these actors do must be a painful experience. But they never betray Lawrence's truth by attempting to alleviate it with sentimentality, caricature or the suggestion of false hope. They do not, in short, patronise these people.

There are many incidents in the three plays one will never forget: to name just one from each, the reconciliation between son and mother in *A Collier's Friday Night*; the blood-chilling moment when the husband screws up the wife's treasured prints and throws them on the fire in *The Daughter-in-Law*; the ritual washing of the dead body which concludes *Mrs Holroyd*. Above all, however, one remembers a whole world, and this is the great achievement of Peter Gill and his dedicated cast.

On the Letters

Letters of the Artist as a Young Man

Paul Delany*

If D. H. Lawrence had ended up as one of that mildly ludicrous type, the Ancient British Intellectual, he would have been 94 this Tuesday. Cambridge University Press has chosen to mark the day by publishing this first volume of a definitive edition of his writings. Like many "major literary events," this one is well seasoned with irony. In adult life, Lawrence himself never celebrated his birthday, and kept the date a secret; he cared nothing for "first or last editions"; and after his disastrous visit of March 1915 he loathed Cambridge and everything it stood for. The list could go on; nevertheless, one should not lose sight of the basic truth that Lawrence's letters are among the finest in the English language and have much to gain from the scholarly presentation given them in this new edition.

The previous collections, by Aldous Huxley in 1932 and Harry T. Moore in 1962, were landmarks in the development of Lawrence's reputation; but between them they include less than half of his letters, and each volume is slanted toward the particular view of Lawrence held by its compiler. The Cambridge edition will require its seven editors to follow a common style set by its general editor, James T. Boulton of the University of Birmingham; and it will solve the problem of selection by printing every word of every surviving letter—over 5,500 in all.

As Lawrence's youth is revealed in ever closer detail, what pattern emerges? A revolutionary Frenchman once claimed that we are all born geniuses, then become stupid; and there may be some confirmation of this in the iron law of biography, that the earlier part of anyone's life will almost always be the most interesting—the years before the successful public figure puts on his mask (not to mention the lamentable conclusion, when his face has grown to fit it). Nonetheless, this record of Lawrence's life up to the age of 28 seems to evolve in a contrary direction. From the beginning, these letters reveal a young man of intelligence and sensitivity;

*Review of *The Letters of D. H. Lawrence, Volume I: September 1901–May 1913*, ed. James T. Boulton (New York: Cambridge University Press, 1979). Reprinted from the *New York Times Book Review*, 9 September 1979, pp. 3, 44, by permission of the periodical and the author.

but also a priggish, laborious and self-consciously literary young man. "I shall never do anything decent," Lawrence admitted to one of his editors, "till I can grow up and cut my beastly long curls of poetry." Despite the myth that his talent was born rather than made, we can now see that it took him years of plodding, and many false turns, before he could gain the full use of his gifts.

How was he able, eventually, to succeed? Not, certainly, by the conventional path of an arduous and self-effacing literary apprenticeship. "We have to hate our immediate predecessors," he told his mentor Edward Garnett, "to get free from their authority." Lawrence did not seek self-realization through art, but through experience; and these early letters show how hard it was for him to gain experience of the kind and scale that he demanded. They also show his courage in seizing his opportunities, once they appeared, and the price in sickness and ostracism that he had to pay for them.

During this phase of his life, Lawrence felt he owed everything, even his very identity, to the women he had known; he told Jessie Chambers that she was "the anvil on which I have hammered myself out." Though there are some fine letters to male friends in this volume, they are outnumbered and overshadowed by the letters to women — despite the loss of what would have been the most important ones. Three women with whom Lawrence had affairs (Jessie Chambers, Agnes Holt, and Alice Dax) destroyed the letters he sent them, while Lawrence himself apparently destroyed his letters to his mother after her death.

Lawrence's alliance with his mother against his father began virtually in the cradle, and when he left home he carried on the quarrel by denigrating the "man's world" of Edwardian society. He told his suffragist friend Blanche Jennings, an obscure post-office clerk, that at Nottingham University College he had been "bitten so deep with disappointment" when the august professors turned out to be "quite small men." On first frequenting London he seemed most impressed by "women such as I have never seen before, beautiful, flowing women"; whereas H. G. Wells, whose novels he much admired, was in the flesh no more than "a funny little chap . . . no glow about him."

It is hardly surprising, then, that Lawrence should achieve a deeper and more conscientious rendering of female experience than any male English novelist (Richardson perhaps excepted). A great share of the credit, certainly, should go to his mother Lydia, that extraordinary and tragic figure: One of her gifted sons died young, the other had just gained his first major literary success — the publication of his first novel, *The White Peacock* — when she died at 59. Her influence guaranteed that Lawrence could never be a genuinely proletarian writer; for Lydia was middle-class to the core, though her marriage to a miner cast her into an oppressively close relation with her husband and her five children. A visit to the shoe-box house where Lawrence was born suggests how claustrophobic that intimacy must have been. Her son's talent promised Lydia a vicarious escape from the humiliation of being de-classed; yet it was the density of emotional life in a working-class household that shaped Lawrence's particular sense of life as a series of obscure and internecine psychological combats. In all his early work — the three novels culminating in *Sons and Lovers* and the constant flow of short stories and poems — he strove to decipher the hidden forces beneath the everyday forms of social life, and to salvage an authentically personal consciousness from the tumult of will and desire in which he was immersed.

The solicitude of his mother, and of his childhood sweetheart Jessie Chambers, at once nourished Lawrence and made him feel impaired in his manhood. A week before his mother's death he proposed to an attractive fellow-student, Louie Burrows; he claimed that he needed her love to deter him from suicide, yet she must have been inwardly dismayed by his avowal that "I must feel my mother's hand slip out of mine before I can really take yours. She is my first, great love." In the following year Lawrence remained emotionally irresolute and unsatisfied, paying court to several women while nominally pledged to Louie. The crux of the matter was that none of them was willing to give him the sexual consummation he craved; if any had yielded unreservedly, he might well have spent years with her as an obscure country school-teacher, writing only in his spare time and constrained by a woman whose views were narrower than his own. Instead, Frieda Weekley decided, on a few hours' acquaintance, that this importunate young student of her husband's was worth turning her life upside down for — the rest is history.

"History with a vengeance" one might say of the present volume, the first of eight in the Cambridge series. Up to a fifth of the 579 letters in this volume, which ends with the appearance of *Sons and Lovers*, are previously unpublished or have appeared incomplete (though it is annoying to find that the editor gives no comprehensive identification of the material that appears here for the first time). There is, in fact, important new material in the correspondence with Helen Corke, Blanche Jennings, and Robert Reid (a Congregational minister with whom Lawrence argued out his loss of faith): one gets a fuller picture of several of Lawrence's friendships, notably that with Ezra Pound, and there are many interesting illustrations, including a colored miniature of Lawrence that Louie Burrows owned (could it have been by her cousin Marguerite? Professor Boulton gives no clue). Still, the main value of the book lies in the commentary and in the insights that are made available when we can see all the surviving letters gathered into a coherent, chronological body of evidence. We can now observe Lawrence, for example, wooing four women at once (in February 1912) — each ignorant of the role of the others — like a burglar who tries one door after another, hoping to find one unlocked. This pattern would be repeated often in his life.

The editorial commentary arouses more mixed feelings. It is sharply incongruous to see Lawrence's vital personality so cribbed and confined by the scholarly apparatus; he would, of course, have detested the whole enterprise — though that need not be a final criticism of such posthumous tributes. In any case, Professor Boulton has labored devotedly to provide us with chronologies, maps of every place Lawrence went, lists of his college textbooks, glosses on Midlands slang and thousands of other facts. Too many, I suppose, for some tastes and most purses.

What is more important, though, is the *kind* of facts that Professor Boulton has chosen to admit to this monumental work — and what he has left out. We learn, for example, that Tom Smith became Deputy Director of Explosives in World War II; that is an extremely marginal fact about Lawrence, though he was friendly with Smith at college. On the other hand, when it comes to some of the central facts of Lawrence's youth, Professor Boulton often says very little — about Lawrence's love entanglements at Croydon, for example — or nothing at all, as in the case of the chronology of Lawrence's affair with Alice Dax. Professor Boulton's blinkered approach to his task is perhaps most evident in his flat assertion that Lydia Lawrence died of carcinoma of the stomach; this is what the death certificate said, indeed, but we are given no hint of the weighty evidence that she died from an overdose of morphine, deliberately given her to end her suffering by Lawrence and his sister Ada. Professor Boulton is a marvel of industry when collecting information, but much less impressive when having to interpret what he has assembled.

Sifting through this mass of evidence about Lawrence's early environment, one still feels fascinated — and perplexed — that he rose so far above his origins. The narrow horizons of life in the mining village of Eastwood, his hard-driven work as a teacher, the puritan hesitancies of his sweethearts: all kindled in Lawrence an overwhelming desire to shatter the whole frame of life as he had known it. Jessie Chambers, he complained to Edward Garnett, had "bottled [him] up till [he] was going to burst." The unleashing of his creative energies in 1912 was sparked by his realization that consciousness and sensuality need not be at odds — a lesson first taught him by Frieda, then soon reinforced by his first contact with the landscape and culture of Italy. It was in Italy, too, that Lawrence confirmed his status as a major novelist by writing the final version of *Sons and Lovers*. As he looked homeward from his villa above Lake Garda to the mining country, Lawrence wondered why his fellow Englishmen could not share his passion for self-transcendence. In his darker moods he would roundly curse them all, "the slimy, the belly-wriggling invertebrates"; at another time he might grandly promise "to bludgeon them into realizing their own selves."

It may be true that Lawrence naively overestimated the sensuousness of Italy; and almost everyone thought he overestimated Frieda, though to him she was proof that "All women in their natures are like giantesses. They will break through everything and go on with their own lives." Even

Frieda herself saw the flaw in that argument: "Lawrence approaches all people (women especially) as if they were Gothic cathedrals," she told David Garnett, "then he finds that they are little houses and hates them for it!" This trait caused endless grief to both Lawrence and those around him: his passionate insistence that life must be *big*.

But how exhilarating still to encounter, near the end of this volume, the letters Lawrence wrote to England while on his German and Italian honeymoon in 1912. The son of a man who could barely read, Lawrence here reveals in an effortless mastery of language — a gift granted him, he feels, by Frieda, his newly won muse. "Never, never, never could one conceive what love is, beforehand, never," he told an Eastwood confidante, Sallie Hopkin; "Life *can* be great — quite godlike." Yet his personal exultation is counterpoised with the brilliant description of the Bavarian countryside that precedes it — a set piece that reminds us that when Lawrence was writing at the top of his powers, the recording eye and the informing vision were seamlessly fused.

Two years earlier, when mired in unsatisfying love affairs with Jessie Chambers and Louie Burrows, Lawrence had lamented to Helen Corke that "I wish, from the bottom of my heart, the fates had not stigmatized me 'writer.' It is a sickening business. . . . The literary element, like a disagreeable substratum under a fair country, spreads under every inch of life, sticking to the roots of the growing things." In his letters, though still inescapably a writer, he came closest to shedding the burden of that stigma. Unlike his novels, which were usually several times rewritten, his letters allowed him to immerse himself in the flux of unconsidered moments of being. Since he blithely threw away every letter that was sent to him, he presumably would have cared little if his own had met with the same fate; yet in the long run, it may turn out that in his letters he will best be known, admired, and even justified.

General Essays

Lawrence's Quarrel with Tenderness

Mark Spilka*

I

Late in *Lady Chatterley's Lover* the heroine compliments the hero for a quality which other men lack, the courage of his own tenderness, which "will make the future." The tenderness she has in mind is frankly physical, as when he puts his hand upon her "tail" and says she has a "pretty tail." Her lover accepts and expands upon her sentiments: "natural physical tenderness," even between men, means bodily awareness and aliveness, means keeping literally "in touch" with others; sex itself is only the closest touch, the closest form of natural communion—"And it's touch we're afraid of. We're only half-conscious, and half-alive. We've got to come alive and aware. Especially the English have got to get into touch with one another, a bit delicate and a bit tender. It's our crying need."[1]

This connection of tenderness with wholeness and aliveness, awareness and communion, is new in Lawrence's fiction. Tenderness implies personal feelings, affections, soft sentiments from the conscious heart; and Lawrence usually speaks for dark impersonal passions from unconscious depths. Tenderness is, moreover, a conventionally romantic feeling, an aspect of romantic love; and Lawrence usually speaks against conventional romance. Yet *Tenderness* was his first title for *Lady Chatterley's Lover*, and courage for it his lasting theme. That tenderness should require courage is the telling point: it means that tenderness inspires fear, that tender feelings are somehow frightening and difficult to express. Such fear is not uncommon. I. A. Richards speaks of the "widespread general inhibition of all the simpler expansive developments of emotion . . . among our educated population"; Ian Suttie speaks, more broadly, of "the taboo on tenderness" throughout our Puritan culture.[2] It was this general social condition which Lawrence was confronting. But he was also confronting his own deepseated fear of "simple" and "expansive" feelings. The courage to confront them came late in life, too late perhaps for

*Reprinted from *Critical Quarterly* 9 (Winter 1967):363–77, by permission of the journal and the author.

consequential change: and yet he did make a place for tenderness in his fiction. How he made it, and what he actually made, are questions which may accordingly tell us much about Lawrence, and something more about ourselves, if we can agree that Lawrence explores and clarifies pervasive modern problems.

II

His quarrel with conventional romance may be illustrated by a late story, aptly called "In Love," where he deals with modish attitudes of the 1920's. Hester and Joe, the engaged couple in the tale, are to spend a weekend together on the little farm Joe has started. Though Hester likes the farm, she is upset by the prospect of making love to Joe. Before their engagement she liked him well enough; there had never been "anything messy to fear from him. Nor from herself." But now that cuddling and petting have started, "she couldn't stand him." To be stroked and cuddled was, she felt, humiliating, insulting, awful, ridiculous; to be "in love" was to lose self-respect: it was SPOONING, it was Rudolph Valentino, it was messy and rather sickening, "As if one were a perfectly priceless meatpie, and the dog licked it tenderly before he gobbled it up." Thus, when Joe begins his doggy business on the sofa, Hester sickens:

> She endured his arm round her waist, and a certain pressure of his biceps which she presumed was cuddling. He had carefully knocked his pipe out. But she thought how smug and silly his face looked, all its natural frankness and straightforwardness gone. How ridiculous of him to stroke the back of her neck! How idiotic he was, trying to be lovey-dovey! She wondered what sort of sweet nothings Lord Byron, for example, had murmured to his various ladies. Surely not so blithering, not so incompetent! And how monstrous of him, to kiss her like that.
> "I'd infinitely rather you'd play to me, Joe," she snapped . . . "I'd love to hear some Tchaikowsky, something to stir me up a bit."[3]

While Joe plays stirring music, Hester slips out of the house, climbs a tree to elude her lover, and questions her normality: "Because the majority of girls must like this in-love business, or men wouldn't do it. And the majority must be normal. So I'm abnormal, and I'm up a tree." When she climbs down, however, Joe confesses that he never was "in love . . . that way"; he merely thought it was "expected." He sees his error now, and she too sees more deeply:

> Why had he tried that silly love-making game on her? It was a betrayal of their simple intimacy. He saw it plainly, and repented.
> And she saw the honest, patient love for her in his eyes, and the queer, quiet central desire. It was the first time she had seen it, that quiet, patient, central desire of a young man who had suffered during his youth, and seeks now almost with the slowness of age. A hot flush went over her heart. She felt herself responding to him . . .

"You know, Joe," she said, "I don't mind what you do, if you love me *really*."[4]

To be "in love," then, in a conventionally romantic way, is to obstruct the deepest feelings, to insult the deepest self. To feel *real* love is to reach "that quiet, patient, central desire" which makes "simple intimacy" possible. Personal closeness depends here on release of deeper, more impersonal feelings. In the modish '20's, after artificial "spooning," it takes a healthy quarrel to release them. Or so the story argues.

III

The difficulties of pre-modern lovers are another matter. In the early novel, *Sons and Lovers*, Paul Morel and Miriam Leivers are late-Victorians, intensely spiritual mates whose chaste relations proceed on a high plane of consciousness. They share intellectual and aesthetic interests; they love old churches and medieval ruins; they commune soulfully with nature and each other. But when love becomes physical, their communion stops:

> He courted her now like a lover. Often, when he grew hot, she put his face from her, held it between her hands, and looked in his eyes. He could not meet her gaze. Her dark eyes, full of love, earnest and searching, made him turn away. Not for an instant would she let him forget. Back again he had to torture himself into a sense of his responsibility and hers. Never any relaxing, never any leaving himself to the great hunger and impersonality of passion; he must be brought back to a deliberate, reflective creature. As if from a swoon of passion she called him back to the littleness, the personal relationship. He could not bear it. "Leave me alone—leave me alone!" he wanted to cry; but she wanted him to look at her with eyes full of love. His eyes, full of the dark, impersonal fire of desire, did not belong to her.[5]

When she finally submits to passion, as if to a sacrifice, Paul realizes "that she had not been with him all the time, that her soul had stood apart, in a sort of horror. He was physically at rest, but no more. Very dreary at heart, very sad, and very tender, his fingers wandered over her face pitifully. Now again she loved him deeply. He was tender and beautiful."[6]

But his tenderness becomes a "gentle reaching-out to death." Miriam has tried to keep their love intensely personal, has been unable to join him spiritually in "dark, impersonal" desire, unable to respond in kind. There has been no exchange, no communion, and though she responds now to his "tenderness," he accepts her "love" as death.

Miriam is clearly a spiritual vampire, one who "wheedles the soul out of things," as Paul observes. Though he joins her at first in absorbing intimacy, he also resists suffocation and rightly seeks release. In his affair with Clara Dawes he seems to find release in "dark, impersonal" passion. Clara is an early version of the "lost girl," the modern feminist who denies the womanhood she desires. Paul sees through her aloofness, responds to her defiance with pagan flower dance and carnation-smashing love in wooded groves. After their first "baptism of fire in passion," their warmth and gaiety affect their tearoom hostess, who gives them benedictive flowers. Later, in Clara's rooms, Paul affirms her womanhood, heals her hurt pride "with an infinite tenderness of caress"; and their ensuing gaiety pleases Clara's mother. Yet aside from these moments their love remains impersonal. When Clara pursues him at work Paul becomes extremely vexed:

> "But what do you always want to be kissing and embracing for!" he said. "Surely there's a time for everything." . . .
> "Do I always want to be kissing you?" she said.
> "Always, even if I come to ask you about the work. Work's work—"
> "And what is love?" she asked. "Has it to have special hours?"
> "Yes; out of work hours."
> "And you'll regulate it according to Mr. Jordan's closing time?"
> "Yes; and according to the freedom from business of any sort."
> "It is only to exist in spare time?"
> "That's all, and not always then—not the kissing sort of love."[7]

Paul may be right about love and work, but even on holiday he sets the night aside for love and keeps the day free: "Lovemaking stifles me in the daytime," he complains, and deliberately pushes Clara towards her estranged husband. Her possessiveness, and her inability to give him balance, are immediate causes for his discontent; but as he sees himself, his mother's hold is the ultimate cause. Though I have elsewhere argued that Clara, like Miriam, defeats herself, and that Mrs. Morel remains "the most vital woman in the novel," she is also the most destructive sweetheart.[8] Paul feels that he cannot give himself in marriage while his mother lives; he might have said, more appropriately, that he cannot *be* himself, express his passions and affections freely, because his mother has usurped his ego. The murkiness and confusion which many critics find in *Sons and Lovers* may be traced, I think, to Lawrence's failure to define Paul's egocentric needs. We can see how Clara and Miriam fail him, and how his mother almost kills him, but why he almost fails himself remains obscure.

Significantly enough, Paul's career as an artist is vaguely presented. Though Lawrence knew something about painting, he seems to have faked Paul's talent for it. We see no development in Paul's style; we see few examples of his art. Painting seems more like a hobby than a career for Paul; it engrosses him less vividly than his work at the factory. What we do see, however, is his artistic dedication to his mother. When he wins prizes in a student exhibition, his mother takes them as her own achievement: "And Paul felt he had done something for her, if only a trifle. All his work was hers." When, at 23, he wins first prize and twenty guineas for a landscape, his mother responds so wildly that Paul is "shocked and frightened":

She flew to him, flung her arms round him for a moment, then waved the letter, crying:

"Hurrah, my boy! I knew we should do it!"

He was afraid of her—the small, severe woman with greying hair suddenly bursting out in such frenzy . . . [He] was afraid [too] lest she might have misread the letter, and might be disappointed after all. He scrutinised it once, twice. Yes, he became convinced it was true. Then he sat down, his heart beating with joy.

"Mother!" he exclaimed.

"Didn't I *say* we should do it!" she said, pretending she was not crying . . .

"You didn't think, mother—" he began tentatively.

"No, my son—not so much—but I expected a good deal."

"But not so much," he said.

"No—no—but I knew we should do it."[9]

They get over the "stress of emotion" by quarreling about the money. Then Paul's father enters, and though he shares their excitement and pride, he also indicates its cost:

His black arm, with the hand all gnarled with work lay on the table. His wife pretended not to see him rub the back of his hand across his eyes, nor the smear in the coal-dust on his black face.

"Yes, an' the other lad 'ud 'a done as much if they hadna ha' killed 'im," he said quietly.

The thought of William went through Mrs. Morel like a cold blade. It left her feeling she was tired, and wanted rest.[10]

William, the older son, had been Mrs. Morel's "knight who wore *her* favour in the battle." Her hold on his spirit had split and killed him; her selection of that son as lover, and her rejection of her husband and his distasteful work, are repeated now as Paul is rewarded for his prize with the gift of William's evening suit. The living son in the dead son's clothes aptly signifies usurped identity; and the intense emotion, undercut by the cold blade of death, amply clarifies Paul's fear of tender love.

Early in childhood Paul had sensed his mother's suffering as that of a brave woman deprived of vital rights: "It hurt the boy keenly, this feeling about her that she had never had her life's fulfilment: and his own incapability to make up to her hurt him with a sense of impotence, yet made him patiently dogged inside. It was his childish aim." Plainly his "childish aim" comes straight from his mother, though she does not enforce it until William dies and she takes Paul as the favored son. In the years that follow there is abundant gaiety between them, and her fresh responsiveness contrasts with Miriam's cloying ways: yet their close affection, born of intense suffering, is always mixed with her own driving needs. Thus she proves a jealous and demanding sweetheart. With Miriam, her rival for Paul's soul, she disapproves of tender love; with Clara she approves only of passion. Paul's tenderness comes through, significantly, with permissive older women like the tearoom hostess and Clara's mother, or in safe arenas like the factory, where he plays the foreman's role. But under pressure his affections flag and his ego wobbles or collapses. Thus Clara is unable to "keep his soul steady," to keep him balanced and intact, as their affair progresses; and Miriam is unable to pull him together, to mother him into selfhood, when his mother dies. His supineness with Miriam is revealing:

> She felt that now he lay at her mercy. If she could arise, take him, put her arms around him, and say, "You are mine," then he would leave himself to her . . . She was aware of his dark-clothed, slender body, that seemed one stroke of life, sprawled in the chair close to her . . . It called to all her woman's instinct . . . She knew she ought to take it up and claim it, and claim every right to it. But—could she do it? Her impotence before him, before the strong demand of some unknown thing in him, was her extremity . . .
>
> "Will you have me, to marry me?" he said very low . . . She pleaded to him with all her love not to make it *her* choice. She could not cope with it, with him, she knew not with what . . .
>
> "Do you want it?" she asked, very gravely.
>
> "Not much," he replied, with pain.
>
> She turned her face aside; then, raising herself with dignity, she took his head to her bosom, and rocked him softly. She was not to have him, then! So she could comfort him. She put her fingers through his hair. For her, the anguished sweetness of self-sacrifice. For him, the hate and misery of another failure. He could not bear it—that breast which was warm and which cradled him without taking the burden of him. So much he wanted to rest on her that the feint of rest only tortured him. He drew away. . . .
>
> It was the end then between them. She could not take him and relieve him of the responsibility of himself.[11]

Yet why should Miriam relieve him of self-responsibility? What "unknown thing" speaks *strongly* for such privileged weakness? Lawrence's lapse into special pleading reveals Paul's lapse into infantilism and self-negation. His mother has appropriated more than his prizes and affections: she has appropriated his ego, has knighted him in love as well as battle, has given him fatherhood without selfhood and without real self-assurance. No wonder, then, that Lawrence would oppose love with individuality, not hate, in later works, and would move to an extreme defense of individuality, an extreme separation too of tender and impersonal modes of love.

IV

He defined these extremes most sharply in *Women in Love*. In this novel there are again two women, spiritual and sensual, in the hero's life. Hermione Roddice is the spiritual vampire, the upper-class intellectual who resembles Miriam Leivers in hyper-conscious intimacy. Ursula Brangwen is sensual and emotional, like Clara Dawes, an uprooted independent woman with romantic predilections. The hero, Rupert Birkin, is articulate and insightful, like Paul Morel, but more messianic, and more consciously concerned with selfhood. Thus he rails against depleting modes of intimacy in Hermione and Ursula; he sees both women as Great Mothers, horrible and clutching, lusting for possession, viewing men as appendages rather than independent beings, and insisting on "horrible" fusion:

> Hermione saw herself as the perfect Idea, to which all men must come: and Ursula was the perfect Womb, the bath of birth, to which all men must come! And both were horrible. Why could they not remain individuals, limited by their own limits? Why this dreadful all-compre-hensiveness, this hateful tyranny? Why not leave the other being free, why try to absorb, or melt, or merge? One might abandon oneself utterly to the *moments*, but not to any other being.[12]

Birkin has come a long way from Paul's regressive lapse. He links lusting mothers with depleting intimacy; he links robust selfhood with enriching love. Indeed, he calls for "paradisal entry into pure, single being, the individual soul taking precedence over love," accepting permanent connection with others, but never losing "its own proud singleness, even while it loves and yields." The attempt to preserve the self from absorbing intimacy, yet still allow for love, is clear.

Birkin must literally preserve himself from Hermione's destructive love. He is almost killed when she bashes his head with a ball of lapis lazuli. The destructive potential in Ursula's love is less obvious. Its romantic basis is suggested, in the chapter called "Island," by the paper boats she makes from purple wrappings for chocolates. The island itself is a romantic site, a place where Chateaubriand's lovers, Paul and Virginia, might hold "Watteau picnics." Birkin rejects this pleasant view, however, and makes "island" stand for selfhood. He fashions a flotilla of daisies, individualistic flowers, for which Ursula's paper boats provide romantic escort. The precedence of daisies over purple boats, of individuality over love, is eventually conceptualized by Birkin. But Ursula believes meanwhile in "unspeakable intimacies" and "complete self-abandon"; she believes that love surpasses individuality and calls for "absolute surrender to love." The results of such surrender are conveyed, in the chapter called "Water-Party," by the drowning of Diana Crich and her boyfriend, the young man choked by Diana's arms around his neck. Birkin eludes that fate by pressing for impersonal union. "There is," he tells Ursula, "a real impersonal me, that is beyond love, beyond any emotional relationship. So it is with you . . . And it is there I would want to meet you—not in the emotional, loving plane, but there beyond," in the unknown plane where each acts in accord with "primal desire." Here Birkin wants the "quiet, patient, central desire" of the tale, "In Love." But he defines it as a "strange conjunction," an equilibrium which avoids merging and fusing, "a pure balance of two single beings: — as the stars balance each other." His views are modified, ultimately, to allow for "the yoke and leash of love," which he accepts in the chapter called "Excurse," where Ursula accepts the primacy of selfhood. But it is love as a bond, a binding yoke, which Birkin acknowledges, and his stress on impersonal desire prevails.

The same stress informs his brotherhood rites with Gerald Crich. Again he wants "An impersonal union that leaves one free" and avoids "sloppy emotionalism." That affection should be primary, in a male relationship, and sensual warmth secondary, seems self-evident; it accords, moreover, with the purposive or spiritual role which Lawrence assigns to brotherhood: yet Lawrence relies on sensual relations and draws away from feared affections; he creates blood rites for brotherhood, strange wrestling scenes, from which each character turns, more plausibly, toward heterosexual affairs.

Gerald is oddly like Paul Morel in his relations with Ursula's sister, Gudrun Brangwen; he reaches finally an infantile dependency which resembles Paul's relapse with Miriam. But Lawrence now sees that state as one of helpless self-exposure:

> A strange rent had been torn in him; like a victim that is torn open and given to the heavens, so he had been torn apart and given to Gudrun. How should he close again? This wound, this strange, infinitely-sensitive opening of his soul, where he was exposed, like an open flower, to all the universe, . . . this disclosure, this unfolding of his own covering, leaving him incomplete, limited, unfinished, . . . this was his cruelest joy. When then should he forego it? Why should he close up and become impervious, immune, like a partial thing in a sheath, when he had broken forth, like a seed that has germinated, to issue forth in being, embracing the unrealised heavens.[13]

But it is death toward which Gerald yearns, the mystery of his own destruction and annihilation; the open flower, the vulnerable and dependent self, invites extinction. Still, his resemblance to Paul suggests how Lawrence divides himself between his heroes and makes of their affinity a dramatization of his own dilemmas. Birkin is his older self, seeking singleness of being; Gerald, his youthful self, seeking annihilation in dependent love: and Birkin oddly cannot save his friend. Not so oddly, though, if dependence is a necessary part of married love, and if Birkin's stress on selfhood and otherness, on polarization of impersonal selves, is too extreme. The affections find no free release, only grudging acceptance, in this radical scheme, and emotional dependence — which threatens Paul and destroys Gerald — finds only dramatic expression. Lawrence would not compose his famous essay, "We Need One Another," for some years to come. But at this stage he could at least assert his "central law" of isolate selfhood, whereby "each organism is intrinsically isolate and single in itself"; and in stressing *impersonal* singleness, in defining a second ego at impersonal planes of being, he could give metaphysical expression to that unthinking process by which we do accept ourselves.

V

Alfred Kazin traces Lawrence's sense of authority, his pride in his own powers, his prevailing righteousness, to his mother's love. Agreeing with Freud that the mother's favorite becomes a "conqueror," he sees Lawrence as the favored son who confidently assays the world, and who recreates his mother's love in all his works.[14] It seems more plausible, however, to see Lawrence's career as a *reaction* to his mother's love, an attempt to reclaim the masculine heritage which she denied him and the selfhood she absorbed. Certainly Lawrence did gain confidence from his mother; his moral sureness, his spiritual strength, owe much to her Congregational firmness. But righteousness is a dubious asset, as Lawrence came to know. In describing Rupert Birkin, in *Women in Love*, as "a Sunday-school teacher, a prig of the stiffest type," he was criticizing his maternal heritage. In decrying self-importance, in *The Man Who Died*, he was castigating the moral egoism of his mother's son. This correlation is made openly in "The Real Thing," a late essay in which righteous mothers are said to produce sons incapable of feeling, animated by self-will and by secret ambition to impose themselves on the world and other people. Lawrence calls their condition "the final state of egoism," as opposed to "the real thing," by which he means a man's faith in himself, his belief "in his own life-flow." Quite clearly it is egoism which derives from mothers and faith in self which sons and fathers alike must find. In other words, Lawrence consciously discredits his maternal sense of authority, and consciously affirms his lost masculine heritage. Indeed, he speaks directly of his childhood, of that early "fight for righteousness" "our mothers" made, as they tried to improve "our fathers" and make life "better" for the children:

> We know now this ethical excuse was only an excuse. We know now that our fathers were fought and beaten by our mothers, not because our mothers really knew what was "better," but because our fathers had lost their instinctive hold on the life-flow and the life-reality, that therefore the female had to fight them at any cost, blind and doomed. We saw it going on as tiny children, the battle. We believed the moral excuse. But we lived to be men, and to be fought in turn. And now we know there is no excuse, moral or immoral. It is just phenomenal. And our mothers, who asserted such a belief in "goodness," were tired of that self-same goodness even before their death.[15]

Plainly Lawrence too is tired of maternal righteousness. He speaks of the need for men to die, to be born again with "a different courage," if the fight between the sexes is to cease. In the meantime young men cling desperately to their wives, hate them with the cold hate of ill-treated children, the egoistic sons of egoistic mothers:

> The young men know that most of the "benevolence" and "motherly love" of their adoring mothers was simply egoism again, and an extension of self, and a love of having absolute power over another creature. Oh, these women who secretly lust to have absolute power over their own children — for their own good! Do they think the children are deceived? Not for a moment! You can read in the eyes of the small modern child: "My mother is trying to bully me with every breath she draws, but though I am only six, I can really resist her" . . .[16]

The personal note is unmistakable. Lawrence too resists his mother's egoism, resists it in tales and essays of his middle and final years, resists it in himself and seeks rebirth into "a different courage" and a different faith. Paul Morel's disguised aggression, in hastening his mother's death, emerges sharply now in tales like "The Rocking-Horse Winner," "Rawdon's Roof," "Mother and Daughter," where usurping mothers are deftly satirized for destroying or enslaving children. At the same time men like Lawrence's father emerge as sensual and unruly heroes — grooms, gypsies, gamekeepers, in whom the "life-flow," the old masculine warmth and wildness, is still intact, while the old unmanliness, the old brutality and cravenness, is shorn away. In *Oedipus in Nottingham* Daniel Weiss sees the culmination of this process in *Lady Chatterley's Lover:* "The shift from the parricidal Paul Morel running to his mother's arms while the father whines in the kitchen, to the 'great blond child-man,' Clifford Chatterley, fondling the housekeeper's breasts while the gamekeeper waits in the Park, represents the total dilapidation of Lawrence's Oedipal longings and the perfection of his reactive anti-Oedipal vision of life. Along with the heroic contempt for the mother image in absolute decay comes the full identification with the once-despised father."[17]

The reaction is thematic as well as psychological. In *Women in Love* Lawrence had affirmed isolate selfhood as "the central law of life" and had established star-equilibrium, or polarization, to preserve it from engulfing love. With selfhood affirmed, he could attend more confidently to his "secondary law of life," that individual fulfillment comes through contact and communion with others. This law operates even in early works: but in the late period there comes a remarkable relaxation and shift of emphasis. In "The Real Thing" Lawrence blithely contradicts his early views on selfhood: "Man and woman are not two separate and complete entities," he argues; they "are not even two separate persons: not even two separate consciousnesses, or minds. In spite of vehement cries to the contrary, it is so. Man is connected with woman for ever, in connexions visible and invisible, in a complicated life-flow that can never be analysed." This from the creator of star-equilibrium, for whom merging and fusing seemed horrible! In "We Need One Another" the contradiction is more openly acknowledged:

> We may as well admit it: men and women need one another. We may as well, after all our kicking against the pricks, our revolting and our sulking, give in and be graceful about it. We are all individualists: we are all egoists: we all believe intensely in freedom, our own at all events. We all want to be absolute, and sufficient unto ourselves. And it is a great blow to our self-esteem that we simply *need* another human being. . . . [It] is terribly humiliating to our isolated conceit.[18]

From isolate selfhood to isolate conceit, from proud singleness to overweening individualism, from impersonal union to the greatest fraud of all, reduction "to our . . . elemental selves." The extremes of *Women in Love* have been abandoned. The new goal is relationship, through which we have "our very individuality." Lawrence has recovered his father's masculine warmth and wildness, has rejected his mother's egoism and relaxed his own defensive individualism; he is ready now for contact, for sprays and vibrations from living fountains, for outflow and inflow, for true human relationship. And so he writes a novel called *Tenderness*.

VI

Oliver Mellors, the gamekeeper in that novel, is by profession a keeper or protector of life; he lapses frequently into vernacular speech, the dialect of the lower classes; he goes about his work "solitary and intent, like an animal that works alone"; he speaks for and conveys warmhearted love. In his work, in his dialect, in his love-making he resembles Paul Morel's father in *Sons and Lovers*, the man whose "sensuous flame of life" attracts Mrs. Morel, whose children love him when he works dexterously in the home or tells animal tales of the pit-horse Taffy and the mouse who climbed his arm. He had "a warm way of telling a story," Lawrence writes, and was "peculiarly lavish" at such times "of endearments to his second son," i.e. Paul. The warmness of Morel's father, his attractive masculine traits, seem present now in Mellors, and Lady Chatterley likes them. When she comes upon him washing himself behind his cottage, she has what Lawrence calls "a visionary experience":

> He was naked to the hips, his velveteen breeches slipping down over his slender loins. And his white slim back was curved over a big bowl of soapy water, in which he ducked his head, shaking his head with a queer, quick little motion, lifting his slender white arms, and pressing the soapy water from his ears, quick, subtle as a weasel playing with water, and utterly alone . . . She saw the clumsy breeches slipping down over the pure, delicate, white loins, the bones showing a little, and the sense of aloneness, of a creature purely alone, overwhelmed her. Perfect, white, solitary nudity of a creature that lives alone, and inwardly alone. And beyond that, a certain beauty . . . a lambency, the warm, white

flame of a single life, revealing itself in contours that one might touch: a body![19]

Mellors' aloneness here, his sensuous flame of life, his animal quickness and singleness, are qualities of the father. The same qualities are reflected as Mellors builds coops for the coming chicks and Connie, watching him, is again touched by his aloneness, quickness and intentness. His animal singleness differs from Birkin's proud singleness, in *Women in Love*, in visual immediacy, in sensual appeal, and more than this, in vulnerability, as hinted by the exposed loins and bones; it contrasts, moreover, with that spiritual sense of authority which leads, for Lawrence, to egoism and self-importance. Mellors has his share of maternal egoism; his occasionally shrill preachments suggest that kind of false sufficiency to many readers: but his immediate appeal for Connie is that of masculine integrity and warmth. She turns in spring from the coldheartedness of Wragby Hall to the new life, the hatching chicks, the promise of creative love, at Mellors' hut. And new life comes as Mellors fetches a chick for her, with "sure gentle fingers," from under the pecking mother hen:

> "There!" he said, holding out his hand to her. She took the little drab thing between her hands, and there it stood, on its impossible little stalks of legs, its atom of balancing life trembling through its almost weightless feet into Connie's hands. But it lifted its handsome, clean-shaped little head boldly, and looked sharply round, and gave a little "peep."
> "So adorable! So cheeky!" she said softly.
> The keeper, squatting beside her, was also watching with an amused face the bold little bird in her hands. Suddenly he saw a tear fall on to her wrist . . . She was kneeling and holding her two hands slowly forward, blindly, so that the chicken should run in to the mother-hen again. And there was something so mute and forlorn in her, compassion flamed in his bowels for her . . . Her face was averted, and she was crying blindly, in all the anguish of her generation's forlornness. His heart melted suddenly, like a drop of fire, and he put out his hand and laid his fingers on her knee.
> "You shouldn't cry," he said softly.[20]

Connie's "crying need," like that of her generation, is for tender love. Mellors responds to it out of that sexual sympathy which, for Lawrence, "is just a form of warmheartedness and compassionateness, the most natural life-flow in the world." That Mellors can speak for such compassion is important. His feelings are no different from Paul Morel's, in *Sons and Lovers*, as he watches Clara Dawes kneeling among the flowers and suddenly scatters benedictive cowslips over her arching neck and body. But Paul's tenderness is not an articulated value, and in the works that follow, only the heroines speak for tender love; as we have seen, the heroes accept it grudgingly as the lesser part of equilibrium. That grudging compromise is replaced now by Mellors' open affirmation. The man speaks for warmheartedness; he is able to accept it as part of his masculine strength; he is even able to accept connection, or dependence on another, as a heartfelt need.

Lawrence shows this effectively as an artist; yet, ironically, he fails to see it in essays of this period. In "The State of Funk," for instance, he claims that accepting sexuality releases natural "blood-sympathy," makes us warmer and more sympathetic toward others; and in "A Propos of *Lady Chatterley's Lover*," he holds that freeing the mind from "fear of the body" releases tender love.[21] It would seem more relevant, however, to free the self from maternal dominance, or from fear of feelings which the mother once usurped. If men must renew faith in themselves, and if Lawrence renewed that faith, in *Lady Chatterley*, through identification with his father, then his affections were released through strengthened masculinity and selfhood, not through sexuality. He had long accepted the body and its sexual needs; now he accepts his masculine heritage, accepts himself as vernacular spokesman for warmhearted love. The sensual and unruly father has finally displaced the righteous mother: thus Mellors can love warmly without fear.

Yet not entirely. Mellors shies away when Connie describes their union as "just love"; and he hates "mouth kisses" as too personal. He also wants support from other men in the fight "to preserve the tenderness of life, the tenderness of women, and the natural riches of desire." His tenderness takes courage, as Connie says. There is also something limited or limiting about it. Ideally his love for Connie should radiate outward and enrich relations with the world: actually it stops more or less with Connie. These lovers touch each other, but do not reach beyond themselves. Perhaps they ask too much of warmth, of touch, to rest the future on it. Or perhaps they ask too little about its nature, to rest so much upon it. Elsewhere Lawrence argues, for instance, that "All the emotions belong to the body," including even "the higher emotions."

> And by the higher emotions we mean love in all its manifestations, from genuine desire to tender love, love of our fellow-men, and love of God: we mean love, joy, delight, hope, true indignant anger, passionate sense of justice and injustice, truth and untruth, honour and dishonour, and real belief in *anything:* for belief is a profound emotion that has the mind's connivance.[22]

VII

What Lawrence wants, apparently, is to release a whole range of spiritual possibilities by accepting the sensual basis of emotion. The aim is laudable; but when he tries to reach that wider range, in *Lady Chatter-ley*, he releases only tender love. It may be that the emotions themselves must be accepted, and not merely their sensual basis. It is one thing, after all, to accept the flesh, another to be bound by it: and Lawrence does seem bound at times by fleshly warmth. It may be, too, that "touch" itself must be accepted on emotional grounds which Lawrence cannot quite acknowledge. Thus Ian Suttie argues that "love in all its manifestations" begins not simply with the body, but with the body's history, with the nurturing process in infancy, when the body first responds to love, and we learn to distinguish self from other. If this is true, then "touch" begins with maternal and presexual relations, and "sexual sympathy" becomes a late development of such relations.[23] There exists, in other words, an original maternal heritage which Lawrence only partially reclaims.

This hypothesis helps to explain, at any rate, why Lawrence stops short of his apparent goals. He sees, wisely enough, that sex is only "the closest of all touch," that touch is a continuum, sensual rather than sexual, which runs through close relations; but he does not see that touch, as the medium for tender feelings, originates with the mother who usurped his selfhood and his manhood. One critic argues that Lawrence returns to the female principle in *Lady Chatterley's Lover*, that the body and its emotions are feminine in his psychology, while the spirit and its drives are masculine.[24] The trouble with this formula is that Lawrence took his spiritual cues from his mother, his sensual cues from his father. In *Lady Chatterley* he breaks his mother's spiritual hold, accepts his father's role in work and love, and asserts his masculine selfhood. It remains true, however, that the love he accepts is tender, warm, gentle, and in that sense maternal; it is nurturing love, released by masculine strength and confidence — the return of the repressed affections of childhood which a strong man may indulge. Its contrast, in the novel, is Clifford Chatterley's infantile love with Nurse Bolton, his complete abject dependence and regression. Mellors can be tender, even dependent, without regressing; he can indulge the sensual sympathies which Clifford paradoxically denies while wallowing in maternal love. But Lawrence's reaction to such love is so intense he cannot see its bearing on Mellors' courage; his understandable bitterness against usurping mothers leaves him, finally, on the threshold of discovery, unable to cross. He sees only Clifford's weakness, his infantile dependence on nurturing love; he cannot see that Mellors' strength converts the same conditions into masculine warmth, by which a man may offer nurturing love without losing male identity; nor can he see finally, that tenderness, founded in touch, is the true maternal heritage by which — according to Suttie — we claim the deepest love and release the highest feelings: consequently he cannot quite release those wider possibilities which his views entail.[25] But it is enough perhaps that he widens love to include the tender and dependent feelings, enriches love with newfound masculine warmth, and deepens it with genuine desire. Certainly no other modern writer has portrayed love's sensual and emotional range so vividly, nor, finally, with so much courage.

Notes

1. D. H. Lawrence, *Lady Chatterley's Lover* (New York: Grove Press, 1959), p. 334.

2. I. A. Richards, *Practical Criticism* (New York: Harvest, n.d.), pp. 253–254; Ian D. Suttie, *The Origins of Love and Hate* (New York: Agora, 1966), pp. 63–77.

3. Lawrence, *The Woman Who Rode Away and Other Stories* (New York: Berkley, 1956), p. 96.

4. *Ibid.*, pp. 105–106.

5. Lawrence, *Sons and Lovers* (New York: Compass, 1958), p. 284.

6. *Ibid.*, p. 286.

7. *Ibid.*, p. 355.

8. Mark Spilka, *The Love Ethic of D. H. Lawrence* (Bloomington: Indiana University Press, 1955), p. 74.

9. *Sons and Lovers*, p. 253.

10. *Ibid.*, p. 254.

11. *Ibid.*, pp. 417–418.

12. Lawrence, *Women in Love* (New York: Compass, 1960), p. 301.

13. *Ibid.*, p. 437.

14. Alfred Kazin, "Sons, Lovers and Mothers," *D. H. Lawrence and "Sons and Lovers": Sources and Criticism*, ed. E. W. Tedlock, Jr. (New York: New York University Press, 1965), pp. 238–250.

15. Lawrence, "The Real Thing," *Phoenix: The Posthumous Papers of D. H. Lawrence*, ed. Edward D. McDonald (New York: Viking, 1936), p. 198.

16. *Ibid.*, pp. 199–200.

17. Daniel A. Weiss, *Oedipus in Nottingham: D. H. Lawrence* (Seattle: University of Washington Press, 1962), p. 109.

18. Lawrence, "We Need One Another," *Phoenix*, p. 188.

19. *Lady Chatterley's Lover*, pp. 75–76.

20. *Ibid.*, pp. 134–135.

21. Lawrence, *Sex, Literature and Censorship*, ed. Harry T. Moore (New York: Twayne, 1953), pp. 66–67, 94.

22. *Ibid.*, p. 96.

23. Suttie, *The Origins of Love and Hate*, especially pp. 7–8, 20–21.

24. H. M. Daleski, *The Forked Flame: A Study of D. H. Lawrence* (London: Faber and Faber, 1965), p. 15.

25. Here I contradict my early views on the role of touch, in *The Love Ethic of D. H. Lawrence*, pp. 192–193; but then this whole essay is hopefully an advance beyond such views.

D. H. Lawrence's
Dual Myth of Origin
David J. Gordon*

As the nightmare of the Great War began to fade, Lawrence made his most searching attempt in discursive form to probe the question of where he and we had gone wrong. Was mankind fated after all to self-division and endless discontent, or could the path be discovered that would lead us back, or forward, to completeness of being? Before the war, while drafting *The Rainbow*, he had tackled the question in his "Study of Thomas Hardy." Only sporadically about Hardy, the essay is a kind of symbolic history which prophetically envisions a restoration of the almost lost balance between the enduring vital forces of neglected Law and triumphant Love, between sensual stability and spiritual striving. During the war, principally in "The Crown" (1915), he tried again. His mood was darker: *The Rainbow* had been suppressed; the unexpectedly prolonged and horrible fighting between his homeland and Frieda's exacerbated him; he was humiliated by poverty, ill-health, and probably also by marriage and (as the rejected prologue to *Women in Love* suggests) by his growing awareness of his homosexual bias. But, determined to rise above despair, he fused bits of pre-Socratic philosophy and romantic tradition into a picture of life as an inescapable warfare of opposites—yet opposites that could be held in a constructive and creative polarity by a transcendent "crown." After the war—convinced by it, above all, that men enjoyed hate and destruction while idealizing love and peace—it was the stimulus of Freud's psychoanalysis, the challenging idea that our conflicts are rooted in the situation of childhood, that prompted the author of *Sons and Lovers* to another, more concrete assault on the problem. He would have to provide an alternative account of the process of repression in order to construct an antitragic picture of human nature and destiny.

As critiques of Freud, *Psychoanalysis and the Unconscious* and *Fantasia of the Unconscious* (written in 1919–1920) are too ill-informed to be of any value. But they have the explanatory value of a strong myth. They are deeply congruent with the fertile thought of Rousseau (although Lawrence does not seem to have studied Rousseau) as well as with the doctrine of various contemporary Freudian revisionists who teach "the abolition of repression." Lawrence crudely understood psychoanalysis to assert that the repression of incestuous wishes in childhood was the simple cause of a thwarted sexual life in adulthood; it therefore followed, although Freud failed to realize it, that the recovery of psychic health required the clearly unworkable tactic of liberating or acting out these wishes. But, despite the inadequacy of this objection, Lawrence understood only too well that a man could suffer profoundly from the residue of

*Reprinted from *Sewanee Review* 89 (Winter 1981):83–94, by permission of the journal and the author.

his childish attachment to his mother. *Something* was uneasily repressed — *that* much of Freud seemed true to him. The question was whether this repression was inevitable and therefore a man's true fate. Could not we conceive an alternative myth of origin that would make the restoration of psychic wholeness imaginable?

Like Rousseau, Lawrence speculates that our fundamental nature is good, innocent, pristine, and that what corrupts us are false ideals of education, false social relations. The heart — or the blood — speaks truly, and must do so, because there is no original flaw in nature. All our unhappiness comes from our judgments and is corrigible. With a corrected understanding and above all with a sufficient strength of will, we do not need to accept as our fate either Christianity's original sin or Freud's everyday unhappiness. We can in fact turn damnation into salvation. For what else is damnation but a fate dictated from outside, beyond the control of our will? And what else is salvation but a fate we freely choose?

A Freudian could salvage some of this — much of our unhappiness, he might say, does indeed come from our judgments — but he would add that our judgments to some extent function below the level of consciousness and that our feelings, *as* we become aware of them, are sometimes already attached to inappropriate ideas instead of to others that have undergone repression. He might, in short, find Rousseau and Lawrence psychologically naive. It is therefore necessary to point out that their conception is not as simple as it appears, that (although it unquestionably diverges from Freud's) it does not entail a simpleminded antithesis between good feeling and bad thought. They understood very well that the two overlap, that the passions themselves could be corrupted. If man's instinctual nature is to be a guide — not because it is irrational but because its report is immediate, as Jean Starobinski explains in his splendid book on Rousseau — a true feeling has to be distinguished from one falsely heightened by fantasy or by some social ideal. The spiritual battle, then, is between two kinds of overlapping consciousness, the natural and the social. Challenging Freud, Lawrence postulates that repression actually occurs by a secondary process. Parents themselves are so infected by a false social morality that they unwittingly convey to the child a teaching that distorts his naturally wholesome sensuality and aggressiveness. As Philip Rieff puts it in his keen introduction to Lawrence's books on psychoanalysis, "the incest taboo articulates the training in possessive love with which modern mothers, no longer libidinally related to their husbands, manage to keep their sons even after they become mothers-in-law." Thus the cardinal rule of pedagogy, for Rousseau as well as Lawrence, was to let the child alone, to refrain from any imposition of one's will, and to restrain him only by allowing him to see that his capricious or egoistic behavior is inconsistent with natural necessity.

The opposition of natural necessity and human desire did not seem to Rousseau and Lawrence the source of our conflicts. One accepts the unalterable. What torments the human animal is the conflict between a deeply positive, inherently moral will and a bullying all-too-human social will that is confused with it. Everything in their doctrine depends on the validity and cogency of this distinction, and one can touch it at its most vulnerable point by suggesting that, in practice, this is an elusive distinction.

How can we know that we are motivated by the true rather than the false will? How can Rousseau and Lawrence know? Although they recognized that in principle they had to be touched by the same pitch as were others in their society, and so might not be able to judge truly, they tended in practice to ignore this scruple and to place a too confident trust in the authority of their own opinions. The result is that we often perceive in their work a discrepancy between what they are telling us or trying to show us and what they are really showing us or allowing us to see. In *Women in Love*, for example, Lawrence tells us that Gerald, unlike Birkin, is damned because he will not see and follow the true path to salvation; but he shows us that Gerald's doom is already determined by his family history. If we are to be convinced that Gerald's will need not be chained by the childhood shooting of his brother (according to Birkin it is not an accident, for "it all hangs together in the deepest sense"), then it would help to see in Birkin's story how it is possible to transcend the condition of childhood. Lawrence first assigned Birkin a family history (see the rejected prologue), then deleted it, leaving only the recent struggle with Hermione as a weak suggestion of a determining past. In short here, as elsewhere in Lawrence, insistent hopefulness is combined peculiarly with profound despair.

Starobinski distinguishes a pessimistic and an optimistic version of Rousseau's central myth of origin:

> La première affirme que l'âme humaine a *dégénéré*, qu'elle s'est défigurée, qu'elle a subi une altération, à peu près totale, ne jamais retrouver sa beauté première. La seconde version, au lieu d'une déformation, évoque une sorte d'occultation: la nature primitive persiste, mais *cachée*, entourée de voiles superposés, ensevelie sous les artifices, et pourtant toujours intacte. Version pessimiste et version optimiste du mythe de l'origine. [The first affirms that the human soul has *degenerated*, that it has been disfigured, that it has undergone a nearly total alteration, never to find again its pristine beauty. The second version suggests the idea of concealment rather than deformity: pristine nature persists but is *hidden*, covered by veils, buried under artifices, yet always intact. The pessimistic and the optimistic versions of a myth of origin. (Author's translation)].
>
> (Jean Starobinski, *Jean-Jacques Rousseau:*
> *La Transparence et l'obstacle* [Paris: Librairie Plon, 1957], p. 16.)

I would give this excellent distinction a psychological turn and apply it to

Lawrence as well. *Theoretically* both Rousseau and Lawrence are opti-
mists: salvation is always possible; the hidden core is incorruptible. But
experientially both are pessimists, great poets of despair, for the process of
degeneration was always advancing, and the hope of recovery had to be
placed in the more and more distant past or more and more distant future.

This theoretic aspect of Lawrence's myth of origin is evident in his
imaginative as well as in his discursive writing. The novels and tales are
full of an odd contradictoriness between a felt pessimism and a willed
optimism — odd because contradictoriness in a work of imaginative literature is a matter not of logically inconsistent statements but of notably
different degrees of convincingness between effects. Enlisting his famous
dictum — "Never trust the artist. Trust the tale" — and using these terms
properly — as a distinction between pressures *inside* a work and not, as it is
commonly used, between what *is* said inside and outside — we may say
that the Lawrentian *tale* is essentially a tragic action but that the teller or
artist tries to turn it sharply away from tragedy.

We can adduce ready, if rough, evidence of this combination of felt
tragedy and willed antitragedy from Lawrence's best novels: *Sons and
Lovers*, *The Rainbow*, and *Women in Love*. As observation and demonstrated event, the Morels and their deteriorating marriage are utterly
convincing, but the narrator cannot refrain at times from telling us what
they *ought* to have felt and done, how it *ought* to have gone. Again the
tragic romance between Paul and Miriam is palpable imaginative truth,
whereas Paul's romance with Clara bears numerous marks of mere
fantasy-enactment. Finally, the anguished reaction of Paul to his mother's
death is far more credible than its abrupt contradiction in the novel's
forced conclusion: "But no, he would not give in. Turning sharply, he
walked towards the city's gold phosphorescence. His fists were shut, his
mouth set fast. He would not take that direction, to the darkness, to follow
her. He walked towards the faintly humming, glowing town, quickly."

In *The Rainbow* Lawrence had learned to integrate these contrary
impulses to some extent, especially in the first half of the novel, which is
distanced from present time and thus protected by irony from the burden
of his immediate desire. In the story of the earlier Brangwen generations,
he expresses a measure of unforced joy in sexual love, although — or
because — the incompleteness of those relationships is clearly marked.
Ursula's story, however, must have an open future, and the effects
sometimes jangle. We believe in her anger and frustration as such, but
some of the presented causes of these emotions — Skrebensky's inadequacy
or the disappointment of the classroom experience — do not account for
their intensity. It is as if Lawrence is unwilling or unable to discover
objective correlatives, and Ursula's perorative vision of a "new creation" is
almost as arbitrary and abrupt as the ending of *Sons and Lovers*. *The
Rainbow* is essentially a tale of degeneration, but the teller punctuates it

with rhapsodies on the hidden incorruptible core or seed—a conspicuous image in the novel—which contains the promise of rebirth.

The central action of *Women in Love* turns on the contrast between the tragic love of Gerald and Gudrun and the metatragic love of Birkin and Ursula, and a good reason for considering this the best of Lawrence's novels is that in it his sense of the tragic and his will to transcend the tragic are interrelated with some energy. Yet the one undermines the other more than is recognized. The only really tender moment of the Birkin-Ursula relationship (in the chapter "Excurse") is purchased by a heap of quarreling, and the relationship is finally left not so much open-ended, which has become the received view, as frustratingly incomplete.

I am suggesting that a characteristic difficulty of reading Lawrence is the gulf that we perceive between the despair he felt and the hope he wanted to feel—a gulf that, in the high romantic tradition, he would not bridge by trying either to accept the one or to modify the other. Understandably some critics (e.g. T. S. Eliot) speak of him as a great pessimist, whereas others (e.g. Diana Trilling) call him a supreme optimist. The question is whether we are attending chiefly to the tale or to the teller, both amply expressed in the text. This explains the curiously abrupt changes of tone that we find all through Lawrence's work, not only in terminal passages. Consider the opening of *Lady Chatterley's Lover*: "Ours is essentially a tragic age, so we refuse to take it tragically." It becomes clear that "so we refuse" means "so we must or ought to refuse" ("We've got to live, no matter how many skies have fallen"), but it follows so abruptly from the opening clause that we are inclined for a moment to suppose that Lawrence meant "so we should be realistic and *not* refuse." Or consider this passage in *Fantasia of the Unconscious*, which begins by idealizing marriage and within a paragraph, almost within a sentence, turns into a grotesque *de*-idealization: "The best thing I have known is the stillness of accomplished marriage, when one possesses one's own soul in silence, side by side with the amiable spouse, and has left off craving and raving and being only half one's self. But I must say, I know a great deal more about the craving and raving and sore ribs than about the accomplishment."

Yet Lawrence was a resourceful artist and found means by which he could at least partially circumvent his ineluctable imaginative commitment to a tragic fate, and express a felt rather than a merely willed joy. As has often been noted, he could describe birds, beasts, and flowers with friendly attentiveness and delight. But a novelist cannot neglect human relationships for long. Lawrence therefore devised a particular kind of irony, most notably in the climaxes of his shorter fictions, which allowed him to celebrate love as a moment of emergence precariously situated in a sea of circumstance; an ironic social perspective protests, as it were, a direct expression of desire. The naive lovers in "The Thorn in the Flesh" annihilate the world in their spontaneous embrace, but the young man's danger (he is a soldier who has struck a superior and run away) and a practicable way of meeting it are nicely indicated in the wordless little final confrontation between the young woman and the baron who employs her. In "The Horse Dealer's Daughter" the abrupt emergence of love between a sullen death-haunted woman and the depressed doctor who rescues her from a muddy pond and removes her clothes brings, at the end, joy and fear together; the glad lovers are almost comically frightened by the sudden loss of a familiar pattern of responses, which makes each an awesome stranger to the other. After reading "The Fox," we can hardly say whether the new love between the demonic young man and the belatedly awakened woman, achieved after many pages, is self-validating or absurd; Lawrence gives us simultaneously the vitalistic perspective which endorses it and the worldly point of view from which it seems unlikely. Even his fablelike tales, though less bound by realistic expectations, contain a similar irony. The climactic coupling of The Man Who Died and the priestess is appropriately symbolic of seasonal and quasi-divine rebirth, but his decision to leave her and return the following year is also motivated by a worldly recognition that domestic familiarity would tarnish the splendor of their intercourse.

Lawrence was most truly a priest of love when he could present the erotic moment as a nascent potentiality untested by worldly experience and in danger of being destroyed by it. The risk of sentimentality is present, especially in the longer fictions where worldly circumstances must be developed and cannot simply loom as a threat to the claims of immediate feeling. In *Lady Chatterley's Lover*, for example, we may wonder whether the forces opposing the lovers have been fairly presented, whether the demonstrated impediments to their love are as external in origin as Lawrence seems to think they are.

In any case, and for all his resourcefulness, the gulf always remained between the optimistic teller and the pessimistic tale. I would therefore question Paul Delany's argument, in his fine book *D. H. Lawrence's Nightmare*, that the experience of war radically altered the artist's vision. On the one hand Lawrence's hopefulness never died: his work in the twenties begins with a challenge to Freud's pessimistic picture of human fate and ends (in *Assorted Articles* and "A Propos of *Lady Chatterley's Lover*") with Rousseauistic affirmations of the natural goodness of man. On the other hand Lawrence was always committed—in his imaginative as distinct from his intellectual will—to the pessimistic version of his myth of origin. As I have suggested, he could only really imagine joy when confronting a nonhuman world, a world tinged with the glamor of an unrecoverable past, or, most important, when dramatizing love as pure potentiality, as (in Wordsworth's phrase) a something evermore about to be. His fictions are most successful, as Delany himself shows in regard to *Women in Love*, when these contrary wills are brought to bear closely on one another.

In Lawrence there is a joy implicit on every page, in the vivacity and plasticity of the writing. No doubt one could mount a sophisticated argument here, making the point that this love of language rather than the fatality of sex or the will to self-transcendence was his true subject. But, although this joy is fundamental to his claim on our attention, such an argument is not illuminating from a literary point of view. Even the darkest literary visions—Hardy's, Kafka's, Beckett's—are not written, because they *cannot* be written, out of *flat* despair. A radiance lies at the heart of even the gloomiest work of genuine imagination. But this fact, at least in the case of Lawrence, has primarily a psychological interest. *Sons and Lovers* is an interesting document from this psychological point of view because it shows that the very relationship with his mother that blighted Lawrence was also the source of his amazing self-confidence and sense of a special destiny. But he was reluctant to develop this aspect of the matter as a literary motif. In fact, quite like Rousseau, he was always troubled by the idea of celebrating art and language as such. In a remarkable passage in *The Confessions* Rousseau speaks of his six years of eloquence as originating in his head rather than his heart, as a kind of unnatural phenomenon, a temporary and problematic transcendence of nature. A comparable passage in Lawrence may be found in his letter (of 1915, to Ottoline Morrell) about Van Gogh, in which he speaks of even great art as provisional and faute de mieux, the better thing being a fully achieved culture in which *being* would at last replace *knowing*. Both writers, in other words, were aware of a discrepancy between their ideal of unselfconscious simplicity and the strenuous effort of mind which was the only means available to them of bringing it nearer to realization.

I do not want to belittle the importance of the strong intellectual will that Lawrence brought to the novel, for it helped to alter significantly the novel's form. If romance and sexual love were subjects that chose him, he in turn helped to change permanently the way in which they were treated. Jessie Chambers, the great friend of his youth, noted in her careful memoir that the narratives that moved the young Lawrence most of all were tales of tragic love like *La Dame aux Camélias, Tristan, Carmen, The Mill on the Floss*, and *Anna Karenina*. After a performance of *Dame aux Camélias*, she writes, "he rushed from place to place and found himself battering at the doors until the attendant came and let him out, adding, 'I feel frightened. I realize that I, too, might become enslaved to a woman.' " As a mature critic Lawrence attempted repeatedly to honor the strength yet expose the perversity of stories of destructive passion—for example in Hardy, Poe, and Tolstoy. The vigorous yet desperate attack on "modern tragedy" in *Fantasia of the Unconscious* is typical:

> When sex is the starting point and the returning point both, then the only issue is death. Which is plain as a pike-staff in *Carmen* or *Anna Karenina*, and is the theme of almost *all* modern tragedy. Our one hackneyed, hackneyed theme. Ecstasies and agonies of love, and final

passion of death. Death is the only pure, beautiful conclusion of a great passion. Lovers, pure lovers should say, "Let it be so."

And one is always tempted to say, "Let it be so." But no, let it not be so. Only I say this, let it be a great passion and then death, rather than a false or faked purpose. Tolstoi said "No" to the passion and the death conclusion. And then drew into the dreary issue of a false conclusion. His books were better than his life. Better the woman's goal, sex and death, than some *false* goal of man's. . . .

But still — we *might* live, mightn't we?

His own early novels — the first (*The White Peacock*), second (*The Trespasser*), and even the third (*Sons and Lovers*) — continue the nineteenth-century fictional tradition of tragic sexuality. But *The Rainbow* and *Women in Love* break new ground. In them Lawrence invents new ways of presenting character and organizing plot that reduce the pressure of cause-and-effect logic and give greater sanction to the immediacy of feeling, before it is exposed to reflective judgment. These books are major instances of the twentieth-century interest in spatial form. They discover new uses of romantic irony.

Lawrence is both a last witness to a major nineteenth-century tradition — Gerald Crich in *Women in Love* is perhaps the last fully tragic figure in the history of the romantic novel — and an important innovator. Although he was not the only novelist responsible for changing its form, it seems to me fair and striking to say that the romantic novel, after him, is required to be essentially ironic rather than tragic in structure. Lawrence wrestled heroically, in and out of fiction, with the Freudian idea of an only partly mitigable fate laid down by the past, but, as with Rousseau, a dual version of a myth of origin — *version optimiste et version pessimiste* — is the legacy he bequeaths us.

INDEX

247